Engaging deeply with both ancient texts and moder
how biblical authors of early Israelite laws dealt wit
ditions of the ancient Near East. She emerges with significant wisdom on an important topic for the church: how inspired authors wrestled with imperial pressures and influences. For anyone interested in the tensions between oppression and liberation in a postcolonial context, this important new study is a must-read.

Christopher B. Hays, PhD
D. Wilson Moore Professor of Old Testament and ANE Studies,
Fuller Theological Seminary, California, USA

Imperial powers tend to pay attention to laws and laws tend to facilitate imperialism. Anna Lo captures this relationship in her careful examination of biblical legal codes. She shows both the conservativism of local elites and their resistance to imperial domination through their development of laws as modeled by empires. This book paves the way for future work on biblical legal texts and postcolonial studies.

Steed Vernyl Davidson, PhD
Professor of Hebrew Bible,
McCormick Theological Seminary, Illinois, USA

Lo offers us a rare find – an extensive study of the Book of the Covenant in Exodus that takes seriously both legal data and sociological theory. Her nuanced presentation is sensitive to the range of viewpoints current in scholarship, and she stakes out her own position by drawing on methods from postcolonial studies and applying them to her investigation in an impressively careful and judicious manner. While one may disagree with aspects of her specific interpretations, Lo is able to show how the biblical authors accepted some facets of the imperial order, as represented by the cuneiform law collections, but earnestly resisted others. The text was thus revolutionary but often in subtle and indirect ways. Lo's contribution is a most welcome addition to the ongoing discussion.

Bruce Wells, PhD
Associate Professor, Department of Middle Eastern Studies,
University of Texas at Austin, USA

From time to time one asks, "Why has nobody written this book before," or "Why didn't I write this book?" This is one of those times. Chung Man Anna Lo's book is a marvelous postcolonial study of the laws in Exodus 19–24. Many readers have wondered about the puzzling way these laws combine visionary insights and oppressive constraints. In a general sense, Jesus explains why they do: the Torah combines God's creation vision with his making allowance for human hardness of heart. Chung Man Anna Lo gives us a concrete twenty-first-century take on that dynamic. I won't be surprised if her anchoring the laws in the eighth and seventh centuries and in the development of scribal culture and literature in that period looks dated when this framework ceases to be scholarly fashion. But that will not take away from the significance and achievement and perception of this work written against the background of postcolonial insight.

John Goldingay, PhD
Senior Professor,
Fuller Theological Seminary, California, USA

The Laws of the Imperialized

Understanding Exodus 19–24 As a Response to Imperial Legal Traditions

Chung Man Anna Lo

Published 2024 by Langham Academic
An imprint of Langham Publishing
www.langhampublishing.org

Langham Publishing and its imprints are a ministry of Langham Partnership

Langham Partnership
PO Box 296, Carlisle, Cumbria, CA3 9WZ, UK
www.langham.org

ISBNs:
978-1-83973-880-7 Print
978-1-78641-004-7 ePub
978-1-78641-005-4 PDF

British Library Cataloguing-in-Publication Data
A catalogue record for this book is available from the British Library

ISBN: 978-1-83973-880-7

Cover & Book Design: projectluz.com

The author would like to thank Brill and the Society of Biblical Literature for permissions to use the translations of the laws from the following publications respectively:

Harry Angier Hoffner, *The Laws of the Hittites: A Critical Edition* (Leiden: Brill, 1997).

Martha T. Roth, *Law Collections from Mesopotamia and Asia Minor*, 2nd ed., Writings from the Ancient World 6 (Atlanta, GA: Scholars Press, 1997).

To Yashar

Contents

Abbreviations

AOAT	Alter Orient und Altes Testament
BAIAS	*Bulletin of the Anglo-Israel Archaeological Society*
BZAW	Beihefte zur Zeitschrift für die alttestamentliche Wissenschaft
CAD	*The Assyrian Dictionary of the Oriental Institute of the University of Chicago*. Edited by Ignace J. Gelb et al. 21 vols. Chicago: Oriental Institute of the University of Chicago, 1956–2010.
COS	*The Context of Scripture*. Edited by Hallo, William W. 3 vols. Leiden: Brill, 2003.
CBQ	Catholic Biblical Quarterly
col.	column
EA	El-Amarna Correspondence
FAT	Forschungen zum Alten Testament
JBL	*Journal of Biblical Literature*
HL	Hittite Laws
JR	*Journal of Religion*
JSOT	*Journal for the Study of the Old Testament*
JSOTSup	Journal for the Study of the Old Testament Supplement Series
LE	Laws of Eshnunna
LH	Laws of Hammurabi
LHBOTS	The Library of Hebrew Bible/Old Testament Studies
LL	Laws of Lipit-Ishtar
LU	Laws of Ur-Namma
LX	Laws of X
MAL	Middle Assyrian Laws

PSD	*The Pennsylvania Sumerian Dictionary*. Edited by Åke W. Sjöberg. Philadelphia: Babylonian Section of the University Museum, 1884–2006. http://psd.museum.upenn.edu/nepsd-frame.html.
RBL	*Review of Biblical Literature*
RIMA	The Royal Inscriptions of Mesopotamia, Assyrian Period
RIMA 2	*Assyrian Rulers of the Early First Millennium BC I (1114–859 BC)*. A. Kirk Grayson. Toronto: University of Toronto Press, 1991.
RINAP	The Royal Inscriptions of the Neo-Assyrian Period
RINAP 1	*The Royal Inscriptions of Tiglath-pileser III (744–727 BC) and Shalmaneser V (726–722 BC), Kings of Assyria.* Hayim Tadmor and Shigeo Yamada. Winona Lake, IN: Eisenbrauns, 2011.
RINAP 2	*The Royal Inscriptions of Sargon II, King of Assyria (721–705 BC)*. Grant Frame. University Park, PA: Eisenbrauns, 2021.
RINAP 3/1	*The Royal Inscriptions of Sennacherib, King of Assyria (704–681 BC), Part 1*. A. Kirk Grayson and Jamie Novotny. Winona Lake, IN: Eisenbrauns, 2012.
RINAP 3/2	*The Royal Inscriptions of Sennacherib, King of Assyria (704–681 BC), Part 2*. A. Kirk Grayson and Jamie Novotny. Winona Lake, IN: Eisenbrauns, 2014.
RINAP 4	*The Royal Inscriptions of Esarhaddon, King of Assyria (680–669 BC)*. Erle Leichty. Winona Lake, IN: Eisenbrauns, 2011.
RINAP 5/1	*The Royal Inscriptions of Ashurbanipal (668–631 BC), Aššur-etel-ilāni (630–627 BC), and Sîn-šarra-iškun (626–612 BC), Kings of Assyria, Part 1*. Jamie Novotny and Joshua Jeffers. University Park, PA: Eisenbrauns, 2018.
SAA	State Archives of Assyria
SAA 2	*Neo-Assyrian Treaties and Loyalty Oaths*. Edited by Simo Parpola and Kazuko Watanabe. Helsinki: Helsinki University Press, 1988.
SAA 3	*Court Poetry and Literary Miscellanea*. Edited by Alasdair Livingstone. Helsinki: Helsinki University Press, 1989.
s.v.	*sub verbo*, under the word

SLEx	Sumerian Laws Exercise Tablet
SLHF	Sumerian Laws Handbook of Forms
VT	*Vetus Testamentum*
VTSup	Supplements to Vetus Testamentum

Introduction

Topic

Being the first legal corpus in the biblical canon, Exodus 19–24 is a law collection that belonged to a people living under the shadow of empire. Noticeably, the literary context depicts a people who have just been liberated from an oppressive empire, while, through most of their history, the people of Israel and Judah continued to endure imperial subjugation. This imperialized social location, together with the liberative narrative, calls for contemplation about the relationship between Exodus 19–24 and extant cuneiform law collections. Whereas scholars focus on imperial influence and legal and literary connections in their comparative studies of these two corpora, I see that the similarities and differences between them reveal how the imperialized people of Israel and Judah wrestled with the legal traditions of empires, as well as the imperial subjugation of their time. This wrestling certainly involved acceptance and ambivalence, but it also unquestionably comprised resistance. This work investigates the dynamic of these responses, inviting attention to the resistive endeavor manifested in this law collection of the imperialized.

Methods and Historical Context (Chapters 1–2)

The key methods of this study are postcolonial analysis of colonized people in the modern context and historical-comparative analysis of biblical and cuneiform law collections, which I discuss in chapters 1 and 2, respectively. The psychology of subjugated people is among the concerns of postcolonial scholars. They observe colonized people's discourse in general and their legal discourse in particular – that is, their written or spoken communications in response to their colonizers at large and those related to law, or exhibiting characteristics of it.[1] These observations offer a crucial perspective for understanding the relationship between Exodus 19–24 and cuneiform law collections, both of which might not be intended for use in court but do reflect legal features.

These observations, though varying, significantly point out that hybridity is a key characteristic of colonized people's response, with which the Exodus corpus resonates. Moreover, these observations reveal the resistive nature of this hybridity. Some scholars further nuance the receptive intent and oppressive consequences of colonized people's mimicry and call for ethical engagement, but they also highlight the resistive endeavor in colonized people's pursuit of difference, inviting scholarly attention. These observations concern both colonized people in general and their elites in particular, shedding light on the authorial motives of Exodus 19–24. They moreover offer a critical lens for reviewing some postcolonial analyses of this corpus. These analyses exhibit the contributions of biblical postcolonial scholars in revealing the imperial features of Exodus 19–24, but meanwhile reflect the necessity to rediscover this corpus's resistive elements. The postcolonial observations of colonized people indeed indicate the importance of attending to the multifaceted nature of the imperialized people's response to the empire and offer guidance for this attention in the study of Exodus 19–24 in comparison to cuneiform law collections.

I integrate these postcolonial observations into the application of historical-comparative analysis for the study of Exodus 19–24, which I discuss in chapter 2. Previous comparative studies have established various approaches to understanding the relationship between this corpus and its cuneiform counterparts. There are also some recent attempts at bringing the subversive nature of the Exodus corpus or its conventional response to cuneiform legal traditions into the scholarly discussion. However, the consideration of the

1. By law, I refer generally to "the system of rules which a particular country or community recognizes as regulating the actions of its members" ("Law," *Oxford English Dictionary*, https://www.lexico.com/en/definition/law). Law, by this definition, may or may not involve judicial functions, such as making court judgments. Thus, while law is usually related to jurisdiction and associated with the courts in today's context, one may also regard custom and tradition as law, just as some colonized indigenous people do, which I discuss in chapter 1.

biblical authors' imperialized social location and how it affects the rhetoric of their law collection is still wanting. To contribute to this area, I carry out a study of Exodus 19–24 in comparison to cuneiform law collections from a postcolonial perspective that attends to the multifaceted nature of the imperialized people's response to the empire. With the propositions on the authorial knowledge of cuneiform legal traditions, which extant cuneiform law collections somehow exhibit, and the authorial awareness of these traditions' imperial nature, I propose that Exodus 19–24 is a work of conservative revolutionists. By conservative, I refer to the hesitancy to deviate from cuneiform legal traditions drastically. By revolutionists, I refer to the biblical authors who endeavored to diverge from those traditions, despite their hesitancy. The corpus of Exodus 19–24 thus reflects how its authors wrestled with the imperial legal metanarrative of their time (see section 2.3.2.3).

The application of this integrative approach to the study of Exodus 19–24 is grounded on the fact that this corpus's authors and their people lived under imperial subjugation for most of their history. Still, dating this corpus to a specific period enhances the understanding of the historical context and the nature of the imperial encounter behind this corpus's composition. Scholars have various understandings of this corpus's unity and dating, but I locate its compilation mainly in the middle of the eighth century to the middle of the seventh century, in view of its relationship with Deuteronomy, the development of scribal culture and literature in Israel and Judah, and the biblical authors' possible exposure to cuneiform legal traditions. This dating does not pinpoint the geographical location of the compilation, and I leave it open due to lack of further evidence, suggesting that it may be Israel or Judah or both. Despite this, this dating significantly indicates a time when Israelites and Judahites lived under the shadow of the Neo-Assyrian Empire. My exploration of how they interacted with the Assyrians through military encounters, diplomatic contacts, and scribal training reveals the imperial subjugation encountered by Israelites and Judahites. It also reflects their exposure to cuneiform legal traditions and suggests their association of these traditions with the imperial legal metanarrative of that time. This exposure under Neo-Assyrian subjugation, in my opinion, induced the multifaceted response exhibited in Exodus 19–24.

I further integrate postcolonial scholars' insights into the understanding of Exodus 19–24's purposes and authors. Through discussing the scholarly debate on this corpus's purposes and a recent application of colonized people's psychology to the study of the Pentateuch, I suggest that the Exodus corpus was intended for multiple purposes. It offered judicial references and wisdom-moral teachings and conveyed religious and political messages. More importantly, it also functioned as the legal discourse of the imperialized. This written communication that exhibits legal characteristics expresses the imperialized authors' response to the imperial legal metanarrative and imperial subjugation, when they sensed the pressure to follow imperial ideology and practices. This written legal communication might concurrently speak to the authors' monarchy, given the similar emphasis of monarchy and empire on royal power and the imperial influence on the Israelite and Judahite monarchies. However, in view of its relationship with imperial legal traditions, I suggest that this legal discourse significantly expressed the authors' response to the empire, and my study particularly focuses on this response.

The Exodus corpus does not identify its authors; however, considering its characteristics and the literary and scribal culture in Israel and Judah in the Neo-Assyrian period, I propose that the authors were Israelite or Judahite scribes who had gone through some training in foreign languages and legal traditions and served the palace or the temple, or both, among the imperialized. They compiled Exodus 19–24 primarily for people with similar training and access to the palace or the temple. Similar to colonized elites in the modern context, these authors might have been torn between pro- and anti-Assyrian positions because of their relationships with the empire, their patronage relationship with their own kings, and their autonomy to express their views toward the empire. These understandings suggest the complexity of Exodus 19–24 as the manifestation of the imperialized people's response to the empire. They also offer an essential background for the historical-comparative analysis of this corpus and cuneiform law collections, which I integrate with postcolonial observations of colonialized people.

Scope and Key Arguments (Chapters 3–5)

Utilizing this integrated approach, I analyze Exodus 19–24 in a particular order and along thematic lines. I begin in chapter 3 with the ordinances in Exodus 21:2–22:16, which exhibit close resemblances to the legal sections of extant cuneiform law collections in terms of both form and content. I focus on ordinances related to slaves and women, as they not only appear throughout Exodus 21:2–22:16 but also attract scholarly concerns about their imperial and oppressive features. The ordinances regarding slaves include those addressing male and female slaves' release and permanent servitude (Exod 21:2–11) and physical assault inflicted by their owners and others' oxen (Exod 21:20–21, 21:26–27, 21:32). I also investigate ordinances concerning kidnapping and theft (Exod 21:16; 22:2), which some scholars associate with the source of the servitude addressed in the ordinances. The ordinances regarding women, meanwhile, include those handling assaults against parents and pregnant women (Exod 21:15, 21:17, 21:22–25) and seduction of unbetrothed maidens (Exod 22:15–16) in addition to those concerning female slaves. I compare these ordinances with laws on similar topics in the Laws of Ur-Namma, the Laws of Lipit-Ishtar, the Sumerian Laws Exercise Tablet, the Sumerian Handbook of Forms, the Laws of Eshnunna, the Laws of Hammurabi, the Middle Assyrian Laws, and the Hittite Laws, informed by the aforementioned propositions on the biblical authors' knowledge of cuneiform legal traditions.

Through this analysis, I argue that while the imperialized authors tolerated debt slavery, as imperial legal traditions do, and accepted their repressive approach to slaves and women in general, they resisted the lack of concern for and negative portrayal of slaves and the particular emphasis on women's social status and patriarchal authority over women in imperial legal traditions. These responses do involve potentially oppressive handling of slaves and women due to the general acceptance of and sometimes ambivalence toward imperial legal approaches to these people, which require a postcolonial inquiry. However, these responses also demonstrate that the imperialized authors did not fully recognize the imperial legal metanarrative of their time, but endeavored to distinguish themselves from it through various divergences. Through these divergences, the imperialized authors urged their elite audience to improve the conditions of slaves and women among their people when they were under Neo-Assyrian subjugation.

In a similar way, I analyze Exodus 20:23–21:1 and 22:17–23:30 in chapter 4. Surrounding the ordinances, these passages contain mainly non-casuistic laws, to which I refer as commandments. I focus on commandments related to services to Yhwh, care for the marginalized, and fighting against enemies, which are among the predominant themes in Exodus 20:23–21:1

and 22:17–23:33. These commandments attract comparatively less attention in comparative studies of the Exodus corpus and cuneiform law collections due to these commandments' apparently distinct form and concerns and their possible redactional features. However, these commandments echo the corresponding themes in the non-legal sections of some cuneiform law collections. The theme of fighting against enemies also particularly attracts postcolonial biblical criticism. Engaging the same mentioned propositions, I compare these commandments with the prologues, superscription, and/or epilogues of the Laws of Ur-Namma, the Laws of Lipit-Ishtar, the Laws of X, the Laws of Eshnunna, and the Laws of Hammurabi.

Based on this comparison, I contend that whereas the imperialized authors were in sympathy with the imperial legal metanarrative in terms of its concern for religious services and the marginalized and its treatments of enemies, they resisted its emphasis on emperors' achievements in these areas. Considering also Neo-Assyrian royal inscriptions and treaties, I argue further that the imperialized authors made use of these imperial legal elements to resist Neo-Assyrian propaganda and subjugation. Again, these responses of the imperialized authors necessitate a postcolonial critique, as they involve acceptance of the hostile attitude toward enemies and an ambivalent shift toward human participation in annihilating them. The call for religious services to Yhwh and care of the marginalized might also involve self-serving motives. Yet, these responses also reveal that the acceptance of the imperial legal metanarrative is a selective one; the imperialized authors endeavored to urge their elite audience to reject the roles of emperors and their gods among the imperialized people. Remaining conservative in departing from the imperial legal metanarrative, the imperialized authors uniquely emphasized the imperialized people's participation in serving Yhwh and building a direct relationship with Yhwh. They also urged their elites to serve Yhwh only, take care of the marginalized, and envision divine subversion of Neo-Assyrian subjugation.

To offer a complete picture of the conservative revolutionists' response to the imperial legal metanarrative, I analyze the surrounding narrative of the ordinances and commandments (Exod 19:1–20:22 and 24:1–18) in chapter 5. Despite scholarly considerations of its redactional features, this narrative essentially identifies the maker, the pronouncer, and the recipient of the commandments and ordinances (the so-called the Book of the Covenant), similar to what the non-legal sections of cuneiform law collections do for their legal sections. By the Book of the Covenant, I refer to Exodus 20:23–23:33.[2]

My analysis thus focuses on the roles of Yhwh, Moses, and the people. It compares the Exodus corpus's descriptions of them with those of the gods, the emperors, and the people in the prologues and epilogues of cuneiform law collections, similar to my analysis of the commandments in chapter 4.

Through this comparison, I argue that while the imperialized authors broadly accepted the hierarchical law pronouncement process and attention to the words of the divine and the lawmaker in the imperial legal metanarrative, they resisted its claim on various dominant roles of the gods and the emperors over the imperialized people. These responses continue to require a postcolonial critique concerning the acknowledgment of the imperial mode of lawmaking, violent and hegemonic characterization of the divine, domination of the people, the subordination of women to men, and potentially oppressive nature of human mediation in actual practice. Yet, they do indicate that the compliance with the imperial legal metanarrative is not a complete one; the imperialized authors expended effort to convey a subversive message to their elite audience against Neo-Assyrian subjugation and to urge them to become mediators who are loyal to Yhwh as well as committed to their people.

This resistance amid acceptance, together with similar responses appearing in the ordinances and commandments, characterize Exodus 19–24 as a work of the conservative revolutionists, who wrestled with the imperial legal metanarrative when they compiled their own law collection primarily for their elite audience during Neo-Assyrian subjugation. By drawing on postcolonial observations of the colonized in modern contexts, but comparing Exodus 19–24 with cuneiform law collections under the Neo-Assyrian

2. There is some variety of opinion concerning its precise limits. Quite a few commentators consider Exod 20:22–23:33 as the Book of the Covenant (for instance, Durham, *Exodus*, 305; Childs, *Book of Exodus*, 451; Lai, *Exodus (I)*, 43; Chiu, *Book of Exodus*, 399). However, David P. Wright defines the Book of the Covenant (or the Covenant Code or the Covenant collection) as Exod 20:23–23:19 (Wright, *Inventing God's Law*, 3). Raymond Westbrook's definition varies among different articles, including Exod 20:22–23:19, 20:23–23:19, and 20:22–23:33 (Westbrook, "What is the Covenant Code," 15; "Biblical Law," 303; "Laws of Biblical Israel," 318). Generally speaking, scholars refer to Exod 20:22/23–23:19/33 as the Book of the Covenant. They usually do not explain the reasons behind their definitions. However, their definitions seem to associate with how they understand the dating of Exod 19–24's different sections and the topic that they aim to study. Regarding my definition, I consider the content of Exod 19–24 and the dating of this corpus's compilation, which I locate mainly in the Neo-Assyrian period.

context, this study invites modern readers not only to caution against the potentially oppressive features of Exodus 19–24 and attend to its literary and legal relationship with extant cuneiform law collections, but also to reflect on the endeavor of the imperialized in expressing their resistance to the empire.

CHAPTER 1

Responses of the Imperialized to Empires

1.1 Introduction

One cannot fully understand the rhetoric of Exodus 19–24 without studying how imperialized people respond to the empires that subjugate them. In this beginning chapter, I thus discuss postcolonial scholars' understandings concerning colonized peoples' response to their colonizers. Although there are some differences between colonialism and imperialism,[1] the rule of empires in ancient Israelite history, including the Assyrians, Babylonians, and Persians, can be defined as both colonial and imperial because they had governance presence in Israel and/or Judah and clear ambition of conquering other lands.[2] Moreover, while there are essential differences between the rule under colonialism and that under imperialism from the rulers' perspective, these differences are not that considerable from the perspective of subjugated peoples.[3] A study of postcolonial understandings of colonized

1. Edward W. Said argues that colonialism is "a consequence of imperialism" that involves "the implanting of settlements on distant territory," while imperialism is "the practice, the theory, and the attitudes of a dominating metropolitan center ruling a distant territory" (Said, *Culture and Imperialism*, 9).

2. Hays, "Isaiah as Colonized Poet," 55–60. John Goldingay also posits that Judah was a colonial entity for its entire history in broad terms, although it was more like a colony in the Persian period in a stricter sense (Goldingay, "Isaiah 56–66," 161).

3. Davidson, *Writing/Reading*, 9.

peoples therefore sheds light on how the people of Israel and Judah responded to empires, with the eventual purpose of fully engaging the rhetoric of Exodus 19–24.

In the following discussion, I first study postcolonial scholars' understandings concerning the characteristics of colonized peoples' discourse in general. Then I examine their views on these peoples' legal discourse in particular. In the last section, I suggest the implications of these understandings for the study of Exodus 19–24, reviewing some postcolonial analyses related to this corpus. This discussion aims to introduce postcolonial scholars' observations, which are vital for the study of Exodus 19–24. It reveals the complexity of imperialized people's response to empires, which calls for an analysis of Exodus 19–24 that is open to the multifaceted nature of the motivation behind this corpus and attends to both the similarities and differences between this corpus and cuneiform law collections.

1.2 Characteristics of Colonized Peoples' Discourse in General

Attending to colonized peoples' response to their colonizers, postcolonial scholars reveal that hybridity is one of the key characteristics of colonized peoples' discourse – that is, their written or spoken communications in response to their colonizer in general.[4] In this section, I discuss postcolonial scholars' understandings of this characteristic. I also examine their observations on the motivation behind, the outcome of, and different approaches of hybridity, and investigate their findings on the colonized elites' responses to their colonizers. These understandings and observations offer a crucial perspective for unfolding the rhetoric of Exodus 19–24, particularly in comparison to cuneiform law collections, as they disclose the dynamics of resistance to and acceptance of the dominant discourse among subjugated peoples.

---

4. Postcolonial scholars suggest that hybridity and its closely related characteristic, ambivalence (which I will discuss momentarily), can be found among both the colonizers and the colonized (Bhabha, *Location of Culture*, 28–56; Ashcroft, Griffins, and Tiffin, *Post-Colonial Studies*, 10). However, in view of my study's purpose, I focus only on the understanding of colonized peoples' hybridity and ambivalence.

1.2.1 Hybridity as a Key Characteristic

The term hybridity refers to "the creation of new transcultural forms within the contact zone produced by colonization."[5] It is closely related to a notable condition of the colonized, namely ambivalence. Ambivalence, a concept first developed in psychoanalysis, describes "a continual fluctuation between wanting one thing and wanting its opposite."[6] It is a "narcissistic reflection of the One in the Other," as Frantz Fanon's psychoanalysis of the colonized Africans in *Black Skin, White Mask* reveals.[7] It is also manifested in "doubling of identity" among subordinate people, according to Homi K. Bhabha.[8] In sum, the colonized take up the ideology and the characteristics of the colonizers, while also retaining their own.

Some postcolonial scholars contend that this navigation between preserving one's own views and approaches and adopting their colonizers' is a continuous process. Bhabha calls this process "negotiation." He also emphasizes that hybridity is opened up by "*negotiation* rather than *negation*" of "contradictory and antagonistic instances," as Fanon's *The Wretched of the Earth* reflects.[9] Postcolonial biblical scholar R. S. Sugirtharajah thus points out that the notion of hybridity "is not about the dissolution of differences but about renegotiating the structure of power built on differences."[10]

A manifestation of this ambivalent negotiation process is mimicry, an overt response of the colonized peoples in which they reproduce their colonizers' traits, but only partially.[11] This hybrid manifestation occurs in different cultural aspects, including languages, literature, habits, and various areas of a society, such as institutions, practices, and politics.[12] It is at work among the diaspora who live under empire, as well as among those who live in colonies.[13] The concept of hybridity is therefore applicable to the study of Exodus 19–24 because it is a literary work of a people living in their own land but subjugated

5. Ashcroft, Griffins, and Tiffin, *Post-Colonial Studies*, 108.
6. Ashcroft, Griffins, and Tiffin, 10.
7. Bhabha, *Location of Culture*, 72; Fanon, *Black Skin, White Mask*.
8. Bhabha, *Location of Culture*, 72.
9. Bhabha, *Location of Culture*, 37–38; Fanon, *Wretched of the Earth*.
10. Sugirtharajah, *Postcolonial Criticism*, 191.
11. Ashcroft, Griffins, and Tiffin, *Post-Colonial Studies*, 125.
12. Ashcroft, Griffins, and Tiffin, 108, 125.
13. Bhabha, *Location of Culture*, ix–x, xxv, 319–28.

by an empire.[14] It also brings up the importance of comparing Exodus 19–24 with cuneiform law collections, which reflect imperial legal traditions,[15] and attending to both the similarities and differences between them in the study of Exodus 19–24's rhetoric.

1.2.2 Motivation Behind, Outcome of, and Approaches of Hybridity

Postcolonial scholars, however, have different understandings of the motivation behind and the outcome of colonized peoples' hybridity. Some advocate its resistive power over the colonial metanarrative, while others point out its compliant, and even oppressive, nature. Accordingly, they also reveal different approaches of hybridity among the colonized. These understandings, nevertheless, work together and offer insight into the relationship between Exodus 19–24 and cuneiform law collections.

1.2.2.1 Hybridity as Resistance

Despite the fact that hybridity involves the adoption of colonizers' traits, some postcolonial scholars argue that hybridity is meant to resist the colonial metanarrative. Bhabha suggests that hybridity is an "in-between" space that enhances the development of a society's new identity, as well as an "anti-dialectical movement" of subordinate people that subverts the binary ordering of power.[16] Robert J. C. Young likewise states that hybridity in its conscious form is a strategy used by the colonized to disrupt homogeneity and reverse the structures of domination established by the colonizers.[17] Bill Ashcroft, Gareth Griffins, and Helen Tiffin point out that the colonized people's hybrid copy of the colonizers can be a menace to the colonizers.[18] These understandings of hybridity invite one to consider the resistive nature of Exodus 19–24,

---

14. About the dating and historical context of Exod 19–24, see §2.3.1.

15. See §2.2.4.

16. Bhabha, *Location of Culture*, 2, 7, 79. Bhabha is aware that pure culture or identity can hardly be found in reality. In other words, hybridity is a common cultural phenomenon, as some postcolonial scholars point out (for instance, Young, *Colonial Desire*, 92; Dewulf, "As a Tupi-Indian," 89). Nevertheless, Bhabha maintains that hybridity has the aforementioned special role in the development of subordinate people's society.

17. Young, *Colonial Desire*, 21–23.

18. Ashcroft, Griffins, and Tiffin, *Post-Colonial Studies*, 125.

as this corpus also reflects both similarities and differences to cuneiform law collections.

Resistive Power of Hybridity

The resistive power of hybridity indeed comes from the exhibition of differences within similarities, according to these postcolonial scholars. "The same, but not quite" is an important phrase that Bhabha uses to explain the strategy of mimicry. He argues that the simultaneous adoption (the same) and rejection (not quite) of colonizers' traits produce slippage that carries the effect of camouflage.[19] It disrupts colonial authority not by obvious opposition, but by causing uncertainty in the structure of colonial discourse.[20] It is thus "at once resemblance and menace."[21] Subordinate people employ it strategically as a secret weapon of revenge.[22] Bhabha offers an illustration from his own colonized context: by acknowledging that they received the Bible from heaven but at a fair held in Hurdwar (a holy city of India), colonized Indians estranged the colonial authority's identity and transformed its power.[23]

This resistive power of hybridity is exhibited further by postcolonial scholars' observations on the limitations of merely asserting difference. These observations mainly focus on literature, which may have limited practical effect in the society in comparison with political projects. Nevertheless, they enhance the understanding of Exodus 19–24, which is also a literary work. Ashcroft, Griffiths, and Tiffin argue that abrogation without appropriation of the colonial values and practices may not surpass the colonial assumption of privilege. In contrast, appropriation effectively attracts audiences who are familiar with the colonial discourse when it also announces the colonized as different.[24] Edward W. Said points out that it is insufficient for the imperialized to proclaim difference only;[25] they need to demonstrate that they have the capacity to develop and become mature, which imperial histories assert as the

19. Bhabha, *Location of Culture*, 121, 128, 130, 172. Bhabha develops this understanding from Lacan, *Four Fundamental Concepts*, 99.

20. Bhabha, *Location of Culture*, 86–88; Ashcroft, Griffins, and Tiffin, *Post-Colonial Studies*, 125–26.

21. Bhabha, *Location of Culture*, 123.

22. Bhabha, "Surviving Theory," 378; Bhabha, *Location of Culture*, 122.

23. Bhabha, *Location of Culture*, 171.

24. Ashcroft, Griffiths, and Tiffin, *Empire Writes Back*, 69, 76.

25. Said, *Culture and Imperialism*, 213.

colonizers' exclusive capacity. They also need to replace imperial narratives of the imperialized with "a more playful or a more powerful new narrative style."[26] For instance, British Indian writer S. Rushdie's *Midnight's Christian* transforms the European and Western discourse into an acknowledgment of the marginalized or the suppressed.[27]

Preference of the Colonized for Hybridity

In their attempts to resist, the colonized thus prefer a hybrid copy rather than a total refusal of their colonizers, according to these postcolonial scholars. Although this preference may not be true among all subordinated people, this observation is crucial for the analysis of Exodus 19–24, as this corpus does carry both similarities and differences in comparison to cuneiform law collections, which reflect the imperial legal metanarrative. Ashcroft, Griffins, and Tiffin argue that while there are times when the colonized refuse to draw on the language and literature of the dominant culture, more often they seek their own advantage by operating within the dominant culture's framework.[28] Ashcroft also finds that although rejection and separation are key manifestations of the resistance rhetoric, the colonized usually appropriate the dominant culture for self-fashioning and self-representation in order to resist the imperial discourse. For instance, in his *Things Fall Apart*, Nigerian writer Chinua Achebe does not "reinstall the 'good' African culture"[29] in response to Joseph Conrad's dehumanization of Africans in *Heart of Darkness*. Rather, he uses English and adopts the form of English literature to present the flaw and complexity of Nigerians and ethical dilemmas in their community. This imitative presentation in turn confirms African culture's complexity and humanity, as well as ambivalence, which subtly resists the imperial binary and colonial stereotyping of Africans.[30]

The concept of "sly civility," which Bhabha uses in his study of the colonized, further explains this hybrid copy of colonizers.[31] Rather than carrying resistance openly, that is, overtly refusing to follow the colonial discourse, the

26. Said, 216.
27. Said, 216.
28. Ashcroft, Griffiths, and Tiffin, "Language," 261–62.
29. Ashcroft, *Post-Colonial Transformation*, 40.
30. Ashcroft, 40.
31. Bhabha, *Location of Culture*, 132–44.

colonized more often outwardly comply with the colonizer's values (civility) but reject them in a subtle way (slyness). For instance, the colonized may address the colonizer as a father and hint that the colonizer is an oppressor at the same time. The former shows the appreciation of the colonizer's governance, while the latter expresses a sense of resistance to their tyranny. By responding ambivalently to the colonizer in this way, the colonized threaten the authority of the colonial power.[32] This concept of sly civility recalls what James Scott calls "hidden transcript."[33] He argues that it is not uncommon to find that some subordinate people, such as slaves, opt for quiet evasion rather than open resistance like protests and revolts.[34] They show consent and obedience to the powerholder in public, but express their objection and indignation in hidden and disguised ways. These hidden ways include approaches that are usually designed to convey multiple meanings, such as folktales, trickster tales, rituals, and so forth. The hidden transcripts also sometimes involve some seemingly fancy imagination, such as believing that some divine power or authorities will soon liberate the subordinate. People are familiar with the meaning(s) of their own circle's hidden transcripts, but cannot easily decipher those of the other.[35]

Transformative Resistance of Hybridity

This observation of "hidden transcript" helps one understand the disguised and creative nature of subordinate people's resistive discourse. It also brings up some subordinate people's approaches, which shed light on passages in Exodus 19–24 related to Yhwh's role. Still, according to some postcolonial scholars, sly civility and hybridity is something more than a hidden transcript. Ashcroft asserts that the colonized selectively consume the colonizers' cultural product, which is transformed in the process.[36] Bhabha points out further that hybridity works toward a cultural translation. It is not merely an appropriation of colonial discourse, but a departure from the habitual rules

32. Bhabha, 138.

33. Scott, *Domination*, 4–5.

34. Scott, *Domination*, 195. For an opposite view, see Sinha, *Slave's Cause*. Sinha reveals a history of abolition in which African Americans involved themselves in open resistance against slavery from the American Revolution through the Civil War. I will also discuss momentarily how some postcolonial scholars advocate openly resisting the colonial discourse.

35. Scott, *Domination*, 3–7, 15–19, 139–49, 162.

36. Ashcroft, *Post-Colonial Transformation*, 41–42.

of transformation that leads to the revision of colonized peoples' system of norms and values. This cultural translation can be found, for instance, in V. S. Naipaul's novels, including *A House for Mr. Biswas*, *The Mimic Men*, and *In a Free State*. Bhabha argues that colonized characters in these novels do not simply bear with "the 'wretched' condition of the Caribbean,"[37] but work toward an incomplete but communitarian life. This incomplete but community-oriented life creatively and humorously challenges the colonizers' value and presupposition of colonized peoples' life.[38] It also helps explain some emphasis on community in Exodus 19–24, suggesting its authors' resistive intent in their response to the imperial legal metanarrative. The potential that some postcolonial scholars see in hybridity, as a response of the colonized, is therefore its pursuit of cultural translation. It reveals the positive and agential value of the whole process that the colonized go through when they wrestle with colonial power.[39]

Utopianism

The utopianism that Ashcroft finds in postcolonial literature casts further light on this cultural translation, as well as the motivation behind the similarities and differences between Exodus 19–24 and cuneiform law collections. Ashcroft notes that while postcolonial utopianism may extend the imperial relationships, it attempts to transform imperial systems to extend beyond the empire and expresses the hope for a better world and the possibility of social change.[40] Thus, it does not follow the stereotype of the colonized as helpless victims. However, it also does not merely advocate for the destruction of the colonial power or fight for a changeless perfect paradise unrelated to the existing society.[41] Instead, colonized writers utilize imperial cultural capital in an adapted and hybrid form, such as creolized English among Caribbean writers, to envision a utopia of alleviating suffering due to exploitation, promoting freedom and self-realization, and working on communal equality and social relations based on cultural and religious principles. This utopianism

37. Bhabha, "Vernacular Cosmopolitan," 140.
38. Bhabha, 140–41.
39. Bhabha, "Surviving Theory," 370.
40. Ashcroft, *Utopianism*, 9, 37–39, 67.
41. Ashcroft, 24, 62, 196.

involves hybridity that points to the possibility of developing a world among the colonized that is different from both the colonizer's and their own.[42]

These postcolonial scholars thus see hybridity as a crucial characteristic of not only colonized peoples' response to their colonizers, but also their resistance to their colonizers. For these scholars, the colonized subvert the colonial discourse when they appropriate dominant values, norms, and texts for the colonizer's purpose in a way that is at odds with the colonizer's intention.[43] This understanding of hybridity invites a comparison of Exodus 19–24 with cuneiform law collections that attends to both the similarities and differences between them and considers the resistive motivation and strategies behind Exodus 19–24.

1.2.2.2 Adoption as Acceptance and Pursuit of Difference as Resistance

This understanding of hybridity, however, attracts some postcolonial scholars' critique. They argue that some manifestations of hybridity can indicate acceptance of, rather than resistance to, colonial discourse. These scholars also highlight the oppressive nature of hybridity, and therefore advocate the pursuit of difference as an effective strategy for resisting the colonial discourse. These observations, however, do not refute the aforementioned understanding of hybridity and instead complement it, offering a more nuanced perspective for analyzing "the same, but not quite" in Exodus 19–24.

Adoption as Acceptance

Studying the literature of the colonized and the phenomena in colonies, these postcolonial scholars find various manifestations of hybridity. They interpret these manifestations in different ways, but all interpretations reflect some kind of acceptance of the colonial discourse in the adoption of the colonizers' traits. These observations are thus particularly important for the understanding of the similarities between Exodus 19–24 and cuneiform law collections. To begin with, Lola Young contends that subordinate people may mimic the dominant only because of their acceptance of the latter's strong influence. She points out that F. C. Welsing's *The Isis Papers: The Keys to the Colors* (1991)

42. Ashcroft, 4, 11, 24, 37, 62, 144, 159, 180.

43. Moore-Gilbert, *Postcolonial Theory*, 131–32.

and C. Barnes's *Melanin: The Chemical Key to Black Greatness* (1995) are examples of this kind of hybridity.[44] These black scientists' works employ scientific methods, such as empirical data, diagrams, and tables, which have their roots in continental Europe, to present their findings on black people's skin coloring. They also follow the ideology that preoccupied European scientists in the eighteenth and nineteenth centuries – the emphasis on the association between race and biological configuration – when they discuss the black people's strengths and weaknesses. However, rather than resisting the dominant paradigm of understanding Africans, these hybrid works homogenize black people as white scientists did. In Young's perspective, these works thus exhibit "the internalization of western or European influence" among the subordinate people.[45] In other words, the colonized adopt the colonizers' approaches because they have accepted them on a deep level.

Adopting the colonial discourse may also be due to other reasons or conditions; however, they still broadly reflect acceptance of the colonizers' values or approaches. Examining various literary works and some cultural phenomena in general, Dimple Godiwala argues that hybridity may be due to recognition for the colonized culture or fluid cultural boundary. Examples of the former are the Indian characters in Naipaul's *The Mimic Men* and Rushdie's *The Satanic Verses*. Godiwala argues that these characters mimic English culture not because they intend to resist the colonial discourse, but because they feel culturally inferior. Their adoption of the colonial habits exhibits the acceptance, and in fact domination, of the colonizer's values in their life.[46] Regarding fluid cultural boundary, Godiwala refers to the colonial situation in Hong Kong. She points out that in the years before the British government handing Hong Kong back to China, not only did Hong Kong people exhibit highly hybrid characteristics, but expatriates did as well. Expatriates, including Filipinos, Indians, Americans, and Europeans, assimilated into the local culture as well as into each other's cultures. This phenomenon suggests that fluid cultural boundary is a characteristic of metropolitan cultures.[47] It also indicates that in colonial contexts, the adoption of different cultures may

44. Young, "Hybridity's Discontents," 159–65.

45. Young, 165.

46. Godiwala, "Postcolonial Desire," 69.

47. Godiwala, 68.

be due to people's openness of accepting to these cultures, rather than their intention to resist them.

In some cases, colonized people's hybridity can merely be due to practical reasons, which again indicates the acceptance of the colonial discourse to a certain extent. Paul Sharrad suggests that this is the case in some Papua New Guinea writings, which borrow Western literary materials without particular rhetorical reasons.[48] One example is Adam Amod's "Once Upon a Time," which directly borrows the lyric of the Australian folksong "The Wild Colonial Boy" in its retelling of a traditional Papua New Guinea story. However, it concludes with a discussion on the origin and difference of local dialects. It also ends with a literary touch echoing the beginning of the story without any reflection on the colonial governance. In view of the incongruity in mixing literary material from different cultural contexts, Sharrad argues that these hybrid writings merely reflect the authors' education contexts – such as English as a Second Language (ESL) writing classes in which students learn to write English by using Western literature to retell traditional stories. He thus calls this hybridity as "a utilitarian appropriation of qualities and objects suited to the situation."[49] Rather than resistive intention, this practical appropriation exhibits an acceptance of the colonizers' cultural products.

These observations suggest that hybridity may be due to the internalization of colonial approaches, recognition of colonial values, fluidity of cultural boundary, and practical considerations, which indicate the acceptance of colonizers' values or approaches. With a focus on colonized peoples' adoption of the colonial culture, these observations nuance the understanding of hybridity. "The same" or the appropriation of the colonizers' traits exhibits certain level of acceptance of colonial practices or values, even though it creates slippage together with the "not quite." These observations thus suggest that it is essential to see the compliant nature of the similarities between Exodus 19–24 and the cuneiform law collections in the study of Exodus 19–24's rhetoric.

48. Sharrad, "Some Pacific Takes," 106–9.

49. Sharrad, 104–9.

Hybridity's Oppressive Nature and Pursuit of Difference as Resistance

In addition to revealing the compliant nature of the colonized people's adoption of the colonial discourse, some postcolonial scholars point out the oppressive nature of hybridity and advocate the pursuit of difference. These arguments not only bring into attention the importance of ethical engagement in understanding hybridity, but also demonstrate the resistive nature of being different from the colonizers, which are vital for the study of Exodus 19–24.

Although in the past few decades the understanding of hybridity as resistance has transformed the concept of hybridity from "a derogatory and supremacist term" to "a subversive byproduct of colonial ideology,"[50] some postcolonial scholars find that the term's racist connotation and its association with oppressive history still limit the resistive power of hybridity. Robert Young reveals that this term originates in the nineteenth-century biological science, which initially devalued non-white and colonized peoples.[51] Anjali Prabhu points out further that the existence of hybrid people, though challenging colonizers' division between themselves and the colonized, in turn led colonizers to set up discriminatory policies on education, marriage, citizenship, and so forth.[52] The notion and the promotion of hybridity are indeed associated with some oppressive history, including colonialism, immigration, and slavery, with which Prabhu urges postcolonial scholars to contend.[53] She thus argues that striving for differences and engaging with colonial history in an ethical way are necessary for resisting colonial power. For instance, Édouard Glissent (an influential figure in Caribbean thought who was born in Martinique and educated in Paris) pursues contradiction and involves his work in an ethical engagement. This ethical engagement aims to stimulate social upheaval, such as the emancipation of the maroon (the runaway slave) from the plantation economy.[54] Fanon's *Black Skin, White Mask* also reveals colonized people's endeavor, which is highly involved with radical social change and ethical engagement that interacts with otherness.[55]

---

50. Roth, *Hyphenating Moses*, 62.
51. Young, *Colonial Desire*. See also Young, *Empire, Colony, Postcolony*, 45–50.
52. Prabhu, *Hybridity*, xii.
53. Prabhu, 16.
54. Prabhu, xiv, 119–20.
55. Prabhu, xiv, 127.

In fact, writers from various colonies see the importance of pursuing differences to the colonized, and some of these writers even practice it. Fanon discloses that while colonized black people try to make themselves white, they know that there is a difference between blacks and whites, and they want this difference.[56] Godiwala also points out that Rushdie puts the Islamic discourse in the center of his text *The Satanic Verses*, rather than mimicking the Western novel. The Qur'an, which Rushdie valorizes, resists Western values and norms, functioning as a counter-discourse.[57] Thus, Godiwala argues that it is the differences, rather than mimicry, that threatens the dominant discourse.[58] In a similar vein, Déwé Gorodé's hybrid fables assert differences between the French and Kanak cultures and the necessity of upholding indigenous culture in Kanak life, even though they contain elements of both French and Kanak myths and identify the mixing of races in Kanak and the influence of Western modernity on Kanak culture.[59] Ngũgĩ wa Thiong'o even emphasizes that writing in the colonizers' languages pays homage to them, handicapping colonized people's revolutionary effort against the colonial power. He asserts that the use of Kenyan languages is essential for African anti-imperial struggles, allowing African people to participate in their national liberation process.[60] He thus not only urges Kenyan writers "to return to the roots," but also announced that *Decolonising the Mind* would be his last work written in English.[61]

Retrieval of Tradition as Open Resistance

Retrieving colonized people's culture and tradition is therefore another form of open resistance, which some postcolonial scholars call for. This strategy notably sheds light on the resistive nature of some ordinances and commandments in Exodus 19–24, which appeal to traditions of the people of Israel and Judah. Ella Shohat emphasizes that the "retrieval and reinscription" of colonized people's past is critical for shaping their collective identity

56. Fanon, *Black Skin, White Mask*, 73, 172.
57. Godiwala, "Postcolonial Desire," 72.
58. Godiwala, 71.
59. Sharrad, "Some Pacific Takes," 113.
60. Ngũgĩ, *Decolonising the Mind*, 26, 28, 41, 45.
61. Ngũgĩ, xiv, 73.

in order to question the colonial hegemony.[62] She suggests that rather than being retrieved statically, fetishistically, and literally, colonized people's past should be presented in the form of "narrated memories and experience."[63] This effort of reclaiming native cultural traditions may not be successful in some colonial contexts. For example, Rey Chow finds that the more Hong Kong people attempt a quest for Chinese identity and culture, the more this quest reveals how Hong Kong people's identity and culture deviates from the Chinese traditional norm.[64] However, the colonized do endeavor to recover and follow their cultural practices, as one can see in Nelson Mandela's work to promote and practice African cultural values in his anti-colonial politics. Elle Boehmer thus comments that by encouraging his people to fight back against the colonizer with minimal violence, Mandela taps his initiative of revolt into "black South Africans' buried histories of resistance" and avoids stooping to the colonizer's tactics.[65]

These pursuits of difference, and the oppressive nature of hybridity in the past, do somewhat challenge the understanding of hybridity as a resistance among the colonized. Nevertheless, resistance carried out in a hybrid way is also a phenomenon in colonies that these postcolonial scholars cannot deny. Shohat admits that hybridity is a reality of colonized peoples' identity "before, during, and after colonialism."[66] She finds that some indigenous people make use of colonial technology in order to preserve their culture. For instance, the indigenous Kayapo in Brazil use video cameras to record their cultural practices to exhibit the importance of preserving their cultural traditions.[67] Similarly, Boehmer notes that Mandela selectively supports the colonizers' values, such as the British understanding of justice and democracy, in his work.[68] Rather than stopping writing in English as he stated, Ngũgĩ continues to publish his work in English, including translating his earlier Kenyan work into English.[69] Postcolonial scholars who advocate open resistance thus

62. Shohat, "Notes on 'Post-Colonial,'" 109.
63. Shohat, 109.
64. Chow, "Between Colonizers," 163.
65. Boehmer, "Revisiting Resistance," 316.
66. Shohat, "Notes on 'Post-Colonial,'" 109.
67. Shohat, 109.
68. Boehmer, "Revisiting Resistance," 316.
69. Ngũgĩ, *Wizard of the Crow*.

also see the inevitable existence of hybridity in colonized peoples' resistive response to their colonizers. These scholars' arguments for difference thus demonstrate the resistive power of deviating from the colonial discourse, which enhances, rather than refutes, the understanding of the "not quite." More significantly, hybridity occurs in Exodus 19–24, which carry both similarities and differences to cuneiform law collections. The oppressive nature of hybridity in the past certainly calls for ethical engagement in the analysis of Exodus 19–24, but the emphasis on difference also urges one to attend not only to "the same," the acceptance of the dominant power, but also to the "not quite," the resistance to it in the study of this work of the imperialized.

1.2.3 Hybridity of Colonized Elites

To unfold the complexity further, postcolonial scholars reveal that different people take different approaches to the colonial discourse. Their observations about colonized elites are particularly significant for the study of Exodus 19–24, as this corpus was likely written by the elite among the people of Israel and Judah, whom some postcolonial biblical scholars deem to be agents for imperial oppression.[70]

Although Sugirtharajah asserts that postcolonialism gives one "the confidence to question the pieties of the powerful,"[71] postcolonial scholars see both the corruption and contribution of colonized elites. On the one hand, there are cases in which colonized elites follow their colonizers' practices and oppress their own people. Fanon sees the gap between the colonized elites and the masses in the African community. He observes that the nationalist bourgeoisie compromise with their colonizer on oppressing the colonized in order to prevent being swept away by the protest of the masses. He also finds that the colonized bourgeoisie take the role of manager for the colonizer, setting up their country as the colonizer's brothel. He argues that the colonized elites' avariciousness in fact makes them more than happy to take up what the colonizer hands out to them.[72] In a similar vein, Chow finds that while some Hong Kong activists seemed to fight for democracy for their people around the time of the handover, they actually carried forward British colonial

70. See §1.4. About the authors' characteristics, see §2.5.

71. Sugirtharajah, *Exploring Postcolonial Biblical Criticism*, 27.

72. Fanon, *Wretched of the Earth*, 62, 127, 152, 154, 175.

ideology. They thus made it even more difficult for Hong Kong people to accept China's governance.[73]

On the other hand, there are cases in which colonized elites fight for their people's well-being and resist following their colonizers' path. Fanon observes that in some underdeveloped countries, some elites, intellectuals, and government officials condemn the colonial rule. Some of them also fight for a planned economy, outlaw profiteers, and encourage the participation of the masses in public affairs.[74] Ngũgĩ finds that some patriotic elites, including students, intellectuals, and soldiers, assist the working people to carry out the resistance tradition in Africa.[75] Said also points out the difference between the power exercised by the Dutch and that exercised by Indonesian successors. The colonized successors are more generous in trade, refraining from imposing a monopoly in the country. They also promote their people's abilities, continuing to use the products of their people.[76] Robert Young contends that the colonized academics still speak for human values that resist colonial and imperial assumptions, even though they are confined by the corporatized university system,[77] and some of their colonial counterparts continue to develop colonial tools to stereotype the colonized.[78]

Ngũgĩ thus suggests that there are different strands among the colonized bourgeoisie, ranging from "the comprador bourgeoisie" to "the nationalistic or patriotic bourgeoisie."[79] The former act as agent between the colonizer and the colonized and hope that their alliance with imperialism will be permanent. The latter, in contrast, strive for independence from the imperial power.[80] Fanon also frankly points out that because of colonial subjugation, the colonized, especially those who are educated, have to struggle unceasingly

73. Chow, "King Kong," 312. For more examples of comprador intellectuals, see Dabashi, *Brown Skin, White Masks*, 38–64.

74. Fanon, *Wretched of the Earth*, 177.

75. Ngũgĩ, *Decolonising the Mind*, 2.

76. Said, *Culture*, 2.

77. Young, *Empire, Colony, Postcolony*, 126.

78. Said notes that rather than scan or subvert academic Orientalism, orientalist scholars, including those who attempt to break the stereotype of the Oriental, keep increasing the effectiveness of academic Orientalism by offering study tools that stereotype the Oriental; Said, *Orientalism*, 276–77.

79. Ngũgĩ, *Decolonising the Mind*, 20.

80. Ngũgĩ, 20.

with the dilemma between being more like their colonizer and identifying themselves more with their colonized fellow.[81] Referring to colonized people's work, Ashcroft, Griffiths, and Tiffin contend that colonized writers inevitably become caught "in the conflict between destruction and creativity"; they "might perish there wrestling multiple-headed spirits," but they might also be able to rejoin their people "with the boon of prophetic vision."[82]

Rev. Tiyo Soga, an early South African Christian convert and minister, is a good example of a colonized leader who wrestled with both colonial values and his own culture. His wrestling exhibits both acceptance of and resistance to the colonizer's traits, offering a useful viewpoint for understanding the motivations behind the similarities and differences between Exodus 19–24 and cuneiform law collections. Although Soga had received European-style education and converted to Christianity, he publicly supported the traditional Xhosa culture and advocated preserving it. Yet, he also promoted modernization and reform of Xhosa customs and beliefs, which he thought only Euro-Christianity could bring forth.[83] Still, he did not acquiesce to the superiority of colonial culture. He taught Xhosa people that while they should raise hats to chiefs as the white people did, they should not do so to the whites who had a poor reputation. Rather than being simply collusive or simply resistive, Soga's thoughts and writings thus reflect his wrestling with his role as a member and supporter of the Xhosa people and a faithful ordained minister of a European mission.[84]

This wrestling, together with the understanding of hybridity, calls for attention to the multifaceted nature of imperialized peoples' response to empire in the study of Exodus 19–24. This attention will be enhanced by asking some crucial questions about the context of imperialized peoples' discourse, including "Who mixes what, with whom, with what result, for what reasons, motives and interests at which historical moment, in what context?"[85] Still, openness to the complexity of imperialized peoples' discourse is necessary for answering these questions. With a serious consideration of ethical implications, one has

81. Fanon, *Black Skin, White Masks*, 8, 14.

82. Ashcroft, Griffiths, and Tiffin, *Empire Writes Back*, 79; Achebe, *Morning Yet*, 67.

83. Griffiths, "Conversion," 69–71, 76, 82.

84. Griffiths, 69, 75–76.

85. Broeck, "White Fatigue," 53.

to attend to the wrestling of the imperialized, to both their adoption of and differentiation from the imperial discourse. Acceptance of, resistance to, and thus ambivalence toward the imperial power all possibly take place among the imperialized, reflecting their endeavor to live under the shadow of empire.

1.3 Legal Discourse of the Colonized

The multifaceted nature of colonized peoples' response to their colonizers is also revealed in their legal discourse, that is, their written or spoken communications related to law or exhibiting characteristics of it. Postcolonial understandings of legal discourse shed further light on the rhetoric of Exodus 19–24, although some notes about their limitations on the analysis of this biblical corpus are also necessary. To begin with, law is not a static concept. In modern colonized contexts, understanding of law and the relationship between law and people may also differ from those in the ancient world. Specifically, postcolonial studies mainly deal with law that has legislative functions, while biblical scholars have basically excluded the possibility that stipulations or stipulation-like elements in Exodus 19–24 were meant to be used in court.[86] Moreover, colonizers' domination of colonized peoples' legal discourse during the modern colonial period is somewhat different from the relationship of the people of Israel and Judah to the empire in relation to Exodus 19–24. Degree of colonizers' domination of colonized peoples' legal discourse in modern contexts distinctively ranges from complete domination to recognition of indigenous legal traditions.[87] An example of the former is Mozambique, whose laws were made in Portugal and whose legal offices were Portuguese. An example of the latter is India, whose legal practices were tolerated by the British government despite the existence of some colonial mediation that led to hybrid legal discourse, such as Anglo-Hindu law. In between these two ends of the spectrum is a kind of negotiation between the colonizer and the colonized, such as that which occurred in many parts of Africa. The colonizers established institutions of governance according to

86. See §2.4.1.

87. Baxi, "Postcolonial Legality," 542–43.

colonized Africans' customs, such as chieftainship, in order to accommodate indigenous elites' interest.[88]

Despite these differences between Exodus 19–24 and colonized people's legal discourse, the Exodus corpus is similarly a work of subjugated people.[89] The Book of the Covenant likewise exhibits legal characteristics and might have been intended to be a reference work for judges.[90] Hence, postcolonial studies of colonized peoples' legal discourse, especially those concerning contexts in which the colonized had participation in the formation of their law, still offer insight into Exodus 19–24's rhetoric. These studies reveal the roles of law among the imperialized and demonstrate the importance of attending to various faces of their legal discourse.

1.3.1 Importance of Law to the Colonized

Law, as a system of rules, plays a vital role in a colonized society. While some postcolonial scholars suggest that a few postcolonies suspended legalities after experiencing colonial overrule,[91] others argue that the colonized usually do not denigrate the importance of law, especially when they need to relate to the colonizers and other postcolonies.[92] In addition to regulating the behavior of the colonized and the relationships among them, law in fact preserves ideals, such as freedom and justice.[93] Moreover, law establishes colonized peoples' identity, just as much as it is established according to their identity.[94] Introducing the law of her people (the Tangankald people, an aboriginal people in Australia), Irene Watson states that, "The law is who we are, we are also the law."[95] Dianne Otto asserts that law has a constitutive role in defining the colonized.[96] Brinkley Messick even demonstrates that the opportunity for

88. Baxi, 542–53.

89. See §2.3.

90. See §2.4.3.

91. Comaroff and Comaroff, "Law and Disorder," 11. Following Comaroff and Comaroff, I use the term "postcolonies" to refer to places that were previously colonized. For other understandings regarding the notion of the postcolony, see, for instance, Ashcroft, Griffins, and Tiffin, *Post-Colonial Studies,*175–78.

92. Sinha, "Perspective," 24.

93. Davies, *Asking the Law Question*, 6.

94. Davies, 314.

95. Watson, "Indigenous Peoples' Law-Ways," 39.

96. Otto, "Subalternity," 162.

the colonized to implement their own law, even only a part of it, manifests their legitimacy in governing themselves and thus a kind of independence from the colonizer.[97] Hence, anthropologists advocate that "law is not only practice and process, but also discourse, code, and communication."[98] Similar to the nature of literature which Ngũgĩ indicates,[99] law is a critical tool in developing colonized people's cultural ethos and values.[100] Ratna Kapur also significantly points out that law is "an important site of politics and the struggle over meaning."[101] These understandings are particularly crucial for unfolding the wrestling of the imperialized authors that Exodus 19–24 reflects, as they suggest this corpus's political nature and its intimate connection with their authors' identity in relation to the empire.

1.3.2 Hegemony and Resistance in the Legal Discourse of the Colonized and their Elites

Indeed, similar to colonized peoples' discourse in general, their legal discourse, including their law, is not singly purposed. Legal scholars do point out that law has some negative features related to power, including its function of upholding arrangements of powers for states and certain classes. However, Susan F. Hirsch and Mindie Lazarus-Black contend that law, by nature, "is simultaneously a maker of hegemony and a means of resistance."[102] This is also the case for colonized people's legal discourse. On the one hand, the hegemonic power is at work in legal procedures, such as the regulation of positioning, language, and timing.[103] It is also revealed in oppressive power structures that law maintains in human history, such as slavery.[104] In some postcolonies, legislation related to women, including trafficking of and violence against them, is still greatly confined by oppressive colonial ideology.[105]

97. Messick, *Calligraphic State*, 51.

98. Hirsch and Lazarus-Black, "Performance and Paradox," 5.

99. Ngũgĩ, *Decolonising the Mind*, 99.

100. Davies, *Asking the Law Question*, 301.

101. Kapur, *Erotic Justice*, 50.

102. Hirsch and Lazarus-Black, "Performance and Paradox," 9. See also Merry, "Colonial and Postcolonial Law," 575.

103. Hirsch and Lazarus-Black, "Performance and Paradox," 10.

104. Kapur, *Erotic Justice*, 22.

105. Kapur, 2–4.

There is also oppression caused by the use of legal violence among the police.[106] Some postcolonies, such as the Mugabe regime and South Africa during apartheid, even set up laws to foreclose the possibility of political resistance and to legitimize violent action against critics.[107] The observance of the laws in fact exhibits inequality between the colonizers and the colonized. Colonizers' law is usually regarded as "universal, metropolitan and advanced," while colonized peoples' law as "local, indigenous, and backward."[108] Therefore, it is not uncommon for the colonized to find that they are bound to follow colonizers' laws,[109] including those oppressive to their own people.

On the other hand, colonized peoples' legal discourse does not always equate to coercion or serve only the upper class's interests.[110] Its resistive power is reflected by the fact that law and its implementation also offer platforms for practicing "justice, rights, development, and individual associational autonomy," in addition to governance.[111] It is also a means the colonized and the subordinate can utilize to appropriate, invent, and oppose cultures.[112] For instance, in the postcolonial period, Swahili women brought their legal cases, such as those regarding maintenance payments and domestic abuse, to the Kadhi's Courts, a Kenyan court system that enforces rights of inheritance, family, and succession for Muslims. They did so in order to fight against oppression that they experienced in their society, which was greatly influenced by colonization and patriarchal values. The rulings of most cases favored women's claims; some even immediately led to positive changes in female plaintiffs' lives, such as recovering their dowry.[113] The legal discourse, including the law and its implementation, offers resistive power to the colonized and the subordinate.

Colonized people's legal discourse, therefore, can be a tool for both hegemony and resistance. Its interconnected potential for both power and resistance is reflected further in some policies established in colonies. For instance,

106. Purdy, "Postcolonialism," 203–29.

107. Comaroff and Comaroff, "Law and Disorder," 30; Morton, *States of Emergency*, 94.

108. Strawson, "Palestine's Basic Law," 422.

109. Roy, "Postcolonial Theory," 325.

110. Hirsch and Lazarus-Black, "Performance and Paradox," 4.

111. Baxi, "Postcolonial Legality," 540.

112. Chanock, *Law and Custom*, viii.

113. Hirsch, "Kadhi's Courts," 218.

while Caribbean slave laws mainly aimed at suppressing the enslaved so that they would not revolt and their masters would not lose their "property," these laws also offered freedom to some slaves, as some of the laws protected slaves from their masters' inhumane conduct. In view of the intense legal arguments involved before the liberation took place, one may regard this liberation as a development within the scope of the law rather than something inherent in the law; however, the law did offer a platform for it to occur.[114] Thus, colonized people's legal discourse can be an artifice for the powerful to legitimately seize benefit for themselves and, at the same time, a weapon used by the weak to fight back against authority and reclaim resources and rights.[115]

In a similar vein, colonized elites' intentions in the formulation of the legal discourse are not one-sided. Otto argues that nationalist elites usually assumed the colonizers' position that ignored the interests of the subaltern, as the strategy of the New International Economic Order (a set of legal proposals suggested by some postcolonies in the 1970s) reflects.[116] Balakrishnan Rajagopal also suggests that elites of both European countries and postcolonies relied heavily on the presentations of the postcolonies as deficient and uncivilized when they developed international legal order.[117] However, Upendra Baxi finds that the colonized elites in some colonies, such as India, have diverse interests in relation to their roles, such as missionaries, commercial or industrial leaders, and law reformers. The networks formed by these elites introduce reform models for their law, which enhance the development of colonized people's legal profession and their independence from their colonizer, even though these elites take into account their collective interests.[118] These observations on the colonized elites and the hegemonic and resistive nature of colonized peoples' legal discourse, like those concerning colonized people's discourse in general, urge openness and attention to the multifaceted nature of the imperialized authors' intention and Exodus 19–24's rhetoric in response to imperial legal discourse.

114. Lazarus-Black, "Slaves, Masters," 258, 264.

115. Comaroff and Comaroff, "Law and Disorder," 31.

116. Otto, "Subalternity," 164.

117. Rajagopal, "Locating the Third World," 1–20.

118. Baxi, "Postcolonial Legality," 543.

1.3.3 Colonized Peoples' Responses to Colonizers' Legal Discourse

Observations on colonized peoples' various approaches to colonizers' legal discourse urge this attention further. Some colonized people adopt colonizers' law indiscriminately due to the cultural pressures of the colonial presence. Others endeavor to distinguish their legal discourse from the colonizers'. Still, quite a few of the colonized appropriate the law of their colonizers in order to resist the colonial legal discourse.

An example in which the colonized simply adopt their colonizers' law is the formation of policy in Tanganyika, which exhibited a tendency to imitate English court's procedures since the early colonized period. The assimilation became even more serious later when African lawmakers progressively departed from their traditions and followed Western law more closely in the treatment of their customary laws.[119] A reason behind this acceptance is a significant phenomenon that colonized peoples face the pressure to follow colonizers' standards in order to be regarded as civilized. This is especially the case when nation-statehood is enforced among them in a standardized way despite their diversity.[120] Indeed, there are cases when colonized people's law may not be recognized unless it is consistent with the colonizer's law. An example is Aboriginal customary law under the Western Australia legal system, in which the recognition of colonized people's law is confined by a dominant legal paradigm formed by the colonizer.[121] Although there is no evidence for similar legal pressure on the people of Israel and Judah, this observation invites consideration of possible pressure behind the similarities between Exodus 19–24 and cuneiform law collections.[122]

Some colonized peoples, nevertheless, endeavor to maintain the distinctiveness of their legal discourse. Some even emphasize the difference between their law and their colonizers' law in order to resist the assimilation into the colonial legal culture. Sri Lanka had a constitution that was mainly affected by Sinhalese Buddhism (the major religion of native people in Sri Lanka), rather than by Roman Catholicism or Protestant Christianity (the

119. Chanock, *Law and Custom*, 60.

120. Otto, "Subalternity," 151.

121. Roy, "Postcolonial Theory," 353–54. A similar situation occurs when indigenous people fight for legitimacy in claiming their land, see Young, *Empire, Colony, Postcolony*, 32.

122. See §2.4.7.

colonizers' religion), even though Sri Lanka was colonized by different countries.[123] Watson, a member of Aboriginal Peoples in Australia, even emphasizes that her people have had their own legal system since the beginning of their existence and contends that their law is different from that of their colonizer. Aboriginal Peoples' legal systems are embedded in their relationships to the natural world, operating in "a natural system of obligations and benefits."[124] Unlike the colonizer's law, their law serves to maintain the continuity of life.[125] Their law is also creatively presented in stories and songs; thus, Aboriginal People know law through living, rather than legislation.[126] These distinctive features of Aboriginal People's legal system resist the colonial claim that Aboriginal Peoples are uncivilized people without law and society. They challenge the colonizer's justification for occupying Aboriginal Peoples' land. They also encourage Aboriginal Peoples to preserve their own law, urging them not to look for legal guidance from their colonizer, but from their own traditions.[127]

Notably, some colonized peoples even reinvented customs in order to establish their own legal system when they were colonized. Martin Chanock observes that small-scale African monarchies, which formed the African legal system's foundation, multiplied enormously during the colonial period.[128] Seizing upon the opportunity offered by the colonizer's need for local legal assistance, African lawmakers made use of customs and gave them new content in order to maintain their collapsing hierarchies and social order. For instance, they idealized traditional understandings of the relationship between men and women in marriage and made rules out of them in order to deal with adultery. Although some urban men used these rules to establish control over women, these rules were aimed to preserve the position of legal authority and to stabilize city dwellers' morality. This customary law not only better met the people's need, representing sensitive responses to living interests, but also expressed "continuing Africanness," resisting English law's

123. Silva, "Ontological Approach," 190.

124. Watson, *Aboriginal Peoples*, 5.

125. Watson, "Indigenous Peoples," 48.

126. Watson, *Aboriginal Peoples*, 12–13, 31, 77.

127. Watson, 1, 18–20, 164.

128. Chanock, *Law and Custom*, 34.

"innovating foreignness."[129] These observations on the use of traditions for the formation of colonized peoples' legal discourse in order to resist the colonizers' echo the understandings of colonized peoples' discourse in general. They again shed light on some ordinances of Exodus 19–24, which relate to their authors' traditions, and indicate the importance of attending to the resistive nature of differences between Exodus 19–24 and cuneiform law collections, amid the similarities between them.

The importance of this attention is demonstrated further by the fact that some colonized peoples partially adopt the colonial legal discourse in order to resist the colonizer's legal discourse. Some incorporate colonial legal language in their legal documents to protest their subordination. Others transform the colonial legal discourses to negate their colonizers' logic.[130] This hybrid legal discourse may disprove the colonizer's perception of colonized peoples' legal underdevelopment. For instance, the translation and reinterpretation of Islamic law based on an English legal framework compelled the Europeans to admit that Islamic societies practiced the rule of law before colonialization.[131] The hybrid legal discourse also manifests a new moral perspective, even though it seems to repeat imperialism. This is the case in the policies formulated by G77 (the Group of 77), a coalition of developing nations. Appropriating liberal legal concepts, these policies strive for self-determination, nondiscrimination, state sovereignty, and so forth. By partially replacing some of the colonizer's principles, such as freedom and reciprocity, with principles that are beneficial to postcolonies, such as protection and non-reciprocity, these policies promote solidarity in law concerning international economics.[132] These observations, like those concerning hybridity in colonized people's discourse in general, suggest the importance of studying the interaction between similarities and differences that the corpus of Exodus 19–24 reflects in comparison to cuneiform law collections. They also invite serious consideration of the resistive force in Exodus 19–24.

129. Chanock, 22, 24, 193, 237.

130. Hirsch and Lazarus-Black, "Performance and Paradox," 10.

131. Strawson, "Islamic Law," 121–22.

132. Otto, "Subalternity," 156–59.

1.3.4 Continuity and Discontinuity of Colonizers' Legal Discourse

Because of the dual nature of colonized peoples' law (hegemonic and resistive) and their various approaches to colonizers' legal discourse, one can see both continuities and discontinuities of colonizers' legal discourse in that of the colonized. Colonized people's legal discourse may maintain some oppressive legal practices of their colonizer, such as debt bondage and gender-based wage differentiation, but at the same time it attempts to break the colonizer's hegemonic practices, for instance, introducing redistribution of property in their society. Colonized people's legal discourse may also preserve the use of violence against the marginalized in view of the landowning classes' interest, but meanwhile extend the colonizer's notions of rights to the marginalized, such as penalizing forced labor and human trafficking.[133]

These continuities and discontinuities may reflect different psychological states of the colonized and various functions of their legal discourse. They may exhibit a kind of anxiety of the colonized, who are unable to decide, establish, and locate their place and time, and are therefore caught up between the colonizer's notions of legality and their own people's fight for justice.[134] They may also manifest the aforementioned wrestling of the colonized, who simultaneously accept and resist the colonial metanarrative, if not break the binary division between the colonizer and the colonized. A thorough study of the context, which engages with colonized people's legal discourse "as a complex, multiple and contingent discourse whose meaning is susceptible to context, cultural histories and the legacies of the past,"[135] will certainly enhance the understanding of colonized peoples' legal discourse. However, this study will not be fruitful unless one attends to the multifaceted nature of colonized peoples' response. This attention is similarly essential for unfolding the complex rhetoric of imperialized people's hybrid legal discourse, including Exodus 19–24, which disclose an endeavor to resist imperial metanarrative, albeit in a conservative way.

133. Baxi, "Postcolonial Legality," 545–47.

134. Perrin, "Approaching Anxiety," 27–28.

135. Kapur, *Erotic Justice*, 50.

1.4 Implications for Analysis of Exodus 19–24

Postcolonial scholars' understandings of colonized peoples' discourse in general and their legal discourse in particular thus call for an analysis of Exodus 19–24 that has the following characteristics: being open to the multifaceted nature of authorial motivation behind this corpus, attending to both the similarities and differences between this corpus and cuneiform law collections, and studying in detail the complex rhetoric in response to the imperial legal discourse that these similarities and differences suggest. A review of postcolonial analyses in relation to Exodus 19–24 will help understand the importance of this openness and attention further.

Notably, no detailed postcolonial analysis of Exodus 19–24 as a whole has been published so far. However, some postcolonial biblical scholars, including Musa W. Dube, Gale A. Yee, Shiju Mathew, and R. S. Wafula, have offered chapter-length analyses that cover various sections of this corpus. These analyses have brought the imperial features of Exodus 19–24 into scholars' attention. A further question is if these imperial features intertwine with resistive elements beyond the scope of their projects. These elements would suggest that this corpus reflects its authors' wrestling in their response to imperial legal traditions rather than merely their compliance with them.

1.4.1 Musa W. Dube's Analysis of Exodus as an Imperializing Text

Dube's analysis is a chapter of her *Postcolonial Feminist Interpretation of the Bible.*[136] With the title "Method in Ancient Imperializing Texts," her analysis aims to demonstrate how to unfold literary-rhetorical presentations that legitimize the possession of inhabited lands in imperializing texts. Dube argues that Exodus, along with Joshua 1–12, is an excellent example of such text. She does note that some scholars date the final form of Exodus to the sixth century BCE, which indicates the historical context of the biblical text. However, she argues for a focus on its rhetoric, which by itself has a function of empowering people to participate or overcome colonialism. Despite the awareness of this dual function, she contends that Exodus's presentations reveal characteristics of imperializing texts. These presentations authorize travel from Egypt to Canaan, construct a flat image of Canaan and its inhabitants,

136. Dube, *Postcolonial Feminist Interpretation*, 57–83.

build up the Israelites' special identity, and reveal shifts between subjugation and domination among Israelite women.

In regard to authorizing travel, Dube not only refers to the repeated command, "let my people go," in the first half of Exodus, but also compares the descriptions about slavery in the narrative with those in the ordinances. A notable argument she presents is that while the narrative depicts divine liberation of Israelites from slavery, the divine-given ordinances (Exod 21:1–11) do not abolish the institution. Thus, she asserts that rather than a statement against slavery, the description of the Israelites as slaves is merely a literary-rhetorical device that aims to attract sympathy for the Israelites and moves the plot of the conquest plan.

Concerning the image of the land and its people and the identity of the Israelites, Dube first reveals the negative characterization of the Canaanites in Exodus 23:23–33, in addition to the uniformly positive descriptions of Canaan in Exodus. She points out the repeated references to different people groups in the descriptions of the God-given land, including that in Exodus 23:23, asserting that these references indicate Exodus's emphasis on God's authorization to colonize an inhabited land. She then argues that this emphasis comes with a negative characterization of the inhabitants. This characterization begins in the depiction of the Sinai covenant, which warns the Israelites against having other gods or making any idol (Exod 20:2–6, 20:23; 23:13). This warning, Dube contends, is then connected to Canaan's inhabitants in Exodus 23:23–33. This passage creates a contact zone between the colonizer (the Israelites) and the colonized (the inhabitants of the land) and casts the latter negatively. The inhabitants will make the Israelites sin against God, and their religious belief will be a snare to the Israelites. Thus, they shall be blotted out. In contrast to this negative image of the land's inhabitants, Exodus constructs a special identity for the Israelites, according to Dube. She asserts that through God's word in Exodus 19:5–6, the Israelites become a chosen and holy race, an identity that early chapters of Exodus hint at and later chapters continue to define.

Finally, Dube asserts that Exodus's description of women exhibits shifts between subordinate and dominant roles. She argues that women first share the colonized role with their male counterparts under the oppression of Egypt. They then particularly become the colonizer when they fight for independence. However, when they begin their journey in the wilderness, their role is submerged by the patriarchy. Dube points out that not only do men take up leading roles and hold special relations with God from that point onward, but the announcement of the law and the law itself reveal patriarchal division (Exod 19:15; 20:17). Dube thus argues that Exodus characterizes Israelite women contradictorily as both "colonizing race-privileged subjects" and "colonized patriarchal objects."[137]

Dube's analysis does bring into attention the imperial features of Exodus, as her chapter aims to. It also reveals the complexity of Exodus's characterization of women, which sheds light on their struggle with their subordinate and dominant statuses. A further question is whether similar complexity also occurs among the male characters or even among the text's authors. If Exodus is a literary-rhetorical product of a certain historical moment, one also has to seriously consider whether Exodus is merely an imperializing text or a text of the imperialized. An equally necessary question for investigation is if this text reflects any similarities, and differences, to imperial texts of its time – for instance, cuneiform law collections. It is not uncommon for a text of the imperialized to reveal imperializing elements, which Dube reveals, as the aforementioned postcolonial understandings suggest that it is a characteristic of imperialized peoples' discourse. Nevertheless, a text of the imperialized may also exhibit resistance to the imperial metanarrative, which a study that only focuses on imperializing features will not be able to unfold. This resistance is actually part of the dual function that Dube introduces in her argument for the focus on the text's rhetoric. To fully understand this rhetoric, attention to the social location and the complex nature of the text's authors and the study of both similarities and differences between that text and corresponding imperial texts are necessary.

1.4.2 Gale A. Yee's Postcolonial Analysis of Exodus 19–20 and Related Passages

Yee's analysis is an encouraging attempt that exhibits consideration of Exodus's hybrid nature and its authors' social location. Nevertheless, her emphasis is still on the imperial tendency of both the authors and the rhetoric of Exodus 19–20 and related passages. Her chapter analyzes postcolonial biblical

137. Dube, *Postcolonial Feminist Interpretation*, 75.

criticism in the festschrift *Methods for Exodus*.[138] In addition to an introduction to postcolonialism and postcolonial biblical criticism, this chapter offers a postcolonial analysis of Exodus 1–2 and 19–20. This analysis begins with a discussion of these texts' historical context in the Persian period. Her understanding of the Jewish elites is noteworthy. It is based on biblical studies regarding the economic and religious life in Yehud, as well as postcolonial studies, including Bhabha's understanding of mimicry. However, Yee argues that Jewish elites were "mimic men" who not only served as agents of the Persian Empire but also oppressed their own people by imposing various taxes on them.[139] Darius, the Persian king, permitted his colonies' local elites to standardize their ancient stories and codify their laws, but confined their work within his empire's interest. Yee thus states that the Pentateuch, including Exodus, is "a product of colonial hybridity," preserving the Jewish community's identity and serving the Persian Empire's interests.[140]

This understanding of the biblical authors' imperial tendency introduces Yee's postcolonial interpretation of Exodus 1–2 and 19–20. Notably, this interpretation first exhibits a shift in Yee's thought, but she then gives a similar view of Exodus 19–20's and related passages' imperial characteristics. She begins her interpretation by pointing out that although the canon was a tool of the Persian Empire and Jewish elites, Exodus 1–2 and 19–20 reflect both the voices of the empire and those of resistance. Yee asserts that this hybridity offers the texts the potential for deconstructing imperial ideology and revealing subaltern voices. She then demonstrates this potential in her discussion of Exodus 1–2. She points out that this passage reflects, for instance, binary descriptions of the Egyptians and the Israelites, characterization of the Pharaoh as a stupid ruler, midwives' mimicry of Egyptian prejudices against the Israelites, and so forth. These presentations, she argues, mock empire and resist imperial intents and purposes, even though they would gratify the Persians' desire for claiming superiority and control over all of their colonies, including Egypt.

Yee's analysis of Exodus 19–20 and related passages, however, does not follow this attention to the texts' dual function. Rather, it unfolds only these

138. Yee, "Postcolonial Biblical Criticism," 193–233.

139. Yee, 211.

140. Yee, 213.

passages' imperial features. Comparing the covenant in Exodus with Hittite suzerainty treaties, Yee suggests that the story of deliverance is only a prologue to the pronouncement of the law in Sinai, which sets up a vassal/king relationship between Israel and God. In this comparison, she also argues that the Sinaitic covenant carries "the imperial ethos of domination and subordination."[141] She then contends that the commands concerning the Canaanites, including the passage in Exodus 23, express that "the imperial God YHWH thus gives the Israelites a religious warrant to conquer indigenous peoples, colonize their lands."[142] She adds that the Exodus/Conquest traditions in the Torah and the Former Prophets were reinterpreted and used by Jewish elites for justifying their possession of the lands and economic exploitation of the indigenous Jews in Yehud.

This interpretation of Exodus 19–20, the covenant, and its epilogue appropriately considers the importance of reading the text from the marginalized, an approach which Robert Allen Warrior advocates in response to liberation theologies that indiscriminately regard Exodus as a model of liberation.[143] This interpretation also supports part of Yee's conclusion that the Bible can be appropriated for legitimating oppression. Nevertheless, given the texts' hybrid nature, which she rightly emphasizes in the beginning of her analysis, this interpretation reasonably makes one wonder about those passages' possible voice of resistance. Her presentation of Jewish elites similarly invites queries regarding the "not quiteness" of their mimicry, as well as the multifaceted

141. Yee, 223.

142. Yee, 224.

143. Yee, 226; Warrior, "Canaanites, Cowboys, and Indians," 261–65. The reading of Exodus from the Canaanites' perspective is first advocated by Said in his response to Walzer's work, although Said does not explain this reading in detail (Said, "Michael Walzer's 'Exodus and Revolution,'" 86–106; Walzer and Said, "An Exchange," 246–59; Walzer, *Exodus and Revolution*). For a critical review of the exchange between Said and Walzer, see Walhout, "*Intifada* of the Intellectuals," 327–50. For a critique of Said's and Warrior's works as canonical references for postcolonial biblical studies, see Roth, *Hyphenating Moses*, 48–54. Laura E. Donaldson offers a helpful explication of the Canaanite reading in "Postcolonialism and Biblical Reading," 10–12. For more about reading Exodus from the marginalized, see articles in Sugirtharajah, *Voices from the Margin*, 150–200. Among them, Naim S. Ateek's article is particularly related to the Exodus passage concerning the Canaanites (Ateek, "Palestinian Perspective," 165–70). He argues that there is liberation and hope in the new exodus in Isaiah, but not in the promised land in Exod 23. This argument is similar to that of Pui-Lan, *Discovering the Bible*, 98–100. Helpful overviews of the development of postcolonial biblical studies in response to liberation theology include Collin, *Bible after Babel*, 53–74; Roth, *Hyphenating Moses*, 8–43; Segovia, "Introduction," xi–xiv, xix–xxv.

characteristics of colonized elites, which postcolonial scholars point out. These lacunae will not be filled unless one is open to the multifaceted features of the authorial motivation behind Exodus 19–24. A more nuanced study of both the voices of the empire and those of the resistance in this corpus is also essential for this task.

1.4.3 Shiju Mathew's Postcolonial Womanist Reading of the Book of the Covenant

Similar to Dube's and Yee's arguments, Mathew contends that the laws in Exodus concerning women exhibit imperial and oppressive characteristics. His analysis of the Book of the Covenant is part of his comparative study, *Biblical Law Codes in Creative Tension: A Postcolonial Womanist Reading.*[144] Dating the Book of the Covenant to the eighth century BCE, Mathew asserts that its treatment of women is more oppressive than that of the Deuteronomic Code and the Holiness Code because of a more intense colonial experience under the Assyrian conquest. He points out that a comparison between the Book of the Covenant and cuneiform law collections indicates the impact of ancient Israelites' interaction with the imperial culture on all aspects of their life, including their legal system. He thus asserts that ancient Israelites mimicked imperial strategies in dealing with women and the land when their nation flourished politically and economically. Similar to Yee, he also suggests that their elites possibly misused and altered laws in order to increase their wealth, which in turn widened the gap between the rich and the poor and exploited the marginalized, as the prophets condemned. Women became victims when the legal system was not intended to protect the weak in the community, according to Mathew.[145]

This understanding of the historical context, which suggests the Book of the Covenant's imperial and oppressive features, leads to Mathew's analysis of women's status first in the cuneiform law collections and laws in Deuteronomy and Leviticus, then laws in Exodus. He studies these laws from a postcolonial womanist perspective, focusing on the relationship between Israelite law collections and colonial powers as well as on the association between the

144. Mathew, *Biblical Law Codes*, 165–211. For a summary of this study, see Mathew, "Law, Land, and Gender," 177–92.

145. Mathew, *Biblical Law Codes*, xx, xxii–xxiii, xxxiii.

subjugation of women in Israelite legal system and the issue of land and economy. He sets his goal to unfold the patriarchal and colonial ideologies in the biblical laws based on intertextual and deconstruction methods.[146] This goal seems to lead Mathew to some interpretations of the Book of the Covenant that consider only this corpus's imperial features.

These interpretations concern various ordinances related to women. Here I review Mathew's analysis of Exodus 21:2–11, 21:20–27, and 22:15–16, in which he offers more detailed explanations. Regarding Exodus 21:2–11 (about male and female slaves), Mathew begins his analysis by pointing out that, like ancient West Asia,[147] ancient Israel did not abolish slavery; its prophets only protested this institution but did not eradicate it. Biblical and cuneiform laws also reflect similar social conditions, such as kidnapping people and selling abducted people. He then strongly criticizes that the ordinances in Exodus 21:3–4 contradict what he calls "the commandment of God" in Genesis 2:24 and exhibits cruelty toward female slaves.[148] He points out that this stipulation does not allow the release of the wife given by the master to the male slave, when the male slave has finished his servitude. This stipulation does not give this wife the freedom of choice but treats her as her slave husband's or her master's property.

Concerning Exodus 21:5–6, in which the slave confesses his love for and his willingness to stay with his master, Mathew contends that the most likely scenario is that the slave fears falling into poverty. Mathew does note the attempt of both Middle Assyrian laws and biblical laws, including Exodus 21:7–11, to mitigate debt slavery's consequence for unmarried women. However, he asserts that the purpose of Exodus 21:7 is to ensure that the women will never escape from men's control. Comparing Exodus 21:7–11 with Deuteronomy 15:12, which allows both male and female slaves to have freedom after they have finished their servitude, Mathew adds that Exodus 21:7 seems to exhibit a "selfish motto" or "a secret male conspiracy" to avoid releasing female slaves.[149] He thus concludes that the Book of the Covenant

146. Mathew, 44.

147. Scholars usually use the term "ancient Near East" to refer to Mesopotamia, Hatti, the Levant, ancient Egypt, Persia, and so forth; however, the term "ancient West Asia" better indicates the region's location for non-Europeans. Mathew uses this term in his study also.

148. Mathew, *Biblical Law Codes*, 190.

149. Mathew, 197.

advocates for and legitimizes slavery, rather than criticizing it. For him, this corpus reflects that injustice prevailed in ancient Israel's social structure in which men, the powerful, had the right to make decisions, marginalizing and subjugating female slaves.

Mathew discusses more deeply the relationship between the Book of the Covenant and imperial legal values in his analysis of Exodus 21:20–27 (about physical assault against slaves and pregnant women) and Exodus 22:15–16 (about the seduction of unbetrothed maidens). He claims that the ordinances in Exodus 21:20–21 project physical assault of slaves as a normal practice. He also asserts that powerful nations' imperialistic tendency to treat slaves as property influenced ancient Israel. Similarly, he comments that Exodus 21:22–25, the talion laws, do not consider women's suffering, but require a fine that their husbands and the judges decide. He also states that monetary compensation was common in cuneiform laws. It is noteworthy that Mathew does point out some differences between Exodus 21:22–25 and the talion laws in cuneiform law collections. Differentiation between free women and female slaves is absent from Exodus 21:22–25; these ordinances also impose punishment on the offender instead of the offender's daughter. However, he does not comment on these differences.

Likewise, Mathew is aware that the ordinances in Exodus 21:26–27 offer freedom to slaves when they lose their eye and tooth because of their master's physical assault, but he explains that this arrangement is only based on a consideration that the cost of eye and tooth is the same as the slave's purchase price. What he emphasizes is that this case does not follow the general principle of talion laws because the offended are not free citizens. He thus concludes that the ordinances in Exodus 21:26–27 reflect slaves' low status in a society full of power control, just as cuneiform laws exhibit. In the analysis of Exodus 22:15–16, which concerns the seduction of unbetrothed maidens, Mathew continues to point out the similarities, but not the differences, between this stipulation and related laws in the Middle Assyrian Laws (MAL A 55–56). He emphasizes that Exodus 22:15–16 are androcentric because these ordinances, again, disregard the voice of the female victim. These analyses exhibit that, for Mathew, only similarities between the Book of the Covenant and cuneiform law collections, and their oppressive features, are meaningful for understanding how the ancient Israelites' legal discourse relates to the imperial one. In his analysis, differences between the Book of the Covenant and cuneiform law collections and the former's liberative features either do not seem to deserve attention, or have to be explained by other non-liberative considerations.

With these observations, Mathew concludes that the Book of the Covenant is both patriarchal and colonial. He not only argues that the casuistic laws conflict with Israel's liberative experience described in the exodus story, but also asserts that the casuistic laws concerning women are not "original" but a product of cuneiform laws' influence.[150] He emphasizes that the Book of the Covenant, like cuneiform law collections, was under rich and powerful people's control. Ancient Israelite elites mimicked their neighboring nations' social departmentalization in order to gain wealth and power, as well as to compete with these nations. Mathew even contrasts the laws in Exodus with God's will: He comments that while God "subverts imperialistic power," curtailing Pharaoh's hegemony, the Book of the Covenant supports "the vested interest of those who subvert the marginalized."[151] Thus, he urges readers of Exodus to deconstruct those laws and consider "more inclusive and life affirming laws" in order to build a strong foundation of a society.[152]

Mathew's study is the only postcolonial analysis of the Book of the Covenant so far. His effort in comparing this corpus with cuneiform law collections for his postcolonial analysis is worth appreciating. This analysis has also called for serious consideration of all people, especially women, in the understanding of the Book of the Covenant. Yet, setting a goal to unfold only the patriarchal and colonial ideologies in the biblical laws hinders him from exploring the possible endeavor of the ancient Israelite elites to alleviate the oppression caused by the corruption of Israelite and imperial social systems. This goal also keeps him from considering the possible liberative and resistive elements in the Book of the Covenant more seriously. While Mathew has observed the ancient Israelites' mimicry of the imperial culture, including their legal discourse, and reviewed Bhabha's contribution to postcolonialism,[153] he only sees the oppressive, but not any resistive, features of the resemblances and differences between biblical and cuneiform laws.

150. Mathew, 211.

151. Mathew, 239.

152. Mathew, 211.

153. Mathew, xx, xxviii, xxxii.

This perspective is reflected not only in his treatment of Exodus 21:7–11 and 21:22–27, which I have discussed earlier, but also by the absence of discussion of Exodus 21:28–32 in his analysis. This passage covers goring oxen laws, which consider both male and female victims, but notably do not distinguish between them in their penalty. Moreover, while these laws resemble the goring oxen laws in the Laws of Eshnunna (LE 54–55) and the Laws of Hammurabi (LH 250–252), their mention of female members of the society is not found in those two cuneiform law collections. This difference between Exodus 21:28–32 and cuneiform laws recall what Bhabha calls "the same, but not quite," which resists the imperial metanarrative, if not produces slippage that carries the effect of camouflage.[154]

An attention to this kind of difference, in addition to the similarities, between the Book of the Covenant and cuneiform law collections helps one to see not only the imperial and patriarchal tendencies of the laws in Exodus, as Mathew argues, but also their resistance to these tendencies. These features may further invite a reconsideration of Mathew's suggestion concerning the elites' abuse of the laws. Rather than reflecting only the ancient Israelite elites' compliance with the imperial practices, the Book of the Covenant exhibits how the imperialized wrestled with the imperial legal metanarrative. To unfold this wrestling, openness to the authors' motivation and detailed examinations of both similarities and differences between this corpus and cuneiform law collections are indispensable.

1.4.4 R. S. Wafula's Postcolonial Analysis of Exodus

Following the trajectory of Dube's, Yee's, and Mathew's analyses, Wafula continues to argue for the oppressive nature of the Exodus story. His analysis is an article in the festschrift titled *Postcolonial Commentary and the Old Testament*,[155] focusing on Exodus's characterization of God and the delineation of his relationship with Moses and the Israelites. He begins his analysis by discussing Dube's observation of how the European imperialists made use of Exodus's descriptions of God as a foundation for colonialization. He then points out the failure of Latin American liberation theology to notice

154. Bhabha, *Location of Culture*, 121–22.

155. Wafula, "Exodus Story," 10–26.

the oppressive nature of Exodus's characterization of God. He thus sets up a goal to study the nature of Yhwh's liberation of the Israelites in Exodus.

A large part of his analysis discusses the first half of Exodus, arguing that Yhwh delivers the Israelites only in order to find a people subservient to his imperial power. In the study of Exodus 19 onward, Wafula continues to address Yhwh's relationships with the Israelites, which he deems to be comparable to imperial strategies: Yhwh wants the Israelites to know him, but does not allow them to come too close. He announces a covenant, so that the Israelites will not keep challenging his authority. He frames the covenant with the statement about his deliverance of the Israelites out of Egypt in order to remind them that they owe him their lives. His commandments against having other gods also warn the Israelites against following any other center of power. Wafula, moreover, asserts that Yhwh's relationship with Moses is similarly imperial: The leadership and worship system that Yhwh provides Moses is hierarchal and confines everyone under Yhwh's rule. Moses is an intermediary who does not serve his people, but fulfills the desire of the imperial power, Yhwh. Wafula's presupposition behind this understanding becomes clear near the end of his analysis. Wafula emphasizes that postcoloniality works because the colonized ruling elite serve their colonizers' interests.

Like Dube, Yee, and Mathew, Wafula has raised awareness of possibly oppressive elements in Exodus 19–24. He also invites a reflection on the descriptions of Yhwh, Moses, and the people in this corpus. A consideration to be taken beyond this awareness and reflection is whether his understandings have fully accounted for the nature of Yhwh's liberation of his people that this corpus reveals. A question worth asking is: If Latin American liberation theology focuses merely on the resistive elements in Exodus, as he points out, does his analysis also similarly concentrate on the compliant elements only? Postcolonial scholars have pointed out the multifaceted nature of the response of the colonized, including their elites, to their colonizers. This finding calls for an analysis of Exodus 19–24 that attends to this multifaceted nature, with a comparison to corresponding imperial legal corpora. This analysis enables one to see not only the ancient Israelite elites' acceptance of imperial practices, but also resistance to them. As conservative as this resistance is, this response reflects the wrestling, rather than total compliance, of the imperialized with the imperial metanarrative. This wrestling is what I aim to present in the following study.

1.5 Chapter Conclusions

Postcolonial studies offer a crucial perspective for examining the rhetoric of Exodus 19–24. The observations about hybridity invite one to seriously consider the resistive power involved in imperialized peoples' mimicry of imperial metanarrative. This resistive power comes from the exhibition of differences within similarities. The imperialized may not fight for a utopia unrelated to the existing society, but they do attempt to transform imperial systems in the hope that this transformation will facilitate changes in norms and values. Admittedly, the adoption of emperors' traits suggests acceptance of them. Hybridity is also associated with some oppressive history. Nevertheless, the imperialized, including their elites, do pursue differences, including retrieving their local traditions, in order to resist empire's dominant discourse. These findings suggest not only the importance of ethical engagement in the study of imperialized people's discourse, but also the necessity of attending to the multifaceted nature of imperialized people's response to empire.

Postcolonial studies of colonized legal discourse also invite this attention. They suggest that despite various degrees of imperial legal domination, law plays a vital role in imperialized people's society. Law is closely associated with their pursuit of freedom and justice, their identity, and their independence from empires. Imperialized people's legal discourse, like their discourse in general, can be both oppressive and liberative. The imperialized, including their elites, can use law to oppress their own people, as well as to resist this oppression. Indeed, they approach the imperial legal discourse in various ways. Some mimic imperial laws indiscriminately. Others are determined to maintain their distinctiveness. Some of them even reinvent customs in order to formulate their laws. However, there are also some imperialized peoples who appropriate imperial laws in order to resist imperial legal conception and values and to develop a legal discourse with a new moral appearance.

These understandings call for an analysis of Exodus 19–24 that is open to the multifaceted motivation behind this corpus and studies in detail the rhetoric expressed by both the similarities and differences between Exodus 19–24 and cuneiform law collections. The postcolonial analyses of Dube, Yee, Mathew, and Wafula have fulfilled the task of postcolonial biblical criticism to expose "the frequent assumption that biblical texts, biblical interpretation, and biblical interpreters are innocent."[156] A further consideration is postcolonial scholars' various understandings of the colonized. These understandings invite exploring various faces of the responses to the empires among the elites of Israel and Judah and examining Exodus 19–24's complex rhetoric in relation to cuneiform law collections. This exploration and examination will unfold this corpus's possible resistive elements, in addition to its imperial and oppressive features.

The corpus of Exodus 19–24, like colonized people's discourse in general and their legal discourse in particular, manifests the wrestling of the imperialized, which involves acceptance of, ambivalence toward, resistance to, and even subversion of the imperial legal metanarrative. This wrestling gives one the impression that the authors of Exodus 19–24 were conservative in deviating from imperial legal traditions, but it concurrently suggests that they attempted to revolt against the imperial legal metanarrative. I demonstrate this wrestling in the following study, beginning with an examination of the relationship between Exodus 19–24 and cuneiform law collections, Exodus 19–24's historical context and purposes, and the social location of this corpus's authors, with an attention to the multifaceted nature of imperialized people's response to imperial power.

156. Sugirtharajah, *Exploring Postcolonial Biblical Criticism*, 54.

CHAPTER 2

Relationship of Exodus 19–24 to Cuneiform Law Collections

2.1 Introduction

Postcolonial findings concerning the multifaceted nature of imperialized people's discourse invite reflection on the relationship between Exodus 19–24 and cuneiform law collections, which biblical scholars have explored for more than a century. This chapter thus begins with a discussion on biblical scholars' key concerns and recent focus and suggest how the postcolonial perspective enhances this exploration. To better understand Exodus 19–24 as a work of the imperialized, I then examine the relationship of the people of Israel and Judah to empire by discussing this corpus's dating and studying how these people related to the Neo-Assyrians. Finally, I investigate the purposes of Exodus 19–24 and the authors' social location, as well as their positions on the empire in light of postcolonial findings.

This chapter posits that postcolonial studies offer a vital perspective for comparing the similarities and differences between Exodus 19–24 and cuneiform law collections. While the people of Israel and Judah lived under the shadow of empire throughout their history, I suggest locating Exodus 19–24's historical context in the mid-eighth century to the mid-seventh century BCE when Israel and Judah were under Assyrian subjugation. I posit that in addition to various purposes, the Exodus corpus represents a legal discourse of the imperialized, given the relationship of Israel and Judah to the empire. I also argue that its authors, despite their elite status, wrestled with how to respond to the imperial legal metanarrative, thus leading to a conservatively revolutionary response reflected in Exodus 19–24.

2.2 Meta-Traditions, Direct Dependence, or Response of the Imperialized?

Since the publication of the Laws of Hammurabi in 1902, scholars have not ceased to explore the relationship between Exodus 19–24 and cuneiform law collections or the legal model behind the composition of Exodus 19–24. There have been thorough reviews of this exploration;[1] thus, here I point out its key concerns and discuss the recent focus on the criteria for determining the relationship, particularly the need to consider the authors' social location. Some recent studies exhibit traces of this consideration, but postcolonial findings urge further analysis of Exodus 19–24 as a work of the imperialized in response to imperial legal traditions, that is, legal traditions belonging to empires.

2.2.1 Key Concerns in Previous Studies

Aside from some early arguments for independent development,[2] scholars have mostly suggested some connections between Exodus 19–24 and cuneiform law collections. These scholars were concerned with the source of their similarities and differences, focusing on when and how the cultural contact occurred between the people of Israel and Judah and their neighbors.

A popular view is the existence of common legal culture behind the Exodus and cuneiform corpora. A classic example is Albrecht Alt's argument in "Die Ursprünge des israelitischen Rechts,"[3] even though scholars have indicated that he failed to consider various forms in the cuneiform corpora and absence of evidence on Canaanite law code.[4] Alt contended that the apodictic laws in the Book of the Covenant were native to the ancient Israelites, but its casuistic

1. For instance, Schwienhorst-Schönberger, *Bundesbuch*, 240–54; Rothenbusch, *Die kasuistische Rechtssammlung*, 23–91; Wright, *Inventing God's Law*, 4–7, 16–28.

2. See Schwienhorst-Schönberger, *Bundesbuch*, 243–46.

3. Alt, " Ursprünge," 1:285–332.

4. Greengus, "Some Issues," 73; Westbrook, "Laws of Biblical Israel," 328. The recent findings of cuneiform laws at Hazor, dated to the Middle Bronze Age, are fragmentary; Horowitz, Oshima, and Vukosavović, "Hazor 18," 158–76; Horowitz, Oshima, and Sanders, *Cuneiform in Canaan*, 86–88.

laws were adopted from the Canaanites shortly after the ancient Israelites had entered into the Levant. He suggested that there was a common legal culture in Mesopotamia and the Levant, transmitted through literary form behind the composition of these casuistic laws, and that these laws reflect a selective reception of that culture.[5] Shalom M. Paul's comparative study is another example of this view. He analyzed the content and formulation of Exodus 19–24 in comparison to cuneiform law collections and suggested that there was an overall cuneiform legal background behind the formation of the Exodus corpus. Dating this corpus to the period around the conquest, he proposed that cuneiform legal traditions reached the biblical authors by various means. He admitted that further investigation is needed to determine what these means were. However, he argued that it was because of an overall cuneiform legal background that the Exodus corpus's casuistic laws exhibit Mesopotamia's legacy.[6]

Later scholars attempted to elaborate more on how a common legal tradition was at work behind the Exodus corpus. An essential example is Raymond Westbrook's studies. His proposal was particularly concerned with how people dealt with legal problems in scribal school settings in the broader region of Mesopotamia, the Levant, the Greco-Roman world, and Egypt. However, his focus was similarly on the contact points between the biblical authors and other legal cultures. He contended that different societies formed similar legal formulations in the process of studying how to deal with different legal circumstances, but each society studied and attempted to resolve these problems independently.[7] In his later work, he further suggested that the affinity of cuneiform laws, biblical laws, and ancient Mediterranean laws involved not only oral transmission and diffusion of written legal form and content, but also intellectual activities in dealing with different problems arising from the same legal topic. He argued that these three levels of affinity led to both similarities and differences between these legal materials.[8]

Some scholars offered even more nuanced hypotheses about how the broader legal culture affected the Exodus corpus's formation diachronically.

5. Alt, "Ursprünge," 290, 297–98.

6. Paul, *Studies in the Book of the Covenant*, 44, 104, 118.

7. Westbrook, *Studies in Biblical and Cuneiform Law*, 1–4, 40; Westbrook, "Nature and Origins," 40–45.

8. Westbrook, "Laws of Biblical Israel," 333–39.

Their focus remained on when and how the contact occurred between the biblical authors and cuneiform legal traditions. A significant example is some earlier works of Eckart Otto, even though some scholars have noted that these works falsely assumed early Israel as an isolated society from its neighbors and the present form of the Covenant collection as a reflection of its composition's circumstances.[9] Otto's emphasis was more on the literary differences between the Book of the Covenant and cuneiform law collections. Referring to the content and what he deemed to be the reflection of ancient Israelite local court practice in the Covenant collection's casuistic laws, he asserted that these laws had their roots in the rural local court setting and were thus native to ancient Israel. He argued that these laws depended on cuneiform legal tradition only in terms of drafting technique, as the scribes drafted and compiled them later in Israel's towns where legal training took place.[10] Another notable example of the diachronic understanding is Ralf Rothenbusch's comparative analysis. Contrary to Otto, he posited that the similarities between the Book of the Covenant and cuneiform law collections came from the influence of cuneiform traditions, which first occurred in the middle to late Bronze Age. He argues that with high literacy, Phoenician cities, particularly Tyros, preserved these traditions and later transferred them to the ancient Israelites, leading to the emergence of legal scholarship in an oral form in the earlier period and the composition of the Covenant collection in the monarchic period.[11]

Other scholars, however, deemed these understandings insufficient for explaining some striking similarities between cuneiform law collections and the Book of the Covenant and argued for direct knowledge of the former in the composition of the latter. Again, their studies focused on when and how the contact took place between the biblical authors and cuneiform law collections. Some also pointed out methodological issues in determining the relationship between the Exodus and cuneiform corpora, which scholars

9. Westbrook, 326–27.

10. Otto, *Wandel der Rechtsbegründungen*, 133–34, 160–70, 173, 179–87; Otto, "Town and Rural Countryside," 4, 16–18, 21. Bernard S. Jackson's latest argument is similar to Eckart Otto's in many respects, although Jackson suggests a five-stage model of development, which allows for some influence from cuneiform legal tradition between the oral and written stages; Jackson, *Wisdom-Laws*, 432–33.

11. Rothenbusch, *Kasuistische Rechtssammlung*, 394–407, 481–99, 513.

continued to explore later. A representative example is Meir Malul's study on the comparative method of the two corpora. He asserted that "the biblical author or editor knew first-hand the Mesopotamian law and that he may have even a copy (or copies?) of them in front of him when he composed or edited his biblical version."[12] His assertion was based mainly on a literary comparison between the goring ox laws in the Covenant collection, the Laws of Hammurabi, and the Laws of Eshnunna. It was also grounded on a discussion of a proper comparative method, including how to identify coincidence and uniqueness.[13] Another example of arguing for direct literary dependence is John Van Seters's study of the Covenant collection, which has received much criticism due to his exilic dating of the Exodus corpus.[14] Based on a literary comparison of their laws and non-legal sections, he argued that Exodus 19–24 borrowed from the Laws of Hammurabi. With a broader goal of demonstrating the late dating of the Yahwist's work, he asserted that the borrowing occurred during the exile period when some ancient Israelites were deported to Babylonia. He deemed this borrowing possible because the stele of the Laws of Hammurabi might survive in Babylonia due to the enthusiasm for venerating the region's ancient past. He also suggested that the author of the Covenant collection had direct access to some Babylonian law collections, in view of the extant copies of the Hammurabi collection and other ancient laws dated to the Neo-Babylonian period.[15]

These studies offer various scenarios for understanding the relationship between Exodus 19–24 and cuneiform laws collections. Despite the aforementioned limitations, these scenarios have pointed out the importance of considering possible cultural contacts between the biblical authors and their neighbors, the period when this contact possibly occurred, the continuity and discontinuity of legal culture in the region, and so forth. What I particularly find to be wanting, however, is a consideration of these authors' social location in relation to empire and how this social location affected their composition of Exodus 19–24 in relation to cuneiform law collections, legal culture, or traditions. With a focus on the time and the way the cultural

12. Malul, *Comparative Method*, 159.

13. Malul, 13–112, 141–42.

14. See, for instance, Levinson, "Is the Covenant Code an Exilic Composition," 272–325; Westbrook, "Laws of Biblical Israel," 328; Wright, *Inventing God's Law*, 22.

15. Van Seters, *Law Book*, 57, 174.

contacts occurred, these studies fail to address how living under the shadow of empire throughout their history would impact the response of the biblical authors in these kinds of contact.

2.2.2 Recent Focus on the Criteria for Determining the Relationship

Following the trajectory of these understandings, recent studies reveal a particular concern about criteria for determining the relationship between the Exodus corpus and cuneiform law collections. These studies exhibit traces of attention to the social location of the biblical authors in relation to empire. However, a deeper reflection on how this social location impacted the manifestation of similarities and differences between the two corpora is still wanting.

The debate between David P. Wright and Bruce Wells, and subsequent studies conducted by William S. Morrow and Pamela Barmash, demonstrate this need. The debate began with Wright's article, in which he argued that the Book of the Covenant depends directly on the Laws of Hammurabi.[16] His argument was mainly based on four observations: the same or nearly the same order in fourteen laws in the two collections' central casuistic laws (Exod 21:2–22:16 and LH 1–282); the correspondences in the materials of these central casuistic laws; similar themes in the apodictic laws in Exodus 20:23–21:1 and the Laws of Hammurabi's prologue; and similar themes and style in the apodictic laws in Exodus 21:17–23:19 and the Laws of Hammurabi's epilogue. Wright explained that although the Covenant collection also bears correspondences with other cuneiform law collections, it has far more similarities with the Laws of Hammurabi, which run through the whole of the two law collections. He also asserted that no other explanations but the direct dependence of the Covenant collection on the Laws of Hammurabi can account satisfactorily for these multiple similarities.[17]

Wells, however, argued against this theory. He criticized Wright for diffusing different degrees of closeness reflected by different types of connection between the two law collections. Wells suggested that there are four different types of connections, namely resemblance, similarity, correspondence, and

16. Wright, "Laws of Hammurabi as a Source," 11–87.

17. Wright, 13, 47.

identicalness.[18] Based on this classification, he demonstrated that quite a few connections in the central casuistic laws that Wright pointed out actually suggest low degrees of closeness. In some stipulations, Wells found that the Covenant collection even exhibits a higher degree of closeness with other cuneiform law collections than with the Laws of Hammurabi. He also saw that the order of the laws in the Covenant collection does not precisely follow that of the Hammurabi collection. Wells understood that there is a continuum in the connections between law collections and agreed that variations in sequence may not totally reject the Covenant collection's dependence on the Laws of Hammurabi. However, he called for a closer match in content and sequence for evidencing the direct dependence model. For Wells, literary dependence is not the only way to explain the two law collections' connections. He contended that "meta-traditions," that is, the sharing of the same legal traditions in a broad sense in Mesopotamia and the Levant, offer a balanced approach for understanding the similarities and differences between the laws in Exodus and various cuneiform law collections.[19]

In response, Wright defended his theory of literary dependence by pointing out weaknesses of Wells's criteria and clarifying evidence concerning the apodictic laws.[20] Wright maintained that Wells overlooked several factors, including the broader collectivity of similarities between the two law collections, the interconnection of numerous literary variables (such as vocabulary, paraphrase, and larger literary context), and the Book of the Covenant's compositional logic that transforms the Laws of Hammurabi. For Wright, Wells's sequential comparison also did not differentiate primary correlation from auxiliary correlation. Primary correlation follows the sequence of the Hammurabi collection, while auxiliary correlation involves material from other parts of the Laws of Hammurabi or from other cuneiform law collections in the expansion of topics according to the thematic sequence of the Hammurabi collection. According to Wright, it became clear that the Covenant collection's apodictic laws, which Wells did not address, correlate with the Hammurabi collection's epilogue in several ways, such as the replacement of Hammurabi and the Mesopotamian gods with Yhwh, and of

18. For their definition, see Wells, "Covenant Code," 89.

19. Wells, "Covenant Code," 116–18.

20. Wright, "Laws of Hammurabi," 211–60.

Hammurabi's temple statue with the altar. Wright argued that the theory of meta-traditions is too abstract for explaining these visible correlations. He thus maintained that the composition of the Book of the Covenant depends directly on the Laws of Hammurabi. He then published a monograph, discussing in detail the similarities and differences between the two law collections and arguing further that the Book of the Covenant "bears the unique fingerprint" of the Laws of Hammurabi.[21]

This study attracted various scholarly reviews. They mostly continued to discuss the number and degree of similarities and differences between the two corpora and the criteria for evaluating these similarities and differences.[22] Among them, Morrow contributed a substantial review in which he insisted on the importance of using formal parallels as bases for determining the relationship between the Book of the Covenant and the Laws of Hammurabi. Accordingly, he developed four criteria: translation or close paraphrase, textual organization, the density of the similarities, and their uniqueness.[23] Based on these criteria, he agreed with Wright that the ordinances in Exodus 21:2–22:16 reflect literary dependence on the Hammurabi collection, but disagreed with him that the apodictic laws do so. In response, Wright published another article in which he emphasized the importance of including hermeneutical transformation as one of the criteria. He demonstrated that this transformation occurs not only in Exodus 21:2–11 and 22–28, but also in the Covenant collection's apodictic laws.[24]

Barmash's recent monograph continued to reflect similar considerations in its argument against Wright's, as well as Wells's, suggestions.[25] This monograph focuses on the Laws of Hammurabi, asserting that this corpus and earlier cuneiform law collections shared a common scribal tradition. With this understanding, Barmash argued that a shared educational tradition, rather than literary dependence or a common legal tradition, was at work in

21. Wright, *Inventing God's Law*, 15.

22. See, for instance, the reviews written by Bruce Wells, *JR* 90 (2010): 558–60; Frank H. Polak, *RBL* 12 (2010): 67–72; L. L. Grabbe, *JSOT* 34 (2010): 163; Meir Malul, *BAIAS* 29 (2011): 155–59; Joel S. Baden, *RBL* (2011): 167–71. For an analysis with a positive outlook on David Wright's monograph, see the review written by Shalom E. Holz, *CBQ* 72 (2010): 820–22.

23. For details, see Morrow, "Legal Interactions," 312.

24. Wright, "Method in the Study," 159–81.

25. Barmash, Laws of Hammurabi.

the composition of later law collections, including the Book of the Covenant.[26] She contended that the ordinances concerning pregnant women and goring oxen particularly originate in this shared educational tradition. According to her, the differences between these ordinances and corresponding cuneiform laws indicate that the biblical author reshaped a repertoire of typical cases just as Mesopotamian and Hittite scribes did. Meanwhile, the widespread concern about the same topics among cuneiform law collections, similar contents (particularly the list of specific bodily injuries), and the similar use of the casuistic form suggest a shared educational tradition.[27]

One of the issues at stake in these studies was, thus, the literary criteria of interpreting the similarities and differences between the Book of the Covenant and cuneiform law collections. Wells has brought to attention the importance of noticing different degrees of closeness between two law collections. He has also correctly noted the similarities between the Book of the Covenant and other cuneiform law collections. His suggestion about how the length and preservation of the Laws of Hammurabi may lead to more connections between the Book of the Covenant and this law collection than other cuneiform laws is worth serious attention. Wright, on the other hand, has reasonably pointed out the importance of considering the collectivity of similarities when one assesses the literary dependency of the Book of the Covenant to the Laws of Hammurabi. Nevertheless, Morrow has demonstrated how to apply a set of criteria for evaluating different parts of the Covenant collection and correctly questioned Wright's analysis and general conclusion. Despite this, Wright constructively emphasized that the two corpora's differences exhibit the former's transformation of the latter. Barmash, meanwhile, introduced the importance of considering the extensiveness of a legal concern across different law collections and its relation to a shared educational tradition. These four scholars' arguments thus have pointed out various vital considerations in examining the relationship between the two corpora, which continue to

26. Notably, William M. Schniedewind similarly suggests a relationship between early Hebrew scribal curriculum and cuneiform curricular traditions. However, he argues for the former's borrowing and adaptation of the latter, and his focus is more on scribal curriculum in general. He briefly comments on the relationship between the Book of the Covenant and the Laws of Hammurabi, and inclines to see that the former is an adaptation of the latter early in the development of the monarchy. However, he admits that how scribes became familiar with cuneiform legal traditions remains a problem. Schniedewind, *Finger of the Scribe*, 1, 153.

27. Barmash, *Laws of Hammurabi*, 256–59.

influence studies of biblical law.[28] However, their focus is mostly limited to the content and literary elements of the law collections.

Notably, Barmash's study did mention Mesoptotamia's political and cultural hegemony.[29] Wright's works also attempted to go behind textual evidence and consider the authors' social location. In his argument for hermeneutical transformation, he stated that "one cannot simply make an estimation on the basis of visible similarities and differences."[30] In his response article, he even commented that the Covenant collection "is a symbolic response to Assyrian hegemony."[31] Then, in his monograph, he posited further that the two law collections' similarities and differences can be understood through postcolonial theory.[32] Notwithstanding, Barmash suggested that the biblical scribes adopted and adapted Mesopotamian learning because they deem it to be prestigious.[33] Wright also focused more on the Covenant collection's attempt to offer a legal corpus more coherent than cuneiform laws. He repeatedly cited Deuteronomy 4:8 to suggest the existence of "nationalistic pride in Israelite and Judean legislation."[34] These suggestions are encouraging attempts to consider the hegemony behind cuneiform law collections and the social location of the biblical authors. However, as my study in chapter one suggests, imperialized people's response to empire is more multifaceted. An understanding of this complex characteristic is essential for better unfolding

28. See, for instance, Skaist, "Ancient Near Eastern Law," 309; Walton and Walton, *Lost World*, 84.

29. Barmash, *Laws of Hammurabi*, 265.

30. Wright, "Laws of Hammurabi," 217. This comment somehow echoes the rejection of equating borrowing to wholesale adoption that Jeffrey H. Tigay raised almost three decades ago (see Tigay, "On Evaluating Claims," 250–55).

31. Wright, "Laws of Hammurabi," 258.

32. Wright, *Inventing God's Law*, 350–51. His argument is based on Morrow, "Resistance and Hybridity," 321–39.

33. Barmash, *Laws of Hammurabi*, 265.

34. Wright, "Laws of Hammurabi," 260; Wright, *Inventing God's Law*, 351. In his response to Morrow, Wright similarly contended that the Covenant collection endeavored to formulate more systematic legislation and adapted cuneiform materials in order to create history that fits Israelite religious and legal perspectives ("Method in the Study," 171, 178, 180). Notably, Wright did mention in an article's footnote that the narrative of the Covenant collection employs Mesopotamian royal ideology to "create a picture of Israelite origins that subversively mimics or flatteringly emulates Mesopotamian ideas" ("Covenant Code Appendix," 68). However, in a more recent article he asserted that the Covenant collection's adaption may not be resistive, but for articulating "a parallel Israelite and particularly Judean identity" ("Adaptation and Fusion," 134).

the rhetoric of Exodus 19–24 and this corpus's relationship to cuneiform law collections.

2.2.3 Trace of Attention to Authors' Social Location and Complex Characteristics

There has been a trace of breakthrough that considers this complex characteristic in relation to the social location of the people of Israel and Judah. Otto's article, "Das Bundesbuch und der „Kodex" Hammurapi: Das biblische Recht zwischen positive und subversive Rezeption von Keilschriftrecht," brought to attention the subversive nature of the Book of the Covenant.[35] He pointed out some particular differences between the Laws of Hammurabi and the Book of the Covenant, such as the protection of higher class people over the lower class versus the consideration of the weak, and the legitimization of the king versus the emphasis of obedience to God. He argued that these differences exhibit the Covenant collection's subversive, rather than positive, reception of the Hammurabi collection.[36] Otto did not explicitly point out the social location of the Covenant collection's redactor in relation to neighboring power. However, dating the Covenant collection's redaction to the eighth century to the seventh century BCE, he suggested a Neo-Assyrian influence on the scribal training in Judah. He also noted that the Book of the Covenant and Deuteronomy were reluctant to follow cuneiform laws' royal ideology.[37]

It is noteworthy that a few years after Otto published this article, Wells, in contrast, suggested that the law in Exodus exhibits conventional characteristics.[38] His study focused on the differences between law collections in the Pentateuch. He accepted the dating of the three law collections offered by recent scholarship: the late eighth century BCE for the Book of

35. Otto, "Bundesbuch," 1–26. Jonathan Vroom also referred to postcolonial theory and suggested that the authors of Exod 21:1–22:16 adapted the Mesopotamian legal genre's form and/or content to promote their national identity. However, he did not elaborate this understanding further; see Vroom, "Recasting *Mišpāṭîm*," 36.

36. Otto, "Bundesbuch," 12, 22–25.

37. Otto, "Bundesbuch," 20–25. Otto pointed out more explicitly the subversion of Assyrian ideology in his study of Deuteronomy ("Assyria and Judean Identity," 339–47). In his article concerning human rights reflected in Deuteronomy, he even suggested that intellectuals of Judah transformed Assyrian ideology into an "anti-imperialistic set of theological ideas" ("Human Rights," 10). For argument against the subversive nature of Deuteronomy, see Crouch, *Israel and the Assyrians*, 18–21.

38. Wells, "Interpretation," 234–66.

the Covenant, the late seventh century BCE for the Deuteronomic Code, and exilic or postexilic period for the Holiness Code. However, unlike other biblical scholars who usually confine their comparison to biblical laws, Wells examined these law collections' characteristics based on a comparison between biblical and cuneiform laws. Comparing the ordinances concerning debt slavery (Exod 21:1–6), theft (Exod 21:37–22:3), and bailment (Exod 22:6–8) with cuneiform laws with similar concerns, Wells argued that the Book of the Covenant exhibits "a general acceptance of previous legal ideas with minimal revisions," which characterizes this corpus as "remarkably conventional."[39] Studying the laws on unsolved homicide, slave manumission, and the unbetrothed maiden, he posited that the law in Deuteronomy tends to redirect and expand older legal traditions. Analyzing the laws regarding levirate marriage, the Jubilee, and talionic punishment, he suggested that the Holiness Code usually redefined previous legal traditions.[40]

Wells's study does enhance the understanding of the interpretive approaches adopted by the authors of the three biblical law collections. It also sheds light on the relationship between biblical and cuneiform laws. Regarding cuneiform laws as sources that reflect legal traditions in broader ancient West Asia, Wells successfully demonstrates that the three biblical law collections exhibit different responses of ancient Israelites to the legal traditions surrounding them. A further question is: while the Book of the Covenant is comparatively more conservative than the other two biblical law codes in deviating from cuneiform legal traditions, does it, when considered by itself, actually conservative in response to those traditions? This question recalls Shiju Mathew's assertion that the Book of the Covenant is imperial and oppressive.[41] However, Otto's study does correctly point out some subversive elements of the Book of the Covenant, which deserve further study.

2.2.4 A Postcolonial Understanding and Propositions of this Study

Postcolonial studies, which discloses the multifaceted nature of colonized people's discourse, invite revisiting all these understandings. As Wright and

39. Wells, 235, 239.

40. Wells, 246–63.

41. Mathew, *Biblical Law Codes*, 211; see also §1.4.3.

Otto point out, the differences between the Book of the Covenant and cuneiform law collections do not necessarily reflect that the former has no direct relationships with the latter. In light of postcolonial findings, the similarities and differences between the two corpora also may not only exhibit that the biblical authors deemed Mesopotamian learning to be prestigious or attempted to write a law collection better than cuneiform law collections, as Barmash and Wright respectively propose. Considering the characteristics of colonized peoples found in postcolonial studies, I argue that similarities and differences between Exodus 19–24 and cuneiform law collections reflect various responses of the people of Israel and Judah to imperial legal traditions, including acceptance, resistance, and ambivalence. These responses exhibit the wrestling of the imperialized people with the imperial legal metanarrative. They also characterize Exodus 19–24 as a work of conservative revolutionists – that is, authors who broadly followed imperial legal values and practices, but endeavored to deviate from them – even though this corpus still adopts the most conventional interpretative approach among biblical laws, as Wells demonstrates.

This perspective will neither evidence the direct access of the biblical authors to the literary form of cuneiform laws, nor demonstrate that there was only a meta-tradition in a broader sense or a shared educational tradition in ancient West Asia. In fact, this perspective cautions scholars against making these arguments simply based on the similarities or differences exhibited in these law collections. If the relationship between the Book of the Covenant and cuneiform law collections involved different levels of affinity, as Westbrook suggests,[42] it is indeed possible that, rather than relating to the cuneiform law collections in one way or another, the authors of Exodus 19–24 had gone through training similar to Mesopotamian scribes' and had both the cuneiform legal traditions in mind and direct access to some cuneiform law collections in hand. This is a legal model that I find to be appropriate for understanding the composition of Exodus 19–24.

Still, one has to seriously consider the lack of solid findings of cuneiform laws in the Levant. The geographical, temporal, and linguistic remoteness of some cuneiform law collections, to which some ordinances in the Covenant

42. Westbrook, "Laws of Biblical Israel," 333–39; see also §2.2.1.

collection bear striking similarities, also deserve attention.[43] Thus, I conduct the following analysis with the proposition that the authors of Exodus 19–24 were familiar with the cuneiform legal traditions that prevailed in ancient West Asia and were aware of their imperial nature, and that the extant copies of cuneiform law collections somehow reflect these traditions. These propositions take into consideration the similarities between Exodus 19–24 and various cuneiform law collections, but do not assume that the biblical authors necessarily had direct literary access to the cuneiform law texts. With these propositions, I demonstrate how the Exodus corpus reflects the wrestling of the imperialized authors, who attempted to resist the metanarrative constituted by imperial legal traditions, albeit in a conservative way.

2.3 Relationship of the People of Israel and Judah to Empire

An examination of Israel and Judah's relationship to empire will offer a crucial backdrop for understanding Exodus 19–24 as a corpus reflecting responses of the imperialized. The people of Israel and Judah lived under the shadow of empires throughout their history. Norman K. Gottwald even contends that "Israel was born as an anti-imperial resistance movement" and continued to live up to this legacy.[44] The imperial presence of Egypt,[45] Neo-Assyria, Neo-Babylonia, and Persia in the Levant and these empires' interaction with the

---

43. For instance, the Laws of Eshnunna and Hittite Laws, as well as legal practice documents from Nuzi and Emar, see Wright, *Inventing God's Law*, 110; Wells, "Covenant Code," 93–110. Regarding the discovery at Hazor, see page 50, note 4.

44. His argument is in view of the emergence of Israel under the Egyptian imperial domination of the Levant and Israel's continuous struggle under different empires; Gottwald, "Early Israel," 9–23. For an overview of different interpretations of the reference to Israel in the Merneptah stele, see, for instance, Miller and Hayes, *History of Ancient Israel*, 39–43.

45. The presence of Egyptian imperial power in the Levant can be traced back at least to the sixteenth century BCE, which creating an imperialized atmosphere in the region and impacting the life of the people there since then (see, for instance, Van De Mieroop, *History of Ancient Egypt*, 151–259; Bright, *History of Israel*, 107–228). For how the local rulers in the Levant in the fourteenth century BCE regarded Egyptian kings as their lords and masters, see some letters from the Amarna archive, EA 104, EA 244, EA 243 (Rainey, *El-Amarna Correspondence*, 1:564–7, 998–1003). Some scholars suggest that the Egyptians also made Judah a vassal shortly before the Babylonians took over the Assyrian imperial rule of the region (see, for instance, Schipper, "Egypt and the Kingdom," 200–226; Perdue and Carter, *Israel and Empire*, 68). Some even argue that Judah was an Egyptian vassal throughout Josiah's reign before the fall of the Assyrians (see, for example, Miller and Hayes, *History of Ancient Israel*, 451–54).

people of Israel and Judah have warranted the analysis of Exodus 19–24 as a work of the imperialized.[46] Nevertheless, dating this corpus to a specific period will enhance the understanding of the historical context and the nature of the imperial encounter behind its composition. Therefore, in this section, I discuss the dating of Exodus 19–24, with which I locate this corpus specifically in the Neo-Assyrian period. I then investigate the relationship between the Neo-Assyrians and the people of Israel and Judah, exploring the characteristics of their contact behind the composition of Exodus 19–24.

2.3.1 Dating of Exodus 19–24

Dating Exodus 19–24 is a challenging task. Various scholars have questioned the validity of the documentary hypothesis for explaining the formation of the Pentateuch,[47] but scholarly understandings of Exodus 19–24's dating still vary. Concerning the Book of the Covenant, suggestions range from the premonarchic period to the postexilic period. Due to ambiguous indications in this corpus, including those seemingly suggesting socioeconomic conditions,[48] its composition date is difficult to determine with certainty. Nevertheless, following some scholars' recent views,[49] I locate the Book of the Covenant's composition to the middle of the eighth century to the middle of seventh century BCE, when Israel and Judah were under the subjugation of the Neo-Assyrian Empire. Some other forms of this corpus or some forms of local rules or customary laws might exist before this period. However, as textual evidence for them and how they related to the current form of the Book of

46. I will discuss the historical relationship of Israel and Judah to Neo-Assyria in §2.3.2. For historical surveys regarding Israel and Judah in relation to Neo-Babylonia and Persia, see for instance, Van De Mieroop, *History of the Ancient Near East*, 289–347; Miller and Hayes, *History of Ancient Israel*, 478–540; Bright, *History of Israel*, 324–402; Perdue and Carter, *Israel and Empire*, 69–128.

47. Alexander, "Composition," 2.

48. Edenburg, "Book of the Covenant," 170; Barmash, "Determining the Date," 238.

49. For instance, Rothenbusch, *Kasuistische Rechtssammlung*, 52; Otto, *Gesetz des Moses*, 126; Wright, *Inventing God's Law*, 3; Wells, "Interpretation," 236. Rainer Albertz also dates the Book of the Covenant to the eighth century BCE and relates it to Hezekiah's reform in his *History of Israelite Religion*, 1:180–86. However, in this latest commentary, he regards Exod 21:1–22:19 as the work of the pre-priestly Exodus composition with older traditions. For him, the pre-priestly Exodus composition most probably occurred in the late exilic period. Despite this dating, Albertz argues that 21:1–22:19 contain three levels of tradition and that 21:12, 21:15–22:16 belong to an older tradition dated to the eighth century BCE (Albertz, *Exodus, Band I*, 20; Albertz, *Exodus, Band II*, 78–85, 90, 99).

the Covenant is still wanting, my study focuses on the dating of this corpus's composition. My dating is based on three main considerations, namely this corpus's relationship with Deuteronomy, scribal development in Israel and Judah, and access to knowledge of cuneiform legal traditions. The first two considerations particularly also indicate the weakness of locating this corpus in other periods. Considering this dating of the Book of the Covenant, together with the connection of it with its surrounding narrative, I also suggest studying Exodus 19–24 as a whole under the Neo-Assyrian context.

2.3.1.1 Dating of the Book of the Covenant

The Book of the Covenant's relationship to Deuteronomy is a crucial consideration in its dating. Studying these two corpora's lexical and syntactical features as well as juridical and cultic conceptions, scholars have demonstrated that the laws in Deuteronomy exhibit development from the Book of the Covenant, not vice versa.[50] This development necessitates a dating of the Book of the Covenant sometime before the end of the seventh century BCE, as scholars generally date most of the laws in Deuteronomy no later than this time.[51]

This consideration reveals the difficulty of dating the Book of the Covenant to the exilic or postexilic period, even though this dating attends to this corpus's literary features and social settings and accounts for its relationship to cuneiform law collections. For instance, Van Seter argues for an exilic dating in view of possible direct access to cuneiform law collections during the Babylonian exile and based on a literary comparison with the Deuteronomic Code and the Holiness Code.[52] The former argument does sound reasonable. However, his approach to the texts, such as translation, emendation, and contextual understanding of the alter law, are demonstrated to be far-fetched,[53] which indicates the challenge of establishing the Book of the Covenant's late dating. Thomas B. Dozeman's commentary classifies the Book of the Covenant as non-priestly history and suggests that its date may be exilic but is more likely to be postexilic. His argument, however, is mainly based on

50. Wright, *Inventing God's Law*, 22–23, 506–7, note 19; Levinson, *Deuteronomy*, 6–10; Levinson, "Is the Covenant Code an Exilic Composition," 272–325; Weinfeld, *Deuteronomy 1–11*, 19–24; Lohfink, "Fortschreibung," 133–81.

51. Wright, *Inventing God's Law*, 23; Otto, "Bundesbuch," 25.

52. Van Seters, *Law Book*, 6–7, 57.

53. Levinson, "Is the Covenant Code and Exilic Composition," 297–315.

the relationship of non-priestly history as a whole to Deuteronomy and the Deuteronomistic history;[54] he does not address the temporal relationship between the Book of the Covenant and Deuteronomy specifically.

Douglas A. Knight resorts to contextual motivation for a postexilic dating of the Book of the Covenant, as well as the Deuteronomic Code, the Holiness Code, and the Priestly Code. He argues that only the Persian period offers a social context that sufficiently explains by whom, why, and how all these legal corpora were systematized to provide a basis for a cultic community. He suggests that it was a time when the biblical authors would have been directly exposed to cuneiform law collections during their long periods of vassalage. He also asserts that the Book of the Covenant looks like customary laws for villages, while Deuteronomy reflects an urban setting.[55] This understanding seems to explain the Book of the Covenant's relationship with both Deuteronomy and cuneiform law collections. However, it unreasonably rules out the need or motivation for developing legal discourse in earlier societies of Israel and Judah. It also does not address the demonstrated relationship between the Book of the Covenant and Deuteronomy, which requires a diachronic explanation that dates the former earlier than the latter.

While this consideration necessitates a composition date sometime before the end of the seventh century BCE, the development of scribal culture in Israel and Judah suggests one not earlier than the eighth century BCE. The use of writing among the people of Israel and Judah did not expand until the eighth century BCE.[56] This scribal advancement is essential for the record of the ordinances, as Rothenbusch points out.[57] Rainer Albertz also reasonably argues that the complicated features of the Book of the Covenant, such as different forms and genres, exhibits this kind of scribal development, which did not happen earlier.[58]

54. Dozeman, *Commentary on Exodus*, 40, 425.

55. Knight, *Law, Power, and Justice*, 18–27.

56. Carr, *Writing*, 164–65. Regarding the prevalent use of the old Hebrew script and evidence of formal scribal training in Israel and Judah in the eighth century BCE, see Rollston, "Scripture and Inscriptions," 457–73.

57. Rothenbusch, *Kasuistische Rechtssammlung*, 52.

58. Albertz, *History of Israelite Religion*, 1:183. Based on the findings at Kuntillet ʿAjrud and cuneiform curricular traditions, Schniedewind suggests that a complete range of education curricula had already been available by the end of the ninth century BCE. However, his evidence is mainly related to the elementary part of the curricula. He admits that his

This consideration puts earlier dating into question, even though this dating acknowledges the influence of the Book of the Covenant on Deuteronomy and contemplates the features of the former's content and its relationship to cuneiform law collections. For instance, Paul and, recently, T. Desmond Alexander, argue for the premonarchic period, as they find that the Book of the Covenant lacks the reflection of the monarchy.[59] In addition to this argument, David M. Carr points out that this corpus reflects a "non-polemical adaptation" of the Laws of the Hammurabi and thus dates it to the tenth century or the ninth century BCE.[60] This view is similar to Martin Noth's and Westbrook's suggestions, which date the Book of the Covenant to the period after the settlement and the tenth century BCE respectively. Their argument concerns the close relationship between this corpus and cuneiform law collections of the second millennium in form and content.[61]

However, as Morrow points out, the lack of references to a monarchy does not suggest that the ordinances presuppose "a society without a monarchy, but a level of social organization in which monarchical institutions were not involved."[62] Furthermore, it may also be a literary approach the authors employed to subvert the imperial promotion of monarchy. In the same vein, the similarities between the Book of the Covenant and cuneiform law collections may reflect the imperialized people's resistive mimicry,[63] rather than "non-polemical adaptation," of the imperial legal discourse. This resistive appropriation more likely occurred later in the monarchical period when the people of Israel and Judah were under a more severe imperial subjugation. Indeed, based on an analysis of Late Bronze and native Hebrew literature in comparison to Akkadian one, Morrow suggests that native Hebrew literature began to appropriate Akkadian texts in "the period of Neo-Assyrian domination over Israel and Judah – not earlier."[64] The expansion of scribal capacity

suggestion concerning the advanced education is conjectural due to fragmentary evidence. Schniedewind, *Finger of the Scribe*, 40, 141.

59. Paul, *Studies in the Book of the Covenant*, 44; Alexander, *Exodus*, 445–47.

60. Carr, *Formation*, 472.

61. Noth, *Exodus*, 174; Westbrook, "Cuneiform Law Codes," 92.

62. Morrow, "Legal Interactions," 326; Seth L. Sanders notably argues that there are several West Semitic ritual texts which do not mention king but were written in scenarios in which kings existed (Sanders, *Invention of Hebrew*, 58–66).

63. See §1.2.2.1.

64. Morrow, "Resistance," 339.

among Israelites and Judahites beginning in the eighth century BCE offered an essential platform for this appropriation.

Deuteronomy's dependence on the Book of the Covenant and scribal development in Israel and Judah have suggested that the mid-eighth century to the mid-seventh century BCE is an appropriate dating for the Book of the Covenant. A further consideration is whether Israelites and Judahites had access to knowledge of cuneiform legal traditions in this period. A notable observation is that other than the Old Babylonian period, the predominance of manuscripts of the Laws of Hammurabi occurred in the Neo-Assyrian period.[65] A fragment of the Middle Assyrian Laws originating in the Middle Assyrian period was also found in a Neo-Assyrian archive.[66] Moreover, there was a Neo-Assyrian scribal school near Haran offering training in cuneiform literature. It was a possible context in which the scribes of Israel and Judah received scribal training offered by the Assyrians and had access to cuneiform legal knowledge, if not the cuneiform law collections themselves.[67] One may argue that the predominance of the Hammurabi manuscripts in the Neo-Assyrian period is an accident of preservation. Further investigation is also needed concerning the access to them and other cuneiform law collections. Nevertheless, these observations suggest the continuous study of cuneiform legal traditions in Mesopotamia and the possible exposure of the biblical authors to related knowledge during the Neo-Assyrian period, which I discuss further in the following sections.[68] They offer potential support for dating the Book of the Covenant to the middle of the eighth century to the middle of the seventh century BCE, in addition to the critical considerations of its influence on Deuteronomy and the expansion of scribal culture among Israelites and Judahites in this period.

65. Levinson, "Is the Covenant Code an Exilic Composition," 293. For more details about the characteristics of these manuscripts, see Wright, *Inventing God's Law*, 106–10.

66. Radner, "Neo-Assyrian Period," 883–84; Wright, *Inventing God's Law*, 110–15.

67. Dalley, "Occasions and Opportunities," 27; Levinson, "Is the Covenant Code an Exilic Composition," 295–96; Wright, *Inventing God's Law*, 98–102.

68. See §2.3.2.3 and §2.5.

2.3.1.2 Compilation of the Book of the Covenant and Surrounding Narrative

With this dating of the Book of the Covenant, a further question is its compilation and the dating of its surrounding narrative. Scholars have long believed that the Book of the Covenant is a unit independent of its surrounding narrative;[69] quite a few scholars also argue for multiple compilation layers and redactions in Exodus 19–24.[70] These understandings do correctly point out features of this corpus: the Book of the Covenant looks self-contained and belongs to a genre distinct from the surrounding narrative; throughout Exodus 19–24, there are also diversity in literary forms and elements, incongruity in its content, themes and motifs relate to those in Deuteronomy and other biblical works, and so forth. However, my key concern is that these features do not necessarily reflect the redaction of Exodus 19–24 that took place at different periods and temporal disconnection between the composition of the Book of the Covenant and of its narrative.[71] Instead, the redaction might have occurred in a compositional process which involved single or multiple writers or editors but in close temporal proximity. Another consideration is that, rather than seeing some passages as late due to their thematic closeness to Deuteronomy or other biblical works, it is also reasonable to regard them as original to Exodus 19–24, which influenced the composition of Deuteronomy or later biblical writings.

There are indeed some observations which suggest the connection between the Book of the Covenant and its surrounding narrative. One of the significant ones is its threefold structure, which some cuneiform law collections also reflect.[72] This narrative offer essential contextualizing information for the Book of the Covenant, including its maker/pronouncer and recipients, similar to the prologue and epilogue of those cuneiform law collections.[73]

69. Alt, "Ursprünge," 285; see also Otto, "Book of the Covenant," 71.

70. For instance, Childs, *Book of Exodus*, 347–58; Otto, *Wandel der Rechtsbegründungen*; Dozeman, *God on the Mountain*, 19; Schwienhorst-Schönberger, *Bundesbuch*, 284–417; Propp, *Exodus 19–40*, 141–54; Oswald, "Lawgiving," 182–92; Albertz, *Exodus, Band II*, 25–31, 78–82, 104–8.

71. For similar concern, see Edenburg, "Book of the Covenant," 160; Barmash, "Determining the Date," 235.

72. Paul, *Studies in the Book of the Covenant*, 27–28.

73. I will examine this in detail in chapter five. For the necessity of having a narrative providing contextualizing information for the Book of the Covenant, see Sarna, *Exodus*, 117;

These features suggest that Exodus 19–24's overall structure in comparison to cuneiform law collection is worth further investigation, as Paul suggests.[74] They, moreover, lead one to consider the composition of the Book of the Covenant and that of its surrounding narrative as an interconnected process occurring in close proximity in time with cuneiform legal traditions in mind, if not as a work finished in one setting with literary reference to cuneiform law collections.

Concerning the diverse literary elements and themes in Exodus 19–24, findings and arguments in relation to cuneiform literature are also noteworthy. Westbrook points out that cuneiform law collections, which offer a relevant framework for understanding the legal development of the Book of the Covenant, actually reflect the use of different forms with pedagogical or rhetorical consideration rather than their use of other legal sources or later redaction.[75] Moreover, Wright not only demonstrates that most of the shift of plural and singular second-person references in Exodus 20:23–23:19 can be explained through literary reasons,[76] but also indicates that passages which some scholars deem to be redactional are the product of their authors' transformation of cuneiform law collections.[77] He finds that Exodus 23:20–33, which some scholars assert to be late, exhibit motifs of Neo-Assyrian royal inscriptions, including some earlier ones, and thus suggests that there were a compositional plan and process of both Exodus 20:23–23:19 and this passage in the same historical period prior to the composition of Deuteronomy.[78]

These considerations and observations do not rule out redactional activity in the compilation of Exodus 19–24. In fact, I agree with some scholars that there are unexplainable linguistic or contextual discrepancies in this corpus.[79] It is also difficult to exclude the possibility of redactional processes in its compilation, given how common they were in the compilation of biblical

---

Wright, *Inventing God's Law*, 333; Oswald, "Exodus-Gottesberg-Erzählung," 39; Oswald, "Lawgiving," 191. Oswald even points out that the theophany in the narrative also requires a purpose or subject matter offered by the law.

74. Paul, *Studies in the Book of the Covenant*, 28.

75. Westbrook, "What is the Covenant Code," 22–32.

76. Wright, *Inventing God's Law*, 324–29.

77. For instance, some sections in the goring ox laws; Wright, *Inventing God's Law*, 209.

78. Wright, "Covenant Code Appendix," 50, 68; Wright, "Origin, Development," 238–41.

79. Morrow, "Generic Discrepancy," 46; Levinson, "Case for Revision," 39; Greengus, "Some Issues," 60–87.

literature of other genres and cuneiform literature.[80] Nevertheless, the considerations of dissociating literary diversity and thematic closeness to later biblical works from the argument for later redaction, together with the observations on the structural, compositional, and literary features of Exodus 19–24 and cuneiform literature, do offer support for analyzing this corpus as a whole in the Neo-Assyrian period. In the following study, I therefore note the diachronic issues of some sections that scholars have raised, but basically locate my analysis of Exodus 19–24 under the backdrop of the Neo-Assyrian period, in the mid-eighth century to the mid-seventh century BCE.

2.3.2 The Assyrians and the People of Israel and Judah

This dating does not pinpoint the geographical location of Exodus 19–24's compilation – it may be Israel or Judah or both.[81] However, this dating certainly indicates a time when Israelites and Judahites lived under Neo-Assyrian subjugation. Understanding further how Israelites and Judahites related to the Assyrians is thus essential for this analysis. This relationship is manifested in various ways, including military sanctions, diplomatic contacts, and scribal training.[82]

2.3.2.1 Military Sanctions

Military sanctions were a critical part of the Assyrian imperial rule of Israel and Judah, which also provide a vital context for other contacts between the Assyrians and the people of Israel and Judah. A brief historical outline offers a necessary background for understanding these military sanctions.[83] Neo-

80. Jackson, *Wisdom-Laws*, 8.

81. Although Judah seems to be a more possible candidate due to its monarchy's longer existence in the period, there is no strong evidence that rules out the composition of this corpus in Israel not long before its fall (722 BCE). Therefore, I leave the location of Exod 19–24's composition and compilation open in this study. I similarly leave the biblical authors' regional origin open. See my following discussion in §2.5.

82. Religious contacts also attract much scholarly attention with various opinions. I deem it to be subordinate to the political relationship of Israel and Judah to Assyria, which is manifested more intensely in military sanctions and diplomatic contacts, and I will discuss it in chapter four.

83. For more surveys about the history of the Neo-Assyrian Empire and its relationship with Israelites and Judahites, see for instance, Van De Mieroop, *History of the Ancient Near East*, 246–88; Miller and Hayes, *History of Ancient Israel*, 360–450; Hays, *Covenant with Death*, 11–21; Perdue and Carter, *Israel and Empire*, 37–68; Frahm, "Neo-Assyrian Period," 161–208; Bagg, "Assyria and the West," 268–84.

Assyrian imperial domination emerged in the Levant in the ninth century BCE and had a direct encounter with Israel and Judah in the eighth century BCE. Assurnasirpal II and Shalmaneser III first consolidated their imperial control from the Zagros Mountains in the east to the Euphrates in the west, and from the Taurus Mountains in the north to the Babylonian border in the south. Then, Tiglath-pileser III and his successors, especially Sargon II, carried out a number of military campaigns to incorporate territories further south of Babylon into their empire, as well as to annex most of the kingdoms in the west.

Israel and Judah became Assyrian vassals in 738 BCE and 733 BCE respectively. Israel joined the anti-Assyrian coalition in the Syro-Ephraimite War afterward, but Tiglath-pileser III defeated the coalition. Shalmaneser V, and perhaps also Sargon II, even besieged Samaria in 722 BCE, made it an Assyrian province, and deported a substantial number of the inhabitants.[84] Judah, on the other hand, refused to join the coalition, but paid tribute to Tiglath-pileser III, under the rule of Ahaz. Nevertheless, it also could not avoid a military encounter with the Assyrians when Hezekiah was more active in taking action against them. Sargon II destroyed Azekah and Ekron due to Hezekiah's involvement in the revolt led by Ashdod in 713–711 BCE. Sennacherib then came up against Judah in 701 BCE.

This siege certainly put much pressure on the people of Judah, even though biblical sources conclude the depiction of it with the withdrawal of Sennacherib's troops in defeat by Yhwh's messenger (2 Kgs 19:35–36//Isa 37:36–37). Sennacherib did end up leaving Hezekiah on the throne. Some scholars even suggest that Sennacherib treated Judah with particular leniency because his father and grandfather were married to Judahite princesses.[85] However, other scholars doubt that these women were Judahites. They also argue that Sennacherib did not capture Jerusalem mainly because of cost and benefit consideration or Judah's submission and reduced territory.[86] Indeed, in this siege, Sennacherib captured Judah's fortresses (2 Kgs 18:13//Isa 36:1), including Lachish, whose people were brutally treated.[87] The biblical account

84. *COS* 2:295–96, Nimrud Prism D & E, col. iv lines 25–41.

85. Dalley, "Waterworks," 119–21; Dalley, "Identity of the Princesses," 171–75.

86. Frahm, "Family Matters," 206–8; Frahm, "Neo-Assyrian Period," 185; Bagg, "Assyria and the West," 272; Elayi, *Sennacherib*, 82–85.

87. Ussishkin, "Sennacherib's Campaign," 75–103; Ussishkin, *Conquest of Lachish*, 73–131.

also describes how Hezekiah confessed his sin, begged Sennacherib to withdraw, and stripped down the doors and doorposts of Yhwh's temple in order to pay the tribute Sennacherib imposed (2 Kgs 18:14–16). These descriptions notably resonate to a certain extent with the Assyrian source, which ends with the deportation of a considerable number of people, the removal of portions of territory from Hezekiah, and the imposition of additional tribute, which Hezekiah paid accordingly.[88] They also reveal that Hezekiah was under heavy imperial pressure due to Assyrian military actions against Judah.

In the following century, Sennacherib's successors Esarhaddon and Ashurbanipal focused more on confronting the Egyptians. However, Judahites still had direct contact with the Assyrians, as Ashurbanipal would have mustered Manasseh for his campaign against the Egyptians. In fact, following Ahaz's path, Manasseh was loyal to the Assyrians when they had substantial control of Judah in terms of economy and politics.[89] This pressure on the subjugated leaders constituted the Neo-Assyrian imperial hegemony of Israel and Judah in the mid-eighth century to the mid-seventh century BCE.

This history reveals that both Israel and Judah did experience pressure or even heavy-handed, if not dictatorial, control from the Neo-Assyrian Empire. Some scholars point out that Assyrian vassals, such as Judah, enjoyed autonomy in the governance of their internal affairs. They also argue that their elites benefited from economic advantages due to the integration of their land into the imperial economic system.[90] However, similar to colonies under indirect rule in the modern context, Israel and Judah might have had autonomy but not independence.[91] Because of the Neo-Assyrian Empire's militaristic nature, Israel and Judah indeed had first-hand encounters with Assyrian terror, which gave them intense experiences of the empire's hegemony. These experiences might not always have led to anti-Assyrian actions, but they were certainly sufficient to touch the nerves of Israelites and Judahites, eliciting both submissive and subversive reactions.

---

88. RINAP 3/1:65–66, Sennacherib 4, lines 49–58. For Assyrian strategies of tribute imposition and deportation and its impact on the subjugated people in general, see Liverani, *Assyria*, 187–94.

89. Miller and Hayes, *History of Ancient Israel*, 428–33.

90. See, for instance, Crouch, *Israel and the Assyrians*, 18–21.

91. Davidson, *Empire and Exile*, 112.

One can understand more about the nature of these experiences through what Marc Van De Mieroop calls "three types of political arrangements," or what Mordechai Cogan regards as the three-stage destruction of petty states' independence.[92] The Assyrians carried out these strategies from the reign of Tiglath-pileser III to ensure the loyalty of their states in the west. In the first stage, the Assyrians allowed their local ruler to remain in charge, but they imposed annual tribute on the vassal states and required them to enlist national troops for the empire's military campaigns. The Assyrians would move forward to the second stage if their vassal states showed disloyalty, such as refusing to pay tribute or joining an anti-Assyrian coalition. They would make these vassals into puppet states by taking military action, deporting their local ruler and his supporters, and appointing a pro-Assyrian local official to rule a reduced territory with more obligations. A further rebellion would lead to the final stage. The Assyrians provincialized the vassals or the puppet states by conquering them, further deporting their people, rebuilding their capital and reconstructing their administration to fit the empire's needs, and appointing a governor who was directly under the empire's control.[93]

As Van De Mieroop and Uriah Y. Kim point out, Israel is a good example of this three-stage political arrangement, or actually destruction.[94] My historical outline also indicates that Judah experienced harsh treatment by Assyria, even though it did not experience this destruction in full force. These experiences of Israel and Judah did compel their leaders to learn an unforgettable lesson about the Assyrians' hegemonic power and intolerance to disloyalty.[95] Thus, for instance, Manasseh chose to submit to Assyria, as Ahaz did, rather than following Hezekiah's resistive path. However, the impetuses that led to these experiences, that is, the rebellion of some leaders in Israel and Judah, also notably demonstrate the anti-Assyrian spirit, rather than total submission, among them in their confrontation with Neo-Assyrian imperial hegemony.

92. Van De Mieroop, *History of Ancient Near East*, 267; Cogan, "Judah," 406. For more about Assyrian military strategies, see Fuchs, "Assyria at War," 380–401.

93. Van De Mieroop, *History of Ancient Near East*, 267–68; Cogan, "Judah," 406.

94. Van De Mieroop, *History of Ancient Near East*, 268; Kim, *Decolonizing Josiah*, 214.

95. Kim, *Decolonizing Josiah*, 214.

2.3.2.2 Diplomatic Contacts

In addition to military subjugation, diplomatic contacts with Assyrian officials also offered crucial opportunities for Israelites and Judahites to learn about Assyrian imperial propaganda and hegemony.[96] The transmission of Assyrian imperial ideology in these diplomatic contacts might occur through oral transmission, probably with translation to Aramaic, which compelled various responses to the empire. One of the important diplomatic contacts was the journeys of tribute-bearing emissaries to Assyria. In these journeys, the emissaries very likely saw Assyrian monuments along the way to Assyria and obtained information about them from Assyrian officials. Moreover, they received entertainment from the Assyrian rulers in reception rooms decorated with texts and images when they arrived at Assyrian palaces and had extensive interaction with Assyrian officials. The emissaries usually stayed in a Mesopotamian capital for a substantial time – usually two weeks, but some stayed more permanently – when they met Assyrian governors and thereby became exposed to imperial ideology.[97] Other diplomatic contacts include emissaries' *ad hoc* journeys to Assyria for delivering tribute during Assyrian military campaigns, special occasions such as Assyrian palace dedications, and Assyrian officials' trips to the vassals for negotiations when the vassals withheld tribute.[98] If the discovery of the treaty tablet at Tell Tayinat suggests a usual Neo-Assyrian practice,[99] these diplomatic contacts may even include the continuous exhibition of Assyrian treaties in the vassals. These contacts offered substantial opportunities for the Assyrians to present their ideology to the emissaries or representatives of Israel and Judah.

These contacts might fill the officials of Israel and Judah with awe of, or even admiration for, the Neo-Assyrian Empire, as the Assyrians usually entertained them lavishly and honored them when they visited Assyria.[100] These officials might also be expected to transmit Neo-Assyrian ideology

---

96. Morrow, "Tribute from Judah," 186, 190. Morrow discusses the diplomatic relations between Judah and Assyria, but most of the textual evidence he uses is also applicable to Israel.

97. Morrow, "Tribute from Judah," 187–90. For more about the Assyrian monuments and palace art, see Aster, "Transmission," 14–18, 22–29.

98. Morrow, "Tribute from Judah," 190–92.

99. Lauinger, "Esarhaddon's Succession," 87–90. For more about this treaty, see Lauinger, "Neo-Assyrian *adê*," 99–115; Lauinger, "Neo-Assyrian Scribes," 285–314.

100. Parpola, "Assyria's Expansion," 101.

positively back to their homeland and to encourage their people and kings to remain loyal to the empire.[101] However, as these kinds of encounters, like those between the colonial power and the colonized in modern contexts, very likely involved differences in power, they also led to the marginalization of Israelites and Judahites, thus inducing possible resistance among them.[102]

An example is the encounter described in 2 Kings 18:17–37 (//Isa 36:2–22) concerning the speech of the Rabshakeh.[103] Sennacherib commissioned him to go to Jerusalem together with two other Assyrian officials and a great Assyrian army. This encounter recalls the type of diplomatic contacts that involved Assyrian officials' trips to the vassals for negotiations, even though the Rabshakeh's speech is not about tribute, but about surrender. This encounter also exhibits the exposure of Judahites, not only their officials, to forceful Assyrian rhetoric. Notably, while Hezekiah's officials requested the Rabshakeh to speak in Aramaic so that his speech would not reach the Judahites in general, the Rabshakeh refused to do so and continued to speak in the language of Judah in a loud voice (2 Kgs 18:26–28). This interaction evidences that Judahites in general had opportunities to learn about Assyrian imperial propaganda directly from the Assyrians. It also suggests that diplomatic interactions between the Assyrians and the people of Judah involved differences in power and the subjugation of the conquered people.[104] Hezekiah knew of this well and thus commanded his people to keep silent beforehand (2 Kgs 18:36). Both the officials and Hezekiah also tore their clothes after hearing the speech (2 Kgs 18:37–19:1). These responses might not be radically resistive, but they clearly were not totally submissive. Hezekiah's request (2 Kgs 19:3–4) and Isaiah's response (2 Kgs 19:6–7) afterward exhibit at least their hope for the destruction of the Assyrians.

2.3.2.3 Scribal Training

Along with military encounters and diplomatic contacts, scribal training was another possible platform through which Israelites and Judahites learned

101. Aster, "Transmission," 11; Aster, *Reflections of Empire*, 16.

102. Davidson, *Empire and Exile*, 88–89.

103. About this speech's authenticity, see, for instance, Gallagher, *Sennacherib's Campaign*, 189–261. For more analysis about this speech, see Machinist, "Rab Šāqēh," 151–68.

104. About the imbalanced power exhibited in Assyrian siege negotiations in general, see Aster, "Transmission," 39–43.

about and developed responses to Assyrian imperial ideology and culture. The existence of scribal training offered by the Assyrians to Israelites and Judahites is still hypothetical and needs further investigation. However, scholars' arguments for it are worth considering for understanding the reception of Assyrian imperial ideology and culture among Israelites and Judahites.

Wright and Simo Parpola reasonably point out that in order to maintain the stability of the conquered regions and manage the masses there, the Assyrians could not only take military actions against them and collect tribute from them, but had to educate at least some of their people on Assyrian culture, including literature and languages.[105] Indeed, Sargon II claimed in his inscription that it was his mission to indoctrinate foreigners, including subjugated people, with Assyrian culture.[106] The discovery of cuneiform materials in Israel, Judah, and nearby regions also indicates their peoples' exposure to Neo-Assyrian writings, even though there is no clear indication of how well they knew Akkadian.[107] These materials include monumental inscriptions and administrative and judicial documents dating to the reign of Sargon II to that of Assurbanipal.[108] They suggest the opportunity as well as the necessity for Israelites and Judahites, or at least their scribes or officials, to learn Neo-Assyrian writings and Akkadian.[109]

It is noteworthy that despite its decreased use due to Neo-Assyrian preference for Aramaic as the official language,[110] Akkadian was not totally replaced by Aramaic by the late eighth century BCE as some scholars suppose.[111] Some Neo-Assyrian legal texts contain Northwest Semitic names, indicating that some scribes from the west worked with cuneiform documents.[112] There was also a Neo-Assyrian scribal school in Huzirina, a region near Haran, where

105. Wright, *Inventing God's Law*, 99; Parpola, "Assyria's Expansion," 101.

106. Dalley, "Occasions and Opportunities," 27.

107. Morrow, "To Set the Name," 378. For more discussion about Judahite scribes' knowledge of Akkadian cuneiform texts, see also Hays, *Covenant with Death*, 23–25.

108. Horowitz, Oshima, and Sanders, *Cuneiform in Canaan*, 5, 38–39, 42–44, 54–62, 101–9, 131–12, 157.

109. Wright, *Inventing God's Law*, 99.

110. Morrow, "To Set the Name," 377–78.

111. Dalley, "Occasions and Opportunities," 26. For more about the continuous use of Assyrian language until the middle of the first millennium BCE, see Luukko and Van Buylere, "Language and Writing," 314.

112. Wright, *Inventing God's Law*, 100.

students continued to copy cuneiform literature even at the time when the Neo-Assyrian Empire reached its end.[113]

If the scribal training that the scribes and officials of Israel and Judah received from the Neo-Assyrians carried on some core elements of the Old Babylonian scribal curriculum, they would learn various types of cuneiform literature, such as letters, hymns, and treaties in the elementary stage.[114] In a more advanced stage, they would even draw up administrative and legal documents in addition to copying famous royal inscriptions and study lexical lists and administrative procedures.[115] This curriculum might have included the study of some cuneiform law collections and related legal traditions.

Suggesting this possibility is Neo-Assyrian preservation of cuneiform law collections from previous periods, including the Laws of Hammurabi and the Middle Assyrian Laws, even though the Neo-Assyrians did not compile their own law collection.[116] These law collections and related legal traditions significantly represented Neo-Assyrian legal knowledge. The scribes and officials of Israel and Judah might also regard them as a reflection of imperial legal metanarrative. The medium of learning this metanarrative might not be Akkadian but a language with which the scribes and officials of Israel and Judah were familiar, such as Aramaic, especially in the early stage of the training. Still, this possible scribal training offered them the opportunity to acquaint themselves with and reflect on imperial legal traditions. Their responses might vary because of Assyrian imperial rule and military actions, as well as their direct encounter with the Assyrians in diplomatic relations, but these responses certainty affected how Israelites and Judahites formulated their own law collection, their own legal discourse, even though they maintained a particular scribal-education apparatus of their own.[117]

113. Dalley, "Occasions and Opportunities," 26–27.

114. Carr, *Writing*, 22.

115. Carr, 24.

116. Radner, "Neo-Assyrian Period," 883–84; Levinson, "Is the Covenant Code an Exilic Composition," 293; Wright, *Inventing God's Law*, 106–115.

117. Carr, *Writing*, 115.

2.4 Purposes of Exodus 19–24

An examination of the purpose of Exodus 19–24 will offer another essential foundation for understanding these responses and the relationship between Exodus 19–24 and cuneiform legal traditions. Scholars, again, have various proposals in view of cuneiform law collections' purposes and biblical literary traditions. In this section, I aim to demonstrate that while most of these suggestions have shed light on the nature of Exodus 19–24, no single one of them suffices for explaining the multifaceted characteristics reflected in this corpus. Considering multiple purposes, namely judicial references and wisdom-moral teachings with religious and political purposes, is a perspective I suggest. Together with the discussed relationship between the Assyrian Empire and the people of Judah and Israel, this perspective also opens a path for understanding Exodus 19–24 as a legal discourse of the imperialized.

2.4.1 Law Used in Court

To begin with, some scholars associate Exodus 19–24's legal section, especially the casuistic laws, with the law used in court. Most scholars have ruled out this possibility due to observations of biblical and cuneiform sources. However, the arguments for and against this proposal are fundamental for understanding other suggestions for the purpose of Exodus 19–24. Demonstrating the difference between the source of the casuistic laws and that of apodictic laws, Alt asserts that the casuistic laws in the Book of the Covenant are rooted in "der konkreten Wirklichkeit des Rechtslebens" (the concrete reality of legal life).[118] For him, the word משפטים in Exodus 21:1 indicates that the following laws were written for the local secular jurisdiction to administer justice. He even suggests that the judicial community would bring up these laws when they gathered in the gate and sought judgment for a case.[119] A few scholars follow this understanding. For instance, Hans Jochen Boecker agrees with Alt's differentiation between casuistic and apodictic laws and contends that the casuistic laws in the Book of the Covenant belonged to a practical work for jurisdiction.[120] Klaus-Peter Adam also studies the teaching on the application of homicide law in 1 Samuel 26 based on the proposition that the

118. Alt, "Ursprünge," 324.

119. Alt, 289.

120. Boecker, *Recht und Gesetz*, 132–33.

legal traditions behind the Book of the Covenant were orally handed down from daily legal practice.[121]

The difficulty of this understanding is the lack of evidence from both biblical and cuneiform sources, as various scholars point out. Bernard S. Jackson notes that biblical passages describing instructions to judges (for instance, 2 Chr 19:5–7 and Deut 16:18–20) do not mention their compliance with a written law.[122] He therefore comments that court use of the Book of the Covenant's casuistic laws is "thoroughly anachronistic and speculative."[123] Michael LeFebvre even argues that the Torah was re-characterized as legislation later, which did not occur until the Hellenistic period.[124] Jonathan Vroom similarly contends that the perception of biblical law as legally binding did not emerge until early Judaism.[125] A crucial starting point of these arguments is that the laws of Mesopotamia, Asia Minor, and Egypt were not legislative or regarded as having binding obligations.[126] Some scholars have pointed out evidence for cuneiform law collections' non-legislative role. For instance, there are many discrepancies between the Laws of Hammurabi and various legal documents,[127] even though some land leases seem to be consistent with this law collection.[128] At best, Paul only suggests that one can "infer" the Laws of Hammurabi as "a legal compilation of customary laws, which incorporates reforms and amendments."[129] Martha T. Roth also only points out that some Old Babylonian letters suggest "interpretative possibilities" that some later legal decision-making referred to the Laws of Hammurabi or judgments pronounced earlier by the king.[130] Thus, there is little evidence supporting the proposal that Exodus 19–24's legal section was the law used in court.

121. Adam, "Didactic Case Narrative," 99.

122. Jackson, "Ideas of the Law," 187–88.

123. Jackson, *Wisdom-Laws*, 54.

124. LeFebvre, *Collections*, 259.

125. Vroom, *Authority of Law*, 211.

126. LeFebvre, *Collections*, 8–15, 40–48, 258–59; Vroom, *Authority of Law*, 50.

127. Eilers, *Gesetzstele Chammurabis*, 8–9. See also Barmash, *Laws of Hammurabi*, 231–46 for gaps between this law collection and various cuneiform documents.

128. Petschow, "Die 45 und 46," 181–212. Ilan Peled, however, is correct to suggest that cuneiform law collections reflect the social elites' main legal notions, which the wider social circles knew and practiced in some ways. In his recent study, he points out other examples of consistency between cuneiform laws and documents (Peled, *Law and Gender*, 6–8).

129. Paul, *Studies in the Book of the Covenant*, 24–25.

130. Roth, "Law Collection of King Hammurabi," 22–29.

2.4.2 Scribal Exercise

In view of this, some scholars argue that the legal section of Exodus 19–24 and that of cuneiform law collections were merely scribal exercises. This proposal represents another end of the pendulum, which also does not receive much scholarly support, but reflects some important considerations. One of the significant studies belongs to F. R. Kraus, who focuses on the characteristics of the Laws of Hammurabi.[131] Kraus points out that although Hammurabi defined his laws as *dīnāt mīšarim* (which Kraus translates as "gerechte Richtersprüche," that is, just judicial decisions),[132] not all cases recorded in the laws reflect real-life situations. Many laws, such as those concerning the negligence of a house builder (LH 229–231), are actually logical expansions of a single case that aim to offer appropriate judgment for various scenarios related to the case.[133]

Kraus points out that this kind of logical extrapolation was an academic method also used by omen series. Despite the seemingly unrelated nature of law collections and omen series, they both exhibit similar gradation of judgment or gradation of ominous event interpretation. They also present their content in a casuistic style, making them a kind of scientific treaty. Kraus asserts that the development of these scientific treaties occurred in the scribal schools. The Hammurabi collection, for instance, was not only formulated by referring extensively to earlier law collections, such as the Laws of Ur-Namma and the Laws of Lipit-Ishtar, but was also copied during scribal training. For him, this explains why archaeologists have found a number of Old Babylonian school copies of both the Laws of Hammurabi and these earlier law collections.[134]

This suggestion, as Westbrook comments, does offer a reasonable explanation for the emergence of law collections in other nearby regions, including Hatti, Assyria, and Israel/Judah. It is also evident that there were cuneiform scribal schools that offered training on language as well as cultural and literary inheritance throughout Mesopotamia since the second millennium. However, considering omens' function and other cuneiform law collections'

131. Kraus, "Ein zentrales Problem," 283–96.

132. Kraus, 284–85; cf. Westbrook, "Biblical and Cuneiform Law Codes," 7.

133. Kraus, "Ein zentrales Problem," 289; Westbrook, "Biblical and Cuneiform Law Codes," 7.

134. Kraus, "Ein zentrales Problem," 289–90, 293–94.

characteristics, cuneiform law collections, and thus the Book of the Covenant, were unlikely to be pure academic exercises without practical functions.[135]

2.4.3 Judicial References

The function of omens and characteristics of other cuneiform law collections indeed suggest that the purpose of law collections in Mesopotamia and the Levant was to offer judicial references, as Westbrook argues. This is one of the proposals I find appropriate for understanding the purposes of Exodus 19–24. It explains this corpus's legal features, even though there is a lack of evidence for its use in court and some of its ordinances do not seem to reflect real-life situations. Similar to Kraus, Westbrook contends that scholars' evidence does not prove that cuneiform law collections, and thus the Book of the Covenant, were legislative.[136] However, rather than scribal exercises, Westbrook argues that these law collections, including Exodus 21:1–22:16, were reference works for judges in deciding difficult cases.[137] Westbrook's argument, like Kraus's, concerns the characteristics of omen series; however, Westbrook significantly points out that the compilation of the omen lists was applied science, which aimed to offer references for diviners to determine the meaning of an ominous event or feature. This consultation purpose is evident by the fact that Old Babylonian diviners marked the omens they consulted or placed the tablets of those omens in different places, even though these diviners usually did not cite the name of the omen series when they made an interpretation. A similar purpose is applicable to the compilation of law collections, which are actually lists of legal decisions.[138]

A potential argument against this understanding is that, unlike the omen series, direct evidence for judges' consultation of law collections is not available. However, Westbrook reasonably argues that this evidence is absent for various reasons, including limited available cuneiform sources of law collections and the less important role of lawsuits than the omen interpretation in Mesopotamia. Moreover, there is indirect evidence of judges' consultation of law collections. Most Middle Assyrian Law tablets were recovered near the

135. Westbrook, "Biblical and Cuneiform Law Codes," 9.

136. Westbrook, "Cuneiform Law Codes," 76.

137. Westbrook, "Biblical and Cuneiform Law Codes," 10–14.

138. Westbrook, 10.

"Gate of Shamash," which scholars believe to be the courthouse. Later copies of Hittite Laws also exhibit an updating of both language and the law, which indicates the law collection's practical, rather than purely academic, purpose.[139] These characteristics of cuneiform law collections and the function of omen series offer reasonable foundations for understanding the purpose of Exodus 19–24's legal section as judicial references.

2.4.4 Wisdom-Moral Teachings

Understanding Exodus 19–24's legal section as judicial references, however, does not account for various themes and forms in this corpus, which the proposal of wisdom-moral teachings notably considers. This proposal, in my opinion, supplements the understanding of Exodus 19–24's purpose, even though in the first place it seems to argue against the understanding that this corpus's legal section had the purpose of offering references for judges.

One of the scholars who offers this proposal is Anne Fitzpatrick-McKinley, who suggests that the Book of the Covenant was "a list of wisdom-moral rules."[140] She argues that while quite a few scholars relate this corpus to legislation and regard it as a reflection of ancient Israelite society, the legal studies of Alan Watson and anthropological studies of Jack Goody suggest that there is a wide gap between ancient codified law and societal circumstances.[141] She also asserts that the Indian concept of *dharma* and the biblical concept of torah compel one to consider the moral, rather than legal, nature of the Book of the Covenant. According to Fitzpatrick-McKinley, *dharma* refers to a moral obligation growing out of a religious desire for grace. She contends that this concept has great potential for understanding the Book of the Covenant's purpose for two reasons. This concept finds a parallel in the Egyptian concept of *ma'at*, which was related to religious order in addition to legal procedure. It also corresponds somewhat to the idea of *kittum* in Old Babylonia, which she regards to be related to Babylonian wisdom tradition. Regarding the concept of torah, Fitzpatrick-McKinley argues that it emphasizes one's religious duty

139. Westbrook, 11–12.

140. Fitzpatrick-McKinley, *Transformation*, 144.

141. Fitzpatrick-McKinley, 60–82; Watson, *Society and Legal Change*; Watson, *Evolution of Law*; Goody, *Logic of Writing*. For criticism concerning her application of these studies, see Jackson, review of *Transformation*, 327–32.

rather than legal sanction and exhibits a clear orientation toward wisdom, corresponding to the concept of *dharma*.[142]

Studying the Book of the Covenant based on these concepts, Fitzpatrick-McKinley points out that it carries inconsistent rules and vague sanctions and lacks formal court enforcement, but exhibits endeavors to protect moral order. These endeavors include resorting to oath-taking, emphasizing the seriousness of false witness and bribery, appealing to a subjective moral sensibility, and so forth. Fitzpatrick-McKinley thus suggests that the Book of the Covenant was moral teaching of scribes, which can be understood in the wisdom tradition of Mesopotamia and the Levant.[143]

Along a similar line of thought, but going even further, Jackson queries about generalizing the evidence from other cultures or cuneiform law collections to the Exodus ordinances and calls for a consideration of the wisdom tradition within biblical literature.[144] He points out that there are many connections between the ordinances in the Book of the Covenant and wisdom. They include themes, such as enmity, consideration of the neighbor, and equal respect of God and authorities; settings, such as quarreling and agricultural life; and forms, such as the participial form used for describing domestic relations. Moreover, Jackson finds that quite a few cases in the Exodus ordinances resort to custom and resolutions among the involved parties, rather than formulated rules. He thus asserts that, rather than stipulations for third-party adjudication or court procedures, the ordinances in Exodus 21:1–22:16 were wisdom-laws intended for "self-execution" in private disputes, such as those within a family or among neighbors.[145]

The key constraint of Fitzpatrick-McKinley's and Jackson's studies is that their suggestions concerning the non-judicial characters of the Book of the Covenant are contradicted by comparative data and not always evident by the Book of the Covenant itself. Some elements that Fitzpatrick-McKinley regards as evidence for demonstrating the protection of moral order in the Book of the Covenant, such as the use of oath and the rules against false witness and bribery, actually appear commonly in cuneiform law collections and

142. Fitzpatrick-McKinley, *Transformation*, 114–18.

143. Fitzpatrick-McKinley, *Transformation*, 21, 137–40.

144. Jackson, *Wisdom-Laws*, 9, 15.

145. Jackson, 7, 24, 29, 30. 41–43, 56.

are believed to have been carried out in legal settings.[146] As Jackson himself notes, some laws in the Book of the Covenant, such as those concerning debt slavery and seduction of the unbetrothed maiden, also necessitate a kind of institutional involvement, rather than reveals the possibility of self-help execution, because of the power imbalance involved.[147] These observations indicate that this corpus might not be simply intended for self-execution purposes initially.

Nevertheless, Fitzpatrick-McKinley's and Jackson's suggestions significantly introduce a wisdom-moral aspect to the understanding of the Book of the Covenant's purposes. This aspect supplements the suggestion concerning references for judges. In addition to judicial references, the Covenant collection also aimed to offer wisdom-moral teachings, which invited its audience to contemplate personal and moral aspects of interpersonal relationships in their society when they dealt with conflicts among their people, or even between themselves and their people. This audience might not be limited to judges, but include people who received scribal training. The proposal of wisdom-moral teachings thus reveals a wider purpose of Exodus 19–24, beyond judicial consideration.

2.4.5 Propaganda with Religious Features

Similar to this proposal, the suggestion of propaganda considers Exodus 19–24's purposes in a deeper, and even multiple, level(s). Scholars argue for this purpose particularly for cuneiform law collections extant with prologue and epilogue, which I find essential for understanding the purpose of Exodus 19–24 as a whole. A significant argument is from Van De Mieroop's recent study of Babylonian literature, in which he advocates that the nature of the Laws of Hammurabi is primarily propagandistic.[148] He asserts that this law collection's composition began with Hammurabi's order to engrave multiple copies in stone as publicly displayed monuments. He even adds that whether or not the Babylonians could read the text on the steles was insignificant, since

146. For the use of oath, see, for instance, LU 29; LH 20, 103, 131, 249; MAL A 47, C+G 1; HL 75, 169. For laws regarding false witness and bribery, see, for instance, LL 17, LH 3–8. About the judicial practices of oath swearing in ancient Mesopotamia, see, for instance, Greengus, "Legal and Social Institutions," 473–74.

147. Jackson, *Wisdom-Laws*, 394–96.

148. Van De Mieroop, *Philosophy*, 146.

its value was more "rhetorical than real."[149] For Van De Mieroop, the public inscriptions were intended to convey a message that Hammurabi governed everyone in his land according to a logical, defined, and written set of laws. It was only after scribes had seen the monuments that they began to copy the inscriptions and made them a model for later scribal practices.[150]

Whether the Laws of Hammurabi was initially propagandistic as Van De Mieroop suggests is subject to further study, but this law collection's propagandistic intention is without question. Indeed, biblical scholars similarly see the propagandistic characteristics of this law collection. Some of them even find related religious features. For instance, although Paul suggests that the Laws of Hammurabi is a collection of customary law, he emphasizes that its ultimate goal was to offer substantial proof to the gods that the king was a king of justice. He argues that similar to cuneiform royal inscriptions, cuneiform law collections aimed to exalt the king's fame as well as to gain gods' favor for the king.[151] Barmash even identifies the Laws of Hammurabi as a royal inscription and suggests that the corpus as a whole was meant to promote the king's fulfillment of divine mandate to institute justice.[152] These understandings invite a consideration of the purposes of Exodus 19–24, including its legal section and the surrounding narrative, not simply as references for judges and wisdom-moral teachings, but those with religious and propagandistic intentions.

2.4.6 Multiple Purposes

Some scholars in fact see the necessity of exploring the multitude of genres or purposes for both cuneiform law collections and Exodus 19–24, even though they maintain that these law collections are unlikely to be meant for use in court or merely for scribal exercise. Examining the codification and canonization of cuneiform and biblical law collections, Otto points out that a critical problem of previous discussions on these law collections' purpose or genre is treating different options as opposites. He therefore urges scholars

149. Van De Mieroop, 177.

150. Van De Mieroop, 146, 173, 177.

151. Paul, *Studies in the Book of the Covenant*, 21–25.

152. Barmash, *Laws of Hammurabi*, 251.

to consider multiple objectives instead.[153] Otto suggests that cuneiform law collections were primarily school texts for scribes to practice making legal decisions by analogy; however, with the framing of prologue and epilogue, they became royal commemorative inscriptions that justified the king's legal function.[154] This understanding is similar to Jean Bottéro's earlier argument, which suggests that the Laws of Hammurabi was simultaneously a treatise about how to exercise judicial power and a proclamation of the king's glory and achievement as well as an expression of political ideal in pursuing justice.[155] However, Otto posits further that the Book of the Covenant similarly was first collected and edited in the scribal scholarship context, but was then adapted to serve as a presentation of God's will.[156] This proposal recalls Westbrook's summary of his discussion concerning cuneiform and biblical law collections' purpose. Although he advocates that they were reference works for judges, he adds that both the cuneiform and biblical law collections, including the Book of the Covenant, also had secondary purposes. The former were also intended for exalting the king as a judge and serving as school texts, while the latter constituted a religio-historical narrative that replaced the king with God as the lawgiver.[157] These understandings suggest that the corpus of Exodus 19–24 was intended for various purposes. Considering the aforementioned scholarly understandings, I posit that these purposes are judicial-referential, wisdom-moral, religious, and even political.

2.4.7 Legal Discourse of the Imperialized

Although Westbrook and Wells suggest that the Book of the Covenant was used for religious purposes, rather than as royal propaganda,[158] the message of Exodus 19–24 can be religious as well as political, especially in view

153. Otto, "Kodifizierung," 80, 88.

154. Otto, 92–111.

155. Bottéro, *Mesopotamia*, 167–69, 183.

156. Otto, "Kodifizierung," 112.

157. Westbrook, "Biblical and Cuneiform Law Codes," 14. In addition to Otto, Bottéro, and Westbrook, see also Jackson's and Wells's comments concerning the necessity of considering biblical laws' multiple genres or purposes, Berman's argument against making dichotomy between legal and non-legal genres, and Marshall's comment on the genre of Exod 21:1–22:16. Jackson, *Wisdom-Laws*, 71; Wells, "What is Biblical Law," 242; Berman, "History of Legal Theory," 26–27; Marshall, *Israel*, 136.

158. Westbrook and Wells, *Everyday Law*, 130.

of how Israelites and Judahites related to the Neo-Assyrian Empire.[159] The consideration of this corpus's multiple purposes also reveals the potential of regarding Exodus 19–24 further as a legal discourse of the imperialized: that is, the people of Israel and Judah appropriated cuneiform legal traditions' ways of formulating law collections in order to respond to the empire's legal discourse.

Anselm C. Hagedorn's study speaks to this potential.[160] He points out that all colonial contexts exhibit a complex dialectic that leads to a particular response of the colonized: Empires always attempt to create contact zones to reach out to the colonized in various aspects of their society, but these zones are located in power relations that are shifting and unequal. Moreover, in addition to the fact that these contact zones occur both before and after the actual colonial rule, they also tend to indicate the occurrence and nature of colonial rule in the near future. Because of this dialectic, the colonized sense a kind of "imagined pressure" to employ strategies that favor compromise and harmony with the imperial power in order to avoid conflict with it, even though they see the need to find a channel to express their resistance. One of these strategies is the appropriation of the legal system, which fits well into the empire's ideology. The creation of a legal document following imperial legal framework and expressions gives the impression that the colonized submit themselves to the governance of the empire, thus avoiding tension with it. However, this legal document simultaneously offers a platform for the colonized to express their resistance to, or even subversion of, imperial values.[161]

Hagedorn's application of this theory to the Pentateuch as a whole in the Persian period may lead to some queries, but his insight does shed light on Exodus 19–24 under the Neo-Assyrian context. Although there is no evidence that Israelites and Judahites faced the same pressure to follow imperial legal practices, as modern colonized people do,[162] the Assyrians created contact zones of unequal power relations, such as diplomatic encounters and possible scribal training, to cultivate Israelites and Judahites. Moreover, the Assyrians carried out brutal military actions against Israel and Judah in

159. For the political nature of the even wider development of the Hebrew language and its literature, see Sanders, *Invention of Hebrew*, 103–56.

160. Hagedorn, "Local Law," 57–76.

161. Hagedorn, 62, 69, 73–74.

162. See §1.3.3.

order to demonstrate zero tolerance to their rebellion. Facing this dialectic and hegemony, Israelites and Judahites felt the pressure to resort to a strategy that allowed them to avoid further conflict, when they at the same time also wanted to subvert the imperial control.

The appropriation of cuneiform legal traditions allowed the authors of Exodus 19–24 to do so. By formulating a legal discourse that looked imperial, they avoided potential tension with the Assyrian Empire or pro-Assyrian parties among their people, but still had the opportunity to express their resistance to the empire. They could also freely circulate this legal corpus because of its seemingly non-threatening, imperial-like features. This legal corpus was intended to offer judicial references and wisdom-moral teachings for contemplating and dealing with interpersonal conflicts in the society. It, however, also had clear religious, as well as political, if not propagandistic, goals. By replacing the gods and the emperors with Yhwh, Moses, and an emphasis on the people's participation, by following imperial legal ways of structuring law collections, formulating laws, and presenting ideology, but "not quite,"[163] the authors of Exodus 19–24 created a legal discourse for their people. This legal discourse might at the same time speak to the authors' monarchy, given the similar emphasis of monarchy and empire on royal power and the imperial influence on the Israelite and Judahite monarchies. However, in view of its relationship with imperial legal traditions, this legal discourse significantly expressed the authors' response to the empire, which is conservatively revolutionary. This response is the particular focus of my study.

2.5 Authors' Social Location and Positions toward the Empire

The social location of this legal discourse's authors and their position toward the empire are then the final areas that require explanation in order to understand the relationship between Exodus 19–24 and imperial legal traditions. The discussion on the relationship of Israel and Judah to empires, specifically the Neo-Assyrian Empire, has already demonstrated that the status of being imperialized is an important social location of these authors for understanding their response to the imperial power. Together with this broader social

163. A manifestation of "the same, but not quite"; see §1.2.2.1.

location, an exploration of these authors' more specific roles in their society and their characteristics will further exhibit the complexity of their possible positions toward the empire.

The Exodus corpus does not mention anything about its authors. Without further evidence for a more specific dating of this corpus, the authors' regional origin is also uncertain – they may be Israelites or Judahites.[164] The corpus itself and its similarities to cuneiform law collections only suggest that its authors had writing competency and knowledge of legal traditions, including those of cuneiform. The ability to write does narrow down the possible roles of the authors to a certain group of people, who were usually some kind of official, including scribes and priests.[165] Based on some biblical references that hint at the production of written law, some scholars also suggest that priests or temple scribes were the authors of biblical law.[166] Nonetheless, religious institutions were not independent of the palace in Mesopotamia and the Levant, including Israel and Judah.[167] Since the late pre-exilic period, royal and priestly scribal offices also overlapped.[168] It is thus difficult to pinpoint the exact role or work context of Exodus 19–24's authors without further evidence.

Still, one can trace some characteristics of Exodus 19–24's authors. Scribes were unlikely to be independent of the palace or the temple in Israel and Judah, given the limited demand for written documents in the First Temple period.[169] In addition to the aforementioned diplomatic encounter and possible scribal training offered by the Assyrians, it is also likely that there was a "two-track educational system" in late pre-exilic Israel and Judah. This system might include one track focused on local language texts and another on foreign languages and limited foreign language texts, in view of similar training provided in the Sumero-Akkadian tradition and Judahite royal officials' ability to communicate with the Assyrians in Aramaic (2 Kgs 18:26//

164. Given lack of solid evidence, I leave the authors' regional origin open, even though being Judahites or transplanted Israelites in the time of Hezekiah seems to be the most viable hypothesis. For various possibilities, see, for instance, Wright, *Inventing God's Law*, 115–16.

165. Carr, *Writing*, 116.

166. van der Toorn, *Scribal Culture*, 87.

167. van der Toorn, 85.

168. Carr, *Writing*, 119.

169. van der Toorn, *Scribal Culture*, 82.

Isa 36:11).[170] The authors of Exodus 19–24 were thus likely to be scribes who had gone through some training in foreign languages and literary traditions, especially legal ones, in addition to local language and scribal traditions. They might also receive some scribal training offered by the Assyrians and might have heard about, if not participated in, some diplomatic contacts with them. These scribes were obligated to serve the palace or the temple, or both, and they compiled Exodus 19–24 primarily for people with similar training who also served or had access to the palace or the temple.

These authors' stance on the empire, however, varied. Some scholars do argue that these scribes took a pro-empire position in general. In addition to Mathew, who contends that eighth-century Israelite elites imitated the empire to oppress their own people,[171] Carly Crouch also emphasizes that it is problematic to see the elites, who constituted the majority of the literate population in Judah, with any motivation for subverting the Assyrian Empire. She argues that these elites benefited from Assyrian expansion, which integrated the southern Levant into the empire's economic system.[172] Fitzpatrick-McKinley similarly states that scribes in Mesopotamia and the Levant, including Israel and Judah, were "the theoreticians of monarchic power," if not of imperial power. For her, the patronage relationship between the king and the scribes played a crucial part in this role. She thus asserts that the law, being the work of legal elites, was inevitably formulated based on the interest of a small group of powerful people rather than the needs of the masses.[173]

Nonetheless, there are also arguments that reflect the other side of these scribes' attitudes toward the empire. A comparative reference I find noteworthy is the work of Neo-Assyrian scribes. As Jennifer Finn rightly points out, it is always a challenge for scholars to identify the expression of discontent over the emperors among the people of Mesopotamia, especially the elites, because the elites were less likely to involve themselves in overt subversive actions against the emperors on whom they depended for their living and identity. However, some Neo-Assyrian documents exhibit some discernible

170. Carr, *Writing*, 156–57; see also van der Toorn, *Scribal Culture*, 100.

171. Mathew, *Biblical Law Codes*, xx, xxii–xxiii, xxxiii. Gale A. Yee has a similar view but with a focus on Jewish elites; Yee, "Postcolonial Biblical Criticism," 213. See also §1.4.2 and §1.4.3.

172. Crouch, *Israel and the Assyrians*, 19–20.

173. Fitzpatrick-McKinley, *Transformation*, 62, 70, 143, 149.

anti-imperial expressions.[174] Although Assyrian scribes had the responsibility to produce literature for promoting the power of their emperors, they also appropriated the same rhetorical technique to create a discourse that countered it. A usual theme that they employed is the relationship between Neo-Assyrian kings and the Babylonian god Marduk.[175] Scribes wrote about the Assyrian kings' mistreatment of Marduk or copied apparently ordinary letters concerning the negative relationship of a prior Assyrian king with Marduk and appropriated them for critiquing contemporary events. "The Sin of Sargon" contains an example of this type of text. It criticizes Sargon, who actually stands for Sennacherib, for mistreating Marduk:

> [Let me investigate] by means of extispicy the sin of Sargon, my father, let me then find out [the circumstances], le[arn the . . . . . .]; [let me make] the sin he committed against the god an abom[ination to myself], and with God's help let me save myself.[176]

These writings were not an endeavor to rebel or revolt. Still, they were scribal expressions against the imperial metanarrative, which exalted the Assyrian king, even though the scribes had a patronage relationship with the royal palace.[177] This kind of resistive scribal expression was fairly common in Mesopotamia.[178] They are also vital for understanding the position of Exodus 19–24's authors toward the empire.

Similar to these Assyrian scribes, ancient biblical writers were not only affected by the social world where they lived, but also affected it.[179] They had the autonomy to produce that world by presenting their reading of it, which involved various activities, including describing, legitimating, denouncing,

174. Finn, "Marduk."

175. Finn, "Marduk."

176. SAA 3:77, "Sin of Sargon," lines 10′–12′; Finn, "Marduk." For other understandings of this text, see, for instance, Tadmor, Landsberger, and Parpola, "Sin of Sargon," 3–52; Weaver, "Sin of Sargon," 61–66.

177. Finn, "Marduk."

178. In her study of the Gilgameš epic, Tracy Davenport points out that similar resistance occurred since the Sumerian period. She also argues that "The Letter of Gilgameš" indicates the active engagement of the scribal class in the criticism of Assyrian imperialist rule. The scribes might use Gilgameš as a cover to criticize oppressive Assyrian rule in this letter (Davenport, "Anti-Imperialist Twist," 1–23).

179. Yee, "Author/Text/Reader," 118.

satirizing, entertaining, and exhorting.[180] They could also challenge the imperial authority by making use of its culture, including language and traditions.[181] These characteristics of the imperialized biblical authors recall those of the colonized elites in the modern time, who may not be the comprador bourgeoisie hoping for a permanent alliance with the empire, but the patriotic bourgeoisie challenging the imperial power.[182] These characteristics also resonate with those of some professionals working within the machineries of the United States and the United Kingdom today who leaked complaints against their bosses who abused resources.[183] Like these elites and professionals, the scribes who wrote Exodus 19–24 could express their resistance to Assyrian imperial values, even though they were in a position that was supposed to tolerate, if not totally support, them.

In fact, in the Neo-Assyrian period, there were both pro- and anti-Assyrian parties and various responses to the imperial subjugation in Israel and Judah. Kings of Israel were backed by different parties and carried out different policies at different times for various reasons.[184] Isaiah, who served kings of Judah, also notably made different comments about Assyrian threats to different kings: He counseled Ahaz not to join the anti-Assyrian coalition (Isa 8:12) and prophesied that Yhwh would bring the Assyrian king against him (Isa 7:17–25). However, he encouraged Hezekiah that Yhwh would defeat and bring death to the Assyrian king (2 Kgs 19:6–7, 19:20–34// Isa 37:6–7, 37:21–35). Rather than protecting their economic interest, as some scholars assert concerning the elites, the compliance of Manasseh and his officials with the Assyrians might not be "an option but only a means to avoid total annihilation" in view of the end of Israel and Sennacherib's siege of Jerusalem.[185] Just as my discussion on the colonized elites in chapter one exhibits,[186] these observations suggest that the authors of Exodus 19–24 had

180. Yee, 118.

181. Yee, "Postcolonial Biblical Criticism," 199.

182. See §1.2.3 and §1.3.2.

183. Ahmad, *Iraq*, 207. Ahmad discusses the example of David Kelly, a British microbiologist who worked for the British government. Despite life-threatening pressure to keep it confidential, through an investigative journalist he exposed the Prime Minister's false claims regarding weapons placed in Iraq.

184. Miller and Hayes, *History of Ancient Israel*, 369, 374, 376.

185. Parpola, "Assyria's Expansion," 104.

186. See §1.2.3 and §1.3.2.

more complicated responses to imperial legal traditions than some scholars have proposed. These responses lead to the similarities and differences exhibited between Exodus 19–24 and cuneiform law collections, making Exodus 19–24 a representation of conservative revolutionists' response to the empire. The complexity of these responses calls for a more nuanced analysis of Exodus 19–24 in comparison to cuneiform law collections, which I aim to present in the following chapters.

2.6 Chapter Conclusions

A postcolonial perspective that considers the multifaceted nature of the imperialized people's discourse sheds light on the relationship between Exodus 19–24 and cuneiform law collections. Scholarly exploration in the past has offered different models for understanding this relationship, including common legal traditions, evolutionary development, and direct literary borrowing. However, their concern was mainly about how and when cultural contact occurred between the people of Israel and Judah and their neighbors, without considering these people's imperialized social location and its effect on the composition of Exodus 19–24 in relation to cuneiform law collections. The studies of Wright, Wells, Morrow, and Barmash have enhanced the understanding of the criteria for determining possible relationships between these two corpora, including literary dependence, common legal traditions, and a shared educational tradition. Barmash's and Wright's studies also reflect an attempt to consider the hegemony behind cuneiform law collections and the biblical authors' social location, respectively. Still, they lack the attention to the multifaceted characteristics of the rhetoric in the work of the imperialized.

A recent work of Otto, however, reveals an encouraging breakthrough, pointing out the Book of the Covenant's subversive reception of the Laws of Hammurabi. This understanding, together with Wells's study of the three biblical law collections, leads one to explore further the characteristics of the corpus of Exodus 19–24 by itself. In light of the multifaceted nature of imperialized people's discourse revealed by postcolonial scholars, I suggest that the similarities and differences between Exodus 19–24 and cuneiform law collections reflect various responses of the imperialized authors to the imperial legal discourse. These responses characterize Exodus 19–24 as a representation of conservative revolutionists' responses to the empire. I will demonstrate this observation in the following chapters with the proposition that the authors of Exodus 19–24 were familiar with the cuneiform legal traditions that prevailed in ancient West Asia and aware of their imperial nature, and that the extant copies of cuneiform law collections somehow reflect these traditions.

The people of Israel and Judah had a long history of living under the shadow of empire, which provides an essential background for analyzing Exodus 19–24 as a work of the imperialized. Various historical and textual considerations make the dating of Exodus 19–24 to a specific period challenging. However, I propose locating the compilation of this corpus in the middle of the eighth century to the middle of the seventh century BCE, when Israel and Judah were under Neo-Assyrian subjugation. This proposal is mainly based on three considerations: first, the reliance of the laws in Deuteronomy on the laws in Exodus and the general dating of the former to no later than the end of the seventh century BCE; second, the expansion of scribal culture in Israel and Judah and the Hebrew literature's appropriation of Akkadian literature occurred not earlier than the eighth century BCE; and third, the continuous study of cuneiform legal traditions in Mesopotamia and the possible exposure of the biblical authors to related knowledge during the Neo-Assyrian period.

There might be some redactional activities in the compilation of Exodus 19–24, including the Book of the Covenant and its surrounding narrative, in view of their various literary features. However, with the consideration of dissociating literary diversity and thematic closeness to later biblical works from the argument for later redaction, as well as the observations on the structural, compositional, and literary features of Exodus 19–24 and cuneiform literature, I will analyze Exodus 19–24 in its entirety under the backdrop of the Neo-Assyrian imperial rule over Israel and Judah, with notes on the diachronic issues of some sections that scholars have explored.

Under this rule, Israelites and Judahites interacted directly with the Assyrians through military encounters, diplomatic contacts, and possible scribal training offered by the Assyrians. These interactions reveal not only the exposure of Israelites and Judahites to Neo-Assyrian ideology and knowledge of legal traditions, but also different levels of imperial subjugations which induced a multifaceted response of the people of Israel and Judah, including the authors of Exodus 19–24.

In view of its content, cuneiform law collections' purposes, and biblical literary traditions, I suggest that this corpus was intended for various purposes, including judicial-referential, wisdom-moral, religious, and political. Furthermore, Hagedorn's observation on colonized peoples' response to the complex dialectic in their colonial contexts suggests further that the corpus of Exodus 19–24 was intended to be a legal discourse of the imperialized. The authors of this corpus appropriated cuneiform legal traditions' ways of formulating law collections in order to express their resistance to imperial values without causing direct conflict with the empire and the pro-empire parties among their people. Due to this strategy's non-threatening feature, the authors could create and circulate freely a text that served as a reference work for judges and wisdom-moral teaching for dealing with interpersonal conflicts. This text at the same time expressed the authors' religious and political views. Employing "the same but not quite" approach to imperial legal traditions, Exodus 19–24's authors created a legal discourse for their people, which might speak to their own monarchy, but significantly expressed their conservatively revolutionary responses to the empire.

The specific regional origin, role, and work context of Exodus 19–24's authors cannot be pinpointed without further evidence. However, I suggest that these authors were not only part of the imperialized people, but scribes who had received some training in foreign languages and legal traditions and who served the palace or the temple, or both, based on several observations: the characteristics of the corpus itself, the writing competency of the people of Judah and Israel, the necessity of scribes' dependence on royal and religious institutions, and the possible local and Assyrian scribal training in the Neo-Assyrian period. These authors compiled Exodus 19–24 primarily for people with similar training who also served or had access to the palace or the temple.

These social characteristics, however, suggest various possible positions of the authors toward the empire. Some scholars argue that these authors may have been pro-Assyrian because of the benefit that they obtained from the empire. Nevertheless, the work of Neo-Assyrian scribes, the characteristics of biblical writers in general, and the features of colonized people and professionals who work for imperial power today suggest that Exodus 19–24's authors had the autonomy to express their views, including acceptance and criticism, toward the Assyrian Empire. This autonomy is further evident from the existence of both pro- and anti-Assyrian parties and kings in Israel and Isaiah's different responses to Assyrian threat when he counseled different kings. Together with the understanding of Manasseh's motivation of compliance with the Assyrians, these phenomena in Israel and Judah indicate the complexity of Exodus 19–24 as the manifestation of the imperialized people's response to the empire. This complexity not only sheds light on the relationship between Exodus 19–24 and cuneiform law collections, but also invites the following analysis with close attention to the imperialized social location of Exodus 19–24's authors. This analysis will reveal their conservatively revolutionary responses to the empire embedded in this law collection of the imperialized.

CHAPTER 3

Slaves and Women in the Ordinances

(Exodus 21:2–22:16)

3.1 Introduction

In chapters 1 and 2, I discuss postcolonial studies concerning colonized people's responses to their colonizers and the imperialized-imperial relationship between Exodus 19–24 and cuneiform law collections, respectively. These understandings offer a crucial perspective for analyzing the similarities and differences between Exodus 21:2–22:16 and cuneiform law collections. The ordinances in Exodus 21:2–22:16 constitute the central section of Exodus 19–24. They cover issues that cuneiform law collections widely address, using forms and expressions similar to those of their cuneiform counterparts in many ways. These features make Exodus 21:2–22:16 a suitable candidate for inaugurating the analysis of Exodus 19–24 as a manifestation of the imperialized people's response to the imperial legal metanarrative.

In the following analysis, I focus on ordinances concerning slaves and women. These ordinances appear throughout Exodus 21:2–22:16 (21:2–11, 21:15–17, 21:20–32; 22:2, 22:15–16). They also attract scholarly discussion regarding their imperial and oppressive features.[1] I compare these ordinances with extant cuneiform law collections, including the Laws of Ur-Namma (LU), the Laws of Lipit-Ishtar (LL), the Sumerian Laws Exercise Tablet (SLEx), the Sumerian Laws Handbook of Forms (SLHF), the Laws of Eshnunna (LE),

1. Mathew, *Biblical Law Codes*, 165–211; see also §1.4.3.

the Laws of Hammurabi (LH), the Middle Assyrian Laws (MAL), and the Hittite Laws (HL). I investigate the Exodus ordinances' similarities to and differences from these cuneiform law collections from the perspective of imperialized people.

As I discuss in chapters one and two, the authors of the Exodus corpus, who lived under Neo-Assyrian subjugation, might have sensed the pressure to follow imperial legal traditions but at the same time might have desired to differ from them.[2] While the former exhibits their acceptance of the imperial legal metanarrative presented by those traditions, the latter expresses their resistance to it. There might also have been times when the imperialized authors oscillated between following and deviating from the imperial legal metanarrative, revealing their ambivalence toward it.[3] These understandings, together with postcolonial scholars' call for ethical engagement,[4] guide the following comparative analysis. This analysis's propositions are that the Exodus ordinances' authors were familiar with the legal traditions prevailing in ancient West Asia, including their imperial nature, and that the extant cuneiform law collections somehow reflect these traditions.[5]

This analysis demonstrates that, as a work of the imperialized, the Exodus ordinances concerning slaves and women reflect their authors' resistance to imperial handling of related issues in various ways, amid their acceptance of and ambivalence toward it. This "the same but not quite"[6] approach is susceptible to being oppressive toward slaves and women in some cases. Nevertheless, it also reveals endeavors to subvert the imperial legal metanarrative with more liberative and considerate measures. These features of the imperialized authors' response characterize these ordinances as a work of conservative revolutionists, who wrestled with the imperial legal metanarrative when they compiled a law collection primarily for their people who had similar scribal and legal training and access to their palace and temple.[7]

2. See §2.4.7.
3. See §1.2.
4. See §1.2.2.2.
5. See §2.2.4.
6. See §1.2.2.1.
7. See §2.5.

3.2 Ordinances on Slaves

This wrestling is first manifested in the ordinances concerning slaves.[8] The imperialized authors inaugurated their ordinances with those concerning the release and permanent servitude of slaves (Exod 21:2–11). They then addressed offenses against slaves in the following ordinances concerning physical assault, including that inflicted by slave owners (Exod 21:20–21, 21:26–27) and others' oxen (Exod 21:32). In addition to these direct handling of issues and offenses concerning slaves, the authors also dealt with some circumstances that might have led to servitude, namely kidnapping (Exod 21:16) and theft (Exod 22:2).

In the following comparative analysis, I first discuss the prioritization of issues regarding slaves in the Exodus ordinances. Then, I examine the content of related ordinances: first those directly addressing this concern, then those possibly associated with it. This analysis exhibits that while these ordinances broadly resemble various cuneiform laws, they differ in many details. These simultaneous similarities and differences do disclose oppressive elements. Yet, they also reveal the imperialized authors' effort to resist imperial legal handling of slaves, alongside their acceptance of and ambivalence toward it.

3.2.1 Priority of the Ordinances

This resistance amid compliance is first exhibited in the prioritizing of issues related to slaves. While this priority also occurs in an excerpt of the Hammurabi collection, it is unique to the Exodus ordinances as compared to the legal section as a whole in various cuneiform law collections. This uniqueness amid resemblance suggests a selective acceptance of imperial legal traditions with resistance to their lesser concern about slaves.

8. Regarding the translation of עבר, see Williams, "'Slaves,'" 452. I maintain that "slave," rather than "servant," is a better translation in English given the Exodus ordinances' treatments of עבר. The Chinese translation 奴僕 in Chinese Union Version with New Punctuation is an even better rendering, as it expresses the double connotation of עבר: "slave (奴)" and "servant (僕)." Notably, the Sumerian term arad and Akkadian term *wardum* are also applied to an enslaved person and a person of a lesser ranking in different literary contexts. In Mesopotamia, the degrees of servitude and honor for each type of slave in practice indeed varied. See Culbertson, "Slaves and Households," 9, 13; Culbertson, "Life-Course Approach," 35; Tsai, *Human Rights*, 114–15, 123.

Acceptance of the Imperial Legal Metanarrative

Comparing the Book of the Covenant and the Laws of Hammurabi, David P. Wright reasonably points out that the ordinances in Exodus 21:1–22:16 exhibit a sequence similar to the laws in LH 117–271:[9]

Debt slavey	Exod 21:2–11	LH 117
Physical assault (and child rebellion)	Exod 21:12–15, 21:17, 21:18–27	LH 192–214
Goring oxen and negligence	Exod 21:28–36	LH 229–230, 250–252
Property issues (on animals and safekeeping)	Exod 21:37–22:14	LH 253–271

This similar sequence of key topics suggests a resemblance between the priorities of the Exodus ordinances and the Hammurabi excerpt over issues surrounding debt slaves. With the proposition that the authors of Exodus 19–24 were knowledgeable about the legal traditions that extant cuneiform law collections somehow reflect, this common priority suggests the imperialized authors' compliance with the imperial legal tradition reflected in the Hammurabi excerpt regarding the priority of the concern about slaves.

Resistance: Prioritizing the Concern about Slaves

Nevertheless, as some scholars correctly contend, no extant cuneiform law collections begin their legal section with laws on slavery.[10] The Exodus ordinances also prioritize different concerns than the entire law section of the Hammurabi collection, which begins with laws handling false accusations.[11] This difference, together with the mentioned resemblance, suggests a selective

9. The following table shows a simplified and modified version of David Wright's comparison (Wright, *Inventing God's Law*, 9).

10. For instance, Averbeck, "Egyptian Sojourn," 155; Sprinkle, *Book of the Covenant*, 62; Sarna, *Exodus*, 118.

11. There are also differences in the order of some individual laws between Exod 21:1–22:16 and LH 117–271 regarding topics other than slaves. For instance, while the Laws of Hammurabi excerpt puts laws concerning the safekeeping of non-animal property (LH 120–126) after the laws on debt slaves (LH 117–119), the Exodus corpus locates corresponding ordinances in its last section concerning property (Exod 22:9–14). The Hammurabi excerpt also does not have a participial section concerning death penalty (Exod 21:12–17) and laws on the bride price of an unbetrothed maiden (Exod 22:15–16), whereas the Exodus corpus

adoption of the legal tradition exhibited in the Hammurabi collection's legal section as a whole, which needs explanation. A possibility is that the biblical authors were only aware of the tradition reflected in LH 117–271. However, the ordinances in Exodus 21:2–22:16 do show similarities to the laws in the Hammurabi collection outside this excerpt.[12] Some of these laws are even located in the beginning (kidnapping, Exod 21:16, LH 14) and the very end (a slave making a declaration, Exod 21:5, LH 282) of the Hammurabi collection's legal section. Hence, the possibility that the biblical authors only had the knowledge of the tradition reflected in the Hammurabi excerpt, but not beyond it, is low.

Scholars, therefore, appeal to the larger literary context and the historical context of Exodus 21:2–22:16 to understand the motivation behind the priority of the ordinances on slaves. Considering the concerns in the commandments preceding and following the Exodus ordinances, Wright suggests that the concern over poverty drove the author to begin the ordinances with debt slavery.[13] Other scholars, such as Richard E. Averbeck, James Williamson, and Nahum M. Sarna, look to the even larger literary context – the announcement of the Decalogue in Mount Sinai and the Exodus event in the first half of the Book of Exodus. They suggest that the priority of the redemptive history is at play in the sequence of the Exodus ordinances.[14] Rainer Albertz refers to eighth-century prophets' words concerning the poor and the oppressed (Amos 2:6; 5:11; 8:6; Mic 2:2, cf. Isa 3:14) and argues that the biblical authors aimed to counteract the devastating social development of their time and better secure the situation of impoverished people, including slaves, in their society.[15]

Notwithstanding, given that the Exodus corpus not only begins with ordinances concerning slaves but also reflects selective adoption of the legal tradition exhibited in the Laws of Hammurabi, I argue that in addition to those internal concerns, the biblical authors also intended to respond to

---

does not contain various laws that the Hammurabi excerpt does have, such as the marriage and inheritance laws (LH 127–191).

12. Wright, *Inventing God's Law*, 9.

13. Wright, 150.

14. Averbeck, "Egyptian Sojourn," 153–55; Williamson, "Priority of the Laws," 100; Sarna, *Exodus*, 118.

15. Albertz, *Exodus, Band II*, 86.

the perspective embedded in the cuneiform legal tradition, which they regarded as a representation of the imperial legal metanarrative of their time.[16] Mimicking partially the tradition reflected in the Hammurabi collection in terms of law sequence, the Exodus ordinances reveal that their authors did not follow imperial legal traditions in putting other concerns before slaves. This divergence certainly relates to the authors' concern about poverty, redemptive history, and the situation of the marginalized people at their time, but it is also associated with the authors' resistance to imperial legal traditions. Amid their acceptance of the imperial legal metanarrative, the imperialized authors resisted downplaying the concern about slaves as their imperial counterparts did.

3.2.2 Release and Permanent Servitude

The content of the ordinances continues to reveal similar resistance to imperial legal traditions alongside acceptance of them. This acceptance, like some colonized people's mimicry of their colonizer,[17] inevitably makes the ordinances not as resistive or liberative as one might hope. As a matter of fact, the introductory ordinances concerning release and permanent servitude (Exod 21:2–11), similar to cuneiform law collections, shy away from abolishing or criticizing the purchase or sale of people into some kind of servitude, if not slavery in the modern sense.[18] Moreover, they reflect strong resemblances to their cuneiform counterparts in handling slaves. Nevertheless, these resemblances appear together with differences, which suggest their authors' resistance to imperial legal approaches to master-slave relationships. This resistance is potentially oppressive, and in some instances even more oppressive than imperial legal traditions. However, it also offers some liberative or protective handling of the relationship between masters and slaves. These features characterize the ordinances as a work of conservative revolutionists who wrestled with imperial legal treatment of slaves, both male and female.

---

16. See §2.3.2.3.

17. See §1.2.2.2.

18. Dube, *Postcolonial Feminist Interpretation*, 62; Mathew, *Biblical Law Codes*, 182; Scholz, "Complexities," 36; Pixley, *Exodus*, 175.

3.2.2.1 Male Slaves (Exodus 21:2–6)

The introductory ordinances concern male slaves (Exod 21:2–6). They first introduce the purchase of a Hebrew male slave and stipulate the length of his servitude, the year his release occurs, and the release of his wife (Exod 21:2–3). The ordinances then address the case in which the slave's wife is given by his owner, specifying that his wife and her children belong to the owner and only the male slave shall be released (Exod 21:4). The last ordinance handles the circumstance when the male slave declares his willingness to continue the servitude, requiring the master to take him before God and pierce his ear to formalize his permanent servitude (Exod 21:5–6).

Exodus 21:2–6

> [2]When you buy a Hebrew male slave, he shall serve six years, but in the seventh he shall go out free without payment.
>
> [3]If by himself he comes, by himself he shall go; if he is the husband of a wife, then his wife shall go out with him.
>
> [4]If his master gives him a wife and she bears for him sons or daughters, the wife and her children shall belong to her master, and he himself shall go out by himself.
>
> [5]And if the male slave clearly says, "I love my master, my wife, and my sons, I will not go out free," [6]then his master shall bring him to God and bring him to the door or the doorpost, and his master shall pierce his ear with an awl, and he shall serve him forever.[19]

Acceptance of the Imperial Legal Metanarrative

Extant cuneiform law collections contain various laws concerning the purchase of slaves, their release and servitude, and their family. Three laws near the end of the law section of the Hammurabi collection (LH 278–280) stipulate handling various circumstances after purchasing a *wardum* (male slave)

19. Unless specified, the translation of Hebrew texts is mine.

or an *amtum* (female slave),[20] each repeatedly beginning their protases by stating this situation:

LH 278–280

> [278]If a man purchases a slave or slave woman and within his one-month period epilepsy then befalls him, he shall return him to his seller and the buyer shall take back the silver that he weighed and delivered.
>
> [279]If a man purchases a slave or slave woman and then claims arise, his seller shall satisfy the claims.
>
> [280]If a man should purchase another man's slave or slave woman in a foreign country, and while he is traveling about within the (i.e., his own) country the owner of the slave or slave woman identifies his slave or slave woman—if they, the slave and slave woman, are natives of the country, their release shall be secured without any payment.[21]

An aforementioned law (LH 117) meanwhile prescribes the servitude length and the release of the persons whom a man sells or gives into debt service, including his wife:

LH 117

> If an obligation is outstanding against a man and he sells or gives into debt service his wife, his son, or his daughter, they shall perform service in the house of their buyer or of the one who holds them in debt service for three years; their release shall be secured in the fourth year.[22]

Some laws in the Ur-Namma collection and one in the Hammurabi collection deal with situations in which male slaves are married to women of various statuses:

---

20. *Wardum* and *amtum* here may refer particularly to chattel slaves. However, one also need to note these terms' fluidity. See page 99 note 8.

21. Roth, *Law Collections*, 132.

22. Roth, 103.

LU 4–5

> [4]If a male slave marries a female slave, his beloved, and that male slave (later) is given his freedom, she/he will not leave the house.
>
> [5]If a male slave marries a native woman, she/he shall place one male child in the service of his master; the child who is placed in the service of his master, his paternal estate, . . . the wall, the house, [. . .]; a child of the native woman will not be owned by the master, he will be pressed into slavery.[23]

LH 175

> If a slave of the palace or a slave of a commoner marries a woman of the *awīlu*-class and she then bears children, the owner of the slave will have no claims of slavery against the children of the woman of the *awīlu*-class.[24]

The Sumerian laws first deal with the case in which an arad (male slave) marries a géme (female slave)[25] and he is granted his freedom (LU 4). Whether restriction on the release is imposed on the male slave or the female slave is uncertain due to the inclusiveness of the Sumerian pronominal suffix.[26] However, this law certainly indicates negative effects on the release of slaves when a male slave marries a woman belonging to a slave owner.

The following law (LU 5) handles the situation where a male slave marries a "native woman," or very likely a "freed woman"[27] or "freewoman."[28] This law focuses on the handling of their children. The treatment imposed at the end of the law, "he will be pressed into slavery," is subject to interpretation due to Sumerian sentence structure and the lacunae of the text.[29] However, the

23. Roth, 17.

24. Roth, 115.

25. Similar to *wardum* and *amtum*, arad and géme here may refer particularly to chattel slaves, but one also need to note these terms' fluidity. See page 99 note 8.

26. Some scholars consider the male slave as the one prohibited from leaving the house; see Kitchen and Lawrence, *Treaty, Law and Covenant*, 59; Wilcke, "Gesetze in sumerischer Sprache," 535. For opposite views, see Yaron, "Quelques Remarques," 131–42; Westbrook, "Female Slave," 160; Civil, "Law Collection," 246.

27. Civil, "Law Collection," 246, 254.

28. Kitchen and Lawrence, *Treaty, Law, and Covenant*, 58.

29. Civil translates this statement together with the preceding one as "No son of a freed woman will become a slave without the acquiescence of the master" (Civil, "Law Collection,"

preceding statement indicates that the master does not own the children, even though a male child of the woman has to serve the master. The Hammurabi law (LH 175) similarly handles children of a woman who belongs to the free-person class but is married to a slave. This law clearly states that the slave owner has no claim on her children.

Finally, two laws at the end of the Hammurabi collection's legal section require action taken before the god (LH 281) and address the declaration of a slave in direct speech (LH 282):

LH 281–282

> [281]If they are natives of another country, the buyer shall declare before the god the amount of silver that he weighed, and the owner of the slave or slave woman shall give to the merchant the amount of silver that he paid, and thus he shall redeem his slave or slave woman.
>
> [282]If a slave should declare to his master, "You are not my master," he shall bring charge and proof against him that he is indeed his slave, and his master shall cut off his ear.[30]

The instruction to bring the charges or proof before the god or swear an oath before or by the god is fairly common in cuneiform legal traditions. In addition to the Laws of Hammurabi, which Wright suggests,[31] such instruction appears also in the Laws of Eshnunna,[32] the Middle Assyrian Laws,[33] and the Hittite Laws.[34] Some of these laws also relate to *wardum* or *amtum*.[35] Likewise, declarations of similar types also occur in other cuneiform law

---

246); Kitchen and Lawrence translate them as "the (other) sons of the freewoman, will not be(long) to ('with') the master, that they should be compelled into slavery" (Kitchen and Lawrence, *Treaty, Law, and Covenant*, 59).

30. Roth, *Law Collections*, 132.

31. LH 9, 23, gap cc, 106, 107, 120, 126, 240, 266, and 281 require handling the case before the god. LH 20, 103, 131, 249 require swearing an oath by the god. David Wright addresses most of the laws in the first category in his discussion concerning Exod 21:3–6 except LH gap cc and 107; Wright, *Inventing God's Law*, 135.

32. LE 22, 37.

33. MAL A 47, C 1.

34. HL 169.

35. LH 20, LE 22.

collections:[36] In addition to the Hammurabi collection,[37] these declarations also appear in the Laws of Lipit-Ishtar,[38] the Middle Assyrian Laws,[39] and the Hittite Laws.[40] Among them, LH 282 contains one made by a male slave concerning his relationship with his owner.

These laws indicate that cuneiform legal traditions are concerned with cases about the purchase of slaves, release and servitude of persons sold into debt service and their family, and handling of slaves in various situations, including where the male slave makes a declaration about his relationship with his owner. Furthermore, these cuneiform laws reflect that the Exodus ordinances resemble them in various ways. As Wright notes,[41] the Exodus corpus similarly formulates its introductory ordinance with a protasis about slave purchase (Exod 21:2; LH 278–280). The Exodus ordinances also similarly specify the servitude length, the release year, and the release of the wife (Exod 21:2–3; LH 117).[42] The following ordinance addresses the effect on the release of the male slave, his wife, and their children if his wife is given by his owner, as cuneiform laws handle similar issues related to wives of different statuses (Exod 21:4; LU 4–5; LH 175).[43] The stipulation about the master's ownership of the wives even resembles the restriction in LU 4, while that of the children reflects a principle inverse but similar to LU 5 and LH 175.[44] Finally, the male slave's declaration and the handling of bringing him

36. The following laws do not include laws clearly indicating declarations related to oaths or made before gods.

37. LH 9, 49, gap a, gap e, 126, 142, 159, 161, 168, 170, 171, 192.

38. LL 11. It also occurs in other Sumerian laws, including SLEx 4', 5', 6', 7' and SLHF 3:16–17, 4:1–9, 4:17–18.

39. MAL A 17, 18, 19, 22, 24, 41, 45, 47, 48.

40. HL 40, 41, 55, 74, 75, 95, 149, 198.

41. Wright, *Inventing God's Law*, 125.

42. For similar observation, see Chirichigno, *Debt-Slavery*, 218; Wright, *Inventing God's Law*, 133; Wells, "Interpretation," 238.

43. David Wright has changed his approach to LU 4 from regarding it as basically about the same issue as Exod 21:4 (Wright, "Laws of Hammurabi as a Source," 16) to minimizing its correlation with Exod 21:4 (Wright, *Inventing God's Law*, 415, note 65). Alongside this change is his argument that Exod 21:4 refers to LH 119 and LH 175 (Wright, *Inventing God's Law*, 138–39). In contrast, Wells argues that LU 4 exhibits closer connection to Exod 21:4 than LH 119 and 175 (Wright, "Covenant Code Appendix," 95). However, the translation of LU 4 that Wells cites treats the pronominal suffix as feminine. While Wells claims that it is Wright's translation, Wright's translation actually includes pronouns of both genders.

44. David Wright calls the relationship between LH 175 and Exod 21:4 a "conceptual inversion" (Wright, *Inventing God's Law*, 138–39).

before God also resemble cuneiform laws (Exod 21:5–6; LH 281–282).[45] These similarities suggest that the imperialized authors broadly accepted cuneiform legal traditions, which they regarded as the reflection of the imperial legal metanarrative under the ruling of the Neo-Assyrian Empire.[46] This acceptance includes the formulation of the laws regarding male slaves and the concerns and handling related to the release and servitude of males slaves and their families. It indicates that the imperialized authors tolerated slave purchase and related repressive practices, as imperial legal traditions did.

Resistance: Emphasizing the Audience's Responsibility

Alongside this acceptance, there is, however, resistance, as several differences from the cuneiform laws indicate. The first such difference is the use of second-person reference in the introductory ordinance's protasis, "When you buy a Hebrew male slave" (Exod 21:2). This use does not appear in the mentioned cuneiform laws, including those in LH 279–280, which contain similar protases but use the third-person reference *awīlum* (free person) only. Some scholars consider the second-person reference in Exodus 21:2 as a result of redaction;[47] however, others see the rhetorical intentions of the original authors. Shalom M. Paul asserts that this reference is a component of "injunctions for moral behavior," which cuneiform law collections lack.[48] Wright suggests that this reference not only offers a bridge for the altar laws (Exod 20:24–26) but also targets the national community, emphasizing a communal orientation of the ordinances.[49] According to Dale Patrick, this reference indicates that the ordinances beginning in Exodus 21:2 are a corpus intended for reading out before the audience.[50]

Mieke Bal's understanding of "focalization,"[51] in my opinion, further explicates the rhetorical use of this second-person reference in Exodus 21:2 for addressing the audience. Her study of narrative is applicable to the ordinances,

45. Jackson, in contrast, regards the declaration in Exod 21:5 as a speech-act that should have existed before the ordinance was written (Jackson, *Wisdom-Laws*, 108).

46. See §2.3.2.3.

47. Schwienhorst-Schönberger, *Bundesbuch*, 309, 311; Otto, *Wandel der Rechtsbegründungen*, 35.

48. Paul, *Studies in the Book of the Covenant*, xviii. See also Tsai, *Human Rights*, 76.

49. Wright, *Inventing God's Law*, 124. See also McConville, "Singular Address," 23–25.

50. Patrick, "Who is the Revolutionist," 158.

51. Bal, *Narratology*, 145–60.

which do exhibit narrative elements.[52] Bal attends to the character whose viewpoint directs the narrative (focalizer) and the object or the character on whom this viewpoint focuses (focalized object). She also underlines the distinction between the viewpoint of those who speak and listen (internal focalizer and focalized object) versus those who simply see (external focalizer and focalized object).[53] Exodus 21:2 does not explicitly identify Yhwh (Exod 20:22) as the focalizer; however, the focalized object, "you" (indicated by the pronominal suffix of the verb קנה, to buy), suggests that the ordinances concerning slaves begin with an internal focalized object. As an internal focalized object, the audience of the Exodus ordinances is not an outsider who only sees the ordinances, watching what a person has to do after purchasing a slave, as the audience of the cuneiform laws does. In contrast, as the introductory ordinance, Exodus 21:2 demands the audience to be an insider who actively listens to the following ordinances in order to learn the proper way of handling the release and servitude of their slaves. This internal focalization may indicate the imperative and moral nature of the treatment of slaves, as Paul asserts. It may also be directed at the national community, as Wright suggests, if one considers the larger literary context (Exod 19–20 and 24). The comparison between Exodus 21:2 and its cuneiform counterparts in terms of their focalization, however, demonstrates the imperialized peoples' emphasis on their own involvement and responsibility, which the cuneiform laws do not emphasize.

This distinction is especially significant if the Exodus ordinances' authors and primary audience were people who had scribal and legal training and access to the palace or the temple, just as cuneiform law collections had a purpose of offering references to judges.[54] It is reasonable to suspect that the motivation behind the ordinances involved these people's self-economic interests, as they themselves were probably slave owners. However, rather than following imperial legal traditions to simply present the ordinances as something that their judges or they themselves could read as outsiders, the imperialized authors persuaded similarly elite people to take full responsibility in treating their slaves properly after they had purchased them. Alongside

52. Bartor, *Reading Laws*, 5–6.

53. Bal, *Narratology*, 145–60.

54. See §2.4.3 and §2.5.

their compliance with the imperial legal formulation of the law's protasis, the imperialized authors resisted the imperial legal underemphasis on the audience's involvement in handling their slaves' release and servitude.

Resistance: Hebrew Rather than Other Slaves

The following reference to עבד עברי (a Hebrew male slave, Exod 21:2) reflects another element of resistance to cuneiform legal traditions, though subtly with a certain degree of oppression. Scholars have much debate about the use of this reference, arguing between addressing a social class and referring to an ethnic group.[55] What they have not noticed is while the use of עברי (Hebrew) to qualify the slave does not find a counterpart in the mentioned cuneiform laws, a similar expression occurs in the Middle Assyrian Laws:

MAL A 44

> If there is an Assyrian man (*Aššurayau*) or an Assyrian woman (*Aššurayītu*) who is residing in a man's house as a pledge for a debt, for as much as his value, and he is taken for the full value (i.e., his value as pledge does not exceed that of the debt), he (the pledge holder) shall whip (the pledge), pluck out (the pledge's) hair, (or) mutilate or pierce (the pledge's) ears.[56]

Though this law does not handle debt slaves *per se*, but a person who resides in another person's house as a pledge, it does concern how one should treat the person involved in a debt, as does Exodus 21:2. It also addresses that person as *Aššurayau* and *Aššurayītu*, which are rare expressions in MAL A but Exodus 21:2 similarly uses.[57]

This juxtaposition between עבד עברי in Exodus 21:2 and *Aššurajau* and *Aššurajau* in MAL A 44 reasonably leads one to consider the use of עבד עברי more as an expression of ethnic identity[58] than of social class. Similar to the cuneiform law, Exodus 21:2 confines the type of slave whom it addresses to

55. For recent summaries of this discussion, see Williamson, "Priority of the Laws," 106; Alexander, *Exodus*, 472.

56. Roth, *Law Collections*, 170.

57. Another similar reference occurs in MAL A 24, which addresses "the house of (another) Assyrian (*Aššuraye*)" and handles a man's wife who withdraws herself from him.

58. For more arguments for this phrase's gentilic use, see Wright, *Inventing God's Law*, 126–27; Alexander, *Exodus*, 472.

its own people; however, Exodus 21:2 specifies the slave as Hebrew in contrast to Assyrian, divergent from the cuneiform law. Given the proposition concerning the biblical authors' knowledge of legal traditions reflected in extant cuneiform law collections, this similarity and difference suggest a response to the legal tradition which the Middle Assyrian law somehow exhibits. The use of עבד עברי in Exodus 21:2 reflects its compliance with the imperial legal exclusion of people of other ethnicities in its ordinances – an exclusion that some scholars, such as Cheryl B. Anderson,[59] deem to be oppressive, as it suggests that only Hebrew people are afforded protections stipulated by the ordinances, while other enslaved peoples are left to be vulnerable. Yet, this expression also reveals its authors' resistance to the imperial legal tradition in considering only the imperial people in its laws. This resistance is particularly striking under the Neo-Assyrian context. Rather than compiling their ordinances for the Assyrians (the people of the ruling empire), the biblical authors expressed they were intended for their people, the imperialized, and are concerned with how to properly handle those who fall into debt service among the imperialized people.

Resistance: Servitude Length, Tradition, and Release

The specification on the servitude length manifests a similar instance of resistance to cuneiform legal traditions, reflecting further the wrestling of the conservative revolutionists with imperial legal traditions. Like LH 117, Exodus 21:2 specifies the servitude length and the release year. However, Exodus 21:2 sets a longer period of servitude than does LH 117. To understand the motivation behind this servitude length, scholars have brought up various associations with the biblical authors' traditions, including the symbolic use of the number seven,[60] the numerical pattern of using the seventh year in Exodus 23:10–11 and 12,[61] the cessation of cultivating one's field in the seventh year and exploiting one's work animals and worker on the seventh day in these laws,[62] the observance of the Sabbath,[63] and so forth. These observa-

59. Anderson, *Ancient Laws*, 41.

60. Sprinkle, *Book of the Covenant*, 65.

61. Wright, *Inventing God's Law*, 127.

62. Albertz, *Exodus, Band II*, 87.

63. Chirichigno, *Debt-Slavery*, 224; Carpenter, *Exodus 19–40*, 74–76; Alexander, *Exodus*, 472.

tions suggest that the retrieval of the tradition of Israel and Judah is at play in the determination of the servitude length in Exodus 21:2.

Retrieval of tradition occurs in other ordinances in the Exodus corpus also with clear protective intent. The ordinance on unpremeditated homicide allows the offender to flee to a place that Yhwh sets (Exod 21:13), an arrangement native to the people of Israel and Judah.[64] It protects the life of the unpremeditated offender, with which cuneiform law collections are not concerned. Similarly, the ordinances on goring oxen uniquely require the oxen to be stoned to death (Exod 21:28–32). This requirement was probably motivated by the traditions of Israel and Judah concerning the bloodguilt that the ox has acquired and the hierarchy of creation that the ox has violated.[65] It also associates with communal concerns, protecting the community from the goring ox and inviting the community to serve as corporate executioner.[66] The appeal to traditions in the debt slavery ordinances thus suggests that the six-year servitude may involve protective considerations for the slave, for instance, to secure his livelihood. However, unlike these ordinances, which explicitly reflect protective and liberative considerations behind their retrieval of traditions, there is no other evidence for similar concern about the slave regarding the six-year servitude. Therefore, one may still suspect that this servitude length has potential for being more oppressive, or at least more repressive,[67] than the cuneiform law, if only because it requires more service from the enslaved person.

Notwithstanding, the three occurrences of יצא (to go out) in Exodus 21:2–3 suggest a liberative consideration for the slave in the ordinances as a whole, if not in the determination of the six-year servitude in particular. These occurrences contrast with LH 117, which only mentions the release

64. Greengus, *Laws in the Bible*, 155; Alexander, *Exodus*, 481; Albertz, *Exodus, Band II*, 90; Jackson, *Wisdom-Laws*, 122–26; Wright, *Inventing God's Law*, 158.

65. Paul, *Studies in the Book of the Covenant*, 79–81; Finkelstein, *Ox that Gored*, 27–29; Dozeman, *Exodus*, 537; Greengus, *Laws in the Bible*, 176–77.

66. Dozeman, *Exodus*, 537; Houtman, *Exodus*, 3:174; Finkelstein, *Ox that Gored*, 27–29; Propp, *Exodus 19–40*, 233; Sarna, *Exodus*, 128; Greengus, *Laws in the Bible*, 176. Jackson, unlike other scholars, suggests that this requirement may merely be a self-help utilitarian measure for ensuring that the ox will not kill another person (Jackson, *Wisdom-Law*, 257–58). Moshe Greenberg sees it merely as a measure for affirming the value of human life (Greenberg, "Some Postulates," 15–16). However, these suggestions do not explain why the ordinance does not simply require killing the ox, but demands the collective action of stoning it.

67. Wright, *Inventing God's Law*, 306.

(*andurārum*) once at the end of the law. While these occurrences do not necessarily indicate the belief that the Israelite society should be constituted of free people,[68] they disclose a particular emphasis on the release of the male slave and his wife after the six-year servitude in the Exodus ordinances. This emphasis may relate to the inverse rhetorical movement that scholars have noticed. Whereas the ordinances concerning male slaves begin with freedom and end with permanent servitude, the following ordinances concerning female slaves begin with a restriction on freedom and end with freedom.[69] However, the contrasts between the Exodus ordinances and the cuneiform law suggest that this liberative emphasis also associates with the imperialized authors' response to the imperial legal tradition reflected in this cuneiform law.

The similarities and differences between Exodus 21:2–3 and LH 117 reveal that while the imperialized authors accepted imperial legal concerns about servitude length and the release year, they did not adhere to the imperial legal stipulation and presentation. The retrieval of their own tradition may be potentially oppressive in view of the longer servitude without clear protective considerations and the authors' and audience's self-interest in maintaining their ownership of slaves, which necessitate an ethical inquiry. However, this appeal to their own tradition is a crucial part of imperialized people's resistance to imperial metanarrative, which postcolonial scholars indicate.[70] The unique emphasis on the release suggests further a liberative component of this resistance. Alongside their compliance with imperial legal traditions, the imperialized authors endeavored to resist the imperial legal underemphasis on the release of the slave and his family, mandating their elite audience to manumit their own slaves and slaves' family accordingly.

Resistance: Positive Rather than Negative Portrayal of Slaves

The portrayal of the male slave in Exodus 21:5–6 further reveals this resistive endeavor. The slave's attitude toward his owner in Exodus 21:5 is totally opposite of LH 282.[71] In Exodus 21:5 the slave declares that "I love my master,

68. Phillips, "Laws of Slavery," 61–62.

69. Alexander, *Exodus*, 478; Arneth, "Exodus," 114; Williamson, "Priority of the Laws," 114; Wright, *Inventing God's Law*, 123; Turnham, "Male and Female Slaves," 548.

70. For instance, Shohat, "Notes on 'Post-Colonial,'" 109; Chanock, *Law and Custom*, 22; see also §1.2.2.2 and §1.3.3.

71. David Wright calls this contrast as "emotional inversion" (Wright, *Inventing God's Law*, 405, note 1).

my wife, and my sons, I will not go out free," whereas in LH 282 the slave says "You are not my master." Exodus 21:6 also demands a procedure that contrasts LH 282's treatment of the slave. Exodus 21:6 requires the master to bring the slave to God and the door or the doorpost and pierce his ear with an awl to formalize his permanent servitude, whereas LH 282 stipulates the owner to bring charge and proof against the slave and cut off his ear as a punishment.

Scholars have much debate on the genuineness of the declaration in Exodus 21:5. Some suggest that economic concern plays a role behind it.[72] Others even regard this declaration as an expression of involuntary last resort in response to the stipulation in Exodus 21:4.[73] This understanding brings up the oppressive nature of Exodus 21:4, which resembles LU 4–5 and LH 175. In fact, while Exodus 21:4 resembles these cuneiform laws in their concerns about the release of male slaves, their wives, and their children, its explicit stipulation on the master's ownership of the wives and the children uniquely emphasize that they cannot go free as the male slaves do, thus indicates a contrast that suggests Exodus 21:4's particularly repressive feature. Nevertheless, other scholars consider the declaration in Exodus 21:5 as the slave's wholehearted announcement of his love for his owner and his family, despite the restriction imposed in Exodus 21:4. They attend to this declaration's wording and the ordinances' larger literary context, which depicts the servant-master relationship between the people and Yhwh.[74]

Without an explicit explanation in the ordinances, the motivation behind this declaration is difficult to determine. What is certain is Exodus 21:5 peculiarly uses an absolute complement אמר יאמר (he clearly says) to introduce this declaration. The use of absolute complement in general may have rhythmic functions.[75] The use of absolute complement particularly in this ordinance also underlines the modality of the action expressed by the verb because of its paronomastic construction.[76] Thus, Exodus 21:5 emphasizes

72. Greengus, *Laws in the Bible*, 87; Matthews, "Anthropology of Slavery," 132; Chirichigno, *Debt-Slavery*, 229; Sarna, *Exodus*, 119.

73. Mathew, *Biblical Law Codes*, 191.

74. Chirichigno, *Debt-Slavery*, 228; Sarna, *Exodus*, 119.

75. Jackson, *Wisdom-Laws*, 131; Yaron, "Stylistic Conceits," 453–54.

76. Waltke and O'Connor, *Introduction to Biblical Hebrew*, 584; Muraoka, *Emphatic Words*, 86; Joüon and Muraoka, *Grammar of Biblical Hebrew*, §123d; Gensenius, Kautzsch, and Cowley, *Gesenius' Hebrew Grammar*, §113m.

that it is under the condition when the male slave makes his own declaration to express his willingness not to go free that this owner can change his servitude from temporary to permanent. This ordinance aims to protect the male slave from being forced into permanent servitude by his master, even though it does not totally liberate him and his family from the restriction that Exodus 21:4 imposes.

Still, this declaration seems counterintuitive, given that the male slave has already fulfilled his debt servitude and gained his freedom. Some scholars, therefore, appeal to the overall theme of the Book of Exodus, arguing that this declaration mirrors the motif of the Israelites being God's servants.[77] While this rhetorical interpretation is possible, the contrast between Exodus 21:5 and LH 282 has more to tell. This contrast suggests that the biblical authors did not follow the cuneiform legal tradition reflected in LH 282 in using a hostile declaration to address the slave's rebellion against his owner. The concern about this rebellion was not uncommon among cuneiform legal traditions, as a Hittite law also deals with slaves who free themselves from their owners, which leads to forced imprisonment in a clay jar (HL 173b). Nevertheless, as the imperialized, the biblical authors positively portrayed that a slave can love his family as well as his master to the extent that he is willing to remain in servitude even though he has the right to go free. This love expresses the initiative that the slave can take in order to alleviate the impact of the restriction in Exodus 21:4 on his family, even though this restriction seems not to give his wife the freedom of choice, just as imperial legal traditions do not.[78] This loving declaration also ends up leading the master to attest before God in a ritual that the male slave will remain in perpetual servitude. This result contrasts with the consequences of the hostile declaration in LH 282 and the rebellious action in HL 173b, namely, the slave owner's accusation against and imprisonment of the slave, respectively.

Notably, the procedure that Exodus 21:6 requires for entering into permanent servitude is not only unique in ancient West Asia,[79] but also in con-

77. Williamson, "Priority of the Laws," 99, 115.

78. Mathew, *Biblical Law Codes*, 190–92.

79. Williamson, "Priority of the Laws," 115. About using brandings or tattoos rather than ear piercing as slave marks in Neo-Assyria, see Reiner, "Runaway," 475–82. Perforation of a person's ears also appears in MAL A 44 and 45; however, it is a punishment for not bringing a slave woman without a veil to the palace for judgment (MAL A 44) and a physical assault

trast to the treatment of the slave that LH 282 stipulates. As Wright notes, LH 282 ends with the owner cutting (*inakkis*, he cuts) the male slave's ear, which concludes the Hammurabi collection's law section with a punishment of the slave. Contrarily, Exodus 21:6 ends with the owner piercing (רצע, he pierces) the male slave's ear with an awl in order to indicate the male slave's self-initiated permanent servitude.[80] As oppressive as Exodus 21:4–6 may appear to be,[81] the divergences occurring in these ordinances reveal that their authors resisted imperial legal traditions by addressing the slave-owner relationship in a positive light.[82]

The Exodus ordinances concerning the servitude and release of male slaves thus disclose their authors' resistance to the imperial legal metanarrative in various ways, indicating that their acceptance of it is a selective one. Their compliance with imperial legal traditions involved broadly with the formulation of the laws concerning slaves, the concerns related to servitude, and the treatments of male slaves and their families. Nevertheless, the imperialized authors resisted imperial legal underemphasis on the elite audience's involvement in handling their slaves' release and servitude and worked against the imperial legal metanarrative's sole concern about imperial people, particularly the Assyrians. They also resisted imperial legal traditions' underemphasis on the release of the slave and his family and subverted their negative portrayal of slaves. This concurrent compliance and resistance reveal some potentially oppressive aspects, including ethnic exclusion, lengthier servitude, and repressive treatment of the slaves' families, which raise an inquiry into possible self-serving motives behind the ordinances and necessitate an ethical critique.

---

that a pledge owner can inflict on his pledge (MAL A 45). See Paul, *Studies in the Book of the Covenant*, 51 for similar observation.

80. Wright, *Inventing God's Law*, 134.

81. Mathew, *Biblical Law Codes*, 191; Marshall, *Israel*, 117.

82. If LH 282 expresses a political message against disloyalty to Hammurabi, as Roth proposes (Roth, "Mesopotamian Legal Traditions," 19), one may go as far as arguing that the imperialized authors resisted such imperial message by hinting at loyalty to Yhwh. Another possible argument is that HL 173b follows a law concerning rejections of kings' and magistrate's judgments (HL 173a), suggesting that imperial legal traditions see a connection between these rejections and slaves' rebellion. However, considering the content of the ordinances on slaves surrounding Exod 21:5–6, I tend to think that these ordinances and the resistance are more about the handling and portrayal of slaves rather than the imperialized people's relationship with God.

However, they also suggest the conservative revolutionists' effort, including retrieving their own tradition, in resisting the imperial legal metanarrative.

3.2.2.2 Female Slaves (Exodus 21:7–11)

Like those concerning male slaves, the ordinances on female slaves (Exod 21:7–11) carry similarities to as well as differences from various cuneiform laws, revealing their authors' simultaneous acceptance of and resistance to the imperial legal metanarrative. These ordinances begin with one that restricts the release of a woman sold into slavery by her father as a slave (Exod 21:7). Then, they address the case in which the master no longer likes her (Exod 21:8) and the situation where he designates her to his son (Exod 21:9). The remaining ordinances handle circumstances when the master or the son marries another woman and when he does not provide for the female slave accordingly (Exod 21:10–11).

Exodus 21:7–11

> [7]And when a man sells his daughter to be a female slave, she shall not go out as the male slaves go out.
>
> [8]If (she is) bad in the eyes of her master, who for himself[83] has designated her, then he shall let her be redeemed; to a foreign people he shall not have authority to sell her, because of his treachery against her.
>
> [9]And if for his son he designates her, according to the ordinance of the daughters he shall deal with her.
>
> [10]If he takes another (woman) for him, he shall not take away her food, her clothing, and her עֹנָה.
>
> [11]And if these three things he does not do for her, then she shall go out without payment, for no money.

83. About reading the text as לוֹ (for himself) rather than לֹא (not), see Chirichigno, *Debt-Slavery*, 248; Wright, *Inventing God's Law*, 144. For an opposite view, see Williamson, "Priority of the Laws," 118. Jan A. Wagenaar even suggests retaining לֹא but emending יעדה (he has not designated her) to ידעה (he has not had intercourse with her) (Wagenaar, "Annulment," 225–26). In my opinion, while this emendation follows the Peshitta, it does not consider the parallel expression in Exod 21:9. Wagenaar also unnecessarily sees this emendation as a way to compare Exod 21:8 to Hittite laws dealing with bride price (HL 29–30). For other arguments against this emendation, see Chirichigno, *Debt-Slavery*, 248.

Acceptance of the Imperial Legal Metanarrative

Various cuneiform laws address the servitude and release of female slaves or women sold into debt service. The aforementioned law LH 117 addresses the situation where a man sells his family, including his daughter, to debt service. The mentioned Sumerian law LU 4 handles the case in which a male slave marries a female slave, which will lead to a restriction on the release of either of them. Moreover, some cuneiform laws allow redemption of female slaves or women pledged to creditors under particular conditions. In LH 119, the *awīlum* has the right to redeem the *amtum* he sold into debt service but had borne him children. Likewise, the mentioned law LH 281 allows the owner to redeem his native *wardum or amtum* purchased by the people of Hammurabi. A Middle Assyrian law, meanwhile, gives a man the right to redeem his sister who resides in the creditor's house as a pledge and whose father is dead (MAL A 48).

LH 119

> If an obligation is outstanding against a man and he therefore sells his slave woman who has borne him children, the owner of the slave woman shall weigh and deliver the silver which the merchant weighed and delivered (as the loan) and he shall thereby redeem his slave woman.[84]

MAL A 48

> If a man <wants to give in marriage> his debtor's daughter who is residing in his house as a pledge, he shall ask permission of her father and then he shall give her to a husband. If her father does not agree, he shall not give her. If her father is dead, he shall ask permission of one of her brothers and the latter shall consult with her (other) brothers. If one brother so desires he shall declare, "I will redeem my sister within one month;" if he should not redeem her within one month, the creditor, if he so please, shall clear her of encumbrances and shall give her to a husband. [. . .] according to [. . .] he shall give her [. . .][85]

84. Roth, *Law Collections*, 103–4.
85. Roth, 173.

These laws indicate that cuneiform legal traditions are concerned with the sale of one's daughter, consider restrictions on the release of female slaves, and commonly allow redemption of affected women under certain additional conditions. The Exodus ordinances resemble to these laws in several ways. As Wright points out, just as the Hammurabi law handles persons sold into debt service, including daughters, the Exodus ordinances deal with a woman sold by her father to be a slave (Exod 21:7; LH 117).[86] Similar to the Ur-Namma law, which possibly prohibits the female slave from leaving the household, the Exodus ordinance imposes restrictions on her release (Exod 21:7; LU 4). The Exodus ordinances also allow the female slave to be redeemed only when the owner dislikes her, as the cuneiform laws do for female slaves and women pledged to creditors only under additional conditions (Exod 21:8; LH 119, 281; MAL A 48). These similarities suggest that the imperialized authors accepted the imperial legal metanarrative broadly regarding its concerns and handling of female slaves or women affected by conditions related to debt. This acceptance, like that reflected in the ordinances concerning male slaves, indicates that the imperialized authors tolerated the sale of women and related repressive treatments of them, as imperial legal traditions did, necessitating feminist and postcolonial critiques.[87]

Resistance: Stay as First Wives

The Exodus ordinances, however, differ from cuneiform laws in various ways, which suggest this acceptance is embedded with resistance. The first difference concerns the restriction on the release of the female slave. Exodus 21:7 specifies that she shall not go free as male slaves do, contrasting with LH 117, which requires the release of whoever the man sells into debt service, including his daughter. This contrast suggests that the biblical authors did not follow the cuneiform legal tradition's handling of daughters sold into debt service. However, this resistance makes Exodus 21:7 look oppressive due to the restriction on the release. Indeed, Exodus 21:7's treatment of the female slave seems harsher than that offered by its cuneiform counterpart, when the latter does not impose such a restriction.

86. Wright, *Inventing God's Law*, 124.

87. Dube, *Postcolonial Feminist Interpretation*, 62; Mathew, *Biblical Law Codes*, 182; see also §1.4.1 and §1.4.3.

This possibly oppressive restriction draws one's attention back to the nature of a man's sale of his daughter, regarding which the Exodus ordinance shows acceptance of the cuneiform legal tradition reflected in LH 117. Some scholars suggest that the sale reflects generational, rather than gendered, authority.[88] Some argue that both the sale and the restriction were meant to be protective measures for securing the daughter's future against poverty[89] or indicate a matrimonial bond, such as concubinage, for avoiding sexual exploitation of female slaves.[90] Yet, others, including postcolonial biblical critics, point out that the sale of one's daughter to be a slave and the restriction on the release of her manifest subordination of women to men, which is unfair to or even harmful for women.[91] The Exodus ordinances are susceptible to this kind of subordination, as they only address a father's sale of his daughter (not a mother's sale of her daughter or son) and their authors and primary audience were likely men who were household heads with the rights to sell or the ability to purchase these women.

Without further contextual evidence, the nature of this sale and restriction is difficult to ascertain.[92] One may refer back to the possible similarity between Exodus 21:7 and LU 4, arguing that the restriction on the release in the Exodus ordinance is as repressive as that in the Sumerian law. Nevertheless, the comparison of Exodus 21:7–11 with other cuneiform laws suggests the restriction's resistive and protective intent. In addition to LU 4, the requirement of not letting the female slave go free in Exodus 21:7 also resembles LL 28 and LH 148. These cuneiform laws stipulate that the affected wife shall not be evicted from the house or shall stay in the quarters. Moreover, ordinances following Exodus 21:7 exhibit other resemblances to these two cuneiform laws. The condition in Exodus 21:8, "if she is bad in the eyes of her master," is similar to that in LL 28, where one of the conditions of the wife is literally "losing her eye" or "offending her husband's eye" (tukum-bi lú-ù

88. Pressler, "Construction of Gender," 56.

89. Sarna, *Exodus*, 120; Gane, "Social Justice," 24; Pressler, "Wives and Daughters," 162.

90. Alexander, *Exodus*, 475–76; Westbrook, "Female Slave," 150–55; Paul, *Studies in the Book of the Covenant*, xxi.

91. Mathew, *Biblical Law Codes*, 194–97; Marshall, *Israel*, 118; Anderson, *Women*, 112; Peled, *Law and Gender*, 30.

92. Regarding the unsettling debate about double potential of selling one's children, including daughters, into domestic slavery from the Sumerian to the modern contexts (for instance, Hong Kong in the colonial period), see Culbertson, "Life-Course Approach," 33–48.

dam-nitadam-a-ni igi-ni ba-ab-gi$_4$).[93] The condition in which the master or his son marrying another woman and the requirement of continuous provisions to the female slave in Exodus 21:10–11 also resemble those in LL 28 and LH 148. In LL 28, the man has the right to marry a healthy woman, but his second wife should support the first wife in addition to not evicting the first wife from the house. According to Paul, there is even a variant of LL 28 which requires the man to support both the new and the first wife.[94] In LH 148, the protasis addresses a man, whose first wife has a disease, deciding to marry another woman. This law requires him to support his first wife for the rest of her life in addition to letting her stay in his house.

The Exodus ordinances also carry resemblance to other cuneiform marriage laws with respect to the designation of the female slave for the master himself and the son. The meaning of יעד (to designate) is in dispute among scholars.[95] However, the wording of the protasis in Exodus 21:8 (לו יעדה, for himself he designates her) and especially that in Exodus 21:9 (ואם־לבנו ייעדנה, if for his son he designates her) resemble the protases in LH 155–156 (*šumma awīlum ana mārišu kallatam iḫīrma*, if a man for his son a bride he chooses).[96] These cuneiform laws deal with a man having sexual intercourse with the bride that he chooses for his son and require punishing the man and compensating the woman. Considering the condition in these cuneiform laws, together with the preceding law (LH 154) which deals with incest, Wright argues that Exodus 21:9, particularly its requirement of treating the female slave according to the ordinance of the daughter, is to "prohibit daughter-in-law incest."[97] Nevertheless, as the connection in the wording of the conditions alone does not necessarily suggest that the Exodus ordinances and the cuneiform laws deal with the same condition, his argument is subject to further evidence. Still, the condition and the wording in LH 155–156 suggest that the descriptions concerning the designation of the female slave in Exodus 21:8–9 resemble these cuneiform marriage laws.

---

93. Scholars have varied understandings of the wording in LL 28's protasis (Paul, *Studies in the Book of the Covenant*, 56; Kitchen and Lawrence, *Treaty, Law, and Covenant*, 79) and Roth translates it idiomatically as "loses her attractiveness" (Roth, *Law Collections*, 31).

94. Paul, *Studies in the Book of the Covenant*, 56.

95. See, for instance, Fleishman, *Father-Daughter Relation*, 44–45.

96. Translation is mine.

97. Wright, *Inventing God's Law*, 148.

The Exodus ordinances, therefore, resemble these cuneiform laws in various aspects. In addition to the requirement of not letting the female slave go free, these resemblances include the unfavorable condition of the female slave, the situation where the owner or his son marries another woman, and the language of designation. However, these cuneiform laws are concerned with women in marriage. They aim to protect them from abandonment or exploitation, especially in the case of retaining the first wife, which unquestionably has a protection intent to secure her livelihood in the household she originally entered.

Notably, extant cuneiform law collections do not secure a similar kind of support for female slaves or women sold into debt service, even though reproductive function and sexual exploitation of female slaves did exist in Mesopotamia.[98] The Hammurabi collection does prohibit the slave owner's wife from selling the *amtum*, even if the *amtum* aspires to have equal status with her (LH 146). Nevertheless, this law concerns specifically an *amtum* who has borne children for her owner. It indeed stipulates that the slave owner's wife shall reckon the *amtum* with other *amātum* (female slaves). The subordinate law (LH 147) even allows the owner's wife to sell the *amtum* if the *amtum* has not borne children for her owner. Cuneiform law collections thus do not usually demand the owner to keep his female slave in his household in order to secure her livelihood, even though they regard it necessary for a husband to do so for his first wife.

The nuance between Exodus 21:7–11 and LL 28 and LH 148, therefore, suggests that the restriction on the female slave's release is the imperialized authors' particular extension of the imperial legal treatment of a first wife to the female slave. This extension is echoed further by the language of designation in Exodus 21:8–9, which resembles the cuneiform laws dealing with the bride of one's son (LH 155–156) and suggests another extension of the imperial legal handling of a wife to the female slave.[99] These extensions do not necessarily indicate that the Exodus ordinances regard the affected

98. Seri, "Domestic Female Slaves," 56, 59.

99. Some scholars, however, suggest that this language indicates directly the marital relationship between the female slave and her owner or his son; see Paul, *Studies in the Book of the Covenant*, 54; Chirichigno, *Debt-Slavery*, 248; Tsai, *Human Rights*, 86. Tsai also points out the use of the marriage language in Exod 21:10 (אמ־אחרת יקח־לו, if he takes another [woman] for him) as a basis for her argument.

woman as a wife *per se* or that Exodus 21:7 is a marriage law or intended only for women sold for marriage.[100] In contrast to some Neo-Assyrian contracts, which clearly state the sale's marital purpose and address the woman as a wife,[101] Exodus 21:7 specifies that the man sells the daughter to be a אמה (female slave) without further explication, indicating that this ordinance deals with women sold by their father to be slaves in general, if not with all female slaves. The inverse rhetorical movement between the ordinances on male slaves and female slaves (Exod 21:2–6 versus Exod 21:7–11) and the redemption and release in Exodus 21:8 and 11 express further that the Exodus ordinances regard the affected woman as a slave.[102] However, these extensions reflect resistance to imperial legal traditions' lack of consideration for female slaves or women sold for debt service. They also suggest the protective nature of Exodus 21:7's restriction on the release of the affected woman, which secures her livelihood in the household she first enters.

Hence, while Exodus 21:7 deals with a case in which a man sells his daughter to be a slave as LH 117 does, it places a restriction on her release, which this cuneiform law does not consider. This restriction possibly resembles that in LU 4. However, this restriction (Exod 21:7), the unfavorable condition of the woman (Exod 21:8), and the situation where the man marries another woman (Exod 21:10) also resemble those in LL 28 and LH 148. Still, the Exodus ordinances deal with female slaves, whereas these cuneiform laws handle first wives. Similar resemblances and differences also occur between Exodus 21:8–9 and LH 155–156 regarding the language of designation. These resemblances and differences suggest that while the imperialized authors complied with the imperial legal tolerance for selling one's daughters, they resisted the imperial legal stipulation on the release of these women like their male counterparts. This resistance may be oppressive, given no such restriction on the release of male slaves in the Exodus ordinances and the likelihood

100. Van Seters, "Law of the Hebrew Slave," 542; Van Seters, "Law of the Hebrew Slave: A Continuing Debate," 173; Doorly, *Laws of Yahweh*, 15; Wagenaar, "Annulment," 222; Gane, *Old Testament Law*, 110. Joseph Fleishman goes as far as suggesting that Exod 21:7–11 reflect a prohibition from selling a daughter as slave, but not from such sale as a concubine; Fleishman, "Law of Exodus," 47–64; Fleishman, *Father-Daughter Relation*, 16.

101. Kwasman, *Neo-Assyrian Legal Documents*, 253–54, no. 214. Van Seters ("Law of the Hebrew Slave," 542) and Wagnenaar ("Annulment," 221) cite this contract as one of the evidences for the marital nature of the sale in Exod 21:7.

102. Pressler, "Wives and Daughters," 163–64; Barmash, "Daughter Sold," 55.

of the authors and audiences being the father or the male owner of these women. Nevertheless, the comparison between Exodus 21:7–11 and LL 28 and LH 148 suggests that this resistance is an extension of imperial protection for first wives to female slaves. This extension indicates the protective intent of the restriction on their release. It also reveals the imperialized authors' resistance to imperial legal traditions' lack of consideration for female slaves.

Resistance: Protect and Release like Women of Non-Slave Statuses

A similar extension appears in the rest of the ordinances concerning the female slave, demonstrating this resistance further. While the stipulation on her redemption (Exod 21:8) exhibits resemblance to various cuneiform laws (LH 119, 281; MAL A 48), the Exodus ordinances uniquely prohibit the owner from selling her to a foreign people after he has designated her to himself (Exod 21:8). They also distinctively require the owner to treat her according to the ordinance of the daughters if he designates her to his son (Exod 21:9). The exact meaning of עם נכרי (a foreign people, Exod 21:8) and the content of משפט הבנות (ordinance of the daughters, Exod 21:9) are uncertain.[103] However, the related prohibition and requirement both undoubtedly emphasize the owner's responsibility to protect the female slave. Exodus 21:9 even extends a daughter's rights to her.

The resemblances between Exodus 21:10–11 and various cuneiform laws reveal nuances that suggest further the extension of the cuneiform legal protection for women of non-slave statuses to the female slave. These nuances first concern the provision for her (Exod 21:10). The meaning of the third item in the list, ענה, is subject to debate.[104] However, a threefold list related to the provision for women of various statuses occurs in several cuneiform law collections.[105] In LL 27, a man should provide "grain, oil, and clothing"

103. For various views on עם נכרי, see Wright, *Inventing God's Law*, 145, 418, note 85. See also, Sarna, *Exodus*, 121; Williamson, "Priority of the Laws," 119. For those on משפט הבנות, see Paul, *Studies in the Book of the Covenant*, 55; Pressler, "Wives and Daughter," 159; Jackson, *Wisdom-Laws*, 92, note 74; Wagenaar, "Annulment," 228.

104. Wright, *Inventing God's Law*, 146. For a recent summary of the debate, see Alexander, *Exodus*, 477–78. See also John Goldingay's recent translation, which regards it as "time"; Goldingay, *First Testament*, 72.

105. Paul also includes MAL A 36, which concerns how a woman should live if her husband travels abroad without sending her "any oil, wool, clothing, or provisions, or anything else (*la šamma la šapāte la lubulta la ukullâ la mimma*)" (Paul, *Studies in the Book of the Covenant*, 56–58). However, this law contains five items instead of three. David Wright only

(še-ba i-ba sig-ba-ni) to a prostitute who bears him a child, even though she will not stay with the family. In LE 32, a man should give the wet nurse other compensation if he does not provide her "food, oil, and clothing" (*epram piššatam lubuštam*) for three years.

Similarly, LH 178 requires the brothers of female cult or palace personnel to provide their sister "food, oil, and clothing allowances" (*ipram piššatam u lubūšam*) according to her inheritance's value, if their father did not grant her authority to give her estate to others before he died. This law then repeats the same phrase in order, specifying that if the brother does not provide his sister with the three things, the woman shall rent her estate to whoever she wants and earn her living from her tenant, even though her brothers remain to possess this estate. This freedom of leasing the estate is actually what the woman was supposed to have if her father has granted the estate to her before he died.

The reference to שלש־אלה (these three) in Exodus 21:11 is not as specific as this repeated phrase in LH 178, since it may refer either to the three items of the provision or to the three subordinate ordinances in Exodus 21:8–10.[106] However, similar to LH 178, Exodus 21:11 gives the affected woman freedom if the threefold requirement is not fulfilled. This freedom, which Exodus 21:11 specifies as without requiring payment, is given to male slaves in the introductory ordinance (Exod 21:2). This requirement of offering freedom also notably finds a resemblance in LH 149. This law follows a mentioned law requiring the retention and support of the first wife (LH 148), but stipulates that if the wife does not want to stay in her husband's house, she can leave.

Exodus 21:10 thus resembles LL 2, LE 32, and LH 178 in requiring a threefold provision for the affected woman. Like LH 178, which grants certain freedom to her if the threefold provision is not offered, Exodus 21:11 also requires the release of the woman in a similar condition. Moreover, this requirement is similar to LH 149, which allows the woman to leave her husband's household. Yet, while these cuneiform laws offer the provision and freedom to women of various statuses or occupations, including prostitutes who bear the man a child (LL 27), wet nurses (LE 32), female cult or palace personnel (LH 178), and wife (LH 149), the Exodus ordinances offer them

discusses LH 178, but lists LL 28, LE, 32, and MAL A36 in the endnote (Wright, *Inventing God's Law*, 146, 419, note 91).

106. Alexander, *Exodus*, 478; Williamson, "Priority of the Laws," 120–21.

to the female slave.[107] The requirements of continuous provisions for and release of the female slave in Exodus 21:10–11 thus reveal that the authors did not follow cuneiform legal traditions in offering these protections only to women of non-slave statuses, but required their elite audience to extend these protections to the female slave.

The differences amid resemblances between Exodus 21:7–11 and cuneiform law collections therefore reflect that the imperialized authors extended the provision to include the female slave and resist imperial ways of offering certain protections to women of non-slave statuses only. This endeavor directs the ordinances from not allowing the female slave to go as the male slave does (Exod 21:7) to requiring the release of the female slave without payment (Exod 21:11) just as the beginning of the Exodus ordinances does for male slaves (Exod 21:2). Together with those concerning male slaves, these ordinances recall the continuities and discontinuities of the colonial legal discourse in the legal discourse of the colonized in modern contexts.[108] They also manifest the work of conservative revolutionists who lived under the shadow of the Neo-Assyrian Empire. The imperialized authors broadly accepted the imperial legal tolerance for practices related to slavery and debt service. They sometimes even diverged from the latter in ways that are potentially oppressive, which require a postcolonial inquiry. Nevertheless, they concurrently underlined the responsibility of slave owners, particularly the elite audience, and brought up consideration for the imperialized, rather than the people of the Neo-Assyrian Empire. They also upheld their own tradition, ameliorated the image of slaves, and urged their elite audience to be responsible for the female slave's well-being. These endeavors resisted imperial handling of male and female slaves, even though they remained conservative in departing from imperial practices drastically.

---

107. According to Paul, there is a Neo-Babylonian document which describes the provision of *epri piššatum ù* [túg]*lubuštum* ("food, oil, and clothing") to a slave (Paul, *Studies in the Book of the Covenant*, 59). However, in addition to the fact that it is a later cuneiform document, it is also notable that this document is a contract which deals with a special situation: the slave decided to seal a contract with the household which agreed to offer him the provision, after the original household failed to provide for him according to a similar contract. Moreover, the slave is a man, rather than a woman. For the text, see Peiser, *Texte juristischen*, 244–47, no. 44.

108. See §1.3.4.

3.2.3 Physical Assault

After the introductory ordinances regarding release and permanent servitude, the concern about slaves appears again in the following ordinances concerning physical assault. These ordinances continue to show both similarities and differences to various cuneiform laws, suggesting that the biblical authors simultaneously took up and departed from elements prevalent in cuneiform legal traditions. These departures are liberative in some cases, but susceptible to being oppressive in others. Yet, they all reflect that the imperialized authors did not fully accept the imperial handling of physical assault against slaves, but expended effort to resist it.

3.2.3.1 By Slave Owners (Exodus 21:20–21, 21:26–27)

Exodus 21:20–21 and 26–27 address physical assault against male and female slaves caused by their owner. The former deals with assaults resulting in immediate or eventual fatality. The latter handles assaults leading to bodily damages. Preceding these ordinances are those concerning capital offenses, including homicide (Exod 21:12–16), and non-fatal assault against other persons in general (Exod 21:18–19). In between these ordinances are those regarding assault against pregnant women, which end with talion laws (Exod 21:22–25).

> Exod 21:20–21, 21:26–27
>
> > [20]And when a man strikes his male slave or his female slave with a rod and he dies under his hand, he shall be surely avenged.
> >
> > [21]However if he survives a day or two, he shall not be avenged; for he is his silver.
> >
> > [26]And when a man strikes the eye of his male slave or the eye of his female slave and destroys it, he shall send him off free for the eye.
> >
> > [27]And when he knocks out the tooth of his male slave or the tooth of his female slave, he shall send him off free for the tooth.

Acceptance of the Imperial Legal Metanarrative

Extant cuneiform law collections contain various laws on fatal and bodily assault against slaves or persons distrained due to debt. Preceding the mentioned law concerning a man selling his family into debt service (LH 117), two laws in the Hammurabi collection handle the death of a distrainee: first due to natural causes (LH 115), then due to physical assault (LH 116). The latter specifically considers beating as one of the causes of the death. It also requires the execution of the distrainer's son, if the distrainee is the debtor's son. Two laws in the Hittite collection addresses fatal assault against an ARAD (male slave) or a GÉME (female slave) (HL 2, 4). Each of these laws follows those concerning fatal assault against free persons (HL 1, 3). The law in HL 4, following the wording of HL 3, specifies the situation as someone striking an ARAD or a GÉME to death.

LH 115–116

> [115]If a man has a claim of grain or silver against another man, distrains a member of his household, and the distrainee dies a natural death while in the house of her or his distrainer, that case has no basis for a claim.
>
> [116]If the distrainee should die from the effects of a beating or other physical abuse while in the house of her or his distrainer, the owner of the distrainee shall charge and convict his merchant and if (the distrainee is) the man's son, they shall kill his (the distrainer's) son; if the man's slave, he shall weigh and deliver 20 shekels of silver; moreover, he shall forfeit whatever he originally gave as the loan.[109]

HL 2, 4

> [2][If] anyone kills [a male] or female slave in a quarrel, he shall bring him (for burial) [and] shall give [2] person (lit. heads), male or female respectively, and he shall look to his house for it.
>
> [4]If anyone strikes a male or female slave so that he dies, but it is an accident, he shall bring him (for burial) and shall give one person (lit. head). He shall look to his house for it.[110]

109. Roth, *Law Collections*, 103.

110. Hoffner, *Laws of the Hittites*, 17, 18.

These cuneiform law collections also address assault leading to bodily damages of slaves. A law in the Hammurabi collection handles physical assault caused by an *awīlum* that affects a *wardum*'s eyes or bone (LH 199). It locates in the middle of laws concerning physical assaults against people of various statuses. Those concerning *awīlum*, including those that involve bodily damages (LH 196, 197, 200, 202), require talion punishments. Some laws in the Hittite collection deal with blinding an ARAD or a GÉME or knocking out his or her tooth (HL 8) and damaging various body parts (HL 12, 14, 16). Each of these laws follows those addressing similar assaults against free persons with higher monetary penalties.

LH 199

> If he should blind the eye of an *awīlu*'s slave or break the bone of an *awīlu*'s slave, he shall weigh and deliver one-half of his value (in silver).[111]

HL 8, 12, 14, 16

> [8]If anyone blinds a male or female slave or knocks out his tooth, he shall pay 10 shekels of silver. He shall look to his house for it.
>
> [12]If anyone breaks a male or female slave's arm or leg, he shall pay 10 shekels of silver. He shall look to his house for it.
>
> [14]If anyone bites off the nose of a male or female slave, he shall pay 3 shekels of silver. He shall look to his house for it.
>
> [16]If anyone tears off the ear of a male or female slave, he shall pay him 3 shekels of silver.[112]

These laws indicate that alongside their attention to physical assault against people in general, cuneiform legal traditions are concerned with that against male and female slaves or persons distrained due to debt. The Exodus ordinances bear a number of resemblances to the cuneiform laws. Exodus 21:20–21 and 26–27 similarly address physical assault against slaves in the middle of ordinances handling physical assault against other people. Besides,

111. Roth, *Law Collections*, 121.

112. Hoffner, *Laws of the Hittites*, 22, 26, 27, 28.

Exodus 21:20's protasis presents the fatal assault against male or female slaves in a way similar to HL 4's protasis does. Exodus 21:20 and 21 also resemble LH 115–116 in handling the physical assault in reverse order: that is, the Exodus ordinances first handle an offense subject to punishment, then an offense not subject to it, whereas the cuneiform laws first address an assault leading to a claim, then a circumstance not leading to it.[113] Furthermore, Exodus 21:20 is similar to LH 116 in indicating the assault related to beating (בשׁבט, with a rod) and requiring a kind of vengeance for the victim's death. To what penalty the absolute complement נקם ינקם (he shall be surely avenged) refers is not explicit; however, attestations of the root in the Old Testament usually refer to capital vengeance.[114] Thus, the penalty required by Exodus 21:20 is similar, in terms of seriousness, to the penalty for killing a distrainee who is the debtor's son in LH 116. Exodus 21:26 and 27 continue to exhibit concerns resembling those in LH 119 and HL 8, handling damage to male or female slave's eyes and teeth. These ordinances also similarly locate after talion laws, as LH 119 locates in the middle of them. These similarities suggest that the imperialized authors accepted the imperial legal metanarrative in many aspects. This acceptance relates to the arrangement of the laws, the way of addressing the affected persons, the conditions of the physical assault, the impact on the slaves, as well as the penalty for fatal cases.

Resistance: Death Penalty for Fatal Assault Against One's Own Slaves

Concurrent with this general acceptance, the imperialized authors, however, resisted imperial legal traditions' silence on physical assault against one's own male and female slaves. This resistance is suggested by the Exodus ordinances' distinctive focus on such cases, rather than physical assault caused by other people as the cuneiform laws do. Indeed, no cuneiform law collection deals with physical assault against one's own slave, whether chattel or debt slaves, not to mention there is no cuneiform law imposing capital vengeance against slave owners because of their fatal assault against their own slave, as Exodus 21:20 requires. Even though cuneiform law collections contain some other

113. Wright, *Inventing God's Law*, 170; Schwienhorst-Schönberger, *Bundesbuch*, 68–70, 312.

114. Alexander, *Exodus*, 483; Wright, *Inventing God's Law*, 174; Sprinkle, *Book of the Covenant*, 100–101. See Chirichigno, *Debt-Slavery*, 149–69, for a review of scholarly understandings and an analysis of this root. See Sarna, *Exodus*, 14, for an argument based on the Samaritan Pentateuch.

laws concerning injury or death of slaves under other circumstances, they all handle cases caused by a person other than their owners, which lead to monetary compensation or replacement of other slaves.[115] The Hammurabi collection does impose capital punishment on fatal assault (LH 116). However, the victim is a distrainee, who does not directly owe a debt to the distrainer, and capital punishment is imposed only when the distrainee is an *awīlum*'s son, not when the distrainee is a slave.[116] The unique concern and requirement of the Exodus ordinances on fatal physical assault against one's own slave may explain the use of a euphemistic term for the death penalty imposed on the slave owner, as this concern and requirement resist imperial legal approach to such offense, unconventionally attending to the slave owner's responsibility. Amid general acceptance, the imperialized authors resisted the lack of concern about slave owners' physical assault against their own slaves in the imperial legal metanarrative, demanding capital punishment from slave owners, including the elite audience, for fatal assault under such condition.

Ambivalence in Handling Non-Immediately Fatal Assault

The treatment in the subordinate ordinance (Exod 21:21) is, nonetheless, far from attentive to slave owners' responsibility, even though it also differs from the mentioned cuneiform laws. Exodus 21:21 states that the owner shall not be avenged if his slave survives a day or two. The meaning of אם־יום או יומים יעמד (if he survives a day or two) is ambiguous. It may indicate a kind of delayed death, somewhat similar to the distrainee's natural death in LH 115, suggesting that the slave's death may not have been directly caused by the owner's assault.[117] That ambiguous phrase may also address the non-fatal nature of the assault, that is, the slave recovers after a day or two.[118] In both cases, a

115. LE 23 (death of distrained female slaves without known cause and the slave owner does not own any claims against the distrainer); LH 213–214, HL 18 (miscarriage caused by physical assault against female slaves); LH 219–220 (death and bodily damages of male slaves caused by physicians).

116. A similar case is LE 24, which requires execution of the assailant, but the victim is a commoner's wife or child and the commoner does not have any claim against the distrainer.

117. For Schwienhorst-Schönberger, this phrase indicates that the slave is able to return to work for a day or two (Schwienhorst-Schönberger, *Bundesbuch*, 64). Some scholars suggest that this phrase indicates the master's intention; for instance, Barmash, *Homicide in the Biblical World*, 124.

118. Chirichigno, *Debt-Slavery*, 175; see also the Common English Bible: "if the slave gets up after a day or two."

deviation from cuneiform legal traditions occurs: If this description indicates a kind of natural death similar to LH 115, Exodus 21:21 reflects a transfer of the lenient treatment of the distrainer (who did nothing to cause the distrainee's death) to the treatment of the slave owner (who strikes his slave some days before he or she dies). If this description refers to a non-fatal physical assault, Exodus 21:21 reveals an inference from cuneiform legal traditions about non-fatal physical assault against others' slaves (LH 199; HL 8, 12, 14, 16). The slave owner would not need to pay the monetary compensation that cuneiform laws required from other assailants, as the slave owes him a debt.[119]

This inference does not necessarily mean that Exodus 21:21 deals with chattel slaves; the motive clause כי כספו הוא (for he is his silver) may indeed refer back to the condition in Exodus 21:2 in which the elite audience buys a slave obligated to a six-year servitude.[120] Nevertheless, this motive clause does emphasize that the slave is the owner's property,[121] which seems to be a principle implied by the mentioned cuneiform laws on non-fatal physical assault against others' slaves. The ordinance also gives the benefit of the doubt to the slave owner, rather than the slave,[122] or implies that the slave owner has the right to non-fatally beat the slave.[123] In any case, a difference from cuneiform legal traditions emerges. However, this difference, unlike the unique concern about and the penalty for fatal physical assault against one's own slave, is intertwined with acceptance of the oppressive imperial approach to dealing with slaves, which is susceptible to the consideration of the elite authors' and audience's interests. This ambivalence, rather than liberating the imperialized from imperial values,[124] leads to oppressive treatment of the subordinate people among them, as some postcolonial scholars assert.[125]

119. For a similar understanding, see Wright, *Inventing God's Law*, 171. Referring to Exod 21:26–27, Scholz regards the penalty in Exod 21:21 as monetary (Scholz, "Complexities," 36). However, the ordinances do not seem to indicate so.

120. For an opposite view, see Chirichigno, *Debt-Slavery*, 149–88. Sarna even suggests that this phrase refers to slaves of foreign origin (Sarna, *Exodus*, 124).

121. Bridge, "Metaphoric Use of Slave Terms," 18.

122. Scholz, "Complexities," 36; Marshall, *Israel*, 120; Sarna, *Exodus*, 124; Patrick, *Old Testament Law*, 76.

123. Referring to Prov 29:19, Albertz even asserts that beating slaves was acceptable in ancient Israel (Albertz, *Exodus, Band II*, 92).

124. Bhabha, "Interrogating Identity," 86–88; Ashcroft, Griffins, and Tiffin, *Post-Colonial Studies*, 125–26; see also §1.2.2.1.

125. For instance, Prabhu, *Hybridity*, 16; see also §1.2.2.2.

Similar to some colonized legal discourse in the modern context, which reflects both continuity and discontinuity of the colonizer's legal discourse,[126] this ambivalence indicates the struggle of the conservative revolutionists in their response to the imperial legal metanarrative. While they uniquely handled physical abuse against one's own slaves, they preserve oppressive imperial values in owner-slave relationships, as some postcolonial biblical scholars contend.[127]

Resistance: Release for Bodily Damages

Notwithstanding, the following ordinances concerning bodily damages to slaves (Exod 21:26–27) reveal a liberative resistance to the imperial legal metanarrative through a requirement different from cuneiform laws. These ordinances demand the release of the injured male or female slave, rather than monetary compensation. It is possible that this distinctive demand is an explication for the preceding talion ordinances, because those ordinances require vicarious punishment or monetary penalty in cases of physical assault against pregnant women, which the biblical authors might deem to be applicable to physical assault against people in general but not to bodily assault against slaves.[128] This distinctive demand may also be explained further by the fact that the assailant that the Exodus ordinances concern is the slave owner, rather than other people as those cuneiform laws address. As some scholars argue, the monetary compensation required of a non-owner is offset by the debt that the slaves owe their owner and led them into servitude; thus, the ordinances require the slave owner to release the slave instead.[129] Yet, this kind of calculation is not reflected in any cuneiform laws. Not only does no cuneiform law collection deal with physical assault against one's own slave, but even cuneiform laws that stipulate talion punishments for bodily assault against free people deal further with bodily assault against others' slaves rather than one's own slaves (LH 199). Cuneiform laws concerning physical assault against one's distrainees (LH 116) also do not deal with assault against their body parts. The mentioned law MAL A 44 (see 3.2.2.1) indeed

126. See §1.3.4.

127. Mathew, *Biblical Law Codes*, 200–201.

128. I discuss these talion ordinances further in the following section concerning ordinances on women.

129. Wright, *Inventing God's Law*, 188; Mathew, *Biblical Law Codes*, 204–6.

grants the creditor the right to physically assault the Assyrian man or woman who resides in a creditor's house as a pledge, to the point of destroying their body parts.

Exodus 21:26 and 27 thus manifest that alongside their sympathy with the imperial legal concern about bodily damages to slaves, the imperialized authors resisted the imperial legal lack of concern about such damages caused by slave owners and explicitly required liberative treatment of the slaves. This "the same but not quite" mimicry, together with that occurring in Exodus 21:20–21, reveals an ambivalent attitude toward the imperial handling of physical assaults against slaves. While Exodus 21:20 particularly attends to slave owners' responsibility for their slaves' death, resisting the imperial legal lack of concern about it, Exodus 21:21 exempts slave owners from any penalty for non-immediately fatal assault, complying with the imperial legal principle of treating slaves as property. Nevertheless, Exodus 21:26 and 27 stipulate the release of the slaves when their owners damage their body parts, resisting again imperial legal traditions' silence on such kind of assault as well as treatment. This ambivalence therefore reveals both oppressive and liberative treatments of slaves, thus both consideration of the elite audience's interests and emphasis on their responsibility. It also discloses how the imperialized authors wrestled to resist imperial legal traditions, despite in a conservative way. This wrestling will be manifested further in the following ordinances concerning goring oxen.

3.2.3.2 By Others' Oxen (Exodus 21:32)

Among the ordinances concerning goring oxen is one dealing with a habitual goring fatal to a male or female slave (Exod 21:32). Before this, a series of ordinances address an ox's first-time goring of men or women, accustomed goring against them, and accustomed goring against sons or daughters (Exod 21:28–31). After this, the ordinances handle fatal damages to others' animals due to open pits and goring oxen (Exod 21:33–35). The similarities and differences between the preceding ordinances and cuneiform laws indicate the biblical authors' particular concerns in handling goring against people in general, which offer a crucial background for understanding these authors' responses to cuneiform legal traditions in handling goring against slaves. Thus, I include these ordinances in the following discussion.

Exodus 21:28–32

> [28]And when an ox gores a man or a woman and he dies, the ox shall surely be stoned and its flesh shall not be eaten, but the owner of the ox is innocent.
>
> [29]And if it is a goring ox in the past, and its owner has been warned, but he does not watch out for it, and it kills a man or a woman, the ox shall be stoned and its owner shall be put to death.
>
> [30]If a ransom is laid upon him, then he shall give the redemption price of his life as whatever is laid upon him.
>
> [31]Or it gores a son or it gores a daughter, it should be done to him according to this ordinance.
>
> [32]If the ox gores a male slave or a female slave, he shall give his master thirty shekels of silver, and the ox shall be stoned.

Acceptance of the Imperial Legal Metanarrative

The Laws of Eshnunna and the Laws of Hammurabi are well known for containing laws dealing with goring oxen that cause death. The laws in LE 53–55 begin with the case in which an ox gores another ox. Then they deal with goring against an *awīlum* by a habitual goring ox and that against a *wardum*. The laws in LH 250–252 begin with accidental goring against an *awīlum*. Laws handling goring against an *awīlum* by a habitual goring ox and that against a *wardum* then follow.

LE 53–55

> [53]If an ox gores another ox and thus causes its death, the two ox-owners shall divide the value of the living ox and the carcass of the dead ox.
>
> [54]If an ox is a gorer and the ward authorities so notify its owner, but he fails to keep his ox in heck and it gores a man and thus causes his death, the owner of the ox shall weigh and deliver 40 shekels of silver.

> [55]If it gores a slave and thus causes his death, he shall weigh and deliver 15 shekels of silver.[130]

LH 250–252

> [250]If an ox gores to death a man while it is passing through the streets, that case has no basis for a claim.
>
> [251]If a man's ox is a known gorer, and the authorities of his city quarter notify him that it is a known gorer, but he does not blunt its horns or control his ox, and that ox gores to death a member of the *awīlu*-class, he shall give 30 shekels of silver.
>
> [252]If it is a man's slave, he shall give 20 shekels of silver.[131]

These laws indicate that cuneiform legal traditions attend to fatal assault caused by goring oxen, whether accidental or habitual, or against an *awīlum* or *wardum*. The Exodus ordinances reflect similar concerns, suggesting that the imperialized authors were broadly in sympathy with imperial legal attention to such kind of assault, including that against slaves.

Resistance: Assault on People Rather than Negligence and Business Issues

Meanwhile, the Exodus ordinances differ from these cuneiform laws in several ways, suggesting their authors' resistance to the imperial legal handling of goring oxen. These differences shed light on the resistance, as well as ambivalence, exhibited in the ordinance dealing with goring against slaves.

The first crucial distinction occurs in the ordinances' sequence, both external and internal. It demonstrates that the biblical authors highly regarded goring oxen cases, including that against slaves, as a physical assault on people rather than merely as business issues and negligence, as cuneiform legal traditions do. In the Eshnunna collection, the laws on goring oxen follow those on physical assault (LE 42–47A), but interrupted by laws of various topic,[132] which indicates a disconnection between the goring oxen laws and those on

130. Roth, *Law Collections*, 67.

131. Roth, 128.

132. They include the types of cases determined by judges and the king (LE 48), the seizing of fugitive slave for personal use (LE 49–50), and the custom for male and female slaves (LE 51–52).

physical assault. The laws concerning goring against an *awīlum* and *wardum* (LE 54–55) are indeed preceded immediately by a law about goring against another ox (LE 53) and followed by laws dealing with negligent owners of vicious dogs and buckling walls (LE 56–58). This sequence suggests a focus on the ox owner's negligence in the laws handling goring against an *awīlum* and a *wardum*. Similarly, the Hammurabi collection separates the laws on goring against an *awīlum* and a *wardum* (LH 250–252) and those on physical assault (LH 195–214) by laws on fees and penalties for different services, including ox rental (LH 215–249). Laws following the goring ox laws reflect similar business transactions (LH 253–270). This arrangement suggests that the Hammurabi collection regards goring against an *awīlum* and a *wardum* as a matter relating to business transactions.

Unlike these two cuneiform law collections, the Exodus ordinances handle goring against people, including slaves, right after physical assault caused by people. The ordinances immediately following Exodus 21:28–32, which concern an open pit (Exod 21:33–34) and goring against another ox (Exod 21:35–36), are related to negligence, similar to the Eshnunna collection. Yet, unlike the subordinate ordinances on goring against people, which begins with אם or או ("if" or "or," Exod 21:29–32), these ordinances about the damage of property begin with כי (when, Exod 21:33), which differentiates them from the preceding ordinances about the loss of human life, including slaves (Exod 21:28–32). This differentiation is evident further in the location of the ordinances concerning the open pit (Exod 21:33–34), which disrupt the goring ox ordinances' sequence (Exod 21:28–32, 21:35–36). This distinction between goring that leads to the loss of human life and goring that leads to the damage of property is absent from the Eshnunna collection. Thus, the arrangement of the Exodus ordinances not only suggests "the relevance of the goring ox laws for the topic of homicide and assault,"[133] but also reflects their authors' resistance to imperial legal traditions in treating goring against people merely as a business issue or negligence and conflating the loss of human life with the damage of property. Amid their acceptance of the imperial legal concern about goring against people, the imperialized authors thus paid particular attention to the loss of human life, including that of slaves. This attention may work against the authors' and their elite audience's economic

133. Wright, *Inventing God's Law*, 227.

interest, as they might own oxen themselves. It, moreover, resists the imperial legal focus on the case's economic aspect, an aspect which empires particularly attend to, including the Neo-Assyrian Empire.[134]

Resistance: Traditions and Community Rather than Ox Owners' Interest

In addition to this attention, the Exodus ordinances also impose punishments different from those of the two cuneiform law collections, reflecting their authors' resistance to imperial legal consideration of ox owners' interest. In the case of first-time goring, while Exodus 21:28 states that the ox owner is innocent, as LH 250 does, the former particularly underlines that the ox shall be stoned (סקול יסקל) and that its flesh shall not be eaten. In the case of accustomed goring, Exodus 21:29 demands that the ox shall be stoned, as well as its owner put to death, contrasting with LE 54 and LH 251, which only impose a monetary penalty. Similarly, the ordinance concerning slaves (Exod 21:32) requires the stoning of the ox in addition to a monetary penalty, when LE 55 and LH 252 prescribe monetary compensation only.

As in the case of male slaves' servitude length, the requirement of stoning the ox to death is related to the retrieval of the traditions of Israel and Judah as well as the consideration of communal well-being and participation.[135] If one considers that the prohibition of eating the ox's meat may be intended to restrain the ox owner from benefiting from the ox in addition to meeting cultic requirements,[136] this prohibition reflects further that the biblical authors gave their tradition precedence over the ox owner's interest. This interest may be something that cuneiform legal traditions attempt to conceal, considering that both LE 54–55 and LH 250–252 do not mention how the goring ox itself should be handled. If LE 53's treatment of the ox, that is, dividing the ox's value, is meant to be applied to LE 54–55, then the intention of protecting the ox owner's interest is even more prominent. The distinction of the Exodus ordinances from the cuneiform laws thus suggests that by appealing to their own traditions and community, their authors resisted the imperial legal attention to economic interest in handling loss of human life.

---

134. Bagg, "Palestine," 121; Berlejung, "Assyrians in the West," 28, 51.

135. See §3.2.2.1.

136. Houtman, *Exodus*, 3:179.

In relation to this resistance is the emphasis on the ox owner's responsibility with a deemphasis of authorities' role. Exodus 21:29, which begins the ordinances on accustomed goring, including that against slaves, does not resort to authorities as the two cuneiform laws do. In LE 54 and LH 251, the ox owner is subject to a penalty if he knows that the ox is a gorer and the *bābtum* has informed him about the ox's tendency to gore. This *bābtum*, which literally means "quarter of a city, neighborhood, ward (as subdivision of a city's population)," refers to authorities with legal power to pass judgment and collect monetary penalties from offenders.[137] These two cuneiform laws thus underline the role of authorities in these cases. In contrast, Exodus 21:29 uses the *hophal* form of עוד to describe the condition in which the ox owner has been warned about the ox's tendency to gore. Although this passive expression implies that someone has warned the ox owner, it does not specify their identity. The use of these unique expressions thus may not only be due to the fact that the Exodus ordinances were intended for people who lived in a more simply organized society than that of the two cuneiform laws, but also aims to emphasize that ox owners are responsible for the death caused by their oxen, regardless of who has warned them. This distinction therefore reflects not only the imperialized authors' resistance to imperial legal emphasis on authorities' role in warning ox owners, but also their stronger concern for the responsibility of ox owners than their imperial counterparts.

Exodus 21:30, which addresses ransom, exhibits this concern further. Although this penalty allows the ox owner to redeem himself from capital punishment and the motivation behind this penalty is difficult to ascertain,[138] the ordinance highlights that the ox owner is subject to others' mercy. Suggesting this emphasis is the fact that this alternative penalty is offered only if a ransom is imposed on the ox owner, which is the predominant concern

137. s.v. "*Babtu*," CAD 2:9–10.

138. Considering some literary criteria and the fact that the Bible, including the homicide ordinances (Exod 21:12–14), usually does not allow monetary compensation for the loss of a human life, some scholars regard the description of this alternative penalty as secondary (Schwienhorst-Schönberger, *Bundesbuch*, 129–62; Otto, *Körperverletzungen in den Keilschriftrechten*, 156–58). However, it is possible that the authors offered this alternative penalty because the death is caused by the ox, not by the ox owner directly. It may also be the case that this alternative penalty is intended to "retreat from the idealistic rigor" of the death penalty imposed in the preceding verse (Wright, *Inventing God's Law*, 211), which exhibits the flexibility of imperialized people's legal discourse.

of Exodus 21:30. Again, the identity of the person who imposes the ransom is not specified; but the use of the *qal* passive form of שׁית underlines that whether the ox owner can redeem himself from the death penalty or not is subject to others' decision. The ox owner does not even know the amount of ransom from the ordinance, as the imperial people do from the cuneiform laws (LE 54; LH 251); he needs to pay whatever is imposed on him (Exod 21:30). This emphasis thus suggests another distinction from the cuneiform laws, which require the ox owner to pay a specific fine only for accustomed goring (LE 54; LH 251), even though the requirement of a ransom in the Exodus ordinance resembles the monetary penalty in these cuneiform laws.[139] This distinction reflects that the imperialized authors not only resisted the imperial legal requirement of monetary compensation only for loss of human life, but also transformed the monetary compensation into a condition in which the ox owner's life and death are subject to others' decision. The ordinances in Exodus 21:28–32 thus reveal that alongside their general acceptance of the imperial legal concern about fatal assault caused by goring oxen, the imperialized authors resisted the imperial legal handling of it. Through appealing to their own traditions, upholding their concern about community, and uniquely addressing the issue of ransom, the imperialized authors paid less attention to ox owners' interest, but more to their responsibility, where imperial legal traditions do otherwise.

Resistance: Attention to Victims of Different Statuses

Whereas the Exodus ordinances do not privilege the ox owner, they particularly attend to victims of different statuses. Unlike the two cuneiform law collections, which refer only to males when they indicate the victim (*awīlum, mār awīlum, wardum, warad awīlum*, LE 54–55, LH 250–252), the Exodus ordinances refer to females (אשׁה, woman, Exod 21:28, 29; בת, daughter, Exod 21:31; אמה, female slave, Exod 21:32) in addition to males (אישׁ, man, Exod 21:28, 29; בן, son, Exod 21:31; אבד, male slave, Exod 21:32). This gender inclusivity resembles that appearing in cuneiform laws dealing with other cases (for instance, MAL A 44, which deals with an Assyrian man or woman who resides in a man's house as a pledge; LH 117, on a man's sale of his son

139. David Wright suggests that this alternative penalty is inspired by the two cuneiform laws (Wright, *Inventing God's Law*, 211).

or daughter into debt service, HL 4, on physical assault against an ARAD or GÉME; and so forth).[140] The mention of both males and females in Exodus 21:28–32 thus suggests that the imperialized authors resisted omitting females or using male terms to imply females, as imperial legal traditions did when they referred to victims of assault by oxen. They extended imperial legal consideration for men and women, sons and daughters, and male and female slaves to the ordinances concerning fatal goring against people in order to draw attention to victims of both genders.

The consideration for sons and daughters evidences this attention to victims of different statuses further. In the case in which an ox gores a son or a daughter, that is, a child of either gender, Exodus 21:31 treats the ox owner in the same way as the case in which an ox gores a man or a woman. Some scholars regard this law as a later addition, especially because it begins with או and the offended (בן/בת), rather than כי/אם and the ox (שור) or the action of goring (נגח), as preceding ordinances do (Exod 21:28–29).[141] However, since the following ordinance, which begins with אם, also mentions the victim first (עבד; Exod 21:32), it is reasonable for one to query if the order of the offender and the victim necessarily suggests later redaction. The particular use of או and emphasis on the offended in fact introduce an ordinance that uniquely gives children the same consideration as adults.[142] While this consideration might not be directed against the talion practice of the empires

140. David Wright notes that this gender inclusivity may be due to the influence of other stipulations in the Hammurabi collection, as well as the native model of the Book of the Covenant reflected in the participial law, Exod 21:17 (Wright, *Inventing God's Law*, 149). However, the examples I list here suggest that this gender inclusivity may not be due to the response to the tradition reflected in the Hammurabi collection only. The gender inclusivity in the participial laws (Exod 21:17, as well as 21:15) also may not suggest a native model, as the participial form is similar to the relative form employed in some cuneiform laws, for instance, LE 13, MAL A 40, and the gender inclusivity occurred in Exod 21:15 and 17 is similar to that in SLEx 4 and LH 192–193. For more about cuneiform law collections' use of formulations other than the usual *šumma*-form, see Westbrook, "What is the Covenant Code," 29; Greengus, "Some Issues," 73; Paul, *Studies in the Book of the Covenant*, 115; Yaron, *Laws of Eshnunna*, 103–5; Meek, *Hebrew Origins*, 72. About the gender inclusivity in Exod 21:15 and 17, see my following discussion in §3.3.1.

141. Both Schwienhorst-Schönberger (*Bundesbuch*, 129–62) and Eckart Otto (*Körperverletzungen in den Keilschriftrechten*, 156–58; *Wandel der Rechtsbegründungen*, 29–30) see various later additions in Exod 21:28–32, including vv. 30–32. However, Rothenbusch does not regard vv. 30–32 as secondary (Rothenbusch, *Kasuistische Rechtssammlung*, 320–21). Yuichi Osumi actually sees a particular unity among vv. 28–36 (Osumi, *Die Kompositionsgeschichte*, 119–21).

142. Dozeman, *Exodus*, 538.

(that is, imposing the death penalty on the ox owner's son or daughter),[143] it is a consideration that imperial legal traditions do not particularly emphasize.

The cuneiform laws' wording may invite suspicion about a similar concern for a son in LH 251, for while the Eshnunna collection uses *awīlum* to refer to the victim (LE 54), the Hammurabi collection uses *mār awīlim* (LH 251). Nevertheless, *mār awīlim* may have various meanings. Its literal meaning, "a son of a free person," deserves attention, as it suggests that the mention of "son" (בן) in Exodus 21:31 may indicate its authors' acceptance of the tradition reflected in the Hammurabi law, if not their direct adoption of the law itself. However, in her recent studies, Martha T. Roth argues that this phrase refers to a dependent, rather than a son, of a free person, in view of the hierarchy exhibited in laws using this phrase.[144] According to her earlier translation, this phrase might even possibly refer generally to a member of the free person class.[145]

It is possible that the Exodus ordinances' authors formulated Exodus 21:31 in response to all these semantic possibilities revealed in the Hammurabi law, as Wright suggests.[146] One may go as far as saying that the biblical authors adapted the language of the imperial legal traditions reflected in the two cuneiform laws, that is, *awīlum* (LE 54) and *mār awīlim* (LH 251), for expressing the imperialized people's concern over victims of different statuses, that is, adults and children. In any case, the Exodus ordinances uniquely handle cases affecting adults and children separately but require the same treatment of the ox owner. This distinction, together with the unique mentions of both males and females, reveals the imperialized authors' resistance to imperial legal traditions' lack of attention to victims of different statuses in handling assault caused by goring oxen.

---

143. Houtman, *Exodus*, 3:176; for an opposite view, see Alexander, *Exodus*, 490.

144. She argues that some laws in the Laws of Eshnunna and the Laws of Hammurabi reflect a hierarchy among statuses, and thus *mār awīlum* or *mār muškēnum* should be understood as a dependent of a household headed by an *awīlum* or a *muškēnum* (Roth, "Errant Oxen Or," 397–404; Roth, "On *mār awīlim*," 267–72; Roth, "On Persons," 219–27). However, some laws she discusses, such as LH 206–208, actually contain different cases, which make the hierarchy that she proposes unsustainable. I therefore maintain that there is still ambiguity on the meaning of *mārum* when it is qualified by certain type of person, such as *awīlum* or *muškēnum*. It may refer to a child, a dependent, or simply a member.

145. Roth, *Law Collections*, 128.

146. Wright, *Inventing God's Law*, 212.

Ambivalence in Handling Goring Against Slaves

This resistance, together with the resistances to the imperial legal concerns about negligence and business issues as well as owners' interest, makes one seriously reflect on the differences and resemblances that occurred in the goring ox ordinance concerning slaves (Exod 21:32). Following the preceding ordinances, Exodus 21:32 uniquely belongs to a section right after ordinances on physical assault against people and distinguished from the following ordinances on negligence. Like the preceding ordinances, Exodus 21:32 also distinctively addresses assault against both male and female slaves and require stoning the goring ox. However, unlike the preceding ordinances on accustomed goring, which impose capital punishment on the ox owner, Exodus 21:32 only requires the ox owner to fulfill a monetary penalty, just as the two cuneiform laws do. These differences and similarities again reveal resistance to imperial legal traditions amid acceptance of them. The imperialized authors resisted to treat the loss of slaves' life caused by goring oxen as simply negligence or business issues as imperial legal traditions do. Moreover, they extended imperial legal considerations for both males and females to such loss and continued to appeal to their own tradition and their concern about community in this case. However, the imperialized authors concurrently followed imperial legal traditions in requiring monetary penalty rather than capital punishment from the ox owner when the victims are slaves.

Notably, Exodus 21:32 demands the ox owner to pay the slave owner thirty shekels of silver, exactly the same as LH 251 does for goring against a son/dependent/member of a free person/the free person class. With the proposition about the authorial awareness of the legal traditions somehow reflected in extant cuneiform law collections, this similarity suggests that the imperialized authors applied the cuneiform legal tradition's penalty for an assault against a free person to that against a slave. This application suggests that the imperialized authors had a higher regard for the slave's life than their imperial counterpart.[147] Nevertheless, in comparison to the death penalty in the preceding cases (Exod 21:28–31), the monetary penalty in Exodus 21:32 still indicates that the imperialized authors did not value the life of a slave as highly as the life of a free man or a woman, or a son or a daughter. This inferior treatment of slaves is similar to the cuneiform laws. Hence, some

147. For a similar argument, see Wright, *Inventing God's Law*, 225; Sarna, *Exodus*, 129.

scholars argue that Exodus 21:32 still follows the principle that slaves are their masters' possessions;[148] some even assert that this ordinance is intended to apply to chattel slaves.[149] Exodus 21:32 therefore reveals an oscillation between resistance to and compliance with imperial legal traditions, an ambivalence of the imperialized. This ambivalence involves various attempts to resist the imperial legal handling of goring oxen against slaves, namely giving comparatively higher regard for their life, upholding the imperialized people's tradition and concern, and attending to both male and female slaves. However, this ambivalence maintains an oppressive element due to compliance with the inferior treatment of slaves that imperial legal traditions stipulate.

This ambivalence recalls what occurs in the ordinances regarding physical assault inflicted by slave owners. Those ordinances exhibit resistance to the imperial legal lack of concern about such assault by imposing capital punishment to fatal cases and requiring the release of the slaves in bodily damages. However, they reveal compliance with the imperial legal principle of treating slaves as property by exempting slave owners from any penalty for non-immediately fatal assault. These ambivalences involve oppressive treatments of the subordinate people among the imperialized, like some hybrid responses of colonized people in the modern context do, requiring an ethical critique which postcolonial scholars call for.[150] They also echo the continuity and discontinuity of the colonizer's legal discourse witnessed among some colonized people,[151] reflecting the struggle of the imperialized authors, who lived under the subjugation of the Neo-Assyrian Empire. They endeavored to resist the imperial legal metanarrative when they compiled their own law collection, although they remained conservative in doing so.

3.2.4 Other Possibly Related Ordinances

In addition to ordinances directly dealing with slaves, the Exodus corpus also contains two ordinances possibly associated with servitude. Exodus 21:16 handles kidnapping, which may prevent people from being sold into servitude. Exodus 22:2 addresses theft, which may contrarily lead one into

148. Patrick, "Studying Biblical Law," 42; Albertz, *Exodus, Band II*, 96.

149. Averbeck, "Slavery," 426.

150. For instance, Prabhu, *Hybridity*, 16; see also §1.2.2.2.

151. §1.3.4.

such a condition. These ordinances again carry both similarities to and differences from extant cuneiform law collections. The similarities manifest the imperialized authors' broad acceptance of imperial legal traditions. Some similarities in Exodus 22:2 even disclose acceptance that leads to oppression. Nevertheless, the differences meanwhile reveal the imperialized authors' resistance to the imperial legal handling of similar offenses. They also suggest their attention to human trafficking and effort to treat thieves in a more humanitarian way.

3.2.4.1 Kidnapping (Exodus 21:16)

Exodus 21:16 is located among the ordinances concerning capital offenses, preceded by the ordinances regarding the release and servitude of slaves and followed by those handling physical assaults, including against slaves. This ordinance prescribes the execution of the kidnappers whether they have sold the kidnapped persons or still keep them.

Exodus 21:16

> And whoever steals a man, and he sells him or[152] he is found in his hand shall surely be put to death.

Acceptance of the Imperial Legal Metanarrative

The concern for kidnapping appears in various cuneiform laws, which deal with different victims, including slaves (LE 49; HL 20–21) and free persons (LH 14; HL 19a–19b). While the Hittite laws have a particular concern about abduction occurring between the lands of Luwiya and Hatti, LE 49 and LH 14 deal with kidnapping in general. The law in LE 49 gives special attention to a kidnapper being caught with the abducted person. The one in LH 14 imposes capital punishment on kidnapping a free person. The Hammurabi collection even situates this law among various capital offenses (LH 1–25).

LE 49

152. About understanding the conjunction ו as an expression of alternative, see Levinson, "Case for Revision," 46–47.

> If a man should be seized with a stolen slave or a stolen slave woman, a slave shall lead a slave, a slave woman shall lead a slave woman.[153]

LH 14

> If a man should steal the son/dependent/member of a free person/the free person class, he shall be killed.[154]

These laws indicate that cuneiform legal traditions are generally concerned with kidnapping, with some attention to the situation when the kidnapper is found with the abducted person and the requirement of executing the kidnapper if the victim is a free person. Exodus 21:16 reflects similar concerns and punishment, suggesting its authors' acceptance of imperial legal handling of kidnapping to a certain extent.

Resistance: Emphasizing Kidnappers' Responsibility

A slight difference between the Exodus ordinance and the cuneiform laws, however, reflects the imperialized authors' resistance to the imperial legal metanarrative alongside this broad acceptance. In addition to kidnapping a person in general (LH 14; HL 19a–21) and the situation where the victim is found in the kidnapper's hand (LE 49), Exodus 21:16 addresses the scenario in which the kidnapper has sold the abducted person.[155] This meticulous but unique consideration exhibits the effort to ensure the kidnapper is held accountable for his actions against others, which the cuneiform laws do not expend. It also echoes the condition of the introductory ordinance in which the audience buys a male slave (Exod 21:2), but suggests prevention of such sale enabled by kidnapping. This difference might exhibit an extension of the imperial legal handling of theft to kidnapping,[156] for in addition to dealing with a thief caught with stolen grain (LH 253), the Hammurabi collection handle a thief who has sold entrusted animals also (LH 265). More certainly,

153. Roth, *Law Collections*, 66.

154. Translation is mine. Regarding the meaning of *mār awīlum*, see §3.2.3.2 and page 142, note 144.

155. Regarding the two conditions as incompatible, D. Daube, however, argues that the condition in which the kidnapped person is found in the kidnapper's hand is a later addition to the ordinance which begins with a description of kidnapping in general and a condition in which the kidnapper has sold the kidnapped person (Daube, *Studies in Biblical Law*, 95).

156. Wright, *Inventing God's Law*, 198.

this difference reflects a resistance to the imperial legal underemphasis on the kidnapper's responsibility, especially in the situation where the kidnapper has sold the abducted person. It also suggests the imperialized authors' endeavor to curtail kidnapping, including that leading to the sale of people into servitude, among ordinances directly handling slaves, even though they did not totally abolish such sale in other cases.

3.2.4.2 Theft (Exodus 22:2)

Exodus 22:2 indeed requires selling the thief who cannot repay for stolen cattle. This ordinance belongs to the section handling theft and burglary, which follows the ordinances regarding goring oxen and negligence, including goring against slaves. This ordinance is immediately preceded by ordinances dealing with thieves who have slaughtered or sold the stolen cattle and burglars who are struck to death at different times (Exod 21:37–22:2). This ordinance is then followed by an ordinance handling thieves who still hold the stolen cattle in possession (Exod 22:3). The similarities and differences between these surrounding ordinances and extant cuneiform law collections indicate the biblical authors' particular considerations in handling theft and burglary in general, which offer an essential background for understanding the authorial response reflected in Exodus 22:2. Thus, I include these ordinances in the following analysis.

Exodus 21:37–22:3

> [37]When a man steals an ox or a sheep and he slaughters or sells it, five from the herd he shall repay for the oxen and four from the fold for the sheep
>
> [1](If while breaking in the thief is found, is struck, and dies, there is no bloodguilt for him,
>
> [2]If the sun has risen upon him, there is bloodguilt for him). He shall surely repay. If he has nothing, then he shall be sold because of what he has stolen.
>
> [3]If the thing stolen is actually found in his hand, either an ox, a donkey, or a sheep alive, he shall repay double.

Acceptance of the Imperial Legal Metanarrative

Theft and burglary are popular topics in cuneiform legal traditions.[157] For instance, MAL C 5 and 8 deal with thieves who have sold an animal they stole, and require them to repay.

MAL C 5 and 8

> [5][If a man should steal from] a meadow either an ox, or a donkey, or a horse, or any other animal not his own, and then sells it to another man at the prevailing price, and the purchaser is not aware (that it is stolen property) and he gives the man the prevailing price, the seller shall restore the stolen goods, as much as [. . .]
>
> [8][If a man should steal] either [. . .], or an animal, or anything else, and they prove the charges against him and find him guilty, he shall repay [the stolen goods]: they shall strike him 50 blows with rods; he shall perform [the king's service for x days]; the judges . . . shall render this judgment. [But if . . .] he/it should "reach" [. . . (in value?)], he shall return the stolen goods, as much as he stole, to the full value, as much as it may be; they shall impose upon him the punishment determined by the king.[158]

Multiplying the value of the stolen animal in the compensation is not uncommon among cuneiform laws (SLHF 3:13–15; LH 8). Some Hittite laws even demand different amounts of compensation for different types of animals (HL 59, 63, 67).

SLHF 3:13–15

---

157. Animal theft: SLHF 3:13–15; LH 8; MAL C 5, 8; HL 57–59, 63–65, 67–70, 81–83 (also LH 263–265, which address animal loss or theft related to a hired worker); theft or robbery of other objects: LH 6–8, LH 22–23, 259–260 (also LH 253–256, which handle crop theft committed by a hired worker); HL 92, 101–103, 121–133, 142–143; burglary: LL 9, LE 12–13, LH 21–23, HL 93–97. According to Hossein Badamchi, *šarāqum* (usually translated as "to steal") has various connotations, including abduction and false testimony (Badamchi, "Meaning of 'Theft,'" 369–86). However, in this analysis, I only consider cuneiform laws dealing with the taking of other's cattle or objects without permission in view of the content of the Exodus ordinances under investigation.

158. Roth, *Law Collections*, 183, 184.

If he steals a pig, he shall double (its value) as compensation.[159]

LH 8

If a man steals an ox, a sheep, a donkey, a pig, or a boat—if it belongs either to the god or to the palace, he shall give thirtyfold; if it belongs to a commoner, he shall replace it tenfold; if the thief does not have anything to give, he shall be killed.[160]

HL 59, 63, 67

[59]If anyone steals a ram, they used to give 30 sheep. Now he shall give [15] sheep: he shall give 5 ewes, 5 wethers and 5 lambs. And he shall look to his house for it.

[63]If anyone steals a plow ox, formerly they gave 15 cattle, but now he shall give 10 cattle: 3 two-year-olds, 3 yearlings, and 4 weanlings, and he shall look to his house for it.

[67]If anyone steals a cow, they used to give 12 oxen. Now he shall give 6 oxen: she shall give 2 two-year-old oxen, 2 yearling oxen, and 2 weanlings, and he shall look to this house for it.[161]

Noticeably, LH 8 specifies how to handle the thief who cannot repay. A similar specification also appears in LH 256, which deals with a theft committed by a hired worker.

LH 256

If he is not able to satisfy his obligation, they shall have him dragged around through that field by the cattle.[162]

Dealing also with hired workers, LH 253 addresses a situation where the stolen seed and feed are found in their possession:

LH 253

159. Roth, 49.

160. Roth, 82.

161. Hoffner, *Laws of the Hittites*, 71, 75, 77.

162. Roth, *Law Collections*, 129.

> If a man hires another man to care for his field, that is, he entrusts to him the stored grain, hands over to him care of the cattle, and contracts with him for the cultivation of the field—if that man steals the seed or fodder and it is then discovered in his possession, they shall cut off his hand.[163]

In addition to theft, cuneiform law collections also deal with burglary. The Laws of Eshnunna and the Laws of Hammurabi particularly contain laws requiring the execution of the burglar. The former imposes such punishment to the burglar seized at night but not daytime (LE 12–13). The latter demands such punishment for breaking into a house in general (LH 21).[164]

LE 12–13

> [12]A man who is seized in the field of a commoner among the sheaves at midday shall weigh and deliver 10 shekels of silver; he who is seized at night among the sheaves shall die, he will not live.
>
> [13]A man who is seized in the house of a commoner, within the house, at midday, shall weigh and deliver 10 shekels of silver; he who is seized at night within the house shall die, he will not live.[165]

LH 21

> If a man breaks into a house, they shall kill him and hang him in front of that very breach.[166]

These laws indicate that cuneiform legal traditions are generally concerned with theft and burglary. They usually require repayment for theft, and some of them multiply the value of the stolen animal depending on the animal type. The handling of thieves who cannot repay is also among their concerns. Execution of burglars is not unusual under cuneiform legal traditions, and the time when the burglary occurs is also a consideration. The Exodus ordinances carry a number of resemblances to these laws: concern about theft

163. Roth, 128.

164. The laws in LL 9 and HL 93–97 also handle burglary in general, but only require monetary penalties or bodily disfigurement.

165. Roth, *Law Collections*, 60–61.

166. Roth, 85.

and burglary, consideration of how a thief deals with a stolen animal, various requirements for repaying for the stolen animal, attention to the killing of the burglar at different times, and specification on how to treat a thief who cannot repay. Resemblances to cuneiform law collections thus occur not only in the ordinances concerning animal theft (Exod 21:37; 22:2b–3), but also in those concerning burglary (Exod 22:1–2a), which appears to be an interpolation or later addition.[167] These resemblances suggest an original connection of Exodus 22:1–2a to the surrounding ordinances in Exodus 21:37 and 22:2b–22:3. They also reflect that the imperialized authors were in sympathy with imperial legal understanding and treatment of animal theft and burglary in many aspects.

Resistance: Responsibility of Burglars and the Burglarized

Like other ordinances concerning slaves, this sympathy appears alongside resistance, which the ordinances' differences from the cuneiform laws indicate. A significant difference concerns the orientation of the burglary ordinances,[168] which offers a crucial background for understanding the requirement of selling the thief in Exodus 22:2. The cuneiform laws focus on the punishment of the burglar, whether monetary restitution or execution, whenever the crime was discovered. In contrast, Exodus 22:1 and 2 focus on the treatment of the burglarized who has fatally struck the burglar, stating bloodguilt is not involved in general, but is involved when it happens in the daytime. With this focus, the Exodus ordinances express that trespassing others' property is not an offense as serious as premeditated homicide, assaults against one's parents, or kidnapping, which all necessitate capital punishment (Exod 21:12, 21:15–17). However, with this focus, the Exodus ordinances simultaneously bring up the responsibility of the burglar, as well as that of the burglarized. The killing of the burglar involves no bloodguilt, if the burglarized kills the burglar at night, when the burglarized can hardly discern the nature of the breaking in; but the burglarized is responsible for the killing if he meets the burglar at daytime, which would allow the burglarized to identify that the

---

167. Greengus, *Laws in the Bible*, 211; Jackson, *Wisdom-Laws*, 306; Levinson, "Case for Revision," 48–51; Paul, *Studies in the Book of the Covenant*, 86. Daube, however, suggests that the ordinances in 22:2b–3 belong to later amendment (Daube, *Studies in Biblical Law*, 93). Against diachronic understandings of these ordinances, Baruch Halpern suggests that the ordinances are dealing with the liability of the burglar instead (Halpern, "Housebreaking Law," 247–50). However, the word דמים (bloodguilt) makes Halpern's reading very unlikely.

168. For similar understanding, see Paul, *Studies in the Book of the Covenant*, 87.

breaking in is burglary.[169] Thus, while burglary does not necessitate capital punishment, the burglar should still be responsible for his own crime against others. Meanwhile, although the burglarized is the victim at risk of losing his property, he still needs to value the burglar's life. This difference from the cuneiform laws thus reflects that the imperialized authors resisted imperial legal handling of burglary or nocturnal burglary as serious as a capital offense and their sole focus on the burglar's responsibility. While this difference does not suggest the Exodus ordinances' unconditional protection of human life,[170] it reveals their unique attention to the burglar's life as well as their endeavor to balance the responsibility of the burglar and the burglarized for it.

Ambivalence in Handling the Thief

The surrounding ordinances concerning theft (Exod 21:37; 22:2–3), including the requirement of selling the thief (Exod 22:2), reveal similar attention and endeavor, although this requirement concurrently exhibits oppressive features and compliance with imperial legal traditions. Exodus 21:37 handles not only the thief who sells a stolen animal (MAL C 5), but also the one who slaughters it. This additional consideration, similar to that in the kidnapping ordinance (Exod 21:16), expresses a particular emphasis on ensuring that the thief is held accountable for his theft, which the cuneiform law does not attend to. Yet, despite this emphasis on the thief's responsibility, the following ordinance does not impose life-threatening penalties on the thief who cannot afford the repayment, as their cuneiform counterparts do. Whereas LH 8 and LH 256 impose the death penalty and severe corporal punishment respectively on such thief, Exodus 22:2 demands to sell the thief. This requirement is notably the same as that in LH 54, which deals with the destruction of others' crops due to negligence.[171]

169. For similar understanding of the reason behind different treatments of burglary in Exod 22:1–2, see Alexander, *Exodus*, 493; Barmash, *Homicide*, 124. For other reasons, see Albertz, *Exodus, Band II*, 98 (the burglarized has opportunities to capture the burglar alive in daytime); Wright, *Inventing God's Law*, 260 (the burglar may intend to commit a crime beyond burglary at night); Paul, *Studies in the Book of the Covenant*, 87 (the burglarized might resort to homicide); Greenstein, "If the Sun Shone," 41 ("the sun has risen upon him" refers to sometime after the burglary occurs, when the killing is not a defense of property or life).

170. Rothenbusch, *Kasuistische Rechtssammlung*, 31.

171. See also Wright, *Inventing God's Law*, 234–35.

LH 54

> If he cannot replace the grain, they shall sell him and his property, and the residents of the common irrigated area whose grain crops the water carried away shall divide.[172]

Exodus 22:2 thus imposes on the thief a punishment that the cuneiform law demands in the case of negligence, requiring a lighter penalty from the thief than cuneiform laws do. This punishment expresses concern about the offender's life, which the burglary ordinances have already exhibited. The following ordinance continues to reveal this concern. While LH 253 requires cutting off the hand of the thief who still keeps the stolen object, Exodus 22:3 only demands monetary compensation. The ordinance that handles the thief who cannot fulfill their repayment (Exod 22:2) is thus surrounded by ordinances demonstrating concern for the thief's life. This concern is a motivation behind the requirement of selling the thief, to which cuneiform laws handling similar situations do not attend.

The sale of the thief, however, deserves some critique: while it saves the thief from corporal punishment, it does treat the thief as property.[173] Some scholars even associate this sale with Exodus 21:2, positing that the thief becomes a temporary slave in this case.[174] The similar treatment in LH 54, moreover, suggests the imperial nature of this requirement. The handling of the thief in Exodus 22:2, therefore, reveals that the imperialized authors resisted the imperial legal lack of concern about the life of such an offender, despite their general acceptance of the imperial legal concern about theft under different scenarios. However, their "the same but not quite" adoption remains oppressive, as they maintain some aspects of imperial legal traditions. This oscillation between accepting and resisting imperial legal traditions reveals the imperialized authors' ambivalence. This ambivalence potentially increased the incidence of people being sold into servitude, which the kidnapping ordinance particularly attempts to avoid. However, like this ordinance and other ordinances directly dealing with slaves, this ambivalence

172. Roth, *Law Collections*, 91–2.

173. Bridge, "Metaphoric Use of Slave Terms," 18.

174. Jackson, *Wisdom-Laws*, 299–302; Wright, *Inventing God's Law*, 234. Referring to Exod 22:1–3, Isaac Mendelsohn regards punishment for larceny as a means of acquiring slaves enumerated in the Pentateuch (Mendelsohn, *Slavery*, 1–6).

also indicates the imperialized authors' endeavor to work against the imperial legal metanarrative and to ameliorate the handling of the affected person when they compiled a law collection primarily for their own elite people during the ruling of the Neo-Assyrian Empire, even though this endeavor remains a conservative one.

3.3 Ordinances on Women

This conservatively resistive endeavor is also at work in the handling of women among the Exodus ordinances. They deal with women in cases concerning slaves, namely the release and servitude of male slaves' wives and daughters sold to be slaves (Exod 21:3–4, 21:7–11) and physical assault against female slaves by their owners and by others' oxen (Exod 21:20–21, 21:26–27, 21:32). They are also concerned about women in general when they address assaults against parents (Exod 21:15, 21:17), physical assault that leads to miscarriage (Exod 21:22–25), death caused by goring oxen (Exod 21:28–31), and the seduction of unbetrothed maidens (Exod 22:15–16). The Exodus ordinances thus deal with women of different statuses and roles, including slaves, slaves' wives, wives in general, mothers, and daughters.

In the previous section, I unfolded the endeavor of the conservative revolutionists in some of these ordinances. Those concerning slaves' wives (Exod 21:3–4) do reflect an acceptance of imperial legal handling of them and repression of the wives given by slave owners. However, the following ordinance regarding the male slaves' decision to stay (Exod 21:5) suggests subversion of the negative portrayal of slaves in the imperial legal metanarrative. This resistance brings about the male slaves' role in alleviating the restriction's impact on their wives. Similarly, the ordinances handling daughters sold as slaves (Exod 21:7–11) exhibit compliance with the imperial legal tolerance of such situation, which is oppressive to those daughters. Nevertheless, these ordinances simultaneously disclose resistance to imperial legal traditions' lack of consideration for female slaves by extending their protection for first wives and women of non-slave statuses to these daughters.

The ordinances concerning physical assault inflicted by slave owners (Exod 21:20–21, 21:26–27) consider such offense against both male and female slaves and impose the same penalties on the slave owners in both cases. The ordinance addressing non-immediately fatal assault (Exod 21:21) does indicate compliance with the imperial legal principle of treating slaves as their owners' property, which is oppressive to both male and female slaves. Yet, overall, the ordinances manifest resistance to the imperial legal lack of concern about physical assault against male and female slaves caused by slave owners. This resistance uniquely brings about the execution of slave owners in cases of fatal assault (Exod 21:20) and the release of the male and female slaves who have sustained bodily damage (Exod 21:26–27). The goring oxen ordinances meanwhile particularly reflect resistance to imperial legal traditions' omission of females or use of male terms for implying females in the address of the victims (Exod 21:28–32). These ordinances do reveal acceptance of the imperial legal handling of goring against slaves with monetary compensation, which seems to equate enslaved people with fiscal property. However, they also indicate resistance to the imperial legal presentation of the death caused by goring oxen merely as negligence and business issues and the imperial legal consideration of the ox owners' interest. These resistances disclose a unique concern about human life of both genders.

In the following analysis, I examine other Exodus ordinances concerning women in general. These ordinances do suggest the subordination of women to men in some cases, but they also exhibit resistance to imperial legal traditions amid acceptance of them, revealing the imperialized authors' concerns for women. These features characterize further the Exodus ordinances as a work of the conservative revolutionists among the imperialized.

3.3.1 Assaults against Parents (Exodus 21:15, 21:17)

Exodus 21:15 and 17 deal with assaults against parents, both fathers and mothers. It is possible that both ordinances are concerned with the refusal to accept parental authority,[175] but Exodus 21:15 particularly handles physical assault, while Exodus 21:17 deals with dishonoring or repudiating (קלל; curse) parent in a non-physical way.[176] These ordinances follow those concerning homicide and surround the one handling kidnapping, constituting a section dealing with capital offenses. This section is preceded by the ordinances addressing servitude and followed by those handling other physical assaults. As

175. Fleishman, "Offences Against Parents," 7–37.

176. Propp, *Exodus 19–40*, 213–14; Alexander, *Exodus*, 482.

aforementioned, these ordinances are concerned with both men and women, including male and female slaves, pregnant women, and sons and daughters.

Exodus 21:15, 21:17

> [15]And whoever strikes his father or his mother shall surely be put to death.
>
> [17]And whoever curses his father or his mother shall be put to death.

Acceptance of the Imperial Legal Metanarrative

Both Sumerian and Akkadian laws handle assaults against parents (SLEx 4; LH 192–193, 195). The Sumerian law and LH 192–193 handle children's rejection or hatred of an adopted father or mother, while LH 195 deals with children's physical attack against their father, without specifying whether he is a biological or adoptive father.

SLEx 4

> If he (the adopted son) declares to his father and mother, "You are not my father," or "You are not my mother," he shall forfeit house, field, orchard, slaves, and possessions, and they shall sell him for silver (into slavery) for his full value.[177]

LH 192–193, 195

> [192]If the child of a courtier or the child of a *sekretu* should say to the father who raised him or to the mother who raised him, "You are not my father," or "You are not my mother," they shall cut out his tongue.
>
> [193]If the child of a courtier or the child of a *sekretu* identifies with his father's house and repudiates[178] the father who raised him or the mother who raised him and departs for this father's house, they shall pluck out his eye.

177. Roth, *Law Collections*, 44

178. The primary meaning of *zêru* is "to dislike, to hate, to avoid." See "*zêru*," *CAD* 21:97–99. See also Kitchen and Lawrence, *Treaty, Law, and Covenant*, 161; Richardson, *Hammurabi's Laws*, 103.

[195]If a child should strike his father, they shall cut off his hand.[179]

These laws indicate that cuneiform legal traditions are concerned about assaults against parents, both mentally and physically. Resembling the cases that these laws handle, the Exodus ordinances suggest that the imperialized authors accepted the imperial legal concern about assaults against parents.

Resistance: Seriousness of Assaulting One's Father and Mother

Nevertheless, the Exodus ordinances differ from their cuneiform counterparts in some ways, which indicate their authors' resistance to imperial legal ways of handling assaults against parents. Rather than stipulating property forfeiture, sale into slavery, or bodily mutilation as the cuneiform laws do, Exodus 21:15 and 17 prescribe capital punishment. This unique penalty underlines the seriousness of both physical and mental assaults against parents in a way that the cuneiform laws do not emphasize, even though LH 195 also deals with parents not limited to adopted ones as the Exodus ordinances do. Moreover, unlike LH 195, which only spells out the physical assault against a father, Exodus 21:15 addresses that against the mother also. If this consideration is due to the fact that the biblical authors were aware of the legal traditions somehow reflected in SLEx 4 and LH 192–193, which handle both parents in cases concerning verbal and emotional assaults, Exodus 21:15 reflects an extension of this imperial consideration to the case on physical assault. This extension expresses gender equality or inclusiveness for all ordinances concerning parents,[180] to which the imperial legal tradition reflected in LH 195 does not attend.

3.3.2 Physical Assault against Pregnant Women (Exodus 21:22–25)

Another significant series of ordinances dealing with women is Exodus 21:22–25, which handles physical assault against pregnant women. The main ordinance (Exod 21:22) addresses assault that affects the pregnancy and requires a fine. The subordinate ordinance (Exod 21:23–25) tackles additional afflictions and presents the penalties in a talion formula. These ordinances are preceded

179. Roth, *Law Collections*, 120.

180. Paul, *Studies in the Book of the Covenant*, 65; Anderson, *Women*, 28; Peled, *Law and Gender*, 34.

by those concerning physical assault in general, including that against male and female slaves, and followed by those concerning bodily damages against them and fatal goring against male and female of various statuses.

Exodus 21:22–25

> [22]And when men fight and they knock a pregnant woman and her children come out but there is no other harm, he shall surely be fined according to what the husband of the woman laid upon him and/or he shall give as mediators determine.
>
> [23]But if there is harm, then you shall give life for life,
>
> [24]eye for eye, tooth for tooth, hand for hand, foot for foot,
>
> [25]burn for burn, bruise for bruise, wound for wound.

Acceptance of the Imperial Legal Metanarrative

A number of cuneiform laws deal with physical assault leading to miscarriage. Their main laws handle miscarriage in general and require monetary compensation (LL d; LH 209, 211; MAL A 50; HL 17). Their subordinate laws then address other scenarios and demand different penalties (LL e; LH 210, 211; MAL A 50–51; HL 17).[181]

LL d–e

> [d]If [a . . .] strikes the daughter of a free person and causes her to lose her fetus, he shall weigh and deliver ½ mina of silver.
>
> [e]If she dies, that free person shall be killed.

LH 209–212

> [209]If a free person strikes the daughter of a free person and causes her to miscarry her fetus, he shall weigh and deliver 10 shekels of silver for her fetus.
>
> [210]If that woman has died, they shall kill his daughter.
>
> [211]If he causes a daughter of a commoner to miscarry her fetus by a blow, he shall weigh and deliver 5 shekels of silver.

181. Translation of the following laws is mine.

[212]If that woman has died, he shall weigh and deliver 30 shekels of silver.

MAL A 21, 50–51

[21]If a free person strikes the daughter of a free person and causes her to miscarry her fetus, and they prove the charges against him and find him guilty, he shall give 2 talents 30 minas of lead; they shall strike him 50 blows with rods; he shall perform the king's service for one full month.

[50][If a free person] strikes [a woman] causing her to miscarry [her fetus], [the wife of] a free person [. . .] and they shall tre[at him] a[s he treat]ed her; he shall make full payment of a life for her fetus. And if that woman dies, they shall kill that free person; he shall make full payment of a life for her fetus. And if there is no son of that woman's husband, and his wife whom he struck miscarried her fetus, they shall kill the assailant for her fetus. If her fetus was a female, he shall make full payment of a life.

[51]If a free person strikes the wife of a free person who does not raise her child, causing her to miscarry her fetus, it is a crime; he shall give 2 talents of lead.

HL 17

If anyone causes a woman to miscarry, [if] it is her tenth month, he shall pay 10 shekels of silver, if it is her fifth month, he shall pay 5 shekels of silver. He shall look to his house for it.

Noticeably, LL e, LH 210, and MAL A 50 demand execution of the assailant or the assailant's daughter if the assault leads to the death of a woman belonging to a free person. Moreover, preceding LH 209–121 and following MAL A 50 are laws applying the talion principle. Those in LH 196, 197, and 200 address bodily assaults against a free person, whereas MAL A 52 handles the physical assault that makes a prostitute miscarry. This Middle

Assyrian law specifically presents its treatment of the assailant as "blow for blow (*miḫṣī kî miḫṣī*)."[182]

LH 196–197, 200

> [196]If a free person has blinded the eye of another free person, they shall blind his eye.
>
> [197]If he has broken another free person's bone, they shall break his bone.
>
> [200]If a free person has kocked out the tooth of another free person, his fellow of the same status, they shall knock out his tooth.

MAL A 52

> If a free person strikes a prostitute and causes her to miscarry her fetus, they shall inflict upon him blow for blow, he shall make full payment of a life.

These laws indicate that physical assault causing miscarriage and the death of pregnant women is a concern among cuneiform legal traditions. They generally require monetary compensation for miscarriage and demand capital punishment for fatal assault against a woman belonging to a free person, with some application of the talion principle to such losses or other physical assaults. The Exodus ordinances reflect a similar concern and requirement, as well as the use of the talion formula, suggesting the imperialized authors' acceptance of the imperial legal metanarrative to a certain extent.

Resistance: Addressing the Woman According to Her Condition Specific to the Assault

Nevertheless, the Exodus ordinances differ from those cuneiform laws in some ways, which reflect resistance to the imperial legal metanarrative amid this acceptance. Some resistive attempts remain oppressive to women, but others suggest unique considerations for them. One of these attempts concerns the description of the woman. The main ordinance's protasis uniquely describes the woman as אשה הרה (a pregnant woman, Exod 21:22). This qualification contrasts with those in the cuneiform laws, which mostly address the women according to their statuses: dumu-munus lú-ka (the

182. Translation of the following laws is mine.

daughter of a free person, LL d), *mārat awīlim* (the daughter of a free person, LH 209), *mārat muškēnim* (the daughter of a commoner, LH 211); *mārat a'īle* (the daughter of a free person, MAL A 21), *aššat a'ile* (the wife of a free person, MAL A 50–51). The lack of status-related qualification in Exodus 21:22 may be due to the fact that its authors lived in a society less stratified than their imperial counterparts, including the Neo Assyrian Empire. In this case, however, the biblical authors could simply leave out the qualification. If they attempted to find a substitute for the status-related qualification used among cuneiform legal traditions, they could also describe the woman as, for instance, "the wife of a man." Uniquely describing the woman as pregnant suggests a concern for the woman focused on her physical condition specific to the assault, rather than her social status or her relationship with a man.[183] This subtle difference from the cuneiform laws reveals resistance to the imperial legal way of presenting the physical assault against pregnant women, as well as a more caring, if not more respectful, way of addressing them.

Resistance: Involving the Husband and Mediators in Penalty Assessment

The following arrangement of the fine, however, does not continue to express similar care for the women, even though the involvement of women's husband and/or the mediators is also unique to the Exodus ordinance. The meaning of פללים has attracted various scholarly suggestions,[184] as פללים occurs only in Exodus 21:22 in the Old Testament. However, the use of פלל in the Old Testament indicates a meaning related to a kind of intercession or mediation, which is suitable for the ordinance's context.[185] The conjunction ו in the description of the penalty may indicate an alternative rather than consecutive

183. This focus may explain why the Exodus ordinances do not address similar assault against female slaves, as cuneiform laws do (LL f, LH 213–214, HL 18). Another possible reason is the mentioned focus on assault inflicted by slave owners (see §3.2.3.1). Without further evidence, the reason is difficult to ascertain. It might be the case that Exod 21:22–25 also cover female slaves. However, the ordinances handling non-fatal assault, bodily damages, and goring oxen suggest that the biblical authors did treat some assaults against slaves differently. Exod 21:22 indeed refers to the man as the husband (בעל), while Exod 21:8 addresses the man as the owner (אדון).

184. Wright, *Inventing God's Law*, 180; Jackson, *Wisdom-Laws*, 222–27; Paul, *Studies in the Book of the Covenant*, 71–72; Speiser, "Stem *PLL*," 301–6.

185. Bovati, *Re-Establishing Justice*, 175–76; Rothenbusch, *Kasuistische Rechtssammlung*, 276–77; Schwienhorst-Schönberger, *Bundesbuch*, 122. The judicial connotation of this word, which Bible translators usually adopt, is not clear; see Gerstenberger, "פלל *pll*," 567–77.

relationship, that is, "or" rather than "and." But in either case, the penalty is subject to someone's decision, and it is distinct from corresponding cuneiform laws that specify the fine's amount (LL d; LH 209, 211; HL 17) or type ("a full payment of a life," MAL A 50), even though Exodus 21:22 similarly underlines the importance of fining the assailant by using the absolute complement ענוש יענש "he shall surely be fined."

Exodus 21:22 thus has a peculiar emphasis on subjecting the amount of the penalty to someone's decision, similar to the ransom in the goring oxen ordinance (Exod 21:30). However, unlike this ordinance, Exodus 21:22 specifies the persons as the husband and/or mediators. This emphasis possibly reflects the interest of the authors and the audience, who were likely to be husbands or mediators. It may also imply oppression against the woman, as the decision involves her husband and indicates the subordination of women to men.[186] If the mediators are likely to be men, this subordination is even more prominent. Thus, while Exodus 21:22 differs from the cuneiform laws in the compensation arrangement, indicating the imperialized authors' resistance to the imperial legal handling of it for physical assault against pregnant women, this difference reflects a resistance potentially oppressive to these women, putting the decision of their compensation under men's authority.

Resistance: Broader Concern about the Woman's Condition

Despite this, the subordinate ordinance (Exod 21:23–25) continues to reflect differences from cuneiform laws, which express the imperialized authors' broader concern for the assaulted woman. The meaning of אסון is ambiguous due to its rare occurrence in the biblical text.[187] However, based on the use of this word in Genesis 42:4, 42:38 and 44:29 and the content of the talion formula in Exodus 21:23–25, I follow some scholars' suggestion that it refers to harm including but not limited to death.[188] This harm may refer to that afflicted not only on the woman but also on the fetus(es), due to the ambiguous meaning of the phrase ויצאו ילדיה "and her children come

186. Anderson, *Women*, 38; Phillips, "Aspects of Family," 351; Streete, *Strange Woman*, 34.

187. Teeter, *Scribal Laws*, 146–47.

188. Albertz, *Exodus, Band II*, 94; Alexander, *Exodus*, 485. For other understandings, see Jackson, "Problem of Exod. XXI 22–5," 276 (serious injuries to someone not directly involved in the fight); Westbrook, "Lex Talionis and Exodus," 345 (harm caused by unknown assailant); Wright, *Inventing God's Law*, 178; Houtman, *Exodus*, 3:168 (fatal and accidental harm); Cohen, "Ancient Critical Understanding," 437–48 (tragic death).

out" (Exod 21:22). This expression, which has no other occurrence in the Old Testament but somewhat echoes the cuneiform idiomatic expression *ša libbiša uštaddīši* "cause her to drop her fetus" (LH 209, 211),[189] may refer to miscarriage or premature birth.[190] Nevertheless, in either case, the ordinances do consider harm inflicted upon a woman. The handling of this harm in the Exodus ordinances suggests that they cover a broader spectrum of injury to the woman than the subordinate laws of corresponding cuneiform laws, which only handle her death in addition to the loss of the fetus (LL e; LH 210, 212; MAL A 50).

The following talion formula in the Exodus ordinance further evidences this broader concern for the woman's condition. Although this talion formula might be applicable to physical assault in general,[191] the appearance of אסון in both Exodus 21:22 and 21:23 and the absence of a break between Exodus 21:23 and 21:24 suggest that the Exodus ordinance does apply the talion formula to the assault against the pregnant women.[192] Whether the phrase ונתתה "and you shall give" indicates vicarious punishment or a monetary penalty is subject to debate.[193] However, the use of a second-person reference clearly emphasizes the responsibility and involvement of the audience (who were likely to be exclusively men), drawing their attention to the lengthy talion principle that reveals the compensation they would need to make if they

189. Translation is mine. The phrase "*libbiša*" literally means "her heart" but idiomatically refers to the fetus; see "*libbu* in *ša libbiša*," *CAD* 9: 175–76. The laws in MAL A 51–52 have a similar expression: *libbiša ušaṣlīši* (cause her to drop her fetus).

190. For a summary of scholarly understandings, see Alexander, *Exodus*, 483–84. For regarding it as premature birth, see Cassuto, *Exodus*, 275. About the plural reference, ילדיה, which can be understood as multiple pregnancies or a way of referring to the fetus, see Schwienhorst-Schönberger, *Bundesbuch*, 97–98; Schwienhorst-Schönberger, "Auge um Auge," 164–65; Wright, *Inventing God's Law*, 178.

191. Albertz, *Exodus, Band II*, 94–95; Lee, "Diachrony and Exegesis," 50–51; Barmash, *Homicide*, 159.

192. Referring to the Eshnunna collection's structure, Barry L. Eichler even suggests that the ordinances in Exod 21:22–25, including their use of אסון and the talion formula, cover a broad spectrum of the women's injuries in order to create a bridge between the preceding and the following ordinances (Eichler, "Exodus 21:22–25," 24–29).

193. Regarding this phrase and the following talion formula as an indication of monetary compensation, see Wright, *Inventing God's Law*, 182; Lafont, "Ancient Near Eastern Laws," 117; Rothenbusch, *Kasuistische Rechtssammlung*, 58. For their indication of vicarious punishment, see Jackson, *Wisdom-Laws*, 193; Anderson, *Women*, 71. For their ambiguity, see Otto, "Aspects of Legal Reforms," 185; Paul, *Studies in the Book of the Covenant*, 72. For understanding them according to the distinction between restitution and retaliation, see Hayes, *Interpreting Ancient Israelite History*, 260–62.

caused any harm to a pregnant woman during a fight.[194] Moreover, while the talion formula in Exodus 21:23–25 addresses some items that the cuneiform talion laws deal with,[195] it includes more affected body parts and types of injuries than they do: life, eye, tooth, hand, foot, burn, bruise, and wound in Exodus 21:23–25, versus life in LL e, LH 210, MAL A 50, eye, bone, and tooth in LH 196, 197, 200, and blow in MAL A 52.

This lengthy talion principle, together with the concern about harm (injuries not limited to death) to the woman, suggests the Exodus ordinances' attempt to cover the injuries to the woman as comprehensively as possible. This attempt reflects the ordinance's particular concern for the woman's physical well-being, which the ordinance uniquely brings into the male audience's attention and the cuneiform express limitedly. These distinctions from cuneiform laws, together with the address of the woman and the arrangement of the fine, reflect that the imperialized authors resisted imperial legal handling of the physical assault against pregnant women, even though they broadly accepted it. The involvement of the woman's husband and the mediators in the decision of the fine does subordinate the woman to men, but the address of the woman according to her condition specific to the assault and extra attention to her injuries express caring concerns for her, to which the imperial legal metanarrative do not attend.

3.3.3 Seduction of Unbetrothed Maidens (Exodus 22:15–16)

The last ordinances in Exodus 21:2–22:16 continue to deal with issues about women and reflect a similar kind of resistance to imperial legal traditions. Located after property ordinances, Exodus 21:15 handles the situation where a man seduces and sleeps with an unbetrothed maiden by requiring him to pay the bride price for her to be his wife. Exodus 21:16 then tackles the circumstance when the maiden's father refuses to marry her to the man. In this case, the man still has to pay the bride price.

194. This emphasis offers another angle for reflecting on whether the talion law permits people to avenge any assault by means of equivalent retaliation. For a recent ethical discussion of this talion law, see Jacobs, "Talionic Principle," 26–30.

195. This resemblance to cuneiform laws queries the notion that Exod 21:24–25 is a later addition. For this notion, see for instance, Otto, "Town and Rural Countryside," 15. Jackson also argues for the same notion; however, he concurrently suggests that the talion formula as a whole originates in the oral sphere (Jackson, *Wisdom-Laws*, 185–89, 196–207).

Exodus 22:15–16

> [15]And when a man seduces a maiden who is not betrothed and sleeps with her, he shall surely pay the bride price for her to be his wife.
>
> [16]If her father absolutely refuses to give her to him, he shall weight out silver according to the bride price of maidens.

Acceptance of the Imperial Legal Metanarrative

Some Sumerian and Middle Assyrian laws possibly handle cases involving unbetrothed women who are involved in illegitimate sex acts (SLEx 7–8; MAL A 55–56). The Sumerian laws focus on whether the parents identify the man and require them to give their daughter to him in marriage if he declares such a wish. The Middle Assyrian laws similarly demand the father to give his daughter to the man if the man is married. They then require the man to pay triple the maiden's value and marry her if he is single. The laws demand him to make the same payment, even if the maiden's father does not want him to marry her.

SLEx 7–8

> [7]If he deflowers in the street the daughter of a man, her father and her mother do not identify (?) him, (but) he declares, "I will marry you"—her father and her mother shall give her to him in marriage.
>
> [8]If he deflowers in the street the daughter of a man, her father and her mother identify (?) him, (but) the deflowerer disputes the identification (?)—he shall swear an oath . . . at the temple gate.[196]

MAL A 55–56

> [55]If a man forcibly seizes and rapes a maiden who is residing in her father's house, [. . .] who is not betrothed(?), whose [womb(?)] is not opened, who is not married, and against whose father's house there is no outstanding claim—whether within

196. Roth, *Law Collections*, 44.

> the city or in the countryside, or at night whether in the main thoroughfare, or in a granary, or during the city festival—the father of the maiden shall take the wife of the fornicator of the maiden and hand her over to be raped: he shall not return her to her husband, but he shall take (and keep?) her; the father shall give his daughter who is the victim of fornication into the protection of the household of her fornicator. If he (the fornicator) has no wife, the fornicator shall give "triple" the silver as the value of the maiden to her father: her fornicator shall marry her; he shall not reject (?) her. If the father does not desire it so, he shall receive "triple" silver for the maiden, and he shall give his daughter in marriage to whomever he chooses.
>
> [56]If a maiden should willingly give herself to a man, the man shall so swear; they shall have no claim to his wife; the fornicator shall pay "triple" the silver as the value of the maiden; the father shall treat his daughter in whatever manner he chooses.[197]

These laws indicate that cuneiform legal traditions are concerned about handling illegitimate sex acts occurring among unbetrothed maidens, with attention to their marriage, the monetary penalty, and their parents' involvement. The Exodus ordinances reflect a similar concern and attention, with particular resemblances to the Middle Assyrian Laws. The Exodus ordinances use not only the absolute complement מהר ימהרנה (he shall surely pay the bride price for her, Exod 22:15) to emphasize the man's responsibility, but also the noun מהר (bride price, Exod 22:16) to indicate his same liability even if the father refuses to give his daughter to him. These three occurrences of the root מהר resemble the three mentions of the threefold silver in relation to the maiden's value in MAL A 55–56. The handling of the father's refusal with the same requirement on the bride price is also similar to that in MAL A 55. These similarities suggest that the imperialized authors accepted some aspects of imperial legal traditions. This acceptance makes the ordinances susceptible to being oppressive to women. Although the attention on the bride price and the father does not necessarily suggest that the Exodus ordinances

197. Roth, 174–5.

treat the maiden as property,[198] it draws the focus of the ordinances away from the maiden's voice and subjects her to her father's authority,[199] similar to what imperial legal traditions do. The imperialized authors thus apparently do not work against the imperial legal metanarrative to promote the agency of women in their sexual and marital life.

Resistance: Unique Concern about Seduction of Maidens

Nevertheless, the Exodus ordinances address a condition divergent from what the cuneiform laws handle, reflecting that this acceptance is a selective one embedded with resistance. The Sumerian laws deal with rape (SLEx 7–8). The Middle Assyrian laws address non-consensual sex on the one hand (MAL A 55) and consensual sex on the other (MAL A 56). In contrast, Exodus 22:15 and 16 handle a man seducing the maiden. There are various understandings of the meaning of פתה (Exod 22:15),[200] but this word undoubtedly suggests a circumstance where neither the man takes a forcible initiative, nor the woman makes a voluntary offer. The Exodus ordinances thus bring up a circumstance different from the Sumerian laws and somewhat in between what the Middle Assyrian laws handle. This distinctive concern reflects that the imperialized authors resisted imperial ways of addressing illegitimate sexual acts that happened among unbetrothed women, filling the gap in imperial legal traditions.

This resistance is, however, susceptible to being oppressive or even more oppressive than imperial legal traditions. For this legal resistance does not approach rape, which those cuneiform laws do handle. This oppressive nature remains even if the Exodus ordinances were intended to offer a basis for the ordinances on female slaves to impose a restriction on their release and require various protective measures for them,[201] or emphasize the ne-

198. Some scholars suggest that the Exodus ordinances treat the maiden as property; for instance, Houtman, *Exodus*, 3:206; Marshall, *Israel*, 130; Paul, *Studies in the Book of the Covenant*, 96. However, others regard the bride price as a "marriage present" or "the husband's contribution," although there is no strong evidence; for instance, Rendsburg, *How the Bible is Written*, 582, note 22; Davidson, *Flame of Yahweh*, 249; Vaux, *Ancient Israel*, 26–27; Emmerson, "Women in Ancient Israel," 382–83. A better argument against the understanding that the Exodus ordinances treat the maiden as property is the requirement of marrying the maiden; see for instance, Childs, *Book of Exodus*, 477. Notably, marrying the maiden is also a requirement of MAL A 55.

199. Mathew, *Biblical Law Codes*, 208; Anderson, *Women*, 69; Anderson, *Ancient Laws*, 33.

200. Fleishman, "Exodus 22:15–16," 64.

201. Wright, *Inventing God's Law*, 131.

cessity of providing a permanent status to a woman when a man has sexual intercourse with her.[202] Still, this resistance uniquely brings to attention a situation where a man takes an illegitimate initiative to have sex with a maiden or even deceives her into having it.[203] This situation may not be serious enough for attracting legal concern, thus imperial legal traditions do not deal with it, but it still involves men's mistreatment of women, which the imperialized authors particularly addressed.

Resistance: Limiting Father's Role and Authority

In addition to this unique attention, the Exodus ordinances also differ from the cuneiform laws in addressing the father's role in the case and his authority over his daughter. These differences suggest resistance to the imperial legal emphasis on them, even though the ordinances do not mention the mother as the Sumerian laws do and may aim at securing the father's rights.[204] Concerning the father's role in the case, the ordinances peculiarly do not explicitly indicate the father as the bride price's recipient, even though some scholars assume or argue that he is the beneficiary.[205] This lack of specification contrasts with the Middle Assyrian laws, as MAL A 55 not only overtly states that the man shall give the threefold bride price "to her father" (*ana abiša*), but also spells out that "he [the father] shall receive" (*imaḫḫar*) the same threefold bride price if he refuses to give his daughter to the man. These explicit mentions clearly imply that the father is also the recipient of the threefold compensation in MAL A 56. The lack of specification on the bride price's recipient in Exodus 22:15–16, while not indicating that the bride price is for the daughter's benefit,[206] reflects that the Exodus ordinances downplay the father's role in receiving the bride price. This undermining of the father's role is consistent with Bernard S. Jackson's understanding that these Exodus

202. Jackson, *Wisdom-Laws*, 342.

203. Fleishman, "Exodus 22:15–16," 64.

204. Albertz, *Exodus, Band II*, 100.

205. Scholars who assume so include Houtman, *Exodus*, 3:209; Albertz, *Exodus, Band II*, 101; Noth, *Exodus*, 185. Jackson makes such argument based on a rabbinic tradition (Jackson, *Wisdom-Laws*, 376).

206. Scholars who suggest that this bride price was intended for the woman's benefit usually refer to Gen 31:15. Durham, *Exodus*, 327; Vaux, *Ancient Israel*, 27. See also Jackson's discussion in *Wisdom-Laws*, 376.

ordinances aim to infringe on the father's economic interests.[207] It also reveals the imperialized authors' resistance to the imperial emphasis on a father's role in dealing with compensation for sexual offenses against his daughter.

In fact, the Exodus ordinances also put less emphasis on the father's authority in dealing with his seduced daughter. While the absolute complement מאן ימאן (he absolutely refuses) does not represent the two refusals made by the father and the daughter respectively as some rabbis suggest,[208] Exodus 22:16 peculiarly does not explain further what the father can do to his daughter as the Middle Assyrian laws do. Under the condition in which the father refuses to give his daughter to the rapist, MAL A 55 states further that the father "shall give his daughter in marriage to whomever he chooses" (*mārassu ana ša ḫadiuni iddan*). In the case which the maiden willingly offers herself to the man, MAL A 56 also stipulates that the father "shall treat his daughter in whatever manner he chooses" (*māras[su] kî ḫadiuni epp[aš]*). Exodus 22:16's address of the father's refusal without further explanation on what he can do to his daughter again undermines the father's authority over his daughter, as compared to the Middle Assyrian laws.

These differences of the Exodus ordinances from the cuneiform laws therefore suggest that the imperialized authors resisted the imperial legal neglect of men's seduction of unbetrothed women, as well as the imperial legal emphasis on a father's role and authority. The ordinances' silence on rape is potentially oppressive, which necessitates an ethical critique. However, their authors distinctively brought up the case in which a man makes a nonforcible but illegitimate sexual initiative against an unbetrothed woman without putting too much emphasis on the father's role in receiving the bride price and granting him excessive authority over his daughter. This resistance may not appear to be totally liberative by itself and may still raise an inquiry into the self-serving motives behind the ordinances, especially when the ordinances remain compliant with imperial legal traditions in ignoring the maiden's voice. However, it does suggest a resistive and liberative attempt, particularly regarding the underemphasis on the father's economic benefit and his authority over the maiden, which may work against the authors and audience's interests. This attempt, like those manifested in other Exodus ordinances

207. Jackson, *Wisdom-Laws*, 382.

208. Greengus, *Laws in the Bible*, 67.

handling women and slaves, reveals the conservatively revolutionary endeavor of the imperialized authors in response to the imperial legal metanarrative when they compiled a law collection primarily for their elite audience under the shadow of the Neo-Assyrian Empire.

3.4 Chapter Conclusions

Analyzing Exodus 21:2–22:16 from the perspective of the imperialized, this study suggests that the similarities and differences between these ordinances and extant cuneiform law collections reveal the imperialized authors' simultaneous acceptance of and resistance to the imperial legal handling of issues pertaining to slaves and women. The imperialized authors were in sympathy with imperial legal traditions' concerns for slaves and women, their formulation of related laws, and their treatments of these people, to a certain extent. However, they concurrently resisted some imperial legal discriminatory perceptions of and repressive approaches to these people, urging their elite audience to ameliorate these people's conditions among the imperialized.

This "the same but not quite" mimicry remains potentially oppressive to slaves and women in some cases. The Exodus ordinances only deal with maintaining master-slave relationships without abolishing the slavery institution. They are concerned only with native debt slaves and stipulate a longer servitude period than their imperial peers. They, moreover, exempt slave owners from punishment for non-immediately fatal physical assault against their own slaves. They impose a less serious penalty for habitual goring against slaves than they do for such offense against other people. They require selling the thief who cannot make restitution, susceptibly leading him to become a temporary slave. As some scholars note, the Exodus ordinances also do not question male dominance in their society.[209] They do not prohibit fathers from selling their daughters to be slaves, but impose restrictions on the release of these female slaves and slaves' wives. They subordinate pregnant women to their husbands and male mediators. They also ignore unbetrothed maidens' voice and remain silent on their rape. These possibly oppressive treatments raise questions on self-serving motives behind the ordinances. They are also mostly related to the acceptance of or ambivalence toward

209. Ween, *Battered Love*, 86.

oppressive legal principles handed down by the empires. This acceptance and ambivalence amid the attempted resistance manifest the struggle of the imperialized authors.

Even so, the Exodus ordinances reveal resistance to imperial legal traditions, which manifests their effort to handle offenses in more liberative or considerate ways than their imperial counterparts. The ordinances prioritize concerns about slaves. They put a stronger emphasis on slave owners' responsibility to handle their slaves properly and uniquely bring it to the elite audience's attention. They work against the imperial legal metanarrative by focusing on the imperialized people, rather than the imperial people – the Assyrians, who fall into debt service. They subvert the imperial legal metanarrative by appealing to their own tradition for determining the servitude length and emphasizing the release of the male slave and his wife. The positive portrayal of the male slave subverts the negative presentation of slaves in imperial legal traditions, as well as exhibits a possibility for the male slave to alleviate the impact of the restriction on the release of his wife and children. The restriction on the release of the female slave, meanwhile, is an extension of the imperial legal protection for first wives. The rest of the ordinances on female slaves extend further imperial legal protections for women of non-slave statuses to female slaves, offering them freedom when their owners fail to provide these protections.

The Exodus ordinances, moreover, uniquely address slave owners' physical assault against their own male and female slaves and impose capital punishment for fatal physical assault. They even distinctively demand the release of the slaves if their owner destroys their body parts. These ordinances reveal again a stronger attention to slave owners' responsibility to their slaves. They also reflect a liberative approach to injured slaves, which imperial legal traditions do not offer. Likewise, the Exodus ordinances uniquely prescribe stoning of the ox for accustomed goring against male and female slaves just as they do for such offense against other people. The goring oxen ordinances as a whole indeed exhibit their authors' tendency to resist the imperial legal emphasis on economic concerns, which were certainly the key concerns of the Neo-Assyrian Empire also. Like those concerning servitude and physical assault caused by slave owners, these ordinances underscore ox owners' responsibility and the imperialized people's traditions instead. They also emphasize communal participation in the execution of the ox and attend to victims of both genders and different statuses, indicating an attention to the people which imperial legal traditions lack. The ordinance concerning kidnapping continues to show stronger emphasis on the offender's responsibility, preventing the sale of people into servitude, which imperial legal traditions do not particularly address. The treatment of the thief may contrarily increase such sale. Yet, it saves the thief from life-threatening punishments, which imperial legal traditions otherwise impose.

In addition to slaves' wives, female slaves, and female victims of goring, the Exodus ordinances also reflect liberative or considerate resistance to imperial legal traditions in their handling of mothers, pregnant women, and unbetrothed maidens. The ordinances uniquely include mothers when they handle physical assault against parents and impose death punishment on such offense. They also distinctively address the pregnant woman according to her condition specific to the assault, rather than her social status or her relationship with a man. They bring a broader concern about her physical condition to their male audience's attention than their imperial counterparts. The ordinances on the unbetrothed maiden address her seduction, which imperial legal traditions do not handle. They limit her father's role in dealing with the bride price and his authority over her, resisting the imperial legal emphasis on such patriarchal role and authority.

Together with the acceptances of imperial legal traditions, these resistances characterize the Exodus ordinance as a work of conservative revolutionists who wrestled with the imperial legal metanarrative when they drew up a law collection for their own people who worked or had access to the palace or the temple. Their ordinances thus appear to be imperial and oppressive in some aspects due to the authors' conservativeness in resisting imperial legal traditions, as some postcolonial biblical scholars criticize.[210] However, they are also resistive and liberative in many cases in view of the revolutionary perspectives and measures that the authors offered. This observation may not suggest that the ordinances have no intention to "distill some aspirational, utopian statement of community life."[211] Rather, it reflects imperialized people's utopianism, which does not strive for a perfect world isolated from the existing society, but endeavors to alleviate suffering due to exploitation

210. For instance, Mathew, *Biblical Law Code*, 211; see also §1.4.3.

211. Cameron, "Liberation and Desire," 134.

and develop a community diverged from the empire.[212] This observation also offers another understanding of the similarities and differences between the Exodus ordinances and cuneiform law collections. This understanding goes beyond borrowing aiming at writing a better law, meta-legal traditions in a broader sense in ancient West Asia, or a shared educational tradition with prestigious perception of Mesopotamian knowledge.[213] It reveals the wrestling of the imperialized, who broadly maintained imperial logics but also attempted to resist the imperial legal metanarrative when they were living under the shadow of the Neo-Assyrian Empire.

---

212. Ashcroft, *Utopianism*, 63, 118, 161; see also §1.2.2.1.

213. Wright, *Inventing God's Law*, 351; Wells, "Covenant Code," 116–18; Barmash, *Laws of Hammurabi*, 256–59, 265; see also §2.2.2.

CHAPTER 4

Yhwh, the Marginalized, and Enemies in the Commandments

(Exodus 20:23–21:1 and 22:17–23:33)

4.1 Introduction

The perspective of imperialized people enhances not only the understanding of the ordinances in Exodus 21:2–22:16, but also that of the surrounding commandments in Exodus 20:23–21:1 and 22:17–23:33. The concerns of these commandments are apparently distinct from the ordinances. They also find few counterparts in the legal sections of extant cuneiform law collections. Nevertheless, just as the ordinances resemble some cuneiform laws, these commandments echo some themes in the non-legal sections of some cuneiform law collections. These echoes suggest a connection between these commandments and the ordinances, as well as between these commandments and the imperial legal metanarrative exhibited in these cuneiform law collections.[1]

In the following analysis, I focus on three themes, namely services to Yhwh or the gods, care for the marginalized, and fighting against enemies. Cuneiform law collections with extant prologue, superscription, and/or epilogue include the Laws of Ur-Namma, the Laws of Lipit-Ishtar, the Laws of

1. Regarding my propositions on the biblical authors' awareness of cuneiform legal traditions prevailed in Mesopotamia and the Levant and their imperial nature, see §2.2.4.

X,[2] the Laws of Eshnunna, and the Laws of Hammurabi. Among them, the Exodus ordinances exhibit similarities especially to the Ur-Namma and the Hammurabi collections. The Hammurabi collection indeed contains the most complete and lengthiest text of prologue and epilogue.

Utilizing postcolonial observations of colonized people's responses to their colonizers,[3] I compare the similarities and differences between the Exodus commandments and the prologue and epilogue of these cuneiform law collections. This comparative analysis again demonstrates how the imperialized authors wrestled with imperial legal traditions, which they regarded as a representation of the imperial legal metanarrative of their time when they compiled a law collection primarily for their elite audience during the Neo-Assyrian subjugation.[4] Alongside their broad acceptance of the imperial legal metanarrative, the imperialized authors resisted various aspects of it, making their commandments a work of conservative revolutionists.

4.2 Services to Yhwh or the Gods

Services to Yhwh is a predominant theme in the Exodus commandments. Preceded by a description of Yhwh's order for Moses to speak with the Israelites (Exod 20:22), these commandments begin with a concern about making idols alongside Yhwh and making and using an altar for Yhwh (Exod 20:23–26). Concerns related to services to Yhwh appear again in the commandments following the ordinances, which deals with sorcery, bestiality, and sacrifice (Exod 22:17–19), blasphemy against God and leaders and offerings for Yhwh (Exod 22:27–30), and the observance of festivals for Yhwh (Exod 23:14–19). While these religious concerns are distinct from those in the ordinances (Exod 21:2–22:16) and rarely appear in the legal sections of cuneiform law collections,[5] they resemble the theme of emperors' services to the gods in the prologue of some cuneiform law collections. This resemblance, however, occurs alongside differences, manifesting the authors' endeavor to

2. This collection is possibly the ending of the Laws of Ur-Namma (Roth, *Law Collections*, 36).

3. See §3.1 for a summary of these observations. For details, see chapter 1.

4. See §2.3.2.3 and §2.5.

5. Only LH 2 and MAL A 47 reflect a comparable concern with sorcery, and HL 187–188 and 199–200a reveal a concern with bestiality.

resist some aspects of the imperial legal metanarrative, despite their broad acceptance of it.

Acceptance of the Imperial Legal Metanarrative

Although religious motives and cultic laws seem to be absent from cuneiform law collections,[6] the theme of services to the gods appears in the prologues of the Laws of Ur-Namma and the Laws of Hammurabi. The introduction of the Ur-Namma collection, though broken, reveals the emperor's monthly offerings, which include specific amounts of produce and cattle: ". . . Ur-Namma, the mighty warrior, king of the city of Ur, king of the lands of Sumer and Akkad . . . he established 21,600 silas of barley, 30 sheep, 30 silas of butter, per month, as regular offerings . . . in the land" (LU A 1:1–30).[7] After depicting the divine delegation of authority to Marduk and ordination of Hammurabi (LH 1:1–49), the prologue of the Hammurabi collection also proceeds to describe, in the first-person, Hammurabi's works. These works include various services to different temples and gods, namely providing or storing general provisions for the temples or the gods (LH 1:60–62; 2:18–21, 2:44–48, 2:52–54; 3:4–6, 3:43–46; 4:4–6), providing or decreeing pure food offerings specifically for the gods (LH 3:33–35; 4:17–21, 4:36–37), purifying the temple's rites (LH 1:66–2:1), and arranging rituals or ceremonies for a god or a temple (LH 2:63–65; 3:62–64). Maintenance and renovation of the temples are also among these services, including taking charge of or organizing the temples in general (LH 2:66–67; 3:68–69), taking care of a temple at a proper time (LH 2:10–12), increasing a temple's fame (LH 2:29–31), renewing or embellishing certain temples (LH 2:26–28, 2:34–36, 2:60–62), and raising a temple's summit (LH 2:42–43). There are also mentions about setting up a god and making a god famous in certain temples and cities (LH 4:48–52, 4:60–63).

These detailed descriptions reflect that cuneiform legal traditions regard services to the gods and their temples as a crucial component in the non-legal sections of their law collections. They also reveal that the Exodus commandments resemble these cuneiform law collections. Similar to the Hammurabi collection, which mentions the setting up of the gods and the renovation of temples, the Exodus commandments begin with issues about idols and altar

6. Mathew, *Biblical Law Codes*, 57; Paul, *Studies in the Book of the Covenant*, 8–9.

7. Roth, *Law Collections*, 15.

making (Exod 20:23–26). Resembling the two cuneiform law collections, which attend to offerings or provisions for the temples or the gods, the end of the Exodus commandment deals with sacrifice, offerings, and festivals for Yhwh (Exod 22:19, 22:27–30; 23:14–19). With the proposition that the authors of the Exodus commandments were familiar with the legal traditions that these cuneiform law collections somehow exhibit, these resemblances suggest that the imperialized authors recognized the imperial legal concern for religious services and followed imperial legal traditions in addressing this concern in the sections outside the casuistic laws.

Resistance: Yhwh's Commandments rather than Emperors' Propaganda

This recognition, nevertheless, is fused with resistance to the imperial legal metanarrative, as well as Neo-Assyrian emperors' domination over the imperialized. This resistance is reflected by the commandments' divergences from cuneiform law collections. A key divergence is the presentation of the religious services as Yhwh's commandments rather than the emperors' propaganda. While the Exodus corpus presents services to Yhwh mostly in the first-person (Exod 20:23–26; 22:28–19; 23:14–15, 23:18) as the Hammurabi collection does, Exodus 20:22 makes it clear that these religious concerns are the words of Yhwh. Thus, in contrast to the two cuneiform law collections, which proclaim the religious services as what the emperors accomplish, the Exodus corpus presents them as what Yhwh commands his audience to do. Yhwh's commandments to the imperialized thereby take the place of the emperor's propaganda in the laws of the imperialized.

Notably, among these commandments is a prohibition against blaspheming God, followed by a prohibition against cursing a leader (נשׂיא, Exod 22:27). Standing in "the place of the normal word for a monarch,"[8] the reference to a leader does not necessarily indicate "a correspondence between God and the leader."[9] Rather, this reference suggests that the authors had a consideration of political leaders in mind when they composed the commandments, and they placed political leaders after God. Thus, the commandments on the one hand require the audience to respect the leaders among them despite

8. Wright, *Inventing God's Law*, 297.

9. Alexander, *Exodus*, 514.

the necessity of revering God, but on the other hand, they put God above political leaders. This regard for God over political leaders contrasts with the emperors' promotion of their accomplishment by claiming their services to the gods and their temples. This contrast suggests further the imperialized authors' intention to exalt Yhwh over the emperors, reflecting their resistance to the emperor's dominant role advocated by the imperial legal address of religious services.

Indeed, in the prologue, alongside his claim about his services to the gods and their temples, Hammurabi calls himself "god of kings" (*ili šarrī*, LH 3:16),[10] which not only exalts himself above other emperors, but also establishes his status similar to the gods.[11] In the epilogue, Hammurabi also wishes that in the Esagila temple that he loves, his name will be remembered as a blessing forever (*ina Esagil ša arammu šumī ina damiqtim ana dār lizzakir*, LH 47:96–48:1). He then even calls the oppressed man to come before his stela (*awīlum ḫalbum . . . ana maḫar ṣalmaya . . . lillikama*, LH 48:3–6)[12] to praise him (LH 48:20–39),[13] in addition to listening to the reading of his stela (LH 48:13). Hammurabi, therefore, exhorts his people to revere him like the gods alongside declaring his own services to the gods.

The Exodus commandments starkly contrast with these presentations. In the altar commandment, Yhwh promises that wherever he makes

10. For the translation of this phrase, see Kitchen and Lawrence, *Treaty, Law, and Covenant*, 133 and Richardson, *Hammurabi's Law*, 34; in contrast to Roth, *Law Collections*, 78, 140. Roth notes that the emendation which inserts *šubat* (the dwelling of) before this phrase to make it refer to the Ezida temple rather than an epithet of Hammurabi indeed presents some difficulties.

11. Spieckermann, "God and His People," 346.

12. As Martha T. Roth argues, according to the literary context, the passage concerning the oppressed man is "propagandistic and aggrandizing," rather than legal (Roth, "Hammurabi's Wronged Man," 39). Regarding arguments for legal connotations, see Westbrook, "Codification and Canonization," 34–36; Lafont, "Codification et Subsidiarité," 53–55; Driver and Miles, *Babylonian Laws*, 1:41.

13. There is ambiguity on whom the oppressed man blesses in the following lines, "*ina maḫar Marduk bēliya Zarpānītum bēltiya ina libbišu gamrim likrubam*" (Before Marduk, my lord, and Zarpanitu, my lady, may he bless with his whole heart [my translation]; LH 48:41–45). Considering the preceding context, it is reasonable for Roth (*Law Collections*, 135) and Richardson (*Hammurabi's Law*, 123) to see that this blessing is for Hammurabi. Even if this blessing is a prayer in general (see Kitchen and Lawrence, *Treaty, Law, and Covenant*, 179), the praise for Hammurabi still precedes the prayer before the gods, suggesting a stronger emphasis on the former.

his name to be remembered,[14] he will come to the people and bless them (בכל־המקום אשר אזכיר את־שמי אבוא אליך וברכתיך, Exod 20:24).[15] In the commandments concerning festivals, he also demands every male among the audience to appear before him (יראה כל־זכורך אל־פני האדן יהוה, Exod 23:17).[16] The male does not necessarily come before an altar, which suggests a contrast between Yhwh's altar and Hammurabi's statue, as Wright argues.[17] The absence of an explicit reference to the altar and the presence of the direct reference to Yhwh in this commandment suggest an emphasis on appearing before Yhwh himself. This commandment, together with Yhwh's promise in the altar commandment, thus contrasts with Hammurabi's call for remembering his name and coming before his stela. This contrast reveals a resistance that the Exodus commandments assert against the imperial legal metanarrative: Rather than revering the emperor or his stela in response to his propaganda, the audience should worship Yhwh according to his commandments.

As some postcolonial biblical scholars point out,[18] this resistance and the resistance to the emperors' claimed dominant role in religious services, however, might serve the interest of the elite authors, just like the acts of some colonized elites in the modern context.[19] These authors probably worked in the temple or the palace, or both[20] and thus might receive economic benefits from offerings given to Yhwh. The call for worshipping Yhwh might even imply the necessity to revere the human leaders whom these authors claimed to be chosen by Yhwh, thus possibly leading to domination of their people, similar to the imperial subjugation against them. Nevertheless, these resistances also reflect a resistive message that one should not overlook. This message

---

14. For the understanding of אזכיר as causative, see Sarna, *Exodus*, 116. For other understandings, see, for instance, Van Seters, *Law Book*, 62–63.

15. For a similar comparison with LH 47:96–48:1, see Wright, *Inventing God's Law*, 295.

16. Although Alexander suggests that this commandment does not necessarily exclude the female (Alexander, *Exodus*, 524), Mathew is correct to argue that it is androcentric (Mathew, *Biblical Law Codes*, 209). Nevertheless, this commandment does not seem to suggest that the appearance before Yhwh as "rights and privilege" as Mathew argues, but a duty of the males, even though nowhere in the commandments suggests that the participation was voluntary for women, as Patrick notes (Patrick, *Old Testament Law*, 115–16).

17. Wright, *Inventing God's Law*, 294.

18. Yee, "Postcolonial Biblical Criticism," 213, 223; Wafula, "Exodus," 23, 25. See also §1.4.2 and §1.4.3.

19. Fanon, *Wretched of the Earth*, 175; Otto, "Subalternity," 164. See also §1.2.3 and §1.3.2.

20. See §2.5.

was particularly significant for the imperialized authors and their elite audience when they lived under Neo-Assyrian subjugation. Like the emperors presented in the cuneiform law collections, Neo-Assyrian emperors emphasized in their inscriptions their reverence for the gods and their services to the gods, including restoring and building temples, making offerings, and holding festivals.[21] Moreover, Neo-Assyrian emperors demanded vassals to pay annual visits to their court to present tributes not only for economic purposes, but also to express reverence and loyalty to the emperors.[22] Presenting a concern about religious services similar to that in the imperial legal metanarrative but as Yhwh's commandments rather than the emperors' propaganda, the imperialized authors appear to particularly urge their elite audience to serve Yhwh, rather than acknowledging the Neo-Assyrian emperors' contribution in religious services or revering them. Thus, alongside the recognition of the imperial concern for religious services, the imperialized authors subverted the dominant role of the emperors presented by the imperial legal metanarrative, even though the services to Yhwh might be susceptible to benefiting these authors economically and politically.

Resistance: Imperialized People's Obligation rather than Emperors' Accomplishment

This subversion, moreover, is not merely about replacing the emperors with Yhwh, as some scholars suggest.[23] The nuance of this resistance is manifested further by the fact that while cuneiform law collections present services to the gods as the emperors' works, the Exodus corpus presents them as divine commandments for the imperialized people. There are scholarly debates concerning the shift of plural and singular second-person references in the Exodus commandments, which attract attention to the possibility of later redaction.[24] However, these references clearly refer to the Israelites (Exod

21. See for instance, RINAP 1:97, Tiglath-Pileser III 39, lines 15b–16; RINAP 1:118, Tiglath-Pileser III 47, lines 11b–12a; RINAP 2:229, Sargon II 43, lines 57–71; RINAP 2:278–88, Sargon II 65, lines 5, 112–115, 156–161; RINAP 3/1:60, Sennacherib 4, line 1; RINAP 3/2:299, Sennacherib 214, lines 62–69; RINAP 4:14, Esarhaddon 1, col. ii lines 20–24; RINAP 5/1:58, Ashurbanipal 3, col. i lines 14–26.

22. Liverani, *Assyria*, 189–90.

23. For instance, Wright, *Inventing God's Law*, 287.

24. For scholars who argue for later redaction see, for instance, Otto, *Wandel der Rechtsbegründungen*, 40–45, 52. Morrow does not regard this shift as evidence of redaction, but concludes that it indicates generic discrepancy (Morrow, "Generic Discrepancy," 136–51).

20:22) – collectively or individually, rather than to their leader(s) only. Hence, in contrast to the presentation of cuneiform law collections, services to Yhwh in the Exodus commandments are not the accomplishments of the emperors, but the obligations of all people among the imperialized. The imperialized people's participation builds up their own relationship with their God.

This contrast is demonstrated further by some nuances between cuneiform law collections and the Exodus commandments. While Hammurabi claims that he provides or decrees pure food (*mākalī ellūtim*, LH 3:34, 4:36) or pure food offerings (*zībī ellūtim*, LH 4:22) for the gods, Yhwh requires the people to become holy (קדשׁ) for him and not to eat the meat of animal injured in the field (Exod 22:30). Under this requirement, the people themselves become a kind of pure offering for their God. Likewise, whereas the Ur-Namma collection states that Ur-Namma establishes monthly offerings (LU A 1:24) and Hammurabi himself claims that he takes care of the Esagil temple at the proper time (*ūmīšu*, LH 2:10),[25] the Exodus commandments demand the people to make offerings and hold regular festivals for Yhwh (Exod 22:29; 23:14–17). Again, the people themselves – not the emperors nor only their leaders – take on the role of serving God regularly. The concern for services to Yhwh in the Exodus commandments, therefore, not only reveals rejection of the reverence for the emperors by emphasizing the worship of Yhwh, but also expresses resistance to the promotion of emperors' accomplishments in religious practices by highly regarding the imperialized people's participation and their relationship with Yhwh.

Notably, as some scholars point out,[26] the commandments concerning the altar indicate its mundane nature. Yhwh demands the people to make an altar for him out of soil (אדמה, Exod 20:24) and prohibits them from using hewn stone (גזית, Exod 20:25). Yhwh explains that the use of tools on the

---

David Wright, however, offers a thorough analysis on all cases of shift in Exod 20:23–23:19, demonstrating that most of them can be explained through literary reasons other than redaction (Wright, *Inventing God's Law*, 324–29). See also Van Seters's criticism of using the shift as a principle of source division (Van Seters, *Law Book*, 62) and Albertz's (*Exodus, Band II*, 2:110) and Sarna's (*Exodus*, 116, 137) comments on the shift.

25. For the translation of this word, see Kitchen and Lawrence, *Treaty, Law, Covenant*, 111; Richardson, *Hammurabi's Law*, 31; and Viel, *New Complete Code*, 359; in contrast to Roth, *Law Collections*, 77.

26. Alexander, *Exodus*, 454; Chavel, "Kingdom of Priests," 183; Albertz, *Exodus, Band II*, 77; Wright, *Inventing God's Law*, 309.

stone will indeed defile it (Exod 20:25). These commandments may suggest the avoidance of strong human intervention[27] or indicate the importance of Yhwh's natural presence.[28] However, a reading of these commandments as a response of the imperialized to the imperial legal metanarrative has more to tell. This positive commandment on making a simple altar sharply contrasts not only the preceding negative injunction against making gods of silver or gold (Exod 20:23),[29] but also Hammurabi's statements about his contributions for different temples. Hammurabi states that he "drapes the sacred building of the goddess Aya with greenery" (*mušalbiš warqim gigunē Aya*, LH 2:26–28), "renews the Ebabbar temple for the god Shamash" (*muddiš Ebabbar ana Šamaš*, LH 2:34–35), and "raises high the summit of the Eanna temple" (*mullî rēš Eanna*, LH 2:42–43), as well as "surrounds the Emeteursag temple with splendor" (*muštasḫir melimmī Emeteursag*, LH 2:60–62).[30] If these grand renovation works necessitate a complex network led by an emperor, the building of an altar according to Yhwh's commandments, contrarily, is something that any ordinary person or, at most, a small group of people can do.[31] The commandments on the construction of Yhwh's altar thus open up an opportunity for the imperialized people's participation. This contrast reveals that the imperialized authors resisted the imperial claims on the emperors' sole services to gods and their temples.

This resistance might not suggest a more democratized environment because the commandments emphasize the imperialized people's obligation to serve Yhwh. This resistance also might not have made a material difference in reality, for the emperors' accomplishment was likely rhetorical more than actual; that is, despite their claims, their people were the ones who did the services to the gods. Nevertheless, for the Israelites and Judahites living in the Neo-Assyrian period, when the emperors similarly emphasized their services to the gods and their temples, this resistance again importantly expresses the imperialized authors' rejection of Assyrian emperors' propaganda. It also

27. Albertz, *Exodus*, *Band II*, 76.

28. Haak, "Altar," 163.

29. Feder, "Aniconic Tradition," 264.

30. Roth, *Law Collections*, 77–78.

31. Chavel, "Kingdom of Priests," 182–83.

reflects the imperialized authors' regard for the imperialized people when they were under Assyrian subjugation.

In fact, alongside this resistance, some commandments concerning services to Yhwh recall a history that calls for resistance to imperial power and attention to the liberation of the imperialized people. Concerning offerings for Yhwh, the requirement of giving the firstborn (Exod 22:28–29) evokes the Israelites' experience in Egypt.[32] Addressing the festival of unleavened bread, Exodus 23:15 even explicitly explains that the motivation behind the specific scheduling of this annual festival is the anniversary of the Israelites' exit from Egypt. Going out from Egypt signifies not only deliverance from oppression but also the liberation of the imperialized people from an empire. The commandments concerning religious services thus are not merely about serving Yhwh, but also remind the imperialized people of the importance of resisting empires' subjugation.

Amid their acceptance of the imperial legal concern for services to the gods, the Exodus commandments, therefore, manifest a twofold resistance against the imperial legal metanarrative. Religious services are about Yhwh's commandments that call for the worship of Yhwh rather than imperial propaganda that demands reverence for the emperors. They represent also the obligations of the imperialized people, rather than the emperors' accomplishments. These resistances would be oppressive if the elite authors did put them up because of ulterior motives, such as securing their economic benefits or supporting their political patrons. Nevertheless, these resistances uphold the importance of the imperialized people's participation in the services to Yhwh and their relationship with him, which subverts, rather than accepts, the claimed dominant role of the emperor in the religious realm. This subversion, amid recognition of the imperial legal concern for religious services, suggests the imperialized authors' intention to communicate their rejection of Assyrian emperors' propaganda and their regard for the imperialized people to their elite audience.

Resistance: Yhwh Only rather than Many Gods

In addition to this subversion, the Exodus commandments noticeably diverge from extant cuneiform law collections by emphasizing offering

32. Alexander, *Exodus*, 514.

the services to Yhwh only instead of many gods. In his law collection's prologue, Hammurabi claims that he is chosen by Anu (LH 1:45–49) and Enlil (LH 1:45–49, 1:50–53). He then states that he pleases and serves a number of gods, including Marduk (LH 2:7–9), Shamash (LH 2:22–25), Aya (LH 2:26–28), Anu (LH 2:44–48), Ishtar (LH 2:44–48, 2:63–65; 3:53–54; 4:46–47, 4:48–52, 4:60–63), Urash (LH 3:21–23), Nintu (LH 3:33–35), Adad (LH 3:56–57, 3:58–59), Enki (LH 4:17–21), Damkina (LH 4:17–21), Tishpak (LH 4:34–35), and Ninazu (LH 4:36–37). Contrarily, the Exodus commandments prohibit the audience from making idols alongside Yhwh (Exod 20:23), as well as from worshipping any god other than Yhwh (Exod 22:19). This emphasis on not worshipping other gods except Yhwh occurs again in commandments exhibiting other themes (Exod 23:13, caring for the marginalized; Exod 23:24–25, fighting against enemies). This emphasis contrasts with the presentation of the imperial legal metanarrative. It also works against Neo-Assyrian emperors' self-presentations, which similarly emphasize the appointment of the emperors by various gods and the emperors' services to them.[33]

This contrast does not necessarily suggest that there was imperial religious imposition among Israelites and Judahites during the Neo-Assyrian period,[34] nor that religious Assyrianism was the only impetus for this kind of religious commitment among the authors of the Exodus commandments.[35] Indeed, these commandments were rooted in the religion of Israel and Judah and expressed their people's understanding of Yhwh;[36] therefore, it is not surprising

33. For instance, RINAP 1:81–82, Tiglath-Pileser III 35, col. i lines 1–35; RINAP 1:118, Tiglath-Pileser III 47, lines 11b–12a; RINAP 2:225–29, Sargon II 43, lines 1–3, 57–71; RINAP 4:14, Esarhaddon 1, col. ii lines 12–24; RINAP 5/1:58, Ashurbanipal 3, col. i lines 6–26.

34. For recent studies arguing for the absence of Assyrian religious imposition in the eighth century to the seventh century in Israel and Judah, see, for instance, Berlejung, "Assyrians in the West," 32–38, 48–51; Berlejung, "Shared Fates," 151–74; Bagg, "Palestine," 125–26.

35. About evidence of Assyrian religious imposition, see, for instance, Miller, "Shadow of the Overlord," 159–63. Nevertheless, as Miller points out, even if this imposition was absent, the Neo-Assyrian presence in the Levant was sufficient for inducing the religio-political reaction of the people. The Assyrian treaty tablet discovered at Tell Tayinat (Lauinger, "Esarhaddon's Succession," 87–91) even possibly suggests that the Neo-Assyrians continuously reminded the people about their imperial authority through placing their treaty at the subjugated people's temple. For the imperial pressure that Israelites and Judahites faced in the Neo-Assyrian period and their possible responses as the imperialized, see also §2.3.2, §2.4.7, and §2.5. For more about the debate of Neo-Assyrian religious imposition and the imperial religious pressure on Judahites, see Hays, *Covenant with Death*, 25–34.

36. Otto, "Laws of Hammurapi," 505.

that the authors addressed Yhwh only, rather than other gods when they deal with religious services in their law collection. Nevertheless, this contrasting religious expression also does not merely reflect a difference between the belief of Israelites and Judahites and that of the Assyrians, as one may argue. As postcolonial scholars find that colonized people retrieve their traditions in order to resist the colonial metanarrative in the modern context,[37] I see that the imperialized authors in the Neo-Assyrian period made use of their own religious belief to subvert the ideology that the imperial legal metanarrative advocated.[38] In the Laws of Hammurabi, the gods were supposed to be the patron deities of various cities under his imperial rule. Alongside his services to these gods, Hammurabi states his contribution to these cities, proclaiming the territories of his imperial domination.[39] Assyrian ideology similarly exhibits a tight association between the gods and their empire. Religious conviction of the Assyrians was intended for constituting their imperial propaganda,[40] just as the gods listed in the Laws of Hammurabi are part of Hammurabi's imperial proclamation.

The authors of the Exodus commandments thus responded to the imperial claims that emperors made through the religious recognition they gained from their services to the patron gods of different cities. Instead of worshipping different gods in order to gain authority over imperialized peoples, as emperors did, the imperialized authors urged their people, particularly their elite audience, to worship no other gods but Yhwh, their national God. Advocating this belief, particularly the punishment against apostasy (Exod 22:19), may make their law collection sound utopian.[41] Yet, this utopianism, similar to that expressed in postcolonial literature,[42] reveals that the imperialized authors did not follow the imperial legal metanarrative in establishing their power through worshipping a number of gods.[43] Instead, the imperialized authors endeavored to maintain their loyalty to their God in order to

37. Shohat, "Notes on 'Post-Colonial,'" 109; Chanock, *Law and Custom*, 22. See also §1.2.2.2 and §1.3.3.

38. For similar understanding, see Otto, "Bundesbuch," 25.

39. Hurowitz, *Inu Anum ṣīrum*, 22, 75–76; Barmash, *Laws of Hammurabi*, 106–111.

40. Berlejung, "Assyrians in the West," 51.

41. Anderson, *Women*, 36; Patrick, *Old Testament Law*, 108.

42. Ashcroft, *Utopianism*, 4; see §1.2.2.1.

43. Aster, "Shock of Assyrian," 479.

develop their own and their audience's national identity during Neo-Assyrian imperial subjugation.[44]

This endeavor indicates that the acceptance of the imperial legal concern for religious services is a selective one. While the imperialized authors recognized the importance of addressing religious services in their law collection, they resisted the domination over the imperialized people that the imperial legal metanarrative advocates. Through adapting the imperial legal concern for religious services, the imperialized authors urged the audience to worship Yhwh rather than revere emperors, underscored the imperialized people's obligation to serve Yhwh rather than boasted emperors' religious accomplishments, and called for worshipping Yhwh alone rather than promoted imperial authority through services to many gods. One perspective of the postcolonial optic calls for essential attention to the possible ulterior motives behind the promotion of loyalty to Yhwh, which relate to the economic and political interest of the elite authors and audience. However, postcolonial observations of colonized people's response to their colonizers also importantly reveal how the imperialized authors rejected the Neo-Assyrian emperors' propaganda and domination. This resistance amid acceptance will continue to be revealed in another theme of the Exodus commandments, namely care for the marginalized.

4.3 Care for the Marginalized

The theme of care for the marginalized intertwines with that of services to Yhwh in the Exodus commandments. After addressing sorcery, bestiality, and sacrifice (Exod 22:17–19), the Exodus corpus proceeds to deal with the גר (immigrant),[45] the widow, the orphan, and the poor. It prohibits oppression against them, acting like a lender to them,[46] and confiscating their neces-

44. Anderson, *Women*, 36; Patrick, *Old Testament Law*, 107.

45. About the translation and meaning of גר, see the following discussion on the resistance regarding concern for the immigrants.

46. Unlike other alternation between singulars and plurals in the surrounding passages, the second person plural pronoun in Exod 22:24b ("You shall not charge him interest") is more difficult to be explained by literary considerations, thus I do not include this commandment in this discussion. However, as David Wright suggests, it is possible that this use of the plural may simply follow the pattern of alternating between singulars and plurals in Exod 22:22–23 (Wright, *Inventing God's Law*, 328).

sary possessions as pledges for prolonged time (Exod 22:20–26). In between the concerns about blasphemy against God and leaders and offerings for Yhwh (Exod 22:27–30) and those about the observance of festivals for Yhwh (Exod 23:14–19), the Exodus commandments tackle false witnessing, with an attention to the powerless, the needy, and the גר (Exod 23:1–9). The following commandments on the observance of the sabbatical year and day are also particularly concerned with the needy, female slaves' offspring, and the גר (Exod 23:10–13). These concerns, like those about services to Yhwh, resemble the concern for the marginalized in the non-legal sections of some cuneiform law collections. Yet, they also diverge, revealing again how the imperialized authors resisted some aspects of the imperial legal metanarrative amid their recognition of the imperial legal concern for the marginalized.

Acceptance of the Imperial Legal Metanarrative

The theme of care for the marginalized, like that of services to the gods, also appears in the Laws of Ur-Namma and the Laws of Hammurabi. After proclaiming Ur-Namma's offerings, the transfer of kingship to god Nanna and Ur-Namma, and Ur-Namma's contributions to the people and the land, the prologue of the Ur-Namma collection states in the first-person how Ur-Namma did not hand over the marginalized to rich and powerful people. The marginalized markedly include orphans, widows, and poor people: "I did not deliver the orphan [nu-sig] to the rich. I did not deliver the widow [nu-mu-un-su] to the mighty. I did not deliver the man with but one shekel to the man with one mina. I did not deliver the man with but one sheep to the man with one ox" (LU A 4:162–168; C 2:30–39).[47]

Similarly, in the Hammurabi collection's prologue, after stating the divine delegation of authority to Marduk and ordination of Hammurabi and before proclaiming Hammurabi's services to different gods, Hammurabi declares that the gods ordained him to carry out various just acts, including ensuring that "the strong may not oppress the weak" (*dannum enšam ana la ḫabālim*, LH 1:37).[48] Echoing the prologue, Hammurabi states in the epilogue that he indeed established his stela so that "the strong may not oppress the weak" (*dannum enšam ana la ḫabālim*, LH 47:59). He also declares that his stela

47. Roth, *Law Collections*, 16.

48. Translation of the Laws of Hammurabi in this subsection is mine.

shows justice to orphan girls and widows (*ekūtam alamattam šutēšurim*, LH 47:61), as well as the oppressed (*ḫablim šutēšurim*, LH 47:71).

These descriptions indicate that cuneiform legal traditions regard care for the marginalized as a vital component alongside services to the gods. The tradition exhibited in the Hammurabi collection even particularly considers care for the marginalized as a kind of divine mandate. The Exodus commandments thus resemble imperial legal traditions in two ways: These commandments also explicitly deal with the widow (אלמנה, Exod 22:21), the orphan (יתום, Exod 22:21), and the poor (עני, Exod 22:24) or the needy (אבון, Exod 23:6).[49] They also similarly present these concerns as Yhwh's commandments and alongside the commandments concerning the worship of Yhwh. These resemblances suggest that the imperialized authors recognized the imperial legal metanarrative in terms of its attention to the marginalized and its association of this attention to the divine and the services to them.

Resistance: Obligation with Yhwh's Attention rather than Accomplishment with the Gods' Delegation

This recognition, however, is selective; it appears alongside resistance to the imperial legal metanarrative, as some differences from the latter indicate. As the Exodus corpus presents the concern for the marginalized as commandments to the people just as it does for its concern for services to Yhwh, it goes without saying that a noticeable difference again concerns addressing care for the marginalized as the imperialized people's obligation rather than the emperors' accomplishment.[50] Nevertheless, unlike the services to Yhwh, this obligation reveals a particular emphasis on Yhwh's attention to oppression against the marginalized – twice Yhwh states that he will listen to the cry of the marginalized due to the oppression inflicted by the audience (Exod 22:22, 22:26). In the case of widows and orphans, Yhwh even pronounces that he will kill such an audience, which will eventually lead to a kind of *lex talionis* – their wives and children will become widows and orphans, respectively (Exod 22:23).[51]

---

49. On synonymous use of "the poor" (עני) and "the needy" (אבון) see Schwantes, *Das Recht der Armen*, 29–52, 87–99; Houston, *Contending for Justice*, 62.

50. Patterson, "Widow, the Orphan," 228.

51. However, it is not exactly a *lex talionis*, as Jonathan Ben-Dov argues ("Poor's Curse," 437). An exact *lex talionis* should include further the oppression of the oppressors' wives and

This emphasis does not suggest that Yhwh dealt with oppression against marginalized people without human mediation. Contrarily, the commandments surrounding Yhwh's pronouncement indicate the importance of the audience's participation in eliminating such oppression. Some of the elite audience, including the authors themselves, might even have a judicial role in handling cases pertaining to the oppression of marginalized people in Israel and Judah.[52] Still, the emphasis on Yhwh's attention to such oppression conveys a vital message, especially when oppression against the needy, the powerless, and the poor was not uncommon in Israel and Judah (Amos 2:6; 5:11; 8:6; Isa 3:14). Rather than extolling human or leaders' accomplishment in eliminating such oppression, the Exodus commandments strongly urge the imperialized people, including the elite audience, to take care of the marginalized, through underscoring that they are all subject to severe punishment for exploiting these people.

This emphasis contrasts with the presentation in cuneiform law collections. Despite proclaiming concern for the marginalized as a kind of divine mandate, cuneiform law collections basically present the imperial accomplishment of this divine mandate. Notably, divine attention to oppression against the marginalized is not foreign to Mesopotamian literature. For instance, a Babylonian prayer addresses Shamash as "the father of the orphan girl,"[53] and an incantation mentions "the orphan girl" and "the widow" among those who receive protection from Shamash.[54] Counsels of Wisdom, a popular Babylonian collection of moral exhortations, even state that the god will be angry at the oppressors of various marginalized people and that Shamash will repay the oppressors evil.[55] The cuneiform legal concern for the marginalized indeed, to a certain extent, reflects a belief that political success is possible only if the emperors expend effort to protect the marginalized.[56] Yet, cuneiform law collections do not explicitly articulate divine attention to oppression

children after they have become widows and orphans.

52. See §2.5.

53. Horowitz, "Astral Tablets," 196–97, "The Prayer to the Gods of the Night," line 12; Barmash, *Laws of Hammurabi*, 118.

54. Scurlock, *Magico-Medical Means*, 534, no. 226, line 23; Barmash, *Laws of Hammurabi*, 118.

55. Lambert, *Babylonian Wisdom Literature*, 100–101, "Counsels of Wisdom," lines 56–60; Fensham, "Widow, Orphan," 131.

56. Fensham, "Widow, Orphan," 129.

against the marginalized. Instead, they present the gods' involvement merely in ordaining the emperors and focus on the emperors' accomplishments. The Hammurabi collection even calls the oppressed to go before Hammurabi's stela in order to find comfort and praise Hammurabi (LH 48:3–39). This emphasis on imperial accomplishment in care for the marginalized appears also in Neo-Assyrian emperors' self-presentation. Sennacherib, for instance, states that he "goes to the aid of the weak" (*ālik tappût akî*) at the beginning of his inscription, among his various virtues.[57]

Through presenting the concern for the marginalized as Yhwh's commandments to the imperialized people and emphasizing Yhwh's responses to the cry of the oppressed, the Exodus commandments thus again resist the imperial legal emphasis on emperors' contribution, which Neo-Assyrian emperors similarly claimed. While the imperialized authors recognized the imperial legal metanarrative in terms of its concern for the marginalized and its association of this concern with the divine mandate, they appear to underline that care for the marginalized is not the accomplishment of emperors, but the obligation of the imperialized people, including the elite audience.

Resistance: Emphasizing Care for the Immigrants in View of Imperial Subjugation

This obligation to care for the marginalized involves a special emphasis on the גר (Exod 22:20–26; 23:1–9, 23:10–12). The meaning of גר attracts much debate and evidently varies diachronically.[58] However, considering the association between the Exodus experience and גרים/גר in Exodus 22:20 and 23:9,[59] I adopt the traditional definition, "a person who, in order to protect his life and family, looks for a new home,"[60] for my analysis. I also translate

57. RINAP 3/1:60, Sennacherib 4, line 2. See also RINAP 2:229, Sargon II 43, lines 50–52; Esarhaddon might have a similar self-presentation, although the text is somewhat broken: "the one who makes good the damages (suffered by) the weak, [hold the ha]nd of the feeble; . . . [. . .] with [. . .] cripples; . . . .;" RINAP 4:99, Esarhaddon 44, lines 12–13.

58. Achenbach, "*Gêr – nåkhrî – tôshav – zâr*," 29–43; Rendtorff, "*Gēr* in the Priestly Laws," 77–87.

59. For the original connection between the motive clauses and the commandments, see Houten, *Alien in Israelite Law*, 53. For the exilic and post-exilic nature of the Egypt-גר formula, see Ramírez Kidd, *Alterity and Identity*, 36; however, one should scrutinize the reliability of inferring the date of the references in Exodus based on references occurring in other books that have clear dating.

60. Ramirez Kidd, *Alterity and Identity*, 13. For a recent review of studies concerning the meaning of גר, see Glanville, *Adopting the Stranger*, 7–14.

גר generically as "immigrant." One may query if all immigrants experienced marginality in Israel and Judah during the Neo-Assyrian period, especially in view of a wide range of social and economic statuses among immigrants today. However, according to the general connotation of גר, it is reasonable to suggest that these immigrants were typically in transitory residence, differing from the host population and receiving limited legal protection.[61] Their separation from home and relatives also contributed to their social or economic marginality, or both.[62] The Exodus commandments against general mistreatment, legal oppression, and economic exploitation of the immigrants (Exod 22:20; 23:9, 23:12) indeed reflect a response to their marginality in Israel and Judah regarding all these aspects.

Notably, this concern for the immigrants is not unique to the Exodus commandments as some scholars contend.[63] The Eshnunna collection probably requires that resident aliens' wares must be sold at a market rate (LE 41); the Hittite Laws may also impose a penalty for abducting a non-Hittite living in Hatti (HL 19b).[64] The Ur-Namma collection's prologue may even state that the emperor liberated both his people and foreigners in his land (LU A 3:122).[65] This possible statement exhibits that this legal tradition may be

61. Stine, "Your Name," 51.

62. Crouch, *Making of Israel*, 217; Kellerman, "גּוּר *gûr*," 443–44; Spencer, "Sojourner," 103–104.

63. Sneed, "Israelite Concern," 504; Ramírez Kidd, *Alterity and Identity*, 111; Alexander, *Exodus*, 511; Gane, *Old Testament Law*, 295.

64. Awabdy, *Immigrants*, 231–34. However, one should note that the identity or status of the offended in these laws is ambiguous. There is scholarly debate on the meaning of *ubārum*, which ranges from a resident alien to a guest-friend ("ubāru," *CAD* 20:10), and on the exact meaning of the stipulation in LE 41 (Yaron, *Laws of Eshnunna*, 69, 160, 234). The connotation of the Luwian in HL 19b is similarly unclear. The Hittite Laws may deal with them because of the special political connection between Hatti and Luwiya (Hoffner, *Laws of Hittite*, 171). As Awabdy notes, Hatti probably had residents of different ethnicities. However, the law collection only addresses the Luwians. In addition to LE 41 and HL 19b, Awabdy also regards HL 5 (murder of a merchant) as a law concerning foreign residents. Yet, this law does not specify the merchant's ethnicity. The Neo-Hittite version even specifies the merchant as a Hittite. Thus, I do not regard it as a law concerning immigrants. The laws in LH 280 and 281 also seem to deal with a kind of immigrant, but these laws actually stipulate how a slave owner can redeem his slaves of foreign origin.

65. Awabdy, *Immigrants*, 233. One should note that the reference to the foreigner (gi [r_5-ra]) involves reconstruction of the text (Roth, *Law Collections*, 15), although, as Awabdy suggests, the literary context does allow such reconstruction. For other reconstructions, see Kitchen and Lawrence, *Treaty, Law, and Covenant*, 56; Wilcke, "Gesetz in sumerischer Sprache," 531.

concerned with the immigrants, in addition to orphans, widows, and poor people. This concern is distinct from that exhibited in the Hammurabi collection's prologue, which only considers the last three groups of marginalized people, but echoed by the Exodus commandments, which similarly address all four groups.

Despite this similarity, the Exodus commandments repeat the concern for the immigrants (Exod 22:20; 23:9, 23:12), revealing a particular emphasis absent from these cuneiform law collections. A usual scholarly explanation for this emphasis concerns the influx of immigrants due to Assyrian invasions at the end of the eighth century, whether they were from Northern Israel or other regions.[66] However, the Exodus commandments uniquely reiterate another motivation behind this concern when they prohibit the audience from oppressing the immigrants (Exod 22:20; 23:9). A reading of this motivation from the perspective of the imperialized particularly sheds light on these commandments' unique emphasis. Like the motive clause following the commandments on festivals (Exod 23:15), which reminds the audience of liberation from an empire, the motive clauses following the prohibition against the oppression of the immigrants repeatedly recall life under an empire. For the imperialized authors and their audience, the experience of being the immigrants is, therefore, not only about being the people who lived in a new home due to the need to protect their lives and families, or merely about being strangers or Others deprived of rights.[67] Rather, it is also, or indeed more importantly, about being the kind of people who were oppressed by empire. This experience with empire offers a further explanation of why the imperialized authors saw the need to repeat the concern for immigrants, while their imperial counterparts do not. If the reluctance to reiterate or mention care for immigrants in cuneiform legal traditions was associated with a feeling of superiority in imperial cultures, which led to a tendency of keeping a distance from immigrants,[68] the Exodus experience with an empire, in contrast, motivated the imperialized authors of the Exodus commandments to enthusiastically empathize with the immigrants in order to

66. Albertz, "Aliens to Proselytes," 54. For a similar understanding see Crüsemann, "Bundesbuch," 34; although Crüsemann emphasizes the impact of Northern Israel's downfall.

67. Bartor, "Law and Narrative," 212; Tzoref, "Knowing the Heart," 119–31.

68. Ramírez Kidd, *Alterity and Identity*, 114–15.

resist their imperial counterparts' reluctance to do so. This experience also, to a certain extent, resonates with the difficulties that the eighth-century immigrants faced because they were driven out of their homes by the Neo-Assyrian Empire and continued to live under this empire, suffering from its subjugation, together with the people of Israel and Judah.

Still, some scholars suspect that the self-interest of the imperialized elites played a role behind the concern for these immigrants, which one should not overlook.[69] Postcolonial scholars observe that some colonized elites in the modern context follow their colonizers to exploit their peers in order to feed their own avarice.[70] Likewise, the imperialized elites in Israel and Judah in the Neo-Assyrian period might advocate the protection of the immigrants in order to secure cheap labor, especially when under pressure to collect resources for paying tributes to the Assyrians. Some postcolonial biblical scholars even add that care for the immigrants was intended for maintaining the power of the imperialized elites over the immigrants, just as colonizers generally do to the colonized.[71] These motivations suggest that the commandments are potentially imperial and oppressive, despite their overt emphasis on care.

Nevertheless, it is noteworthy that the Exodus commandments demand the primarily elite audience to stop their work on the seventh day of the week so that the immigrants can refresh themselves (Exod 23:12). This requirement not only reflects retrieval of the imperialized people's tradition, similar to colonized people's resistive strategy in the modern context,[72] but also expresses an anti-economic as well as anti-imperial sentiment. Ceasing from work on a weekly basis indeed disrupts the rhythms of production that empire usually endeavors to maintain.[73] It also curtails the exploitation of the immigrants, limiting the imperialized elites' human resources and thus their ability to accommodate the economic demand of the Neo-Assyrian Empire. Hence, while the imperialized elites' self-interest might be at work behind the concern for the immigrants, the unique emphasis of this concern in the Exodus commandments and the requirement that protects the immigrants

69. Sneed, "Israelite Concern," 504.

70. For instance, Fanon, *Wretched of the Earth*, 175; see also §1.2.3.

71. Dube, *Postcolonial Feminist Interpretation*, 79.

72. Shohat, "Notes on 'Post-Colonial,'" 109; Chanock, *Law and Custom*, 22; see also §1.2.2.2 and §1.3.3.

73. Berquist, "Resistance," 55.

from economic exploitation reveal that the imperialized authors endeavored to resist the imperial metanarrative, as well as to limit such oppression among the imperialized.

Amid their general recognition of the imperial legal concern for the marginalized, the authors of the Exodus commandments therefore again resisted the imperial legal metanarrative in two ways: underscoring care of the marginalized as the imperialized people's obligation with Yhwh's attention rather than as the emperors' achievement with the gods' delegation, and emphasizing care of the immigrants with attention to their suffering caused by imperial subjugation, which the people of Israel and Judah similarly experienced. The latter might be motivated by oppressive intents that served the interests of the imperialized elites and the Neo-Assyrian Empire. However, this resistance also involves protective measures for the immigrants, which demand the imperialized elite audience to work against the imperial exploitation of these marginalized people.

4.4 Fighting against Enemies

After dealing with services to Yhwh and care for the marginalized alternately, the end of the Exodus commandments addresses the audience's obedience to Yhwh, expressing a theme of fighting against their enemies (Exod 23:20–23:33). There is much debate about this section's dating, Deuteronomistic characteristics, and relationship with the preceding commandments (Exod 20:22–21:1; 22:17–23:19) and ordinances (Exod 21:2–22:16).[74] However, given the similarity of its theme on confronting enemies to that in the non-legal sections of the Hammurabi collection, it is worth considering the original connection between this section and the preceding commandments and ordinances, as well as examining this section's rhetoric from the perspective of

74. On regarding this section as later addition, see, for instance, Albertz, *Exodus*, 112, 130. Alexander offers a survey of different views and emphasizes this passage's connection with the preceding sections (Alexander, *Exodus*, 528–31). David Wright argues for a single compositional process for this section and preceding sections and dates this process to the Neo-Assyrian period (Wright, "Covenant Code Appendix," 66–68). About Deuteronom(ist)ic characteristics, see, for instance, Feder, "Aniconic Tradition," 257. About the distinctiveness of the motifs used in this section in comparison to those in Deuteronomistic literature, see Ausloos, "Deuteronomi(sti)c Elements," 490–500; Ausloos, "Exod 23, 20–33," 562; Ausloos, "'Angel of YHWH,'" 7; Van Seters, "Terms 'Amorite,'" 70.

the imperialized. This examination indicates that the Exodus commandments do reflect an acceptance of oppressive imperial ideology through their resemblances to the cuneiform legal tradition, which necessitates postcolonial and ethical inquiries. Yet, these commandments also continue to diverge from their cuneiform counterpart, disclosing the imperialized authors' endeavor to resist the imperial legal metanarrative as well as Neo-Assyrian subjugation, which deserves examination.

Acceptance of the Imperial Legal Metanarrative

In the Hammurabi collection, the theme of fighting against enemies first appears in the prologue. Through different words denoting enemies (*nakrum, zā'erum, ayyābum*), this theme explicitly manifests in some of Hammurabi's epithets: "the enemy-ensnaring throw-net" (*sapar nakirī*, LH 2:68), "the fierce wild bull who gores the enemy" (*rīmum kadrum munakkip zā'irī*, LH 3:7–9), the one "who seizes the enemies" (*mutammeḫ ayyābī*, LH 3:47).[75] These epithets appear alongside the pronouncements of Hammurabi's services to various temples and gods[76] and his contributions to different cities, including expanding a city (LH 3:2–5).

In the epilogue, through the word *nakrum*, the theme of fighting against enemies appears again not only in Hammurabi's statement about his contributions to his people, but also in his curses against people who ignore, change, or erase the inscription on his stela. Among statements about his accomplishments and before his statement of concern for the marginalized, Hammurabi declares that with the help of multiple gods, he annihilated enemies above and below (*nakrī eliš u šapliš assuḫ*, LH 47:30–31). This declaration is followed by his statement on ending conflicts, enhancing the land's well-being, and ensuring the safety and prosperity of the settlement's people (LH 47:32–39). In two curses, Hammurabi invokes the god Zababa to ensure the curse recipients' enemies triumph over the curse recipients (*nakiršu elišu lišziz*, LH 50:90–91). He also appeals to the goddess Ishtar to deliver the curse recipients to their enemies' hand (*ana qāt nakrīšu limallīšuma*, LH 51:20–21) and make the curse recipients captives in their enemies' land (*ana māt nukurtišu kamîš līrūšu*, LH 51:22–23). Notably, before these requests, Hammurabi invokes

75. Roth, *Law Collections*, 78–79.

76. See §4.2.

Ishtar to plunge the curse recipients into confusion (*išītam*, LH 51:5). In a preceding curse, Hammurabi similarly calls upon Shamash to confuse (*liši*, LH 50:23) the curse recipients. In both cases, a curse about overthrowing the curse recipients' military follows (LH 51:8–9; 50:24–25), suggesting a connection of this confusion to military effort, even though some translators regard the reference in the invocation of Ishtar (*išītu*, LH 51:5) as one that denotes revolts.[77]

These descriptions reflect that, alongside services to the gods and care for the marginalized, the legal tradition exhibited in the Hammurabi collection regards attention to enemies as another vital element in its law collection's non-legal sections. They also reveal the resemblances of the Exodus commandments to this cuneiform legal tradition. Similar to Hammurabi's statement, Yhwh not only explicitly states that he will become an enemy to the audience's enemies (ואיבתי את־איביך, Exod 23:22) and an adversary to their adversaries (וצרתי את־צרריך, Exod 23:22), but also promises to efface them (Exod 23:23). Like Hammurabi, who relates his enemy-ensnaring character to the expansion of a city, Yhwh will drive out the audience's enemies to ensure the audience's possession of the land (Exod 23:30). Resembling Hammurabi's curse, Yhwh's promise is made under the condition in which the audience attends to Yhwh's envoy and does what Yhwh instructs (Exod 23:21–22). Yhwh also similarly states that he will confuse (המם) the people whom the audience encounters, in addition to making the audience's enemies (איבים) turn their backs before them (Exod 23:27). These resemblances suggest an original connection between this last section of the Exodus commandments with the preceding ones. Moreover, they indicate that the imperialized authors were in sympathy with imperial legal attention to enemies, in addition to religious services and care for the marginalized.

Notably, as some postcolonial biblical scholars contend, with this sympathy, the Exodus commandments offer the imperialized people a template for dealing with their enemies in hostile ways, if not directly grant them a weapon to conquer other peoples in the Levant.[78] These commandments indeed focus

77. See the translations of Kitchen and Lawrence, *Treaty, Law, and Covenant*, 183, and Richardson, *Hammurabi's Law*, 131.

78. Davidson, *Writing/Reading*, 14; Ateek, "Palestinian Perspective," 167; Dube, *Postcolonial Feminist Interpretation*, 64–65; Yee, "Postcolonial Biblical Criticism," 224; see also §1.4.1 and §1.4.2.

on the subjugation of these people, just as the emperor presenting himself as an aggressive adversary to his enemies in the imperial legal metanarrative. This sympathy thus makes the Exodus commandments appear not only to be imperial but also particularly oppressive.

Resistance with Ambivalence: Yhwh's Destruction with People's Involvement rather than Emperors' Work

This oppressive imperial feature may explain a nuance between the two law collections, which suggests that the imperialized authors attempted to distance themselves and their elite audience from the imperial legal emphasis on human effort in destroying enemies. Nevertheless, there is a shift at the end of the commandments toward the imperial legal metanarrative, indicating an ambivalent response that again draws the Exodus commandments fairly close to the oppressive imperial approach to enemies.

The Exodus commandments concerning enemies begin with Yhwh's promise, which expresses that his envoy will go before the audience and Yhwh will efface the enemies (Exod 23:22–23); the only action that Yhwh demands of the audience is to destroy the gods and the pillars of the six people groups and to serve Yhwh (Exod 23:24–25). This emphasis on Yhwh's, rather than the audience's, role in the destruction of their enemies continues when Yhwh reaffirms that he will throw the enemies into confusion and make them flee from the audience (Exod 23:27). Yhwh also explains further how he will gradually drive the enemies out from the land (Exod 23:29). This focus on Yhwh's role to a certain extent resonates with Hammurabi's statement about his annihilation of his enemies with the gods' help (LH 47:30–31) and his invocations of the gods to manipulate the enemies into punishing the disobedient people (LH 50:90–91; 51:20–23). For Hammurabi's statement and invocations express the belief in divine involvement with the destruction and manipulation of the enemies. However, the Hammurabi collection puts much emphasis on the emperor's enemy-destroying character (LH 2:68; 3:7–9, 3:47), his direct contribution to the elimination of the enemies (LH 47:30–31), and his invocation of the gods (LH 49:18–44). Therefore, the Exodus commandments' explicit statements concerning Yhwh's destruction of the audience's enemies still contrast with the imperial legal focus on the human emperor's work.

This emphasis on Yhwh's direct involvement notably also reveals an adjustment of the perspective on Yhwh's role in comparison to the preceding commandments concerning the marginalized. This adjustment indicates further the imperialized authors' intention to highlight the divine role and undermine human participation in eliminating the land's inhabitants. Although the commandments concerning the marginalized exhibit Yhwh's particular attention to marginalized people, these commandments begin with and mostly concern the demand for the audience to take actions to protect them. Contrarily, the last section of the Exodus commandments begins with and continually reiterates Yhwh's destruction of the audience's enemies. The first two-thirds of this section does not even address the destruction of the enemies as the audience's work with Yhwh's monitoring (like the commandments on the marginalized do) or the audience's job with Yhwh's help (like the Hammurabi collection does). These contrasts reflect an internal adjustment of emphasis from calling for human participation in the care for the marginalized to prioritizing Yhwh's role in eliminating the audience's enemies. This prioritization recalls a subtle but resistive strategy that the subordinate people employ in the modern context, that is, envisioning help coming from divine power rather than striving for human endeavor.[79] This adjustment, moreover, suggests a tendency for the imperialized authors in Israel and Judah to deemphasize human participation, including their elite audience's action, in dealing with their enemies. This tendency again works against the imperial legal metanarrative, which carries a belief in divine involvement with the destruction of the enemies but emphasizes the human emperor's effort in it.

Nevertheless, a kind of shift back occurs at the end of the Exodus commandments, which indicates a call for the audience's participation in their confrontation with the land's inhabitants. While Yhwh continues to state that he will set large boundaries for the audience, he also declares that the audience will drive out those inhabitants (Exod 23:31). Whether the *weqatal* of גרשׁ (drive out) suggests a command or simply a future action is subject to interpretation;[80] either way, it indicates the involvement of the audience in driving out the land's inhabitants alongside Yhwh's direct work against them. The end of the commandments even negatively portrays these inhabitants

79. Scott, *Domination*, 148; see also §1.2.2.1.

80. For regarding it as a command, see for instance, New Revised Standard Version, New King James Version, and Chinese Union Version with New Punctuation; for regarding it as a future action, see for instance, New American Standard Bible, Common English Bible, New International Version, and Khmer Old Version.

(Exod 23:33), reinforcing further the necessity for the audience to drive them out. This involvement of the imperialized audience, like that expressed under the themes of services to Yhwh and care for the marginalized, contrasts with the emperor's achievement advocated by the imperial legal tradition, revealing a rejection of the imperial propaganda. Yet, it also suggests a direct human involvement in eliminating other people, which resembles what the imperial legal tradition advocates, manifesting an acceptance or even favorable reception of it.

This favorable reception and the negative descriptions of the inhabitants notably resonate with the presentation of synergy between divine and human kings in war and adverse characterization of enemies in Neo-Assyrian inscriptions,[81] indicating the imperialized authors' compliance with Neo-Assyrian ideology. The shift between resistance and acceptance also reflects a kind of ambivalence of the imperialized authors toward the imperial legal metanarrative in dealing with the enemies by human effort. This ambivalence, like those appearing in the Exodus ordinances concerning slaves, does not totally resist imperial values, as some postcolonial scholars might hope.[82] Rather, it leads to an inquiry about the oppressive nature of the commandments' attention to the enemies, which some postcolonial critics similarly call for in the study of colonized people's hybridity in the modern context.[83] Regardless of whether גרש involves killing or simply refers to casting out, the explicit mention of human involvement suggests a kind of colonialism, as some postcolonial biblical scholars contend.[84] Moreover, it creates "an ethical

81. Crouch, *War and Ethics*, 191–95; Zaccagnini, "Enemy," 413–14; Fales, "Enemy," 428–29; Nowicki, *Enemies of Assyria*, 104–6.

82. Bhabha, *Location of Culture*, 86–88; Ashcroft, Griffins, and Tiffin, *Post-Colonial Studies*, 125–26. See also §1.2.2.1.

83. Prabhu, *Hybridity*, 16; see also §1.2.2.2.

84. Yee, "Postcolonial Biblical Criticism," 227–28; Dube, *Postcolonial Feminist Interpretation*, 64–65. See also Warrior, "Canaanites, Cowboys, and Indians," 261–65; Assmann, *Invention of Religion*, 229. In response to Warrior's article, Charles William Miller suggests a reading of the so-called conquest narrative from the perspectives of both Euro-Americans and Native Americans in "Negotiating Boundaries," 1–12. However, he identifies the reading from the perspective of the Israelites as the reading from the perspective of Euro-Americans. This approach seems to overlook the fact that the Israelites in the Exodus narrative, as well as the people of Israel and Judah in the Neo-Assyrian period, were both people oppressed by empires, whose experience may hardly be comparable with the experience of Euro-Americans. For more responses to Warrior's article, see §1.4.2 page 39, note 143.

slippery slope," which supports the audience's oppression of their enemies.[85] Between their acceptance of and resistance to the imperial legal attention to the enemies, the imperialized authors struggled with the imperialized people's role in dealing with their enemies, making the last section of the Exodus commandments particularly susceptible to being oppressive.

Resistance: Loyal Obedience to Yhwh rather than Emperors

This oppressive feature inevitably draws attention away from resistance to other aspects of the imperial legal metanarrative, which the Exodus commandments put up through further divergences. These divergences indicate that the acceptance of imperial legal traditions is not a complete adoption of them. Rather, it involves appropriation of imperial ideology for conveying resistive messages to the imperialized audience living under the Neo-Assyrian Empire, even though these messages still carry imperial and oppressive sentiment because their authors presented them within the imperial legal framework.

A noticeable divergence is, again, the call for obedience to Yhwh, in contrast to following the emperor's law. Like those occurring in the commandments concerning religious services, this divergence should be subject to postcolonial critique due to possible self-serving motivations behind the promotion of divine governance, which I will discuss momentarily. Yet, it similarly deserves attention because of the resistance to the Neo-Assyrian Empire that it further expresses. This divergence is even more direct than that in the commandments addressing services to Yhwh, thus exhibiting a more intense resistance. While Hammurabi's curses begin with a condition about not attending to the inscriptions on his stela, that is, his law (LH 49:18–38), the Exodus commandments inaugurate their last section by Yhwh's commandment on listening to his envoy's voice (Exod 23:21) and his conditional blessing that demands listening to his envoy's voice and doing what Yhwh speaks (Exod 23:22). This blessing and the envoy's voice (קוֹל, Exod 23:21, 23:22) possibly hint at the observance of the preceding ordinances,[86] which looks similar to Hammurabi's call for following his law. However, the anonymous envoy likely denotes a divine representation of, if not a substitute for, Yhwh, rather than a human leader, given Yhwh saying that his name is within

85. Anderson, *Ancient Laws*, 51.

86. Wright, "Covenant Code Appendix," 65; Dozeman, *Exodus*, 557.

the envoy (Exod 23:21).[87] Yhwh also sets up the condition of his blessing as doing what Yhwh says, in addition to listening to his envoy's voice (Exod 23:22). This condition especially warrants the contrast between the Exodus commandments' focus on obedience to Yhwh and the imperial legal emphasis on following the human emperor.

This focus on obedience to Yhwh and its contrast to the imperial legal metanarrative is revealed further in the following prohibitions against worshipping the gods of the land and commandments on destroying them (Exod 23:24). This loyal obedience to Yhwh is not only an essential condition for Yhwh's blessings (Exod 23:25–26) but also the core reason for driving out the inhabitants in the process of gaining possession of their land (Exod 23:31–33). This religious reason certainly does not offer a more liberative justification for eliminating enemies than the imperial claims do. Instead, it necessitates critique and even rejection from a postcolonial and ethical standpoint. However, this emphasis does strikingly contrast with Hammurabi's reliance on various gods' help in annihilating enemies (LH 47:22–31) and his invocation of different gods to hand over the curse recipients to their enemies (LH 50:81–51:23). This reliance notably also appears in Neo-Assyrian royal inscriptions and treaties in which emperors underscore their destruction of their enemies with the gods' help and invoke various gods to put disobedient people under their enemies' subjugation, respectively.[88] Yet, in opposition to these emperors' faith in a number of gods in the elimination and manipulation of enemies, the Exodus commandments demand the imperialized audience not to bow down to or serve gods of the land but to destroy them and serve Yhwh only, when they confront their enemies and proceed to take possession of their land.

Related to this contrast is a significant observation about the motif of destroying the enemies' gods occurring in some Neo-Assyrian royal inscriptions.[89] This motif appears in the descriptions of the emperors' achievement in military campaigns and the spoils obtained from them. For instance, in the depiction about how he handed Babylon's property to his people and how his

87. Ausloos, "'Angel of YHWH,'" 9. For more about the relationship between Yhwh and his envoy, see Hundley, "Of God and Angels," 12–13.

88. For instance, RINAP 3/2:330–35, Sennacherib 230, lines 2, 5, 63, 114, 121; SAA 2:46–56, Esarhaddon's Succession Treaty, § 42, 48, 80, 86, 90, 95.

89. Wright, "Covenant Code Appendix," 61, 81, 84–85.

people took the city's possessions, Sennacherib states that "My people seized and smashed the gods living inside it (the city)."[90] Similarly, after recounting his annihilation of the people in Elam and how he carried off their possessions to Assyria, Assurbanipal states that "I smashed their gods (and thus) placated the mood of the lord of lords."[91] These descriptions, together with occurrences of other military motifs, reasonably indicate the use of Assyrian royal motifs in the last section of the Exodus commandments and suggest this section's dating in the Neo-Assyrian period.[92] Together with the aforementioned contrast concerning the theme of enemies, these depictions, moreover, suggest that the imperialized authors tactfully appropriated the Neo-Assyrian motif to subvert the reliance on the gods that emperors, including Neo-Assyrian emperors, advocated and to underline the importance of obedience to Yhwh for the imperialized audience.

Again, this emphasis on obedience to Yhwh reasonably leads to a query about what divine governance meant to the imperialized people in Israel and Judah, which deserves reflection. This emphasis might be motivated by the imperialized authors' economic and political interests and might imply subservience to the imperialized leaders who claimed to be chosen by Yhwh. In this case, this obedience would be susceptible to serving not only those leaders' domination of the imperialized people but also their ambition to conquer other people in the Levant. This suspected intention is undoubtedly just as oppressive as the ideology that emperors promoted. Nevertheless, the contrast between the Exodus commandments and the imperial metanarrative certainly indicates the imperialized authors' intent to reject emperors' propagandas, which unquestionably conveys a significant subversive message to the imperialized audience. By requiring listening to Yhwh, particularly destroying the gods of the land, the imperialized authors resisted following the emperors, including their faith in various gods. Amid accepting the imperial legal attention to the enemies in general, the authors of the Exodus commandments urged their imperialized people to show loyal obedience to Yhwh alone when they were subjugated by the Neo-Assyrian Empire.

90. RINAP 3/2:316, Sennacherib 223, line 48; Wright, "Covenant Code Appendix," 81.

91. RINAP 5/1:249, Ashurbanipal 11, lines 119–112; Wright, "Covenant Code Appendix," 84.

92. Wright, "Covenant Code Appendix," 68.

Resistance: Yhwh's Anti-Imperial Blessings rather than Emperors' Curses

Another similar resistance occurs in the nuanced attention to the enemies. In addition to calling himself as an enemy destroyer (LH 2:68; 3:7–9, 3:47) and narrating that he successfully annihilated enemies everywhere with various gods' help (LH 47:22–31), Hammurabi invokes the gods to manipulate enemies in order to punish people who do not follow or preserve his law (LH 50:90–91; 51:20–23). Contrarily, in the Exodus commandments, the theme of enemies and prohibitions on worshipping their gods are basically about Yhwh's blessing of the obedient imperialized audience. Yhwh will become their enemies' enemy, as his envoy will go before the audience when he leads them to the six people groups whom Yhwh will efface (Exod 23:23). Yhwh not only will bless various aspects of the audience's life (Exod 23:25–26) and set large boundaries for the audience (Exod 23:31), but also will make their enemies flee from them and send the hornet to drive them out (Exod 23:27–28).

These blessings are unquestionably beneficial to the audience only and oppressive to their enemies, particularly the inhabitants in the land. From the latter's perspective, these blessings even make the Exodus commandments ones of terror,[93] because they focus on the subjugation of these people, just as the imperial legal metanarrative emphasizes the emperor's destruction of his enemies. Notwithstanding, these peculiar blessings at the same time carry resistive elements. These elements, similar to other divergences of the Exodus commandments from the cuneiform law collection, express the imperialized authors' resistance to Neo-Assyrian subjugation, despite remaining conservative in derailing from the imperial legal framework.

The first resistive element relates to the work of the envoy (מלאך), who will participate in carrying out the blessing (Exod 23:23). The Exodus commandments do not specify his identity. The list of the six people groups, "the Amorite, the Hittite, the Perizzite, the Canaanites, the Hivites, and the Jebusites" (Exod 23:23), is also probably just a general traditional reference to the inhabitants of the Levant for recounting the early history of the people

93. Fernandez, "Exodus-toward-Egypt," 176.

of Israel and Judah.[94] However, among various references to מלאך in the Bible,[95] two of them occur in narratives with military contexts and markedly describe confrontations with empires. In the Exodus narrative, an envoy of God (מלאך האלהים) moved from leading to buffering the Israelites when the Pharaoh and his army pursued them (Exod 14:19). In the narrative of Hezekiah's reign, an envoy of Yhwh (מלאך יהוה) even wiped-out Sennacherib's army (2 Kgs 19:35//Isa 37:36). These two references suggest that the envoy in the Exodus commandments, which is also militarily related, carries an anti-imperial character.

The blessings of the audience's life also similarly suggest resistance to the power and oppression of empire. The mention of food (לחם), water (מים), and illness (מחלה) in Exodus 23:25 recall the Israelites' life in the wilderness after they had escaped from the Egyptians' pursuit (Exod 15:22–27; 16:2–32; 17:1–6), their seemingly comfortable life in the Egyptian empire (Exod 16:3), and the illness that Yhwh inflicted on the Egyptians (Exod 15:26). Moreover, the blessing of the audience's food and water, the removal of illness from them, and the preservation of their lives (Exod 23:25–26) contrast with one of the curses in the cuneiform law collection in which Hammurabi invokes the god to induce "years of famine" (*šanāt ḫušaḫḫim*, LH 49:66–67) and "sudden death" (*mūt niṭil īnim*, LH 49:70) among the curse recipients.[96] Neo-Assyrian emperors notably made similar curses, which invoke the gods to put the disobedient subjugated people into famine and drought as well as pain and illness.[97] The blessings in the Exodus commandments thus resist the imperial power and oppression depicted in the Exodus narrative, eliminating the hardship that the Israelites faced due to the necessity of liberating themselves from imperial oppression, subverting the illusive comfort offered by the empire, and contrasting with the divine punishment against it. These

94. O'Connell, "List of Seven People," 227; Hostetter, *Nations*, 146. Regarding the debate concerning to where or whom the envoy will bring the audience, see Ishida, "Structure," 461–90; Ishida, *History and Historical Writing*, 8–36; Hostetter, *Nations*; Garrett, *Exodus*, 204–205; Dozeman, *Exodus*, 129; Durham, *Exodus*, 32, 129.

95. For surveys of the use of מלאך in the Old Testament, see Ausloos, "'Angel of YHWH,'" 7; Newson, "Angels," 248–53.

96. Roth, *Law Collections*, 137.

97. SAA 2:11, Treaty of Aššur-nerari V with Mati'-ilu, King of Arpad, lines 8′–24′; SAA 2:49, Esarhaddon's Succession Treaty, lines 476–480; Lauinger, "Esarhaddon's Succession," 133, §54 A. A similar curse also appears in an earlier royal inscription: RIMA 2:254, Ashurnasirpal II, A.0.101.17, lines 90–96; Wright, "Covenant Code Appendix," 79.

blessings, moreover, work against the emperor's curse appeared in the imperial legal metanarrative, which the Neo-Assyrian emperors similarly put on their subjugated people.

The blessing about the extensive boundaries of the land further reveals a resistance to imperial subjugation. The list of the six people groups (Exod 23:23) and the summary list (Exod 23:28) may not clearly indicate geographical locations. The appearance of the references to the Amorites and the Hittites in some Neo-Assyrian sources also neither explains other gentilic references in the lists nor suggests a particular response of the Exodus commandments to the Neo-Assyrian sources.[98] However, the large boundaries – which Yhwh promises to set for the audience (Exod 23:31) but the people of Israel and Judah never totally encompassed – cover the lands where the Egyptian Empire carried out numerous military expeditions since the fifteenth century and ruled over in various degrees in the thirteenth and twelfth centuries.[99] Furthermore, these boundaries correspond to the administrative district *Eber-Nāri*/עבר־נהרה (Beyond the River), which was first established by the Neo-Assyrians.[100]

These connections suggest that Yhwh's promise of setting up the large boundaries is about granting the land subjugated by empires to the imperialized audience. They again reveal the resistive nature of Yhwh's conditional blessings in relation to the theme of fighting against enemies. They also suggest further that the acceptance of the imperial legal attention to enemies is an appropriation of this imperial emphasis for subverting imperial subjugation, a strategy that some postcolonial scholars regard as an effective resistance of the colonized to the colonizer.[101] In the case of the Exodus commandments, this appropriation certainly does not eradicate their oppressive feature, especially in terms of affecting other people's lives; it thus necessitates an ethical critique, as some postcolonial critics call for.[102] Yet, this appropriation does

98. About the association between the references to Amorites and Hittites in the Covenant collection and in the Assyrian royal inscriptions, see Van Seters, *Law Book*, 77; Van Seters, "Terms 'Amorite,'" 64–81. For other objections against Van Seters's argument, see Hostetter, *Nations*, 69, 139; Satterthwaite and Baker, "Nations of Canaan," 599.

99. Weinstein, "Egyptian Empire," 1–28; Sarna, *Exodus*, 149.

100. Rainey, "Satrapy," 51; Tuell, "Southern and Eastern Borders," 51; Dozeman, *Exodus*, 559.

101. Bhabha, *Location of Culture*, 86–88; Ashcroft, Griffins, and Tiffin, *Post-Colonial Studies*, 125–26. See also §1.2.2.1.

102. Prabhu, *Hybridity*, xiv, 119–20; see also §1.2.2.2.

reflect the imperialized authors' endeavor to invite their audience to envision the subversion of imperial subjugation, particularly that of the Neo-Assyrian Empire, albeit in a conservative way.

Hence, while the imperialized authors broadly took up hostile attention to enemies in the imperial legal metanarrative, they resisted following it in using the enemies to punish disobedient people. They instead distinctively made use of the confrontation with enemies as Yhwh's blessings for the imperialized people, subverting Neo-Assyrian subjugation. These blessings do necessitate the discussed postcolonial and ethical critique, especially when they appear together with an ambivalent response toward the imperial legal emphasis on the human emperor's effort in the elimination of enemies. This response makes the blessings particularly oppressive to other inhabitants in the Levant, due to the shift from Yhwh's role to the audience's participation in driving out the enemies. These blessings are also tied with the condition of loyal obedience to Yhwh, which would be oppressive to the imperialized people if this divine governance was motivated by the elite authors' self-serving economic and political interests. Nevertheless, the unique details of these blessings, the call for obedience to Yhwh rather than emperors, and the initial distancing from human participation in eliminating the enemies indicate the imperialized authors' attempt to convey a message resistive to imperial subjugation. This message was significant to the imperialized audience in Israel and Judah, inviting them to envisage Yhwh's subversion of Neo-Assyrian subjugation, although it was still framed under the imperial legal paradigm, thus characterizing the Exodus commandments as a conservatively revolutionary response of the imperialized people to the imperial legal metanarrative.

4.5 Chapter Conclusions

Studying Exodus 20:23–21:1 and 22:17–23:33 from the perspective of the imperialized, this analysis demonstrates how these commandments reveal the wrestling of the biblical authors with imperial legal traditions when they compiled a law collection primarily for their elite audience in Israel and Judah during Neo-Assyrian subjugation. On the one hand, these commandments reflect resemblances to cuneiform legal traditions in addressing topics on religious services, care for the marginalized, and fighting against enemies outside the mostly casuistic legal section. These resemblances manifest that the imperialized authors accepted imperial legal traditions' attention to these issues and their approach of locating them in their law collections. On the other hand, these commandments exhibit contrasts to cuneiform legal traditions, indicating that the imperialized authors did not fully acknowledge the imperial legal metanarrative, but endeavored to resist some aspects of it, especially the promotion of the emperors' domination over the subjugated people. Commandments regarding obedience to Yhwh, meanwhile, involve shifts between acceptance and resistance, revealing an ambivalent response of the imperialized authors to the imperial legal metanarrative concerning human participation in the elimination of enemies.

These responses do reveal some oppressive imperial elements, especially examined from a postcolonial optic. The requirements of serving Yhwh and caring for the marginalized lead to a question about the possible self-serving motivations of the elite authors, which would lead to exploitation and domination of the imperialized people similar to and in addition to the imperial subjugation of them. The commandments related to the enemies even exhibit oppressive imperial ideology from the outset due to the acceptance of the hostile attention to them advocated in the imperial legal metanarrative. Despite the initial attempt at moving away from human participation in the elimination of enemies, these commandments end up shifting toward the imperial legal promotion of it and concurrently complying with Neo-Assyrian political ideology. The call for loyal obedience to Yhwh again attracts a query about the imperialized authors' economic and political interests behind the support of divine governance, which would serve further their ambition to conquer other people in the Levant in addition to their domination of their own people. These commandments indeed bless the imperialized audience at the expense of other inhabitants in the Levant, necessitating critique, as well as rejection.

These extensive oppressive elements inevitably overshadow the resistance that the imperialized authors endeavored to put up against the imperial legal metanarrative, as well as Neo-Assyrian subjugation. A significant one is directed to the exaltation of the emperors in the imperial legal metanarrative, which the Neo-Assyrian Empire similarly advocated. Resisting their presentation of religious services, care for the marginalized, and destruction of enemies as the emperors' achievements, the Exodus commandments address these concerns as Yhwh's commandments and conditional promise. This resistance urges the imperialized audience to worship Yhwh, rather than revering the emperors. Making use of their own religious belief, like colonized people retrieving their traditions in modern contexts, the imperialized authors, moreover, appear to demand the imperialized people not to follow the emperors in relying on multiple gods for gaining recognition, but to loyally obey Yhwh, their national God. The commandments concerning the marginalized, meanwhile, remind the imperialized audience of Yhwh's attention to their oppression against these people instead of the emperors' delegated duties in their care. Like colonized people who use their colonizer's culture strategically for anti-colonial resistance, the imperialized authors also appropriated imperial attention to enemies in order to urge the imperialized audience again to obey Yhwh, rather than following emperors' law and reliance on various gods. The conditional blessings, which contrast with the emperors' curses, help the imperialized audience further to envision Yhwh's subversion of the imperial subjugation against them, including that carried out by the Neo-Assyrian Empire.

This resistance is nuanced further by presenting the religious services and care for the marginalized as the people's obligation rather than an emperor's accomplishment. The requirements for the materials of the altar, in fact, allow laypeople among the imperialized to participate in serving Yhwh and establish relationship with him. The association between the Israelites' experience in Egypt and the commandments on offerings and festivals reminds the imperialized audience about the importance of resisting imperial subjugation of them. Yhwh's attention to the oppression against marginalized people, furthermore, calls the imperialized people, particularly their elites, to care for the marginalized. Uniquely repeating the concern about the immigrants among those regarding marginalized people, these commandments associate the immigrants' suffering to imperial subjugation, which the people of Israel and Judah also endured. The imperialized authors, therefore, resisted the imperial legal reluctance to emphasize care for the immigrants. They even required their elite audience to offer a weekly day off to the immigrants in order to work against the economic exploitation of these people, even though there was a tremendous need to accommodate the economic demand of the Neo-Assyrian Empire.

These resistances amid acceptances of the imperial legal metanarrative characterize the commandments in Exodus 20:23–21:1 and 22:17–23:33 as part of the work of conservative revolutionists, just as the ordinances that they surround. The authors' conservativeness in departing from the imperial legal framework explains why the Exodus commandments, particularly those concerning the land's inhabitants, look imperial and oppressive, as postcolonial biblical scholars have noted. However, the authors' revolutionary attempts also make these commandments resistive to imperial exploitation and domination of the imperialized people, as my study unfolds. This comparative analysis, going beyond scholarly arguments about the literary, legal, or educational relationship between the Book of the Covenant and cuneiform law collections, reveals the wrestling of the imperialized authors when they attempted to respond to the imperial legal metanarrative in the composition of their own law collection under the shadow of the Neo-Assyrian Empire.

CHAPTER 5

Yhwh, Moses, and the People in the Narrative

(Exodus 19:1–20:22 and 24:1–18)

5.1 Introduction

A study of the Exodus ordinances and commandments from the perspective of imperialized people is not complete without analyzing their surrounding narrative in Exodus 19:1–20:22 and 24:1–18. As some scholars argue, these ordinances and commandments, which constitute the Book of the Covenant, need a narrative to provide essential contextualizing information.[1] Although it seems to have little connection with the Book of the Covenant and is unlikely to present its original historical setting,[2] the narrative identifies the maker, the pronouncer, and the recipient of the ordinances and commandments. It also constitutes a threefold structure together with the Book of the Covenant.[3] These features notably resemble those of the prologue and epilogue of some cuneiform law collections, warranting further a comparative analysis between

1. Sarna, *Exodus*, 117; Wright, *Inventing God's Law*, 333; Oswald, "Exodus-Gottesberg-Erzählung, 39; Oswald, "Lawgiving," 191.

2. About the lack of connections between the narrative and the Book of the Covenant, see Greengus, "Some Issues," 74; Westbrook and Wells, *Everyday Law*, 130. Concerning the dissociation between the narrative and the historical setting of the Book of the Covenant, see Patrick, "Who is the Revolutionist?," 158.

3. Paul, *Studies in the Book of the Covenant*, 27–28.

this narrative and the non-legal sections of these cuneiform law collections.[4] Utilizing postcolonial understandings of imperialized people, this analysis continues to unfold the imperialized authors' wrestling with imperial legal traditions.

The question is which passages in Exodus 19:1–20:22 and 24:1–18 this study should include. Scholars have diverse opinions on this narrative's composite features. From source analysis and tradition-historical analysis to redaction analysis, scholars have not reached a consensus on the relationship between different passages in the narrative and their date of composition.[5] In view of the possible connections between different passages in this narrative and between this narrative and the Book of the Covenant, such as similar themes, imagery, and language occurring in Exodus 19:3–6, 20:22–26, and 24:3–8,[6] I am inclined to regard most of the passages in Exodus 19:1–20:22 and 24:1–18 as a unit written in the Neo-Assyrian period prior to the composition of Deuteronomy (see the quotation below).[7] Still, as a matter of caution,

---

4. About the lack of links between the non-legal and legal sections of some cuneiform law collections, see Greengus, "Some Issues," 74. For the essential nature of the prologue and epilogue to the entire law collection, particularly in the Laws of Hammurabi, see Bottéro, *Mesopotamia*, 158.

5. For recent discussions of these opinions see Alexander, *Exodus*, 355–58, 360–63, 379–82, 390–98, 433–35, 538–42, 551–52, and Albertz, *Exodus, Band II*, 27–29, 31–38, 107–110, 112–14, 142, 145–48. Alexander argues for the unity of Exod 19:1–20:22 and 24:1–18 and the priority of this narrative over Deuteronomy. Albertz, however, sees various components in this narrative and dates the earliest one to the late exilic period. Still, Albertz suggests that this earliest and substantial component contains older traditions. Dozeman's latest understanding is similar to Albertz, but only divides the narrative into Non-P and P histories (Dozeman, *Exodus*, 37–43, 424–32). This understanding differs from his classic tradition-historical or redaction-critical analysis, which argues for several redaction layers and identifies the earliest tradition as pre-Deuteronomistic (Dozeman, *God on the Mountain*, 19). For earlier but still helpful discussions, see Propp, *Exodus 19–40*, 141–54; Durham, *Exodus*, 258–61, 268–70, 278–83, 302, 340–42; Houtman, *Exodus*, 2:425–39, 3:7–11, 72–74, 284–88, 297–99; Childs, *Book of Exodus*, 344–51, 388–93, 499–502. They express more about the speculative or inconclusive nature of the narrative's composite features and dating.

6. Chavel, "Kingdom of Priests," 186–87, 190–92. Other scholars also identify the parallel between 19:2–8 and 20:21–24:3 (Alexander, *Exodus*, 360; Philips, "Fresh Look," 44–45; Patrick, "Covenant Code," 145–57). John Van Seter, meanwhile, argues for the mixed nature of the storm and fire theophanies (Van Seter, *Life of Moses*, 256). Reading Exod 19:1–20:22 and 24:1–18 with literary techniques, such as synoptic/resumptive repetition, in mind, scholars, such as Sprinkle (*Book of the Covenant*, 17–34) and Chirchigno ("Narrative Structure," 457–79), even see the coherence of the whole narrative. Paul R. Williamson argues further that these literary devices, or source criticism, are "largely unnecessary" for the reading of Exod 19–24, although his chronological reading is theologically oriented (Williamson, "Promised with Strings," 119–20).

7. Passages which I agree possibly to be additions subsequent to the composition of Deuteronomy are Exod 19:20–25, 24:1–2, 24:9–11, and 24:15–18. I do not include them in the

in the following analysis, I always begin with the passages that David P. Wright proposes as the basic surrounding narrative of the Book of the Covenant (in bold type in the quotation).[8] This suggestion considers scholarly proposals regarding the possible existence of two narrative blocks, namely one about the fire theophany and another about the storm theophany, and the original connection between the latter and the Book of the Covenant.[9] This suggestion is also mostly in line with the pre-Deuteronomistic passages proposed by scholars who deem Exodus 19:1–20:22 and 24:1–18 to be composite.[10] Following each analysis of this narrative block, I examine other passages relevant to the discussion, with notes concerning their primary features.

The Narrative of the Book of the Covenant for This Analysis[11]

> [19:1]On the third new moon, after the sons of Israel had gone out of the land of Egypt, on that day they came into the wilderness of Sinai. [2]They set out from Rephidim, came to the wilderness of Sinai, and camped in the wilderness; **Israel camped there before the mountain.** [3]**Moses went up to God.** Yhwh called to him from the mountain, saying, "Thus you shall say to the house of Jacob and tell the sons of Israel: [4]You yourself saw what I did to the Egyptians, and I lifted you on eagles' wings and brought you to me. [5]So now, if you surely listen to my voice and keep my covenant, you shall be for me treasured possession from among

---

following analysis. About their late features, see, for instance, Albertz, *Exodus, Band II*, 49–51, 134–35, 140–41, 151–53.

8. These passages include Exod 19:2b–3a, 9a, 16b–17, 19, 20:18–22a (excluding ואת ההר עשן "and the smoking mountain" in 20:18), and 24:3–8 (excluding ואת כל־המשפטים "and all the ordinances" in 24:3); Wright, *Inventing God's Law*, 338–39, 341–42.

9. According to David Wright, the core of the fire theophany narrative includes Exod 19:10–16a, 18 (Wright, *Inventing God's Law*, 338–39). Scholars, such as Bernard M. Levinson and Ralf Rothenbusch, identify conflicting contents between the two narrative blocks, but suggest that each of them exhibits internal consistency (Levinson, "Is the Covenant Code an Exilic Composition," 280–81; Rothenbusch, *Kasuistische Rechtssammlung*, 546–66). For a summary of this scholarly discussion, see Wright, *Inventing God's Law*, 495–96, note 70.

10. For a detailed review of suggestions on the basic pre-Deuteronomistic narrative, see Wright, *Inventing God's Law*, 496–98, notes 71, 76.

11. The following translation is mine. While David Wrights defines the Book of the Covenant as Exod 20:23–23:19, I define it as Exod 20:23–23:33. For more about various understandings of this corpus's limits, see Introduction, page 7, note 2. Regarding Exod 23:18–33's connection with Exod 22:17–23:17, see §4.4.

all the peoples. For the entire earth is mine, [6]but you will be for me a kingdom of priests and a holy nation. These are the words that you shall speak to the sons of Israel."

[7]So Moses came and called for the elders of the people, and he set before them all these words that Yhwh ordered him. [8]All the people answered together and said, "Everything that Yhwh spoke, we will do." Moses brought back the words of the people to Yhwh. [9]**Yhwh said to Moses, "Look, I myself am coming to you in a thick cloud, so that the people may hear when I speak with you and also may trust in you forever."** So Moses told the words of the people to Yhwh, [10]and Yhwh said to Moses, "Go to the people and consecrate them today and tomorrow, and have them wash their clothes. [11]They shall be ready for the third day because on the third day Yhwh will come down before the eyes of all the people on Mount Sinai. [12]You shall set bounds for the people all around, saying, "Keep yourself from going up the mountain or touching its border. Anyone who touches the mountain shall surely be put to death. [13]No hand shall touch him, for he shall surely be stoned or shot through. Whether animal or human being, he shall not live. When the ram's horn sounds out, they themselves may go up the mountain. [14]So Moses went down from the mountain to the people and consecrated the people, and they washed their clothes. [15]He said to the people, "Be ready for the third day. Do not go near a woman."

[16]It came about on the third day, when it was morning, **there were sounds, lightning flashes, and a heavy cloud over the mountain, and the very strong sound of a horn. All the people who were in the camp trembled.** [17]**Moses brought the people out from the camp to meet God, and they took their stand at the foot of the mountain.** [18]Mount Sinai smoked, all of it, because Yhwh had gone down on it in fire, and the smoke went up like the smoke of a kiln. The whole mountain trembled greatly. [19]**The sound of the horn was getting stronger and stronger. Moses would speak, and God would answer him with the sound.**

[20:1]God spoke all these words, saying, [2]"I am Yhwh your God, who brought you out of the land of Egypt, out of the house of slavery. [3]There shall not be other gods for yourself before me. [4]You shall not make for yourself an image or likeness of anything that is in heaven above, or that is on the earth below, or that is in the water under the earth. [5]You shall not bow down to them, and you shall not serve them; for I, Yhwh your God, am a jealous God, attending to the iniquity of fathers in connection with the sons, with the third and the fourth generations, for those who hate me, [6]but acting in steadfast love to thousands, for those who love me and who keep my commandments. [7]You shall not lift up the name of Yhwh your God in vain, for Yhwh will not acquit anyone who lifts up his name in vain. [8]Remember the sabbath day to consecrate it. [9]Six days you shall serve and do all your work, [10]but the seventh day is a sabbath for Yhwh your God. You shall not do any work, you, your son or your daughter, your male slave or your female slave, or your animal, or your immigrant who is within your gates. [11]For in six days, Yhwh made the heavens and the earth, the sea, and all that is in them, and settled down on the seventh day; therefore, Yhwh blessed the seventh day and consecrated it. [12]Honor your father and your mother, in order that your days may be prolonged on the land that Yhwh your God is going to give you. [13]You shall not murder. [14]You shall not commit adultery. [15]You shall not steal. [16]You shall not bear false witness against another person. [17]You shall not desire the house of another person; you shall not desire the wife of another person, or his male slave, or his female slave, or his ox, or his donkey, or anything that belongs to another person.

[18]**All the people were looking at the sounds, lightning, and the sound of the horn**, and the smoking mountain. **The people looked, shook, and stood at a distance.** [19]**They said to Moses, "You yourself speak with us, and we will listen; God shall not speak with us, lest we will die."** [20]**Moses said to the people, "You shall not fear, for God has come in order to test you, and in order that fear for him will be upon your faces, so you**

do not sin." [21]**The people stood at a distance, and Moses drew near to the darkness where God was.** [22]**Yhwh said to Moses, "Thus you shall say to the sons of Israel:** You yourselves saw that I spoke with you from heaven."

(The Book of the Covenant, Exod 20:23–23:33)

[24:3]**Moses came and recounted to the people all the words of Yhwh** and all the ordinances. **All the people answered with one voice and said, "All the words that Yhwh has spoken, we will do."** [4]**Moses wrote all the words of Yhwh. He rose early in the morning and built an altar beneath the mountain and twelve pillars for the twelve tribes of Israel.** [5]**He sent young men of the sons of Israel, and they offered up burnt offerings and sacrificed well-being sacrifices of bulls to Yhwh.** [6]**Moses took half of the blood and put it in basins, and half of the blood he sprinkled on the altar.** [7]**He took the book of the covenant and read it in the ears of the people. They said, "All that Yhwh has spoken, we will do, and we will listen."** [8]**Moses took the blood, sprinkled it on the people, and said, "Look, the blood of the covenant that Yhwh made with you on the basis of all these words."**

[12]Yhwh said to Moses, "Go up to me on the mountain and be there. I shall give you the tablets of stone and the instruction and the commandment, which I have written to instruct them." [13]So Moses arose with Joshua, his minister, and Moses went up to the mountain of God. [14]To the elders he said, "Stay here for us until we return to you. Here are Aaron and Hur with you. Whoever has issues shall approach them."

Similar to the analysis of the commandments in chapter four, I compare this narrative with cuneiform law collections whose prologue, superscriptions, and/or epilogue are extant, although the following analysis indicates that this narrative resembles mainly the collections of Ur-Namma, Lipit-Ishtar, and Hammurabi. My propositions are that these cuneiform law collections reflect the legal traditions that prevailed in Mesopotamia and the Levant and that the authors of the Exodus corpus were familiar with these legal traditions and their imperial nature, regarding them as a representation of the imperial legal metanarrative of their time.[12]

My analysis focuses on the roles of gods, human leaders, and the people in the pronouncement of the law. An essential background is that the biblical authors, who lived under Neo-Assyrian subjugation, might have felt the pressure to follow imperial legal traditions but concurrently desired to differ from them.[13] According to postcolonial observations of colonized people, the adherence reflects acceptance of the imperial legal metanarrative, while the difference indicates resistance to it.[14] These understandings, together with postcolonial scholars' call for ethical engagement,[15] again guide the following comparative analysis. This analysis continues to reveal how the imperialized authors wrestled with the imperial legal metanarrative when they compiled a law collection primarily for their elite audience, who had scribal and legal training and access to their palace and temple similar to the imperialized authors.[16] This wrestling, like that manifested in the ordinances and commandments, characterizes the narrative of the Covenant collection as a work of conservative revolutionists.

5.2 Gods, Human Leaders, and the People in the Pronouncement of the Law

The suggested basic narrative in the Exodus corpus presents who is involved in the pronouncement of the commandments and ordinances and how this pronouncement works. The narrative preceding the Exodus commandments reveals that this pronouncement involves a top-down process from the divine, to the human leader, then to the people.[17] Yhwh finds a way to show his conversation with Moses to the people (Exod 19:9a). He also tells Moses what he should announce to them (Exod 20:22a). The narrative following the Exodus commandments focuses more on Moses's work related to the pronouncement, with a particular emphasis on "words" (דברים). He recounts Yhwh's words

12. See §2.2.4 and §2.3.2.3.

13. See §2.4.7 and §2.5.

14. See §1.2.2.2.

15. See §1.2.2.2.

16. See §2.5

17. Childs, *Book of Exodus*, 393.

(כל־דברי יהוה "all the words of Yhwh," Exod 24:3) and the people respond to them (כל־הדברים אשר־דבר יהוה "all the words that Yhwh has spoken," Exod 24:3). He also writes them down (כל־דברי יהוה "all the words of Yhwh," Exod 24:4) and reads them in the covenant ceremony (Exod 24:7), which he carries out according to these words (על כל־הדברים האלה "on the basis of all these words," Exod 24:8). All these occurrences noticeably refer to the words of Yhwh, the divine and the lawmaker.

Passages not belonging to the suggested basic narrative offer more details about the pronouncement but still reveal this top-down process involving God, the human leader, and the people. Yhwh calls Moses from the mountain and instructs him what to tell the people (Exod 19:3b). He asks Moses to consecrate the people (Exod 19:10), preparing for the pronouncement of the commandments and ordinances. He also asks Moses to go up to the mountain in order to receive the stone tablets for instructing the people (Exod 24:12). Noticeably, the reference to "words" (דברים) occurs four times in Exodus 19:6–9, two of which refer to Yhwh's words (אלה הדברים אשר תדבר "these are the words that you shall speak," Exod 19:6; כל־הדברים האלה אשר צוהו יהוה "all these words that Yhwh ordered him," Exod 19:7).[18] It then occurs again in Exodus 20:1, which introduces God's pronouncement of the Decalogue (וידבר אלהים את כל־הדברים האלה "God spoke all these words"). It also appears in Exodus 24:14, which refers to the people's issues needing some kind of judgment (מי־בעל דברים יגש אלהם "whoever has issues shall approach them"). These passages, although not belonging to the suggested basic narrative, are regarded by some scholars as the basic text of the Book of the Covenant and/or texts that predate Deuteronomy.[19]

---

18. Two other references refer to the people's words (Exod 19:8–9), which I will discuss in the following analysis.

19. In addition to Exod 19:2b, 16b, 17, 19b; 20:18a, 19–20a, 21; 24:3–8 (which David Wright similarly includes in his basic narrative), Otto Eissfeldt also includes 19:3a, 4–8, 10, 13b, 14; 20:1–17; 24:12, 13b, and 18b in the basic narrative of the Book of the Covenant (Eissfeldt, *Komposition der Sinai-Erzählung*, 5–29). Patrick also argues that, in addition to Exod 20:22–23:19 and 24:3–8, Exod 19:3b–8 belong to the Book of the Covenant's preceding narrative and predate Deuteronomy (Patrick, *Old Testament Law*, 64–65). Dozeman, meanwhile, regards Exod 19:10a–11a, 12a, 13b–15a, in addition to 19:2b–3a, 16a–17 and 24:4a–5, as the work of the Mountain of God tradition, which is pre-Deuteronomistic (Dozeman, *God on the Mountain*, 19). Regarding the Decalogue (Exod 20:1–17), David Wright suggests that it predates Deuteronomy despite probably being secondary to the basic narrative (Wright, *Inventing God's Law*, 342). Concerning the narrative following the Exodus commandments, Propp regards Exod 24:1–15a as the work of a single authorship belonging to E (Propp, *Exodus 19–40*, 147). Joel S. Baden,

This three-tier, top-down pronouncement process, which involves Yhwh, Moses, and the people, and the emphasis on the words resemble the descriptions in the prologue and epilogue of some cuneiform law collections. Nevertheless, these resemblances appear alongside intricate contrasts, manifesting the authors' endeavor to resist the imperial legal metanarrative of their time, amid their acceptance of it.

Acceptance of the Imperial Legal Metanarrative

Providing contextual information for the pronouncement of the law, the prologues of the Ur-Namma, Lipit-Ishtar, and Hammurabi collections all begin with an account of a top-down delegation from the gods to the emperors, who then promote justice accordingly in their lands. The text of the Ur-Namma collection's prologue is broken, and the meaning of some passages is obscure. However, after a brief description of Ur-Namma's kingship and his services to the gods (LU A 1:1–30), this prologue presents An and Enlil's delegation of Ur's kingship to the god Nanna and the divine origin of Ur-Namma's kingship (LU A 1:31–42). With a better-preserved text, the Lipit-Ishtar collection offers an even clearer presentation of this delegation process. Its prologue begins with an account of An and Enlil's delegation of Sumer and Akkad's kingship to the goddess Ninisina (LL 1:1–19). Then it states that An and Enlil call Lipit-Ishtar to the princeship of the land to promote justice there (LL 1:20–37). The Hammurabi collection's prologue follows a similar pattern, recounting Anu and Enlil's delegation of Babylon's kingship to Marduk (LH 1:1–26) and then their calling of Hammurabi to princeship in order to promote justice in the land (LH 1:27–49).

The epilogues of these law collections then focus on the emperors' work, particularly their effort in preserving the law. The Laws of X, which is possibly the epilogue of the Ur-Namma collection,[20] ends with a concern about those who erase the inscription, whom the emperor curses (LX rev. 3':9'–20'). Similarly, after reiterating his work, including the maintenance of justice (LL 21:5–17), Lipit-Ishtar states that he erected the stela when he established justice in Sumer and Akkad (LL 21:36–38). He then blesses those who do not erase the inscription but curses those who do (LL 21:39–60; 22:6–16,

meanwhile, considers Exod 24:11b, 12–15, and 18b as the work of E (Baden, "Rethinking," 186, note 146).

20. Roth, *Law Collections*, 36.

22:34–52). The epilogue of the Hammurabi collection follows a similar pattern, but with a more elaborate account of Hammurabi's work on promoting the observance and preservation of the law. The epilogue begins with a statement indicating that the preceding laws are just decisions that Hammurabi established (LH 47:1–8). After reiterating his various contributions to his people (LH 47:9–58), he states that he has inscribed his words on his stela and set it up (LH 47:74–76). He then calls the oppressed person to read aloud the inscription on his stela and to listen to his words (LH 48:9–12). He also calls future kings to observe what he inscribed on his stela and not to change it (LH 48:59–84). Hammurabi's blessings for those who attend to and preserve his inscription and his curses for those who erase or change it then follow (LH 49:2–51:91).

These prologues and epilogues, moreover, contain some references to "word" (inim in Sumerian; *awātum* in Akkadian) and "words" (*awâtum* in Akkadian).[21] Two references to inim involve some textual reconstructions. One occurs in the Ur-Namma collection's prologue, which addresses Ur-Namma's establishment of justice in the land by Utu's true word (([inim g]i?-na [^{d}Utu(?)]-ta, LU A 3:108–113); another occurs in the Lipit-Ishtar collection's epilogue, which presents Lipit-Ishtar's maintenance of justice by Utu's true word ([inim g]i-na ^{d}Utu-ta, LL 21:5–7). A reference in the Lipit-Ishtar collection's prologue, meanwhile, clearly presents that Lipit-Ishtar established justice in his lands by Enlil's word (inim ^{d}En-líl-lá-ta, LL 1:52–55).[22] The Hammurabi collection's epilogue echoes these references by stating Hammurabi's submission to Marduk's word (*ana awat Marduk*, LH 48:25). Furthermore, there are two occurrences of "word" (*awātum*) that refer to the oppressed person's issue or lawsuit (LH 48:6, 15).[23] The reference

21. See "inim" *PSD*, http://psd.museum.upenn.edu/nepsd-frame.html, for the correspondence between inim and *awātum*.

22. Another reference to inim occurs in the Lipit-Ishtar collection's epilogue, which relates to Lipit-Ishtar's invocation of Utu to remove Utu's word (probably some kind of promise) for the curse recipient (LL 22:34–52).

23. For different translations of these occurrences of *awātum*, see Roth, *Law Collections*, 134; Kitchen and Lawrence, *Treaty, Law, and Covenant*, 177; Richardson, *Hammurabi's Law*, 123. There are three other occurrences of *awātum*: The first refers to Marduk's word in the warning against the removal of Hammurabi's engraved image (LH 47:89). The second refers to the curse recipient's word or case, which Hammurabi invokes the goddess Ninlil to denounce before Enlil (LH 49:81). The third refers to Shamash's word, which Hammurabi invokes Shamash to use to overcome the curse recipient (LH 50:31). David Wright compares the curse related to the

to the plural form, "words" (*awâtum*), even occurs a number of times (LH 47:74, 47:81; 48:12, 48:64, 48:78, 48:99; 49:2, 49:7, 49:18, 49:29), emphasizing the pronouncement made by Hammurabi, the lawmaker.

These descriptions suggest that cuneiform legal traditions regard the origin or the pronouncement process of the law (which involves the gods, the emperors, and their lands) as a crucial component in their non-legal sections. They also exhibit the resemblances of the Covenant collection's narrative to its cuneiform counterparts. Similar to these cuneiform law collections' prologues, the Covenant collection's prelude reveals that the pronouncement of the commandments and ordinances involves a three-tier, top-down process from the divine to the human leader and then to the people. Like the prologues and epilogues of these cuneiform law collections, the Covenant collection's prelude and postscript also respectively emphasize the divine delegation and the human leader's effort to preserve and to draw others' attention to the commandments and ordinances. Moreover, the Covenant collection's emphasis on "words" (דברים) resembles cuneiform law collections' mentions of "words" (*awâtum*) and "word" (inim; *awātum*), which have attracted little scholarly attention.[24] These resemblances suggest that the imperialized authors broadly accepted the imperial legal understanding of the roles of the divine, human leaders, and the people in the law pronouncement and the imperial legal emphasis on the words.

This acceptance reasonably leads to a postcolonial inquiry into the imperial, and even oppressive, nature of the Covenant collection's narrative. The similar emphasis on writing down the law seems to suggest that the imperialized authors acknowledged the imperial mode of lawmaking, as some colonial people do in the modern context.[25] That is, even having depicted that Moses has communicated Yhwh's words to the people and the people have

---

third one with Yhwh's threat against the oppressor of the poor in Exod 22:22–23, 26 (Wright, *Inventing God's Law*, 68).

24. Despite addressing various similarities between the suggested basic narrative of the Book of the Covenant and the epilogue of the Hammurabi collection, David Wright does not make any comparison concerning דברים and *awâtum* between these two corpuses. Rather, he compares the references to *awâtum* in the Hammurabi collection to Exod 23:13a (about the observance of what Yhwh said [מאר]), Exod 23:7 (about false testimony [דבר־שקר]), and Exod 22:8 (about an issue [דבר] concerning property disputes); see Wright, *Inventing God's Law*, 60, 64, 66, 68, 255, 317, 338–42.

25. Chanock, *Law and Custom*, 60; see also §1.3.3.

verbally affirmed their acceptance of those words, the imperialized authors still delineated Moses's efforts to record those words, just as the emperors inscribed their laws. This delineation may reflect these authors' attempt to establish a certain kind of authority for their leader among their people, like the emperors did. The comparable hierarchal understanding of God, the human leaders, and the people, meanwhile, appears to promote imperial domination of the people and subordination of women to men, as postcolonial biblical scholars argue.[26] It may be susceptible to supporting exploitative human leadership in Israel and Judah, if it was motivated by the elite authors' self-interests. Composing their own law collection primarily for their elite peers, the imperialized authors appear to follow imperial approaches to leadership and lawmaking when they were under Neo-Assyrian subjugation.

Resistance: Yhwh and Moses rather than the Gods and Emperors

Amid this acceptance, the Covenant collection's narrative, however, reflects resistance to imperial legal traditions through its intricate divergences. As Naiden notes, "Marduk is not Yahweh, nor is Hammurabi Moses;"[27] these divergences are not straightforward one-to-one contrasts but exhibit a kind of crossover between the roles of the divine and those of the human leaders in the Exodus corpus and cuneiform law collections. This crossover indicates that the imperialized authors did not totally accept the imperial legal metanarrative but endeavored to work against imperial ideology and domination, including that of the Assyrians, even though they expressed this resistance under the framework of the imperial legal metanarrative.

Yhwh, rather than the Gods, is the Delegator – but More

This crossover begins with contrasts between the depiction of Yhwh and those of the gods, which are noticeable but have not received much scholarly attention. These contrasts indicate that the imperialized authors rejected imperial gods' roles among the imperialized people. Contrary to cuneiform law collections, which describe that An(u) and Enlil delegate princeship to the emperors (LU A 1:36–42; LL 1:20–37; LH 1:27–49), the Covenant collection's suggested basic narrative depicts that Yhwh commissions Moses to

26. Dube, *Postcolonial Feminist Interpretation*, 75; Yee, "Postcolonial Biblical Criticism," 223; Wafula, "Exodus," 22; see also §1.4.

27. F. S. Naiden, "Gods, Kings," 83.

pronounce the ordinances and commandments (Exod 19:9a; 20:22a). Rather than stating that the emperors establish justice in the land by the gods' word (inim, LU A 3:108–113; LL 1:52–55; 21:5) or submit themselves to the gods' word (*awātum*, LH 48:25), the suggested basic narrative also emphasizes that what Moses recounts to the people are Yhwh's words themselves (דברים, Exod 24:3–4). Passages other than the suggested basic narrative also reflect these contrasts. The repeated descriptions of Yhwh calling or talking to Moses (Exod 19:3, 19:10; 24:12) and the reoccurrences of "the words" (הדברים) that refer to Yhwh's message to the people (Exod 19:6, 19:7) demonstrate that the human leader receives delegation from Yhwh, rather than the gods of the empires.

The contrast between Yhwh and the imperial gods is not limited to their role as the delegator of the human leaders but occurs also in the descriptions of their roles as a royal figure and a warrior of their people. As mentioned, before stating that the emperors receive princeship from the gods, the three cuneiform law collections begin their prologues by presenting that An(u) and Enlil delegates kingship (nam-lugal or *šarrūtum*) of the lands to other gods (Nanna in LU A 1:31–33, Ninisina in LL 1:1–19, Marduk in LH 1:1–26). The Lipit-Ishtar and Hammurabi collections indeed refer to Enlil and Anu, respectively, as king (lugal, LL 1:3–4; *šarum* LH 1:1–2) in their prologues.[28] Their epilogues then particularly address Ninurta//Zababa as a mighty warrior (ur-sag kala-ga in LL 42:34–52 for Ninurta; *qarrādum rabium* in LH 50:81–82 for Zababa).[29] The Hammurabi collection also states that Zababa and Ishtar bestowed Hammurabi a mighty weapon (LH 47:22–25) and that Ishtar draws out his weapon (LH 50:92–95), indicating these gods' warrior roles.

Contrarily, the Covenant collection presents that Yhwh takes these royal and warrior roles through its description of the theophany. Images in this description, including thunder and lightning (in the suggested basic narrative, Exod 19:16b), and even fire and shaking of mountains (in passages outside the suggested basic narrative, Exod 19:18), occur fairly commonly in different combinations in the depictions of theophany in both Mesopotamian and

---

28. For more about Mesopotamian understanding of the gods' possession of kingship, see Smith, "Concept of God," 19–23.

29. About the relationship between Ninurta and Zababa, see Black and Green, "Zababa," 187.

Ugaritic literatures and do not necessarily relate only to one or the others.[30] More significantly, these literatures suggest that those images carry warrior, and even royal warrior, connotations: The cloud represents a chariot-like vehicle,[31] the thunder and lightning flashes, as well as fire, symbolize the divine's weapons,[32] and the trembling of nature indicates a response to the appearance of war-like gods and Assyrian kings in battle.[33] In the Covenant collection, these images indeed appear together with the description of the sound of the horn (שופר, in the suggested basic narrative, Exod 19:16b, 19:19). As some scholars point out, the blowing of the horn is unusual in the biblical description of theophany,[34] but it occurs in biblical passages describing the introduction of a new king (2 Sam 15:10; 1 Kgs 1:34, 1:39; 2 Kgs 9:13)[35] in addition to those describing festivals.[36] The theophany in the Covenant collection, especially the suggested basic narrative, thus presents Yhwh as a warrior as well as a royal figure, while cuneiform law collections state that the gods take up these two roles.

These parallel contrasts between Yhwh and the imperial gods appear alongside a significant distinction, which is widely noticed in general but deserves explication. Rather than sitting back after the delegation, or merely taking the role as a royal warrior, like the gods do, Yhwh himself formulates the commandments and the ordinances. In cuneiform law collections, An(u) and Enlil basically fade out from the scene after delegating princeship to the

30. For scholars who emphasize the relationship between the Covenant collection's theophany and Mesopotamian literature, see, for instance, Jeremias, *Theophanie*, 78–87; Mann, *Divine Presence*, 96–100; Niehaus, *God at Sinai*, 125–36. For scholars who underscore the relationship between the Covenant collection's theophany and Ugaritic literature, see, for instance, Cross, *Canaanite Myth*, 147–94. See also Van Seters, *Life of Moses*, 254–62 for the relationship between the Covenant collection's theophany and Mesopotamian and Ugaritic literature. Concerning the relationship between the Covenant collection's motif of nature's trembling and Mesopotamian and Ugaritic literatures, see Loewenstamm, "Trembling of Nature," 173–89.

31. Hiebert, "Theophany," 509; Longman and Reid, *God Is A Warrior*, 67–68. For other understandings of this imagery, see, for instance, Burnside, "Hidden Faces," 108. He suggests that the cloud and the smoke indicate Yhwh's hiddenness, but does not consider other images, namely thunder, lightning flashes, and fire.

32. Hiebert, "Theophany," 509; Dozeman, *Exodus*, 19; Jeremias, *Theophanie*, 78–83.

33. Loewenstamm, "Trembling of Nature," 182–83.

34. Van Seters, *Life of Moses*, 268.

35. Brettler, *God Is King*, 129, 133.

36. Van Seters, *Life of Moses*, 268; Propp, *Exodus 19–40*, 164.

emperors to establish justice in the lands. At most, Lipit-Ishtar mentions the gods again when he states that he established justice in Sumer and Akkad by Enlil's and Utu's words (LL 1:52–55; 21:5–7). Ur-Namma also refers to Nanna and Utu when he says that he established justice in the land by their power and word respectively (LU A 3:108–113), while Hammurabi refers to Marduk when he talks about his establishment of justice as Marduk commanded him to do so (LH 5:14–24). All three emperors even invoke various gods, including An(u) and Enlil, to bless rulers who follow the laws the emperors inscribed and to punish those who do not (LX rev. 3:15'–20'; LL 21:36–22:52; LH 49:2–51:91). However, in cuneiform law collections, the gods do not play any direct roles in formulating the law itself.

The Covenant collection, in contrast, underscores that Yhwh is the one who authors the commandments and ordinances. In the suggested basic narrative, Yhwh's lawmaking role is reflected by his command to Moses (Exod 20:22a), which indicates Yhwh himself is the one who formulates the following commandments and ordinances (Exod 22:23–23:33). Moreover, this lawmaking role is revealed by the occurrences of דברים which are specified by the references to Yhwh (Exod 24:3–4, 8) and which refer to the preceding commandments and ordinances.[37] Passages outside the suggested basic narrative also exhibit this contrast between the role of Yhwh and that of the imperial gods. While there are some questions on the exact content of הדברים in Exodus 19:6–7, the occurrence of הדברים in Exodus 20:1 clearly refers to the commandments that follow, indicating Yhwh's role as the lawmaker.[38]

37. There are some debates about the content of these דברים. Considering together with the phrase ואת כל־המשפטים "and all the ordinances," some scholars suggest that these דברים refer to the Decalogue only, while המשפטים refer to the ordinances in Exod 20:23–23:33; see, for instance, Childs, *Book of Exodus*, 505; Levinson, "Is the Covenant Code an Exilic Composition," 281, note 13; Jackson, *Wisdom-Laws*, 453–54, 461–62; Hamilton, *Exodus*, 358. However, in view of the unnecessity for Moses to repeat the Decalogue to the people and the occurrence of the reference המשפטים in Exod 21:1 rather than Exod 20:22, Alexander argues that the phrase כל־דברי יהוה ואת כל־המשפטים "all the words of Yhwh and all the ordinances" refers to Exod 20:22–23:33. The content of these דברים indeed also depends on one's understanding of the composite feature of Exod 19–24. If Exod 24:3 belongs to the basic narrative of the Book of the Covenant as David Wright and some other scholars suggest, these דברים likely refer to the commandments and ordinances in at least Exod 20:22–23:19, if not Exod 20:22–23:33. Nevertheless, in all these cases, the reference to דברים in Exod 24:3 indicates Yhwh's role as the lawmaker.

38. Concerning Exod 20:1–17 as a corpus predates Deuteronomy, see Wright, *Inventing God's Law*, 342.

Introducing these commandments as הדברים that God speaks (וידבר אלהים) without addressing Moses, Exodus 20:1 even suggests that it is not necessary for God to delegate a human leader to pronounce the commandments that he formulates. The Covenant collection thus emphasizes the unique role of the imperialized people's God in lawmaking, contrasting the imperial gods who merely take royal or warrior roles and delegate legal authority to the emperors without involving themselves directly in the lawmaking process.

These contrasts suggest that while the imperialized authors accepted the imperial legal ways of positioning the gods on the top of the three-tier law pronouncement process and emphasizing the divine words/word, they recognized Yhwh, rather than the imperial gods, as the delegators of their human leader and as the royal figure and the warrior of the imperialized people. In addition, they resisted the imperial legal perspective of regarding the gods merely as the delegator or a royal warrior but uniquely presented Yhwh as the lawmaker. These acceptances and resistances, like some in the ordinances and commandments, do require a postcolonial inquiry, because the presentation of the hierarchical law pronouncement process still promotes domination over the imperialized people. The understanding of Yhwh's royal and warrior roles even supports not only monarchical governance but also violence, which empires, especially the Assyrian Empire, tend to inflict on subjugated people. The distinctive understanding of Yhwh as the lawmaker, like the unique attention of Yhwh to the marginalized in the commandments, inevitably leads to the question of how this divine role played out in reality with human mediation. This mediation is susceptible to being oppressive, which I will address further in the following discussion.

Notwithstanding, the resistance reveals that the imperialized authors' response to the imperial legal metanarrative was not a complete acceptance but conveyed a significant subversive message to their elite audience under Assyrian subjugation. Similar to cuneiform legal traditions, Neo-Assyrian inscriptions state that the gods are the delegators of their emperors and have royal and warrior roles.[39] By regarding Yhwh, their national God, as the

39. For instance, RINAP 2:225, Sargon II 43, lines 1–3 (delegators); RINAP 2:282–99, Sargon II 65, lines 64–70 (delegators), lines 156–161, 319 (warriors); RINAP 3/1:60, Sennacherib 4, line 4 (delegators); RINAP 3/2:225, Sennacherib 161, lines 9b–12, 26–32 (royal and warrior roles); RINAP 4:14, Esarhaddon 1, col. ii lines 20–24 (delegators), 30–39 (royal and warrior roles); RINAP 5/1:67–71, Ashurbanipal 3, col. 1 lines 36–96 (delegators and warriors).

God who takes these roles, the imperialized authors expressed their rejection of the gods of the empire and invited their elite audience to do so. Again, this rejection does not necessarily suggest that there was imperial religious imposition or religious Assyrianism among Israelites and Judahites during the Neo-Assyrian period.[40] However, it does indicate the imperialized authors' endeavor to retrieve their traditional belief in order to subvert the Assyrian imperial ideology. This resistance, amid acceptance, foreshadows and concludes the Book of the Covenant, which exhibits similar responses to the imperial legal traditions, including their attention to the gods.[41] It also constitutes subversion of the emperors' roles advocated by the imperial legal metanarrative.

Yhwh, rather than the Emperors, is the Lawmaker – but More

The parallel and distinctive contrasts between Yhwh and the imperial gods indeed reflect those between Yhwh and the emperors. These contrasts exhibit further the crossover between the roles of the divine and those of the human leaders in the Covenant collection and cuneiform law collections. They also indicate that the imperialized authors resisted the dominant roles that emperors, including Assyrian emperors, claimed over the imperialized people. To begin with, the unique role of Yhwh as the lawmaker in the Covenant collection is not only at odds with the role of the imperial gods but also contrasts with the role of the emperors as the lawmaker in cuneiform law collections, which scholars usually emphasize.[42] In cuneiform law collections, the emphasis on the emperors' establishment of justice in their prologue (LU A 3:108–113, A 4:169–170; LL 1:20–37, 1:52–55; LH 5:14–24) indicates that the emperors are the authors of the following laws. The epilogues of the Lipit-Ishtar collection and the Hammurabi collection reveal the role of the emperors as lawmakers even more explicitly. Lipit-Ishtar states that he erected the stela when he established justice in the lands (LL 21:36–38). Hammurabi proclaims that the preceding laws are the just decisions that he established (LH 47:1–8). Conversely, as the aforementioned passages (Exod

40. See §4.2.

41. See §4.2.

42. For instance, Wright, *Inventing God's Law*, 341; Van De Mieroop, *Philosophy*, 150.

20:22a; 24:3–4 [Exod 20:1])[43] exhibit, the Covenant collection portrays that Yhwh himself, rather than the human leader, is the lawmaker.

The emphasis on the "words" in the Laws of Hammurabi and the Covenant collection manifests this contrast even more strikingly, which scholars do not usually note. In the epilogue, Hammurabi not only states that he has inscribed his precious words (*awâtum*) on his stela in order to treat the oppressed fairly (LH 47:71–74), but also proclaims that his words (*awâtum*) are special when he talks about his preeminent position among kings (LH 47:79–81). He thus calls the oppressed person to listen to his precious words (*awâtum*, LH 48:12) and future kings to follow his words (*awâtum*) of justice (LH 48:59–64) and attend to his words (*awâtum*, LH 48:78). After repeating that his words (*awâtum*) are special (LH 48:99), Hammurabi invokes the gods to bless those who attend to his words (*awâtum*, LH 49:2) and do not alter his words (*awâtum*, LH 49:7). He also invokes the gods to punish those who do not attend to his words (*awâtum*, LH 49:18) and alter his words (*awâtum*, LH 49:29). The Hammurabi collection thus strongly emphasizes the emperor's role as the words' author – that is, the lawmaker.

The Covenant collection does not underscore the special nature of the דברים, as the Hammurabi collection emphasizes (*awâtiya šāqurātim*, "my precious words," LH 47:74, 48:12; *awâtūa nasqā*, "my words are special," LH 47:81, 48:99). Nor does the Covenant collection depict Yhwh saying that the דברים is דברי ("my words"), as Hammurabi reiterates (*awâtiya*, LH 47:74; 48:12; 49:2, 49:7, 49:18, 49:29; *awâtūa*, LH 47:81; 48:99). Yet, from the narrator's presentation (Exod 24:3–4 [Exod 19:7])[44] and the people's mouth (Exod 24:3), the Covenant collection reiterates that Yhwh, not the human leader, gives the דברים. Together with other descriptions concerning Yhwh's law-making role, these references to דברים indicate that the Covenant collection underscores Yhwh's role as the lawmaker, which contrasts with the emphasis on the emperors' role as such in cuneiform law collections.

The contrast between Yhwh and the emperors, similar to those between Yhwh and the gods, is not limited to the depiction of their legal role but also occurs in the presentations of their roles as the royal warrior and the deliverer

43. The square parentheses indicate passages not belonging to the suggested basic narrative.

44. For the primary nature of Exod 19:7 in relation to the Book of the Covenant, see page 218, note 19.

for the people. The presentation of the royal warrior role particularly exhibits further the crossover between the roles of the divine and those of the human leaders in the Exodus corpus and cuneiform law collections. Meanwhile, the presentation of the deliverer role has attracted little scholarly attention. The Ur-Namma collection begins its prologue by calling Ur-Namma the mighty warrior (nita kalag-ga, LU A 1:11)[45] and the king (lugal, LU A 1:12) and repeats these roles after proclaiming the divine origin of his kingship (LU A 3:105–107). After presenting his establishment of justice in the land, Ur-Namma states that he has set free the people in Sumer and Akkad (LU A 3:114–124) and liberated other peoples who were under Anshan's subjugation, or literally Anshan's servitude or slavery (nam-arad; LU A 3:125–134). The references to Ur-Namma's royal warrior role involve textual reconstruction, but the text concerning his deliverer role is intact, indicating the certainty of the attribution of this role to the emperor in this legal tradition. Moreover, the Lipit-Ishtar and Hammurabi collections also reflect their emperors' roles as the deliverer and royal warrior, respectively: After declaring his royal role (lugal) and establishment of justice in the land (LL 1:45–55), Lipit-Ishtar states that he has liberated the people of Nippur, Ur, Isin, Sumer, and Akkad, who were under the servitude (nam-arad) of certain people (LL 2:1–15). Amid his claims about his services to the gods, Hammurabi not only calls himself as king (*šarrum*, LH 1:63, 2:22, 3:65; *zēr šarrūtum*, LH 2:13; *ušumgal šarrī*, LH 2:55; *etel šarrī*, LH 3:70; *ašared šarrī*, LH 4:23), but also as the warrior (*qarrādum*, LH 2:32) and the one unrivaled in combat (*qabal la maḫārim*, LH 3:71–72). Noticeably, the emperors take the royal warrior role from and alongside the gods, as my comparative analysis of Yhwh and the gods indicates.[46] In addition to the lawmaker, cuneiform law collections thus present the emperors also as the royal warriors and deliverers for their people.

The Covenant collection, in contrast, presents Yhwh, rather than the human leader, as the one who carries these roles. My comparative analysis of Yhwh and the gods has already unfolded the portrayal of Yhwh as the royal warrior in the description of the theophany, especially in the suggested basic

45. This phrase literally means "strong male" but carries a connotation of mighty warrior; see Roth, *Law Collections*, 15, and Kitchen and Lawrence, *Treaty, Law and Covenant*, 55, 57.

46. See also Hammurabi's statement that he pleases Adad's heart as Adad fights in a city (LH 3:58–61).

narrative. As cuneiform law collections present that the emperors take the warrior roles from and alongside the gods, the portrayal of the Covenant collection is at odds not only with the cuneiform legal understanding of various gods as the royal figure and the warrior of the lands but also with the cuneiform legal presentation of their emperors as the royal warriors. The aforementioned description of the horn's sound in the Covenant collection highlights this contrast with the emperors. While the emperors claim to be the royal warriors in their law collections, the horn's sound in the storm theophany reveals that Yhwh is the new royal warrior.

Passages outside the suggested basic narrative, meanwhile, present that Yhwh, rather than the human leader, is the deliverer of the people. In Exodus 19:4, Yhwh tells Moses to remind the people what Yhwh did to the Egyptians in order to bring the people to Yhwh. In Exodus 20:2, Yhwh even announces himself that he is the God who brought the people out of Egypt from the house of slavery (בית עבדים).[47] Similar statements relating to Egypt also occur in the commandments (Exod 22:20; 23:9, 23:15).[48] However, unlike these commandments, which focus on the people's experience, the narrative emphasizes Yhwh's deliverance of them out of slavery. This emphasis does not only express liberation from slavery related to the exodus story,[49] indicating resistance to imperial subjugation in the history of Israel and Judah. This emphasis also contrasts with the cuneiform legal presentation concerning the liberation of various peoples out of servitude, suggesting a rejection of emperors' claim on such a role in the imperial legal metanarrative. This rejection is crucial for understanding the rhetoric of Yhwh's declaration of his deliverance of the people. Rather than underlining that the people owe Yhwh a favor,[50] the Covenant collection emphasizes the identity of the imperialized people's deliverer – that is, Yhwh, their national God, rather than the emperors.

---

47. For these passages' primary nature, see page 218, note 19.

48. See §4.2 and §4.3.

49. Dozeman, *God at War*, 51–52, 123. Dozeman considers liberation, that is, Yhwh bringing the people out of Egypt, as "a common motif in the Deuteronomistic interpretation of the exodus." Moreover, he argues that priestly tradition also employs this exodus motif, but emphasizes its relation with the people's wilderness journey (for instance, Exod 19:1). However, the contrast that I discuss momentarily suggests that this motif is not necessarily a late addition, at least in the narrative of the Covenant collection.

50. Wafula, "Exodus Story," 22; Watts, *Reading Law*, 95.

These parallel contrasts between Yhwh and the emperors, like those between Yhwh and the gods, appear together with distinctions, further indicating resistance to the emperors' roles. As Marc Zvi Brettler argues, biblical metaphors presenting God as king rarely simply mimic the king;[51] the Covenant collection reveals that Yhwh, unlike the emperors, is more than a royal figure. A significant distinction between Yhwh and the emperors is that Yhwh is the delegator while the emperors are the delegates. As the Covenant collection (including both the suggested basic narrative and passages outside of it) reveals through its parallel contrast that Yhwh, rather than the gods, calls Moses to pronounce the commandments and ordinances, it also emphasizes that Yhwh does not need a higher power's delegation before he carries out the roles of lawmaker, warrior, and deliverer, as the emperors do.

Moreover, while cuneiform law collections state that the emperors have made various contributions to their empires (LU A 3:104–124; LL 1:38–2:15; LH 1:50–5:13) and Hammurabi claims his subjugation of the whole world (*kibrāt erbettim/arba'im*, "the four edges," LH 2:2–4, 5:10–12), the Covenant collection (particularly passages outside the suggested basic narrative) reveals that Yhwh not only possesses the entire land (Exod 19:5) but also has a concern that is not in the emperors' agenda. Exodus 19:6 indicates that Yhwh looks forward to the establishment of "a kingdom of priests and a holy nation" (ממלכת כהנים וגוי קדוש). Remarkably, the terms "kingdom" (ממלכה) and "nation" (גוי) connote Yhwh's expectation as political, but the terms "priests" (כהנים) and "holy" (קדוש) at the same time clearly indicate his concern is religious.[52] Yhwh's speech does not explain further what "priests" and "holy" exactly refer to. However, the following passages suggest that the consecration of the people, which Yhwh asks Moses to do, is an act that enables the people to go up the mountain, offering them the opportunity not only to know

51. Brettler, *God Is King*, 72.

52. Regarding the combination of two religious and two political terms in this phrase, see Albertz, *Exodus, Band II*, 42. About the political nature of ממלכה and גוי, see Paul, *Studies in the Book of the Covenant*, 31. On "the hybrid ideal of the Torah republic" that these terms articulate, see Brett, *Locations of God*, 119. For various understandings of the semantic structure of ממלכת כהנים and the relationship between this phrase and וגוי קדוש, see Propp, *Exodus 19–40*, 157–59; Graupner, "Ihr sollt mir ein Königreich," 33–44.

Yhwh from distance,[53] but to get close to him (Exod 19:10–13).[54] This concern indicates the religious purpose of Yhwh's delegation. Together with Yhwh's role as the delegator, this religious concern suggests that, in addition to the parallel contrast between Yhwh in the Covenant collection and the emperors in the cuneiform law collections, the Covenant collection emphasizes that Yhwh, unlike the emperors, is more than a king.

Being familiar with imperial legal traditions, which the cuneiform law collections reflect, the authors of the Covenant collection, therefore, accepted the imperial legal way of positioning the human leaders in the middle of the three-tier law pronouncement process, but simultaneously did not follow it in recognizing the emperors as the lawmaker, the warrior, and the deliverer of the imperialized people. The imperialized authors also took up the imperial legal emphasis on the lawmaker's words but concurrently did not regard the emperors as the authors of these words. In fact, whereas the imperialized authors perceived that their God Yhwh takes all the roles that the emperors claim, they emphasized that Yhwh is more than a royal figure, having the power to grant delegation to the human leader and carrying a religious concern over the people's relationship with Yhwh himself.

These acceptances and resistances, again, require a postcolonial critique, as they still appear to promote domination over the imperialized people in lawmaking. The dominant and violent nature also remains in Yhwh's royal and warrior roles, if not his deliverer role. This characterization of Yhwh unavoidably continues to invite questions about potentially oppressive practices in the human mediation between Yhwh and the imperialized people in reality, which I will address momentarily. Nevertheless, the resistances do indicate that the imperialized authors' acceptance of the imperial legal metanarrative was not in total compliance with it. While the Covenant collection is not unrelated to royalty, it does compete with the emperors, if not the empires,[55]

53. Wafula, "Exodus Story," 22; see also §1.4.4.

54. Regarding the primary nature of the passages in this discussion, see page 218, note 19. Baruch J. Schwartz helpfully notes that the words "holy" and "priests" are not clear indicators of priestly writing (Schwartz, "Priestly Account," 112–13). For a survey about holiness and consecration in both priestly and non-priestly writing in the Old Testament, see Wright, "Holiness, Old Testament," 237–49.

55. Assmann, *Invention of Religion*, 252.

rather than merely expressing imperial domination and subordination, as some postcolonial biblical scholars argue.[56]

This competition further expresses the significant message that the imperialized authors intended to convey to their elite audience in Israel and Judah, especially when Neo-Assyrian emperors also emphasized their royal, warrior, and deliverer roles.[57] The acceptances and resistances regarding Yhwh's and the emperors' roles, indeed, echo and simultaneously work against the Assyrian theological emphasis on Assur's, rather than the rulers', possession of the true kingship, which the festival exclamation of "Assur is king, Assur is king!" reflects.[58] Characterizing Yhwh in contrast to the presentation of the emperors in imperial legal traditions, the imperialized authors thus urged their elite audience to acknowledge that Yhwh, rather than the Neo-Assyrian rulers, or Assur, is their king, and more than that.[59] This rejection of the Assyrian god and emperors' domination over the imperialized people, through resistances to amid acceptances of the imperial legal metanarrative, set up a vital backdrop for those reflected in the Book of the Covenant, characterizing the Covenant collection as a whole the work of conservative revolutionists. This rejection is also nuanced further by the description of the human mediator in the Covenant collection.

56. Yee, "Postcolonial Biblical Criticism," 223; Wafula, "Exodus Story," 22; see also §1.4.2 and §1.4.4.

57. For instance, RINAP 2:225, Sargon II 43, lines 1–11; RINAP 3/1:60, Sennacherib 4, lines 1–3 (This self-presentation notably includes the lightning imagery); RINAP 4/4:14, Esarhaddon 1, col. ii lines 12–24; RINAP 4/4:105–106, Esarhaddon 48, lines 41, 44; RINAP 5/1:69–71, Ashurbanipal 3, col. 1 lines 36–96.

58. Holloway, *Aššur is King*, xv; Maul, "Assyrian Religion," 348. Regarding possible channels through which the authors of the Covenant collection learned about Assyrian theology, see §2.3.2.

59. One may wonder how this acknowledgement would work in the biblical authors' context among their elite audience. Considering the content of Exod 19–24, I suggest that this acknowledgment might be expressed through following the ordinances in the Book of the Covenant, which the biblical authors characterized as Yhwh's words and endeavored to formulate in ways divergent from the imperial legal traditions. Moreover, this acknowledgment might be expressed through worshiping Yhwh only, according to the commandments in the Book of the Covenant. This acknowledgment might also include refusing to show support for fulfilling Neo-Assyrians' various demands. However, further evidence is needed to pinpoint what exactly they were, given the fact that the corpus of Exod 19–24 does not address them explicitly, probably due to its authors' intention to avoid creating tension with the Assyrian Empire or pro-Assyrian parties among their people, as I discuss in §2.4.7.

Moses, in Contrast to the Emperors, Is Only the Mediator

The Covenant collection's contrast with the emperors is not confined to the presentation of Yhwh. Rather than simply replacing the emperors, or the gods and the emperors, with Yhwh,[60] the Covenant collection also works against the roles of emperors through its portrayal of Moses. This portrayal may simultaneously speak to the biblical authors' monarchy, especially when Moses is depicted as a kind of leader among the people. However, in view of Exodus 19–24's target audience and the fact that there is no further evidence for a specific monarchical context behind this corpus's compilation, here I concentrate on demonstrating how this portrayal manifests further the resistance of the Covenant collection to the imperial legal metanarrative and conveys this resistive message to its elite audience. This portrayal indicates again that the imperialized authors' acceptance of the latter was not total compliance but involved attempts to subvert the nature of human leadership advocated by empires.

Like the descriptions of Yhwh, there are parallel contrasts between the presentations of Moses and the emperors. While cuneiform law collections state that their emperors receive princeship from the gods (LU A 1:31–42; LL 1:20–37; LH 1:27–49), the Covenant collection describes that Moses receives delegation from Yhwh (Exod 19:9a; 20:22a [Exod 19:3b–6, 19:10–13; 24:12]). Whereas its cuneiform counterparts present that the emperors gladden the gods' heart (LL 1:50–51; LH 2:7–9; 3:53–54; 4:46–47), the Covenant collection reveals that Moses has the special privilege to meet and talk with Yhwh on the mountain (Exod 19:3a, 19:9a, 19:19; 20:21 [Exod 19:8, 19:9b; 24:12]). Moses's access to Yhwh is so barrier-free that some scholars deem his ascent to be "almost natural."[61] Moses's continual and active participation in the theophany even gives an impression that the Covenant collection exalts Moses as much as exalting Yhwh.[62] These parallel contrasts between the Exodus corpus and cuneiform law collections indicate the comparability between Moses and

60. Based on the analysis of Exod 20:23–25; 21:1; 22:20–23:19, David Wright argues that the key permutation between the Covenant collection and the Laws of Hammurabi is the replacement of Hammurabi and Mesopotamian gods with Yhwh; while in his study of the basic narrative, he emphasizes the replacement of Hammurabi with Yhwh (Wright, *Inventing God's Law*, 287–300, 341). This emphasis appears again in his latest article (Wright, "Adaptation and Fusion," 91, 136).

61. Polak, "Theophany and Mediator," 131.

62. Mann, *Divine Presence*, 134–38.

the emperors in addition to Yhwh and the emperors. They also reflect the Covenant collection's emphasis on Moses, rather than the emperors, being the divine-delegated human leader of the imperialized people.

Yet, while in cuneiform law collections the emperors are themselves the lawmakers, warriors, and deliverers, in the Covenant collection Moses is only a law pronouncer, if not the servant of the law.[63] The delegation from Yhwh, which indicates what Moses should tell the people (Exod 19:9a; 20:22a [Exod 19:3, 19:6; 24:12]), not only reveals that Moses seems to receive endless tasks from Yhwh,[64] but also demonstrates that Moses is only Yhwh's mouthpiece. Despite the similar emphasis on textuality in lawmaking, Moses in fact merely recounts to the people and writes down Yhwh's words (Exod 24:3–4 [Exod 19:6–7]), contrarily to the emperors, particularly Hammurabi, who inscribes and calls people to attend to his own words (LH 47:71–74; 48:12, 48:59–64, 48:78).[65] At most, Moses is the covenant maker,[66] or actually the covenant ceremony performer, who carries out the ritual to testify to the people's agreement with Yhwh's words, which he only pronounces (Exod 24:6–7). As privileged as Moses's position is before Yhwh, the Covenant collection only regards Moses as the spokesman for Yhwh before the imperialized people.

Moses's mediating, rather than ruling, role is manifested and nuanced further in the presentation of his actions related to the people. In the suggested basic narrative, Moses brings the people out from the camp to meet

63. Paul, *Studies in the Book of the Covenant*, 36. Some scholars argue that in the chapters preceding Exod 19–24, Moses has a role as the people's deliverer (Van Seters, *Life of Moses*, 13–127; Eakins, "Moses," 464). However, Yhwh's calling of Moses in Exod 3, especially Exod 3:8, clearly indicates that Yhwh himself is the deliverer. At most, Moses is depicted only as the human agent whom Yhwh commissions to participate in the work of deliverance together with Yhwh (see, for instance, Exod 3:10, 14:1–15:19). This role is similar to Moses's role as a law pronouncer, rather than a lawmaker, in the Covenant collection. More significantly, despite Moses's participation in the work of deliverance in the preceding chapters, the Covenant collection does not mention his role in delivering the people out of Egypt at all. This absence of mention evidences further the contrast with the emperors' statements on freeing their people. Regarding various images of Moses in the book of Exodus, see also Coats, *Moses*. Regarding different traditions' portrayal of Moses and issues concerning historical Moses, see Beegle, "Moses," 909–16. About extrabiblical traditions and modern interpretations concerning the depictions of Moses, see Houtman, "Moses," 593–98.

64. Albertz, *Exodus, Band II*, 38.

65. These descriptions particularly emphasize the emperor's ruling, rather than mediating, role, even though Hayim Tadmor suggests that Babylonian belief regards the king as a kind of intermediary in the implementation of justice (Tadmor, "Hammurabi," 609).

66. Mathews, *Royal Motifs*, 66.

Yhwh (Exod 19:16b–17), rather than declaring his own services to Yhwh as the emperors do.[67] When the people ask him to speak to them on behalf of God (Exod 20:20), Moses even encourages them not to fear, but to see the appearance of God in a constructive way,[68] even though compelling the people to listen to Moses is the theophany's initial purpose (Exod 19:9a) and their fear seems to be necessary for confirming his mediating role.[69] Notably, following the Exodus commandments, the narrative not only describes that Moses recounts all the words of Yhwh to the people (Exod 24:3) but delineates again that Moses reads the Book of the Covenant to the people (Exod 24:7). This delineation is at odds with Hammurabi's self-presentation, which calls the oppressed person to keep reading aloud the message on Hammurabi's stela in order to listen to Hammurabi's words (*narî šaṭram lištassīma awâtiya šūqurātim lišmēma*, LH 48:9–11). Located between the depiction of Moses sprinkling the blood on the altar and that of Moses sprinkling the blood on the people, this delineation indeed especially emphasizes Moses's role as a mediator who serves both Yhwh and the people, rather than as a ruler who focuses on legitimizing his own rule and orders the people to serve themselves.

Passages outside the suggested basic narrative also reveal this mediating role. Moses not only tells Yhwh's words to the people, according to Yhwh's order, but also brings back the people's words (דברי העם) to Yhwh (Exod 19:8, 19:9b).[70] This description may neither suggest that Moses is identified fully with the people at times,[71] nor portray Moses as an outsider in order to shift the emphasis to the law and Yhwh.[72] Rather, it manifests that the Covenant collection underscores the role of the human leader as the one who

67. See §4.2.

68. There are various understandings of what "to test" (נסות) means, such as declining to ascend the mountain, obeying the Decalogue, and being instructed (Alexanders, *Exodus*, 435; Propp, *Exodus 19–24*, 181–82). Moshe Greenberg even suggests that it refers to experiencing Yhwh palpably (Greenberg, "נסה in Exodus," 275). Adopting Greenberg's translation, Joe Baden suggests further that the Decalogue functions as an experience rather than law (Baden, "Transformation," 66). In any case, Moses's explanation, including that about not sinning, attempts to help the people to see their fear in a positive light in relation to their relationship with God.

69. Albertz, *Exodus, Band II*, 73.

70. About the primary nature of Exod 19:8, see page 218, note 19. About explanations for the repeated description in Exod 19:9b, see Alexander, *Exodus*, 371; Propp, *Exodus 19–40*, 160.

71. Savran, "Theophany," 139.

72. Peter Machinist, "Man Moses," 19, 53.

communicates the people's response to Yhwh, instead of merely following Yhwh's order, as some postcolonial biblical scholars argue.[73] It also contrasts the Hammurabi collection in which the emperor calls the oppressed person to praise him before the gods (LH 48:20–45). Unlike the Hammurabi collection, which presents the emperor as the ruler who asks his people to speak for him before the gods, the Covenant collection thus emphasizes that the human leader is a mediator who speaks on behalf of the people before Yhwh in addition to communicating Yhwh's words to them.

These parallel and distinctive contrasts again suggest that the biblical authors did not completely comply with imperial legal traditions but selectively accepted as well as resisted them. While the imperialized authors accepted the imperial legal understanding that human leaders are involved in the legal tasks assigned by the divine and have special relationships with the divine, they did not recognize the emperors as their divine-delegated human leader or regard the emperors' roles as their human leader's roles. By depicting Moses as the one who carries out various tasks for Yhwh and the people, rather than as a lawmaker, fighter, and deliverer, the imperialized authors appear to emphasize that human leaders only have a mediating role between Yhwh and the imperialized people, rather than a ruling role over the imperialized people.

To a certain extent, this mediating role remains imperial and susceptible to being oppressive, especially from a postcolonial optic. The Yhwh-Moses relationship seems to endorse the imperial practice of having intermediaries who belong to the people but enjoy a privileged relationship with imperial power.[74] This relationship apparently grants power to the human leader no less than that of the emperors. It also potentially encourages human leaders to become a proxy for the emperor in reality, just as the comprador bourgeoisie does for their colonizers or for imperial machinery in the modern context.[75] The divine delegation of the mediator role to Moses, rather than a female leader, moreover, subordinates women to male leadership.[76] Nevertheless, the Covenant collection concurrently envisions these mediators somewhat differently from the emperors characterized in the imperial legal metanarrative and

73. Wafula, "Exodus Story," 23; see also §1.4.4.

74. Wafula, "Exodus Story," 23; see also §1.4.4.

75. Fanon, *Wretched of the Earth*, 154; Dabashi, *Brown Skin, White Masks*, 38–64. See also §1.2.3.

76. Dube, *Postcolonial Feminist Interpretation*, 75; see also §1.4.1.

from the intermediaries that postcolonial biblical scholars note. Rather than aggrandizing themselves by boasting their services to God and their military and liberative works for the people, rather than asking the imperialized people to praise them, and rather than doing nothing for their people but fulfilling the empire's whims,[77] these mediators are supposed to be spokespersons of God as well as the voices of all the imperialized people. They have the role of building the relationship between God and their people, instead of between the emperors and the imperialized.

Again, because the authors of the Covenant collection probably had roles in the palace as well as the temple in Israel and Judah, the role of God's spokesperson still leads to a question about the nature of human leadership in relation to the imperialized people's condition, which I will address further momentarily. Despite this, the somewhat different characterization of the human leader in the Covenant collection continues to reveal the significant message that the imperialized authors attempted to communicate to their elite audience, when the Neo-Assyrian emperors also aggrandized themselves by proclaiming their royal, warrior, and deliverer roles.[78] By characterizing the human leader as the mediator serving both Yhwh and the imperialized people, but not the ruler, fighter, or deliverer, the imperialized authors urged their elite audience to reject Assyrian emperors' claim on the latter roles and their authority over the imperialized people.[79] This rejection further develops the subversion that the imperialized authors had expressed in the parallel and distinctive contrasts between Yhwh and the emperors that are associated with those between Yhwh and the imperial gods. It also reveals the wrestling of the imperialized authors, who endeavored to resist the imperial legal metanarrative about the gods and the emperors, and thus Neo-Assyrian subjugation, albeit in a conservative way.

77. Wafula, "Exodus Story," 23; see also §1.4.4.

78. See page 233, note 57.

79. Again, in the biblical authors' context and among their elite audience, who similarly served the palace and/or the temple, this rejection might be expressed by refusing to show support for fulfilling Neo-Assyrians' various demands (See my discussion on page 233, note 59). According to Exod 19–24's characterization of Moses, this rejection should also mean that the elite audience regarded their own roles as mediators, who served both Yhwh and their people, which I discuss further momentarily.

Resistance: The Imperialized People Are Active Participants

As imperialized people, the authors of the Covenant collection were not only concerned with God and the human leader; the key actors in its narrative include Yhwh and Moses, as well as the people, as Wolfgang Oswald points out.[80] This distinctive emphasis on the people deserves more attention than it has attracted in the comparative study of the Exodus corpus and cuneiform law collections. It discloses further the conservatively revolutionary resistance to the imperial legal metanarrative, which continues to work against the imperial domination over the people of Israel and Judah.

The beginning of the Covenant collection has already manifested its prioritized concern over the people. Rather than inaugurating with statements about the emperors' services to the gods (LU A 1:1–30) and the divine delegation of kingship to other gods and princeship to the emperors (LU A 1:31–42; LL 1:1–55; LH 1:1–49), the suggested basic narrative begins with a description of the people: "Israel camped there before the mountain" (ויחן־שם ישׂראל נגד ההר, Exod 19:2b). After this description the Covenant collection proceeds to delineate Moses's encounter with Yhwh and Yhwh's speech. Passages outside the suggested basic narrative exhibit the same attention to the people in their beginning through details about the people's background and current location (Exod 19:1–2a).[81] The background about having been out of Egypt for a period of time (Exod 19:1) even expresses the anti-imperial sentiment of the people's identity – they are no longer subordinate to an empire. Through these descriptions, the Covenant collection underscores that the people are important participants in the pronouncement process of the commandments and ordinances, contrasting with its cuneiform counterparts, which prioritize the role of the gods and the emperors in the law pronouncement.

This introductory emphasis on the people paves the way for the following descriptions of them in the Covenant collection, which further emphasize the people's participatory role in the pronouncement process and contrast with the cuneiform legal presentation. After introducing their gods and emperors in relation to the establishment of justice, cuneiform law collections

80. Oswald, "Exodus-Gottesberg-Erzählung," 43.

81. While some scholars argue for this passage's additional nature, Alexander reasonably suggests that its repetitive elements offer various information about the people's circumstance (Alexander, *Exodus*, 363).

do mention the people; however, these mentions mainly occur in the declarations of the emperors' works, including deliverance from servitude (LU A 3:114–134; LL 2:1–15) and prevention of oppression (LU A 4:162–168; LH 1:27–49).[82] As discussed, the Covenant collection has exhibited parallel contrasts to these declarations in its prelude (see above) and commandments (see §4.3), respectively, emphasizing Yhwh's, rather than the emperors', roles in these works. In addition to these parallel contrasts, the suggested basic narrative reveals a distinctive emphasis through Yhwh's explanation concerning his plan of theophany (Exod 19:9a). Although Yhwh is on the top of the three-tier pronouncement process and thus seems to have the highest authority in it, he plans to come to Moses in order to ensure that the people will directly hear their conversation. Even though a motivation behind this direct hearing experience is to secure Moses's middle position as the law pronouncer, this experience aims at the people, moving them to trust in Moses. The fact that Yhwh takes the initiative to actualize the people's direct hearing experience indeed demonstrates again that Yhwh is not merely a king sitting on high. This description of Yhwh and his consideration of the need to ensure the people's trust in the human leader reveals that the Covenant collection emphasizes the people's, rather than merely the divine's and the human leader's, participatory role in the pronouncement process.

The description of the people's response to the theophany (Exod 20:18–21) also manifests this distinctive emphasis. Noteworthy is that Yhwh's appearance as a royal warrior receives a negative emotional response from the people, who worry that their direct communication with him will lead to death. Equally significant is that the people have the opportunity to honestly make their response to their direct involvement in the theophany, expressing their preference to have the human leader, rather than God, to speak with them. This response of the people does confirm Moses's role as the mediator according to Yhwh's plan, as Childs notices,[83] but it also simultaneously rejects Yhwh's direct sovereignty over the people, which likewise deserves attention. In both ways, the narrative underscores the point that the people

82. Other works include making family members to sustain each other and imposing fair service on people of different statuses (LL 2:16–40), providing necessities to the people (LH 2:39–41), gathering scattered people and offering them protection (LH 2:49–51, 4:11–13), and so forth (LH 4:29–31, 4:38–39, 4:45, 5:14–24).

83. Childs, *Book of Exodus*, 371–72.

have a decisive role, if not their own initiative, in the pronouncement process of the ordinances and the commandments. Under the narrative's depiction, the people indeed maintain their presence, despite keeping distance, in the pronouncement process, rather than withdrawing from it, after they have made their request to Moses.[84] Unlike cuneiform law collections, which focus on the gods' and the emperors' roles in the law pronouncement and address the people mainly for presenting the emperors' works, the Covenant collection emphasizes that the people, in addition to Yhwh and the human leader, have a vital participatory role in the pronouncement process of the Book of the Covenant.

These contrasts between the Covenant collection and cuneiform law collections, like those concerning Yhwh and Moses versus the gods and the emperors, continue to appear in the presentations concerning the words. As discussed, cuneiform law collections declare that the emperors are the ones who established justice by or submitted to the gods' words (LU A 3:108–113; LL 1:52–55; 21:5–7; LH 48:25). Regarding the emperor's words, the Hammurabi collection also only calls the oppressed person to read them in order to understand his case and calm his heart (LH 48:3–19). The three cuneiform law collections indeed focus on urging future kings or rulers to follow the emperors' words and to preserve their inscriptions (LX rev 3':9'–14'; LL 21:36–60; LH 48:59–49:44). Contrarily, the suggested basic narrative (Exod 24:3) presents a "popular consent" to Yhwh's words,[85] emphasizing that all the people (כל־העם), rather than merely the human leader, observe them. The people even repeatedly agree to act according to Yhwh's words (Exod 24:3; 24:7), rather than merely taking them as a means for calming their hearts.[86]

---

84. Alan Lenzi points out that while the people in Deut 5 withdraw from the scene, the people in Exod 20 still stand at a distance when Moses approaches Yhwh (Lenzi, *Secrecy and the Gods*, 302). Indeed, in Deut 5, Yhwh asks Moses to tell the people to return to their tents, but asks Moses to stay in order to receive the commandments and ordinances (Deut 5:30–31). The Covenant collection thus emphasizes the people's participation in the pronouncement of Yhwh's words.

85. Naiden, "Gods, Kings," 96.

86. For various interpretations of the people's additional response concerning listening to Yhwh's words (Exod 24:7), see Propp, *Exodus 19–24*, 295–96; Albertz, *Exodus, Band II*, 139; Peeler, "Desiring God," 195. In my opinion, this additional response may be a poetic presentation corresponding to the preceding description of Moses reading the book of the covenant "in the ears of the people." In any case, this listening denotes obedience to Yhwh's words, as Propp suggests, rather than merely taking them as a means of comfort.

Passages outside the suggested basic narrative also reflect this contrastive emphasis on the people's participatory role. Despite depicting the need of consecrating the people before they approach Yhwh, which is related to his particular religious concern as discussed, the passages describe that Yhwh's words are for the Israelites (Exod 19:6) and underline that all the people (כל־העם) agree to act accordingly (Exod 19:8). Furthermore, the passages distinctively delineate that Moses brings back the people's words. Repeatedly using "the words of the people" (את־דברי העם, Exod 19:8, 19:9b) to describe the people's response to "the words" (הדברים) spoken by Yhwh (Exod 19:6, 19:7),[87] the Covenant collection reveals that it regards the people's response as important as Yhwh's commandments and ordinances. This emphasis again suggests the Covenant collection's emphasis on the people's active participation in the pronouncement process of Yhwh's words, which is at odds with cuneiform legal focus on the emperors' and future rulers' roles in the observance of the gods' and the emperors' words, respectively.

Indeed, the Covenant collection presents that the people are involved in various ways in this pronouncement process, despite Moses's privileged position before Yhwh. In the suggested basic narrative, after pronouncing and writing down Yhwh's words, Moses builds not only an altar but also twelve pillars for the twelve tribes of Israel (Exod 24:4), signifying the participation of all the people with Yhwh in the covenant-making ceremony.[88] Moreover, rather than preparing the ceremony by himself, Moses sent young men among the people to make offerings and sacrifices to Yhwh (Exod 24:5), particularly contrasting with the emperors' statements about the religious services carried out by themselves alone.[89] Passages outside the suggested basic narrative also depict a similar delegation of Moses's role to other people. Before his final ascent, Moses tells the elders that he has delegated his mediator role to Aaron and Hur (Exod 24:14).[90] With the instruction of having whoever has issues

87. About the primary nature of Exod 19:6–8, see page 218, note 19. About explanations for the repeated description in Exod 19:9b, see page 236, note 70.

88. Alexander, *Exodus*, 544; Peeler, "Desiring God," 192.

89. See §4.2. For various understandings of "the young men" (נערים), including their possible priestly nature, see Alexander, *Exodus*, 544; Propp, *Exodus 19–24*, 294, 601; Nicholson, "Covenant Ritual," 81. In any case, the Covenant collection depicts that Moses delegates religious services to others among the people, contrasting with the emperors' statements about their own services to the gods.

90. Regarding the primary or early nature of Exod 24:14, see note page 218, note 19.

(דברים) to approach Aaron and Hur, this delegation remarkably contrasts Hammurabi's instruction, which calls the oppressed person who has an issue or lawsuit (*awātum*) to come before his own statue (LH 48:3–8). Unlike cuneiform law collections, which put the emperors under the spotlight, the Covenant collection emphasizes that, in addition to the privileged human leader, the people and other leaders among them also actively participate in the pronouncement process of the Book of the Covenant and tasks related to it.

As the ones who were familiar with imperial legal traditions, the authors of the Covenant collection thus resisted them amid general acceptance. On the one hand, they complied with the imperial legal understanding that the people are at the bottom of the three-tier pronouncement process, under the divine and the specially delegated human leaders. They also accepted the imperial legal presentation that the people should have certain responses to the lawmaker's words. On the other hand, the imperialized authors did not regard the people merely as a means for evidencing the emperors' works or as merely reading the lawmaker's words for comfort, as the imperial legal metanarrative does. They began their narrative with the people's circumstances, underscoring that they are no longer subordinate to the empire. They also expressed concern about the people's trust in the human leader and their response to the theophany, emphasized the agreement of all the people with the observance of Yhwh's words, and highlighted various participations of the people throughout the pronouncement process of Yhwh's words.

These emphases may not indicate that the Covenant collection regards the people as the sovereign,[91] or even as able to respond totally freely.[92] Although the narrative depicts the people's seemingly independent decision,[93] it does state Yhwh's demand for obedience,[94] with conditions attached to this demand.[95] Moreover, men still take up more participatory roles than women,

91. Oswald, "Exodus-Gottesberg-Erzählung," 43–44.

92. Assmann, *Invention of Religion*, 234; Ska, "Biblical Law," 155; Patrick, "Who is the Revolutionist," 159.

93. Studying the understanding of freedom in cuneiform culture, Eva Von Dassow defines freedom as "the capacity for independent action" in addition to "having power over oneself" (Von Dassow, "Freedom," 206).

94. Watts, *Reading Law*, 94–95.

95. Wright, "*Raison d'Être*," 52; Levinson, "Sinai Covenant," 49–50.

suggesting subordination of women to male leadership among the people.[96] However, these emphases do indicate that the Covenant collection is not merely about imperial domination and subordination,[97] or about the divine's "absolute 'imperial' authority."[98] Contrarily, through these emphases on the people, the imperialized authors recast imperial legal traditions' limited audiences as the people,[99] as well as framed the Book of the Covenant as divine words whose observance is the matter of all the people. Through this focus on the people, the imperialized authors continued to communicate to their elite audience a vital message against their Assyrian overlords, which they had conveyed through the contrasts between Yhwh and the emperors and those between Moses and the emperors.[100]

Indeed, while some Neo-Assyrian treaties mention the people of subjugated cities among those who should observe the oaths,[101] these treaties prioritize the emperors' dominant role[102] and focus on putting curses on the rebels.[103] Neo-Assyrian inscriptions even reveal that their emperors mainly considered the people as the subject of their lordship,[104] loyal supporters of their kingship,[105] part of their booty,[106] the subjugated that they deported,[107]

96. Dube, *Postcolonial Feminist Interpretation*, 75; see also §1.4.1.

97. Yee, "Postcolonial Biblical Criticism," 223; Wafula, "Exodus Story," 22; see also §1.4.2 and §1.4.4.

98. Schmid, "Biblical Writings," 493.

99. Wright, *Inventing God's Law*, 341.

100. This focus on the people does not necessarily suggest that the biblical authors or their elite audience belonged to a social organization outside of the monarchial period. Rather, it suggests that the biblical authors saw the need to attend to their people and urged their elite audience to do so in order to express their resistance to their Assyrian overlords, even though having a focus on the people was not a usual practice of their monarchy.

101. For instance, SAA 2:9, Treaty of Aššur-nerari V with Mati'-ilu, King of Arpad, col. I lines 10′–35′; SAA 2:45, Esarhaddon's Succession Treaty, lines 1′–10′.

102. SAA 2:45, Esarhaddon's Succession Treaty, lines 1′–10′.

103. SAA 2:9–12, Treaty of Aššur-nerari V with Mati'-ilu, King of Arpad, col. I lines 21′–35′, col. III lines 19′–27′, col. IV lines 4–7, 32, col. V lines 1–7.

104. For instance, RINAP 3/2:61, Sennacherib 4, line 11.

105. RINAP 2:281, Sargon II 65, lines 51–54; RINAP 4:13–14, Esarhaddon 1, col. i lines 50, 80–84.

106. RINAP 1:119–20, Tiglath-Pileser III 47, lines 18–23a, 33–34; RINAP 2:300–306, Sargon II 65, lines 345–349, 420–425; RINAP 3/2:61–63, Sennacherib 4, lines 12–14, 27–28; RINAP 4:16–21, Esarhaddon 1, col. ii lines 75–80, col. iii lines 10–14, col. iv lines 46–52, 70–77; RINAP 5/1:63–77, Ashurbanipal 3, col. iii lines 40–42, col. viii lines 32–42.

107. RINAP 1:121, Tiglath-Pileser III 47, lines 36b–37a; RINAP 3/2: 62, Sennacherib 4, lines 22–24.

targets of or witnesses to their military campaign and slaughter,[108] and forced labor for their building project.[109] By adopting the three-tier law pronouncement process of the imperial legal metanarrative but emphasizing the people's distinctive participatory role, the imperialized authors exhorted their elite audience further to reject the domination over the imperialized people that the Assyrian emperors advocated. The imperialized authors also envisioned, and invited their elite audience to carry out, a meditating role that attends to the people, cares about their responses, and values their participation. Together with the general acceptance of imperial legal traditions, this exhortation and invitation reveal the wrestling of the imperialized authors. They conservatively resisted the imperial legal metanarrative about the gods, the emperors, and the people, when they lived under the shadow of the Neo-Assyrian Empire.

5.3 Chapter Conclusions

Analyzing the narrative of the Covenant collection from the perspective of the imperialized people that some postcolonial studies suggest, this chapter demonstrates how this narrative discloses further the imperialized authors' wrestling with imperial legal traditions when they compiled their law collection primarily for their elite audience during Neo-Assyrian subjugation. This narrative, including both the suggested basic narrative and passages not belonging to it, does reflect similarities to its cuneiform counterparts in the presentation of the three-tier, top-down law pronouncement process and the repeated references to word or words. With the understanding of the authors' familiarity with the imperial legal traditions prevailing in their world, these similarities suggest that the imperialized authors accepted the imperial legal way of addressing the legal pronouncement process in their non-legal sections and presenting this process in a hierarchical way. They also reveal that the imperialized authors acknowledged the imperial legal attention to the words of the divine and the lawmaker and to legal cases or issues that people have.

108. RINAP 2:227, Sargon II 43, lines 27–33; RINAP 2:289–90, Sargon II 65, lines 167–177, 188–194; RINAP 3/2:62, Sennacherib 4, lines 16–17; RINAP 5/1:60–64, Ashurbanipal 3, col. i line 91–col. ii line 1a, col. iii lines 43–52a.

109. RINAP 3/2:67, Sennacherib 4, lines 68–70; RINAP 4:23, Esarhaddon 1, col. v lines 45–53.

The narrative in the Covenant collection, nevertheless, simultaneously exhibits contrasts to the descriptions of the gods, the emperors, and the people in cuneiform law collections. Its characterization of Yhwh contrasts with cuneiform legal presentations of the gods and the emperors, while its portrayal of Moses diverges further from those of the emperors. The emphasis on the people in the Covenant collection is at odds with the subordinate characterization of them in its cuneiform counterparts, which in turn contrasts with their prioritized concern over the gods and focus on the emperors. These contrasts suggest that the imperialized authors resisted imperial legal understanding of the gods, the emperors, and the people.

These acceptances, as well as resistances, reasonably require postcolonial queries. The similar delineation of the ordinances and commandments' preservation suggests that the imperialized authors acknowledged the imperial mode of lawmaking. Together with the comparable hierarchal understanding of the law pronouncement, this delineation seems to promote imperial domination of the people and subordination of women to men. This imperial tendency remains in the contrastive characterization of Yhwh, Moses, and the people, as the imperialized authors still framed it under the hierarchical law pronouncement process. Moreover, the unique understanding of Yhwh as the lawmaker and Moses as the mediator leads to an inquiry about the potentially oppressive nature of human mediation in actual practice. The royal and warrior roles of Yhwh appear to advocate hegemony and violence. The Yhwh-Moses relationship potentially grants imperial power to the human leaders, who usually work as proxies for emperors. The people's response is still subject to Yhwh's conditional demand for obedience.

Even so, the resistances indicate that the imperialized authors did not completely comply with the imperial legal metanarrative but endeavored to convey a subversive message to their elite audience against Neo-Assyrian subjugation. By presenting Yhwh as the delegator, the royal warrior, as well as the lawmaker and the deliverer, with concerns about his people's relationship to him, the imperialized authors retrieved their traditional belief to reject that the gods and emperors of the Assyrian Empire had any roles among their people. To subvert the emperors' roles further, the imperialized authors underlined that human leaders only have a mediating role between Yhwh and their people, rather than being proxies of the emperors or being sovereign over the people. Through prioritized attention to their people and emphases on their liberated status and active participatory roles, the imperialized authors again subverted the domination over the people that the Assyrian emperors advocated, as well as invited their elite audience to become meditators both loyal to Yhwh, their national God, and committed to their people.

These acceptances and resistances, like those exhibited in the ordinances and commandments, characterize the narrative of the Covenant collection as the work of conservative revolutionists. Their conservative emulation explains the imperial outlook of this narrative, as postcolonial biblical scholars note; but their revolutionary diversion expresses resistance to imperial domination over their people, which my study unfolds and calls for attention. This *imperfect* vision is notably a kind of utopianism that some postcolonial scholars find in postcolonial literature.[110] Without fighting for a perfect community unrelated to the existing imperial power structure, the imperialized authors wrestled attention to their people based on their understanding of human leadership and belief in Yhwh, envisioning a world among the imperialized deviating from the empire's, though not totally different from it.

With these hybrid features, the narrative of the Covenant collection inaugurates and concludes the commandments and ordinances which express similar conservatively revolutionary attempts. Analyzing Exodus 19–24 and cuneiform law collections from the perspective of the imperialized, this study offers another understanding of the similarities and differences between them, revealing the wrestling of the imperialized authors with imperial legal traditions that prevailed in their world when they were subjugated by the Neo-Assyrian Empire.

110. Ashcroft, *Utopianism*, 4; see also §1.2.2.1.

CHAPTER 6

Conclusions

I began this study by noting that the corpus of Exodus 19–24 presents a law collection belonging to an imperialized people. Attending to the imperialized social location of the collection's authors, this study set out to investigate how the similarities and differences between Exodus 19–24 and extant cuneiform law collections reflect the wrestling of the imperialized authors with the imperial legal metanarrative and imperial subjugation of their time.

6.1 From the Colonized in Modern Contexts to the Imperialized in Israel and Judah

The first two chapters laid out the methods of this investigation and the historical context of Exodus 19–24, integrating observations of colonized people in the modern context into the understanding of the Exodus corpus and its authors. Chapter 1 pointed out that postcolonial scholars regard hybridity as one of the key characteristics of colonized people's response to their colonizers and highlight its resistive power. They observe, moreover, that the utopianism of subjugated people does not seek an idealized existence unrelated to their existing society but attempts to transform imperial systems in the hope of facilitating changes in norms and values. Some postcolonial scholars correctly identify the receptive intent and oppressive consequences of colonized people's mimicry, which necessitate ethical engagement in the study of subjugated people's hybrid response. However, these scholars also underscore the resistive endeavor in colonized people's pursuit of difference, including the retrieval of their own tradition, which calls for attention to subjugated people's diversion from the metanarrative amid their hybridity.

These observations concern both discourse in general and legal discourse in particular, covering colonized people at large as well as their elites. Legal discourse carries a vital role in colonized people's identity and their pursuit of justice and independence from their colonizers. Moreover, legal discourse can be a means of oppression as well as a tool for resisting this oppression among the subjugated people. The colonized people, including their elites, approach their colonizers' legal discourse in various ways. Some mimic their overlords' legal discourse indiscriminately, while others maintain the distinctiveness of the colonized people's legal discourse. Some colonized people, meanwhile, resort to the colonized people's customs in the formulation of their laws. Some even appropriate their colonizers' legal discourse to resist their colonizers' conceptions and values.

Considering these multifaceted responses of the colonized people to their colonizers' discourse in general and legal discourse in particular, I reviewed the studies of Musa W. Dube, Gale A. Yee, Shiju Mathew, and R. S. Wafula in relation to Exodus 19–24. I suggested rediscovering the resistive elements in this corpus, in addition to the imperial features that these postcolonial biblical scholars have revealed. I argued that postcolonial observations of colonized people indicate the importance of attending to the multifaceted nature of the imperialized people's response to the empire and offer guidance for this attention in the study of Exodus 19–24 in comparison to cuneiform law collections.

Chapter 2 integrated these postcolonial observations into the historical-comparative method that scholars have worked on for more than a century. Albrecht Alt, Shalom M. Paul, Raymond Westbrook, Eckart Otto, Ralf Rothenbusch, Meir Malul, and John Van Seter have offered different models for understanding the relationship between Exodus 19–24 and cuneiform law collections, namely common legal tradition, evolutionary development, and direct literary borrowing. However, while these models suggest how and when cultural contact occurred between the people of Israel and Judah and their neighbors, they do not attend to the imperialized social location of these people, or its effect on the composition of the Exodus corpus in relation to cuneiform law collection. David P. Wright, Bruce Wells, William S. Morrow, and Pamela Barmash have shed light on the criteria for determining possible relationships between these two corpora, including literary dependence, common legal traditions, and a shared educational tradition. Wright's and

Barmash's studies have also attempted to consider the imperialized social location of the biblical authors and the hegemony behind cuneiform law collections. However, their analyses of the multifaceted features of the rhetoric in the imperialized people's work leaves considerable room for additional work.

The chapter also reviewed Otto's and Wells's recent studies, which suggest the Book of the Covenant's subversive reception of the Laws of Hammurabi and the Book of the Covenant's conventional characteristics, respectively. I contended that integrating the aforementioned postcolonial observations into the historical-comparative analysis of Exodus 19–24 and cuneiform law collections enhances attention to the biblical authors' imperialized social location in the understanding of the relationship between the two corpora. With this integrated perspective, I suggested that the similarities and differences between Exodus 19–24 and cuneiform law collections reflect various responses of the biblical authors to cuneiform legal traditions, which characterizes the Exodus corpus as a work of conservative revolutionists. These authors seem to have been hesitant to deviate from cuneiform legal traditions drastically, but did nevertheless diverge from those traditions. To demonstrate this characteristic, I proposed that the authors of Exodus 19–24 were familiar with the cuneiform legal traditions that prevailed in ancient West Asia, which the extant cuneiform law collections somehow reflect, and these authors were aware of these traditions' imperial nature.

To enhance the understanding of the imperial encounter behind Exodus 19–24, I also located this corpus's compilation in a specific historical context, suggesting that this work mainly occurred in the middle of the eighth century to the middle of the seventh century. This dating is based on three considerations, namely the Exodus corpus's relationship with Deuteronomy and Deuteronomy's dating; expansion of scribal culture in Israel and Judah and Hebrew literature's appropriation of Akkadian literature; and the biblical authors' possible exposure to cuneiform legal traditions in the Neo-Assyrian period. There might be some redactional activities in the compilation of Exodus 19–24. However, I suggested dissociating literary diversity and thematic closeness to later biblical works from the argument for later redaction. I also called for attention to the similar structural, compositional, and literary features of Exodus 19–24 and cuneiform literature dated to or accessible in the Neo-Assyrian period. I, therefore, analyzed Exodus 19–24 in its entirety under the backdrop of the Neo-Assyrian imperial rule over Israel and Judah in the mid-eighth century to the mid-seventh century, with notes on the diachronic issues of some sections that scholars have explored.

With this dating in mind, I left open the geographical location of Exodus 19–24's composition and compilation, suggesting that it may be Israel, Judah, or both. I explored the interaction of Israelites and Judahites with the Assyrians through military encounters, diplomatic contacts, and scribal training, demonstrating that the people of Israel and Judah experienced various levels of imperial subjugation from the Neo-Assyrian Empire. Moreover, this exploration suggested that through such scribal training, the biblical authors had exposure to cuneiform legal traditions and regarded them as the representation of the imperial legal metanarrative of their time. I argued that this exposure under Neo-Assyrian subjugation was a critical impetus of the multifaceted response exhibited in Exodus 19–24.

Integrating further postcolonial observations into understanding its historical context, I suggested that the Exodus corpus was intended to be the legal discourse of the imperialized, among the multiple purposes scholars have proposed, including judicial-referential, wisdom-moral, religious, and political. Anselm C. Hagedorn's recent study of the Pentateuch particularly speaks to this potential through its consideration of colonized people's response to the complex dialectic in their colonial contexts. Because of this dialectic, the subjugated people sense the pressure to employ strategies that favor compromise and harmony with the imperial power in order to avoid conflict with it, even though there is no current and direct imposition from their overlords. One of the strategies that the subjugated people employ is the appropriation of the legal system, which resonates with their overlords' ideology. The subjugated people create a legal document that follows imperial legal framework and expressions, which gives the impression that they submit themselves to the empire's governance. However, the subjugated people at the same time make use of this legal document to express their resistance to imperial values.

Drawing on this study, I argued that Exodus 19–24 is a written legal communication that significantly expresses the imperialized authors' resistive response to the imperial legal metanarrative and Neo-Assyrian subjugation, when they sensed the pressure to comply with imperial practices. This legal discourse might simultaneously speak to the Israelite or Judahite monarchy, but my study particularly focused on the imperialized authors' response to the empire in view of Exodus 19–24's relationship with imperial legal traditions. Based on the characteristics of the Exodus corpus and the literacy and scribal culture in Israel and Judah in the Neo-Assyrian period, I proposed that these authors were Israelite or Judahite scribes who had gone through some training in foreign languages and legal traditions and served the palace and/or the temple among the imperialized. They compiled Exodus 19–24 primarily for elites who had a similar background. These authors had special relationships with the empire, a patronage relationship with their own kings, as well as the autonomy to express their views toward the empire. Thus, I posited that they might have been torn between pro- and anti-Assyrian positions, similar to the colonized elites in the modern context. These understandings suggest the complexity of Exodus 19–24 as the manifestation of the imperialized authors' response to the empire, offering an essential background for unfolding their wrestling with the imperial legal metanarrative and imperial subjugation of their time.

6.2 The Wrestling of the Imperialized

Utilizing the historical-comparative approach integrated with postcolonial observations, chapters 3–5 demonstrated how the Exodus corpus exhibits this wrestling. Chapter 3 argued that the comparison of ordinances in Exodus 21:2–22:16 with corresponding cuneiform laws reflects the imperialized authors' resistance to the imperial legal handling of slaves and women amid their general acceptance of it. The imperialized authors followed imperial legal traditions in tolerating debt slavery and broadly accepted their repressive approach to slaves and women. However, the imperialized authors worked against these traditions by prioritizing the concern and owners' responsibility for slaves among the imperialized people, emphasizing their release, and portraying them positively. They also uniquely handled slave owners' physical assault against their own slaves, imposing the death penalty for fatal assault, demanding release for bodily damages, and prescribing stoning of the ox for fatal accustomed goring. In the goring ox ordinances as a whole, the imperialized authors indeed expressed resistance to the imperial legal emphasis on economic concerns, which were among the key concerns of the Neo-Assyrian Empire. In the ordinance regarding kidnapping, the imperialized authors even uniquely addressed the case when the kidnapper has sold the kidnapped, exhibiting their endeavor to prevent the sale of people into servitude.

The imperialized authors, moreover, resisted imperial legal treatment of women in various ways. They extended imperial protections for women in general to female slaves, including restricting female slaves' release and stipulating provisions for them. They offered these women freedom when their owners failed to protect them. The imperialized authors also uniquely addressed mothers and prescribed the death punishment in the ordinances concerning the physical assault against parents. They focused on pregnant women's well-being rather than their social status. They brought up a broader concern about the pregnant women's physical condition than imperial legal traditions did. Concerning unbetrothed women, the imperialized authors distinctively addressed their seduction and de-emphasized patriarchal authority over them.

I pointed out that these responses do potentially remain oppressive to slaves and women because the imperialized authors did not forbid slavery but maintained the master-slave relationships. The imperialized authors were also only concerned with native debt slaves but not with foreign ones. They indeed stipulated a longer servitude length than their imperial counterparts and exempted slave owners from punishment for physical assault against their own slaves that were not immediately fatal. They imposed less penalty for accustomed goring against slaves than they did for such assaults against free people, just as their imperial peers did. Notably, the imperialized authors saved thieves from life-threatening punishment, which cuneiform legal traditions imposed. However, the imperialized authors potentially promoted temporary servitude when they similarly demanded selling thieves who were not able to make restitution. Concerning the treatment of women, the imperialized authors did not prohibit fathers from selling their daughters to be slaves, but they imposed restrictions on the release of slaves' wives and female slaves. They potentially subordinated injured pregnant women to their husbands and male mediators. They also ignored unbetrothed maidens' voices and did not address their rape. These possibly oppressive treatments may be related to the acceptance of or ambivalence toward oppressive imperial legal principles, requiring a postcolonial inquiry. Given the biblical authors' and their audience's elite status, these treatments of slaves and women also raise questions about the self-serving motives behind the ordinances.

Still, in view of the aforementioned resistive responses, I argued that the imperialized authors did not fully recognize the imperial legal metanarrative of their time. Rather, they wrestled to distinguish themselves from it through various approaches, including retrieving their own tradition. Through this wrestling, the imperialized authors urged their elite audience to improve the conditions of slaves and women among their people when they were under Neo-Assyrian subjugation.

Comparing the commandments surrounding these ordinances (Exod 20:23–21:1 and 22:17–23:33) with cuneiform law collections' prologues and epilogues, chapter 4 similarly indicated this conservatively revolutionary response. I contended that whereas the imperialized authors followed the imperial legal approach in attending to religious services, the marginalized, and enemies outside the mostly casuistic legal section, they resisted the imperial legal aggrandizement that emphasized the emperors' own achievements and their relationships with various gods. Considering Neo-Assyrian royal inscriptions and treaties, which express similar emphases, I argued further that the imperialized authors appropriated these imperial legal attentions to resist Neo-Assyrian religious and imperial ideology and their subjugation.

Again, I pointed out that these responses still necessitate a postcolonial inquiry because the imperialized authors took a hostile attitude toward enemies just as their imperial counterparts did. While the imperialized authors initially attempted to move away from human participation in the elimination of enemies, they ended up following the imperial legal promotion of this participation, which resonated with Neo-Assyrian political ideology. The imperialized authors might also serve their own economic and political interests through calling for religious services and obedience to Yhwh and care of the marginalized. These self-interests possibly led to exploitation and domination of the imperialized people and other inhabitants in the Levant, similar to and in addition to the imperial subjugation of them. In fact, the biblical authors blessed their audience at the expense of other people in the Levant, which necessitates not only critique but also rejection.

Yet, the imperialized authors' resistive responses also indicate that their acceptance of the imperial legal metanarrative, as well as Neo-Assyrian ideology, is a selective one. By resisting the imperial presentation of religious services, care for the marginalized, and destruction of enemies as the emperors' achievements, the imperialized authors urged their elite audience to reject the emperors and their gods. Remaining conservative in diverging from the imperial metanarrative, the imperialized authors indeed had a platform for highlighting their emphasis on and offering opportunity for the imperialized people's participation in serving and building a direct relationship with Yhwh. The imperialized authors appropriated imperial legal concerns but retrieved their own religious belief, underscored Yhwh's attention to the oppression against marginalized people, and repeated their concern about the immigrants. They motivated their people to maintain their festivals and offerings to their own God and take care of the immigrants by recalling the oppression that Israelites experienced under the Egyptian Empire and their liberation from it. Unlike their imperial counterparts, the imperialized authors emphasized the blessing, rather than cursing, of their audience. Through this "the same but not quite" presentation, the imperialized authors called their elites to serve only Yhwh, to take care of the marginalized, including the immigrants among themselves, and to envision divine subversion of Neo-Assyrian subjugation.

Chapter 5 demonstrated that the narrative surrounding these commandments and ordinances (Exod 19:1–20:22 and 24:1–18) in comparison to cuneiform law collections' non-legal sections reflects similar resistances amid acceptances. I indicated that this narrative, including both the suggested basic narrative and passages outside of it, does exhibit broad acceptance of the imperial legal metanarrative in terms of its hierarchical law pronouncement process. Furthermore, this narrative shows sympathy with the imperial legal attention to the words of the divine and the lawmaker and the legal issues that people have. Nevertheless, I also contended that this narrative reveals a resistance to the imperial legal claim on the gods' roles as the delegator and royal warrior and the emperors' dominant roles as the royal warrior, deliverer, and lawmaker. It does so through the characterization of Yhwh that contrasts with the presentations of the gods and the emperors in cuneiform legal traditions and Neo-Assyrian inscriptions and through the portrayal of Moses that diverges from those of the emperors. Putting emphasis on the people since its very beginning, this narrative not only works against the prioritized concern over the gods and the focus on the emperors in cuneiform legal traditions and Neo-Assyrian inscriptions and treaties, but also resists the subordinate characterization of the people in them.

I pointed out that these responses require a postcolonial inquiry, particularly into the acceptance of the imperial mode of lawmaking, violent and hegemonic characterization of Yhwh, domination over the people, subordination of women, and potentially oppressive human mediation in actual practice. Yet, the resistive responses concurrently indicate that the compliance with the imperial legal metanarrative is not a complete one. The imperialized authors characterized Yhwh as filling the roles of the gods and emperors. They portrayed Moses as a mediator between God and the people rather than a subservient proxy or a sovereign ruler. The imperialized authors indeed regarded the people as the prioritized concern of their law collection, a people liberated from an empire, and the essential and active participants in the law pronouncement process. Through this resistive characterization, the imperialized authors conveyed a subversive message against Neo-Assyrian subjugation to their elite audience, urging them to become mediators who serve Yhwh and their people rather than the empire.

These resistances amid acceptances, together with those appearing in the ordinances and commandments, characterize Exodus 19–24 as a work of conservative revolutionists, expressing a kind of utopianism that some postcolonial scholars find in postcolonial literature. The imperialized authors did not strive for a perfect community disassociated from the existing social circumstance and structure, while under imperial subjugation and hoping for its subversion. However, they wrestled to reject such subjugation, to alleviate the suffering caused by exploitation and subordination, and to draw attention to the need and voices of the imperialized people. Through this wrestling, the imperialized authors worked toward a society among the imperialized which diverged from the empire's and their own.

Analyzing Exodus 19–24 and cuneiform law collections from the perspective of the imperialized, I therefore argued that the Exodus corpus does not simply reveal borrowing aiming at a better law, a meta-legal tradition in a broader sense in ancient West Asia, or a shared educational tradition with a prestigious perception of Mesopotamian knowledge. Rather, the corpus of Exodus 19–24 represents a law collection of the imperialized, who wrestled to resist the imperial legal metanarrative when they were living under the shadow of the Neo-Assyrian Empire.

6.3 Implications

These findings invite reflections on existing approaches to the study of Exodus 19–24, as well as the contemporary application of this corpus. First, the imperialized-imperial relationship between Exodus 19–24 and cuneiform law collections invites modern readers to continue to contemplate the comparative approach to these two corpora toward which scholars have made valuable contributions in previous decades. Differences between the corpora do not necessarily indicate the absence of a direct relationship. While they may only reflect a universal feature of literary traditions in relation to adaptation, the differences also suggest resistive responses of subjugated people to dominant power, as postcolonial studies indicate. Likewise, similarities do not always point to the same rhetoric and meaning, as these people may transform their acceptance of the metanarrative into part of their resistance to it. These observations call for further consideration on the criteria for determining the relationship between biblical texts and comparative materials. They also invite reinvestigation of the method for inferring rhetoric and meanings of biblical texts based on comparative materials of similar features. In addition to historical and literary data, authors' social location, especially their relationship with the producers of the comparative data, is a factor that deserves serious attention.

Second, as the Exodus corpus involves resistive endeavors in addition to imperial tendencies, it is necessary for modern readers to ponder if a focus on the latter does justice to the rhetoric of the corpus and offers a complete picture for developing an application of it. Postcolonial biblical studies, which I reviewed in Chapter 2, have successfully brought the imperial elements of Exodus 19–24 to light, cautioning readers against applying this corpus uncritically in response to oppression and subjugation. A further question is whether modern readers should then de-emphasize the value of this law collection in their response to hegemony and the metanarrative of their own society. My study revisited the dynamics of the imperial and resistive components in the Exodus corpus in comparison with the imperial legal metanarrative of its time. Through this study, I urge modern readers to attend to the biblical authors' endeavors in addition to their failures. I also invite modern readers, including myself, to reconsider the meaning of this law collection of the imperialized people to us, when we wrestle with power and subordination today.

This calling leads to the final significant point of this study's implications: the contemporary application of Exodus 19–24. Just as biblical scholars have wisely pointed out that "Israel's story is not intended to model normative behavior in all its particulars,"[1] I have to emphasize that my study does not suggest that modern readers should completely follow the path of the authors of Exodus 19–24. Rather, my findings of these authors' response to the imperial legal metanarrative and imperial subjugation offer a platform for modern readers to reflect on their own response to hegemonic domination today. On the one hand, the acceptance of imperial legal traditions allowed the biblical authors to speak against the empire when they sensed the pressure to comply with it or saw the need to avoid creating possible tension between pro- and anti-imperial parties among their people. On the other hand, this acceptance inevitably confined the biblical authors' resistive response to imperial paradigms, including oppressive ones. In a similar vein, the resistance of the biblical authors was a vital step toward actualizing their hope for a more liberative world. However, its effectiveness was subject to their actual practices and how far these practices departed from their own oppressive approaches and the oppressive imperial ideology of their time.

Between acceptance and resistance, modern readers must inevitably wrestle with how far our pendulum should swing. We need to continuously contemplate whether we follow the path of the biblical authors in complying with the dominant paradigm because of circumstances similar to those of the biblical authors in relation to the dominant power, or assertively strive for breakthroughs in view of historical lessons that we have uniquely learned. Some might unconditionally advocate a total departure from the metanarrative, but there are always limitations and pressures in reality which inevitably lead us to acquiesce. Others might unreservedly uphold a complete acceptance of the dominant ideology, but quite often this ideology involves oppressive elements, which necessitate our confrontation or even resistive actions. The question is, should we choose not to resist at all when we cannot find a pure space to do so? Or, should we refuse to comply in any case, even if this refusal may lead to other kinds of oppression? Should we also consider resistance amid acceptance as an option for working toward the subversion of dominant power and oppression, and therefore contemplate how we should

1. Birch, *Let Justice Roll Down*, 43; Anderson, *Ancient Laws*, 9.

do so in an effective and liberative way? These questions are vital for modern readers when we continue to experience some form of imperialism today throughout the globe.[2] By unfolding the resistive responses in addition to those receptive ones, my study attempted to help modern readers not only to identify oppressive imperial values in the biblical text so that we can resist following them, but also to appreciate its effort to work against imperial values and subjugation so that we can reflect on what we can do further to subvert dominant power and oppressive practices in our own contexts.

2. Said, *Orientialism*, xxii; Venn, *Postcolonial Challenge*, 2; Roy, "Postcolonial Theory," 336–37.

Bibliography

Achebe, Chinua. *Morning Yet on Creation Day*. New York: Doubleday, 1975.

Achenbach, Reinhard. "*Gêr – nåkhrî – tôshav – zâr*: Legal and Sacral Distinction Regarding Foreigners in the Pentateuch." In *The Foreigner and the Law: Perspectives from the Hebrew Bible and the Ancient Near East*, edited by Reinhard Achenbach, Rainer Albertz, and Jakob Wöhrle, 29–51. Beihefte zur Zeitschrift für altorientalische und biblische Rechtsgeschichte 16. Wiesbanden: Harrassowitz, 2011.

Adam, Klaus-Peter. "A Didactic Case Narrative on Homicide Law: 1 Samuel 26." In *Law and Narrative in the Bible and in Neighbouring Ancient Cultures*, edited by Klaus-Peter Adam, Friedrich Avemarie, and Nili Wazana, 99–122. FAT 2/54. Mohr Siebeck, Tübingen, 2012.

Ahmad, Aijaz. *Iraq, Afghanistan, and the Imperialism of Our Time*. New Delhi: LeftWord, 2004.

Albertz, Rainer. *Exodus, Band I: 1–18*. Zürcher Bibelkommentare. Zürich: Teologischer Verlag Zürich, 2012.

———. *Exodus, Band II: 19–40*. Zürcher Bibelkommentare. Zürich: Teologischer Verlag Zürich, 2015.

———. "From Aliens to Proselytes: Non-Priestly and Priestly Legislation Concerning Strangers." In *The Foreigner and the Law: Perspectives from the Hebrew Bible and the Ancient Near East*, edited by Reinhard Achenbach, Rainer Albertz, and Jakob Wöhrle, 53–69. Beihefte zur Zeitschrift für altorientalische und biblische Rechtsgeschichte 16. Wiesbanden: Harrassowitz, 2011.

———. *A History of Israelite Religion in the Old Testament Period*. Translated by John Bowden. 2 vols. Louisville: Westminster John Knox, 1994.

Alexander, T. Desmond. "The Composition of the Sinai Narrative in Exodus XIX 1–XXIV 11." *VT* 49, no. 1 (1999): 2–20.

———. *Exodus*. Abingdon Old Testament Commentaries 2. Downers Grove: InterVarsity Press, 2017.

Alt, Albrecht. "Die Ursprünge des israelitischen Rechts." In *Kleine Schriften zur Geschichte des Volkes Israel*, band 1, 278–332. München: C. H. Beck, 1959.

Anderson, Cheryl B. *Ancient Laws and Contemporary Controversies: The Needs for Inclusive Biblical Interpretation*. Oxford: Oxford University Press, 2009.

———. *Women, Ideology and Violence: Critical Theory and the Construction of Gender in the Book of the Covenant and the Deuteronomic Law*. JSOTSup 394. New York: T&T Clark, 2004.

Arneth, Martin. "Der Exodus der Sklaven." *Kerygma und Dogma* 59, no. 2 (2013): 109–24.

Ashcroft, Bill. *Post-Colonial Transformation*. London: Routledge, 2001.

———. *Utopianism in Postcolonial Literature*. London: Routledge, 2017.

Ashcroft, Bill, Gareth Griffins, and Helen Tiffin. *The Empire Writes Back: Theory and Practice in Post-Colonial Literature*. 2nd ed. New York: Routledge, 2002.

———. "Language: Introduction to Part Ten." In *The Post-Colonial Studies Reader*, edited by Bill Ashcroft, Gareth Griffins, and Helen Tiffin, 261–62. 2nd ed. London: Routledge, 2006.

———. *Post-Colonial Studies: The Key Concepts*. 2nd ed. London: Routledge, 2007.

Assmann, Jan. *The Invention of Religion: Faith and Covenant in the Book of Exodus*. Translated by Robert Savage. Princeton: Princeton University Press, 2018.

Aster, Shawn Zelig. *Reflections of Empire in Isaiah 1–39: Responses to Assyrian Ideology*. Ancient Near East Monographs 19. Atlanta: SBL Press, 2017.

———. "The Shock of Assyrian Imperial Ideology and the Responses of Biblical Authors in the Late Eighth Century." In *Archaeology and History of Eighth-Century Judah*, edited by Zev I. Farber and Jacob L. Wright, 475–87. Ancient Near East Monographs 23. Atlanta: SBL Press, 2018.

———. "Transmission of Neo-Assyrian Claim of Empire to Judah in the Late Eighth Century B.C.E." *Hebrew Union College Annual* 78 (2007): 1–44.

Ateek, Naim S. "A Palestinian Perspective: Biblical Perspectives on the Land." In *Voices from the Margin: Interpreting the Bible in the Third World Account*, edited by R. S. Sugirtharajah, 165–70. 3rd ed. Maryknoll: Orbis, 2006.

Ausloos, H. "The 'Angel of YHWH' in Exod. xxiii 20–33 and Judg. ii 1–5: A Clue to the 'Deuteronom(ist)ic' Puzzle?" *VT* 58, no. 1 (2008): 1–12.

———. "Deuteronomi(sti)c Elements in Exod 23,20–33: Some Methodological Remarks." In *Studies in the Book of Exodus: Redaction – Reception – Interpretation*, edited by Marc Vervenne, 481–500. Leuven: Leuven University Press, 1996.

———. "Exod 23, 20–33 and the 'War of YHWH.'" *Biblica* 80, no. 4 (1999): 555–63.

Averbeck, Richard E. "The Egyptian Sojourn and Deliverance from Slavery in the Framing and Shaping of the Mosaic Law." In *"Did I Not Bring Israel Out of Egypt?" Biblical, Archaeological, and Egyptological Perspectives on the Exodus*

Narratives, edited by James K. Hoffmeier, Alan R. Millard, and Gary A. Rendsburg, 143–75. Bulletin for Biblical Research Supplements 13. Winona Lake: Eisenbrauns, 2016.

———. "Slavery in the World of the Bible." In *Behind the Scenes of the Old Testament: Cultural, Social, and Historical Contexts*, edited by Jonathan S. Greer, John W. Hilber, and John H. Walton, 423–30. Grand Rapid: Baker Academic, 2018.

Awabdy, Mark A. *Immigrants and Innovative Law: Deuteronomy's Theological and Social Vision for the* גר. FAT 2/67. Tübingen: Mohr Siebeck, 2014.

Badamchi, Hossein. "The Meaning of 'Theft' in Ancient Near Eastern Law." *Folia Orientalia* 53 (2016): 369–86.

Baden, Joel S. "Rethinking the Supposed JE Document." PhD diss., Harvard University, 2007.

———. Review of *Inventing God's Law: How the Covenant Code of the Biblical Used and Revised the Laws of Hammurabi*, by David P. Wright. *Review of Biblical Literature* (2011): 167–71.

———. "The Transformation of the Decalogue into Law and Covenant." *Maarav* 24 (2020): 63–73.

Bagg, A. M. "Palestine under Assyrian Rule: A New Look at the Assyrian Imperial Policy in the West." *Journal of the American Oriental Society* 133 (2013): 119–44.

———. "Assyria and the West: Syria and the Levant." In *A Companion to Assyria*, edited by Eckart Frahm, 268–84. Blackwell Companions to the Ancient World. Hoboken: John Wiley & Sons, 2017.

Bal, Mieke. *Narratology: Introduction to the Theory of Narrative*. 3rd ed. Toronto: University of Toronto Press, 2009.

Barmash, Pamela. "The Daughter Sold into Slavery and Marriage." In *Sexuality and Law in the Torah*, edited by Hilary Lipka and Bruce Wells, 48–76. London: Bloomsbury, 2020.

———. "Determining the Date of Biblical Legal Texts." In *The Oxford Handbook of Biblical Law*, edited by Pamela Barmash, 233–53. Oxford: Oxford University Press, 2019.

———. *Homicide in the Biblical World*. Cambridge: Cambridge University Press, 2005.

———. *The Laws of Hammurabi: At the Confluence of Royal and Scribal Traditions*. Oxford: Oxford University Press, 2020.

Bartor, Assnat. "Law and Narrative." In *The Oxford Handbook of Biblical Law*, edited by Pamela Barmash, 217–31. Oxford: Oxford University Press, 2019.

———. *Reading Laws as Narrative: A Study in the Casuistic Laws of the Pentateuch*. Atlanta: SBL Press, 2010.

Baxi, Upendra. "Postcolonial Legality." In *A Companion to Postcolonial Studies*, edited by Henry Schwarz and Sangeeta Ray, 540–55. Oxford: Blackwell, 2000.

Beegle, Dewey M. "Moses (Person): Old Testament." In *Anchor Bible Dictionary*, vol. 4, edited by David Noel Freedman, 909–18. 6 vols. New York: Doubleday, 1991.

Ben-Dov, Jonathan. "The Poor's Curse: Exodus XXII 20–26 and Curse Literature in the Ancient World." *VT* 56, no. 4 (2006): 431–51.

Berlejung, A. "The Assyrians in the West: Assyrianization, Colonialism, Indifference, or Development Policy?" In *Congress Volume Helsinki 2010*, edited by M. Nissinen, 21–60. VTSup 148. Leiden: Brill, 2012.

———. "Shared Fates: Gaza and Ekron as Examples for the Assyrian Religious Policy in the West." In *Iconoclasm and Text Destruction in the Ancient Near East and Beyond*, edited by N. N. May, 151–74. Oriental Institute Seminars 8. Chicago: Oriental Institute of the University of Chicago, 2012.

Berman, Joshua. "The History of Legal Theory and the Study of Biblical Law." *Catholic Biblical Quarterly* 76, no. 1 (2014): 19–39.

Berquist, Jon L. "Resistance and Accommodation in the Persian Empire." In *In the Shadow of Empire: Reclaiming the Bible as a History of Faithful Resistance*, edited by Richard A. Horsley, 41–58. Louisville: Westminster John Knox, 2008.

Bhabha, Homi. *The Location of Culture*. New York: Routledge, 1994.

———. "Surviving Theory: A Conversation with Homi K. Bhabha." In *The Pre-Occupation of Postcolonial Studies*, edited by Fawzia Afzal-Khan and Kalpana Seshadri-Crooks, 369–79. Durham, NC: Duke University Press, 2000.

———. "The Vernacular Cosmopolitan." In *Voices of the Crossing: The Impact of Britain on Writers from Asia, the Caribbean and Africa*, edited by F. Dennis and N. Khan, 133–42. London: Serpent's Tail, 2000.

Birch, Bruce C. *Let Justice Roll Down: The Old Testament, Ethics, and Christian Life*. Louisville: Westminster John Knox Press, 1991.

Black, Jeremy, and Anthony Green. *Gods, Demons and Symbols of Ancient Mesopotamia: An Illustrated Dictionary*. Austin: University of Texas Press, 1992.

Boecker, H. J. *Recht und Gesetz im Alten Testament und im Alten Orient*. Neukirchen-Vluyn: Neukirchener Verlag, 1976.

Boehmer, Elleke. "Revisiting Resistance: Postcolonial Practice and the Antecedents of Theory." In *The Oxford Handbook of Postcolonial Studies*, edited by Graham Huggan, 307–23. Oxford: Oxford University Press, 2016.

Bottéro, Jean. *Mesopotamia: Writing, Reasoning, and the Gods*. Chicago: University of Chicago Press, 1992.

Bovati, Pietro. *Re-Establishing Justice: Legal Terms, Concepts, and Procedures in the Hebrew Bible*. JSOTSup 105. Sheffield: Sheffield Academic, 1994.

Brett, Mark G. *Locations of God: Political Theology in the Hebrew Bible*. Oxford: Oxford University Press, 2019.

Brettler, Marc Zvi. *God Is King: Understanding an Israelite Metaphor*. JSOTSup 76. Sheffield: JSOT Press, 1989.

Bridge, E. J. "The Metaphoric Use of Slave Terms in the Hebrew Bible." *Bulletin for Biblical Research* 23, no. 1 (2012): 13–28.

Bright, John. *A History of Israel*. 4th ed. Louisville: Westminster John Knox, 2000.

Broeck, Sabine. "White Fatigue, or, Supplementary Notes on Hybridity." In *Reconstructing Hybridity: Post-Colonial Studies in Translation*, edited by Joel Kuortti and Jopi Nyman, 43–58. Amsterdam: Rodopi, 2007.

Burnside, Jonathan. "The Hidden Faces of the Law-Giver: Revelation and Concealment in the Giving of the Law at Mount Sinai." In *Ben Porat Yosef: Studies in the Bible and Its World: Essays in Honor of Joseph Fleishman*, edited by Michael Avioz, Omer Minka, and Yael Shemesh, 103–20. AOAT 458. Münster: Ugarit-Verlag, 2019.

Cameron, Andrew. "Liberation and Desire: The Logic of Law in Exodus and Beyond." In *Exploring Exodus: Literary, Theological and Contemporary Approaches*, edited by Brian S. Rosner and Paul R. Williamson, 123–53. Nottingham: Apollos, 2008.

Carpenter, Eugene. *Exodus 19–40*. Exegetical Evangelical Commentary. Bellingham: Lexham, 2016.

Carr, David M. *The Formation of the Hebrew Bible: A New Reconstruction*. Oxford: Oxford University Press, 2011.

———. *Writing on the Tablet of the Heart: Origins of Scripture and Literature*. Oxford: Oxford University Press, 2005.

Cassuto, U. *A Commentary on the Book of Exodus*. Jerusalem: Magnes, 1987.

Chanock, Martin. *Law and Custom and Social Order: The Colonial Experience in Malawi and Zambia*. Portsmouth, NH: Heinemann, 1998.

Chavel, Simeon. "A Kingdom of Priests and its Earthen Altars in Exodus 19–24." *VT* 65, no. 2 (2015): 169–222.

Childs, Brevard S. *The Book of Exodus*. Old Testament Library. Philadelphia: Westminster, 1974.

Chirchigno, G. C. *Debt-Slavery to Israel and the Ancient Near East*. JSOTSup 141. Sheffield: Sheffield Academic, 1993

———. "The Narrative Structure of Exod 19–24." *Biblica* 68, no. 4 (1987): 457–79.

Chiu, Andrew. *The Book of Exodus*. Chinese Bible Commentary 3. Hong Kong: Chinese Christian Literature Council, 1993. [Chinese].

Chow, Rey. "Between Colonizers: Hong Kong's Postcolonial Self-Writing in the 1990s." *Diaspora* 2, no. 2 (1992): 151–70.

———. "King Kong in Hong Kong: Watching the 'Handover' from the USA." In *A Companion to Postcolonial Studies*, edited by Henry Schwarz and Sangeeta Ray, 304–18. Oxford: Blackwell Publishers, 2000.

Civil, Miguel. "The Law Collection of Ur-Namma." In *Cuneiform Royal Inscriptions and Related Texts in the Schøyen Collection*, edited by A. R. George, 221–310. Cornell University Studies in Assyriology and Sumerology 17. Bethesda: CDL Press, 2011.

Coats, George W. *Moses: Heroic Man, Man of God*. JSOTSup 57. Sheffield: JSOT Press, 1988.

Cogan, Mordechai. "Judah under Assyrian Hegemony: A Reexamination of Imperialism and Religion." *JBL* 112, no. 3 (1993): 403–14.

Cohen, Chaim. "The Ancient Critical Understanding of Exodus 21:22–25 and Its Implications for the Current Debate on Abortion." In *Mishneh Todah: Studies in Deuteronomy and Its Cultural Environment in Honor of Jeffery H. Tigay*, edited by Nili Sacher Fox, David A. Glatt-Gilad, and Michael J. Williams, 437–58. Winona Lake: Eisenbrauns, 2009.

Collin, John J. *The Bible after Babel: Historical Criticism in a Postmodern Age*. Grand Rapids: Eerdmans, 2005.

Comaroff, John L., and Jean Comaroff. "Law and Disorder in the Postcolony: An Introduction." In *Law and Disorder in the Postcolony*, edited by Jean Comaroff and John L. Comaroff, 1–56. Chicago: University of Chicago Press, 2006.

Cross, Frank Moore. *Canaanite Myth and Hebrew Epic: Essays in the History of the Religion of Israel*. Cambridge, MA: Harvard University Press, 1973.

Crouch, C. L. *Israel and the Assyrians: Deuteronomy, the Succession Treaty of Esarhaddon, and the Nature of Subversion*. Atlanta: SBL Press, 2014.

———. *The Making of Israel: Cultural Diversity in the Southern Levant and the Formation of Ethnic Identity in Deuteronomy*. VTSup 162. Leiden: Brill, 2014.

———. *War and Ethics in the Ancient Near East: Military Violence in Light of Cosmology and History*. Berlin: de Gruyter, 2009.

Crüsemann, F. "Das Bundesbuch: Historische Ort und institutioneller Hintergrund." In *Congress Volume: Jerusalem, 1986*, edited by J. A. Emerton, 27–41. VTSup 40. Leiden: Brill, 1988.

Culbertson, Laura. "A Life-Course Approach to Household Slaves in the Late Third Millennium B. C." In *Slaves and Households in the Near East*, edited by Laura Culbertson, 33–48. Oriental Institute Seminars 7. Chicago: University of Chicago Press, 2011.

———. "Slaves and Households in the Near East." In *Slaves and Households in the Near East*, edited by Laura Culbertson, 1–17. Oriental Institute Seminars 7. Chicago: University of Chicago Press, 2011.

Dabashi, Hamid. *Brown Skin, White Masks*. New York: Pluto, 2011.

Dalley, Stephanie. "The Identity of the Princesses in Tomb II and a New Analysis of Events in 701 BC." In *New Light on Nimrud: Proceedings of the Nimrud Conference, 11th–13th March, 2002*, edited by J. E. Curtis, H. McCall, D. Collon, and L. al-Gailani Werr, 171–75. London: British Institute for the Study of Iraq, 2008.

———. "Occasions and Opportunities: 1. To the Persian Conquest." In *The Legacy of Mesopotamia*, edited by Stephanie Dalley, 9–22. Oxford: Oxford University Press, 1998.

———. "Waterworks in the Time of Hezekiah and Judaean Princesses in Assyria." *Bulletin of the Anglo-Israel Archaeological Society* 18 (2000): 119–21.

Daube, D. *Studies in Biblical Law*. Cambridge: Cambridge University Press, 1947.

Davenport, Tracy. "An Anti-Imperialist Twist to the Gilgameš Epic." In *Gilgameš and the World of Assyria: Proceedings of the Conference Held at Mandelbaum House, the University of Sydney, 21–23 July, 2004*, edited by Joseph Azize and Noel Weeks, 1–23. Ancient Near Eastern Studies Supplement Series 21. Leuven: Peeters, 2007.

Davidson, R. M. *Flame of Yahweh: Sexuality in the Old Testament*. Peabody: Hendrickson, 2007.

Davidson, Steed Vernyl. *Empire and Exile: Postcolonial Readings of the Book of Jeremiah*. LHBOTS 542. New York: T&T Clark, 2011.

———. *Writing/Reading the Bible in Postcolonial Perspective*. Biblical Interpretation Series. Leiden: Brill, 2017.

Davies, Margaret. *Asking the Law Question*. 4th ed. Pyrmont: Thomson Reuters Australia, 2017.

Dewulf, Jeroen. "As a Tupi-Indian, Playing the Lute: Hybridity as Anthropophangy." In *Reconstructing Hybridity: Post-Colonial Studies in Translation*, edited by Joel Kuortti and Jopi Nyman, 81–97. Amsterdam: Rodopi, 2007.

Donaldson, Laura E. "Postcolonialism and Biblical Reading: An Introduction." *Semeia* 75 (1996): 1–12.

Doorly, William J. *The Laws of Yahweh*. New York: Paulist, 2002.

Dozeman, Thomas B. *God on the Mountain: A Study of Redaction, Theology and Canon in Exodus 19–24*. Society of Biblical Literature Monograph Series 37. Atlanta: Scholars, 1989.

———. *God at War: Power in the Exodus Tradition*. New York: Oxford University Press, 1996.

———. *Commentary on Exodus*. Eerdmans Critical Commentary. Grand Rapids: Eerdmans, 2009.

Drivers, G. R., and John C. Miles. *The Babylonian Laws*. 2 vols. Oxford: Clarendon Press, 1952.

Dube, Musa W. *Postcolonial Feminist Interpretation of the Bible*. St Louis: Chalice, 2000.

Durham, John I. *Exodus*. Word Biblical Commentary 3. Dallas: Word, 2002.

Eakins, J. Kenneth. "Moses." *Review and Expositor* 74, no. 4 (1977): 461–72.

Edenburg, Cynthia. "The Book of the Covenant." In *The Oxford Handbook of Biblical Law*, edited by Pamela Barmash, 157–75. Oxford: Oxford University Press, 2019.

Eichler, Barry L. "Exodus 21:22–25 Revisited: Methodological Considerations." In *Birkat Shalom: Studies in the Bible, Ancient Near Eastern Literature, and Postbiblical Judaism Presented to Shalom M. Paul on the Occasion of His Seventieth Birthday*, vol. 1, edited by Chaim Cohen, Victor Avigdor Hurowitz, Avi Hurvitz, Yochanan Muffs, Baruch J. Schwartz, and Jeffery H. Tigay, 11–29. Winona Lake: Eisenbrauns, 2008.

Eilers, Wilhelm. *Die Gesetzstele Chammurabis: Gesetze um die Wenden des dritten vorchristlichen Jahrtausends*. Der alte Orient 31 hft 3/4. Leipzig: J. C. Hinrichs, 1932.

Eissfeldt, Otto. *Die Komposition der Sinai-Erzählung Exodus 19–34*. Sitzungsberichte der sächsischen Akademie der Wissenschaften zu Leipzig 113/1. Berlin: Akademie Verlag, 1996

Elayi, Josette. *Sennacherib, King of Assyria*. Atlanta: SBL Press, 2018.

Emmerson, Grace I. "Women in Ancient Israel." In *The World of Ancient Israel: Sociological, Anthropological, and Political Perspectives*, edited by R. E. Clements, 371–94. Cambridge: Cambridge University Press, 1989.

Fales, Frederick Mario. "The Enemy in Assyrian Royal Inscriptions: 'The Moral Judgement.'" In *Mesopotamien und seine Nachbarn: politische und kulturelle Wechselbeziehungen im Alten Vorderasien vom 4. bis 1. Jahrtausend v. Chr*, edited by Hans Jörg Nissen und Johannes Renger, 424–35. Berliner Beiträge zum Vorderer Orient Texte 1. Berlin: Dietrich Reimer Verlag, 1987.

Fanon, Frantz. *Black Skin, White Mask*. Translated by Charles Lam Markmann, 1967. Reprint ed. London: Pluto Press, 2008.

———. *The Wretched of the Earth*. Translated by Constance Farrington. New York: Grove, 1963.

Feder, Yitzhaq. "The Aniconic Tradition, Deuteronomy 4, and the Politics of Israelite Identity." *JBL* 132, no. 2 (2013): 251–74.

Fensham, F. Charles. "Widow, Orphan, and the Poor in Ancient Near Eastern Legal and Wisdom Literature." *Journal of Near Eastern Studies* 21, no. 2 (1962): 129–39.

Fernandez, Eleazar S. "Exodus-toward-Egypt: Filipino-Americans' Struggle to Realize the Promised Land in America." In *Voices of the Crossing: The Impact of Britain on Writers from Asia, the Caribbean and Africa*, edited by F. Dennis and N. Khan, 176–86. London: Serpent's Tail, 2000.

Finkelstein, J. J. *The Ox that Gored*. Transactions of the American Philological Association 71. Philadelphia: The American Philosophical Society, 1981.

Finn, Jennifer. "Marduk, the Scribes, and the Problem of the Neo-Assyrian King." *Ancient Near East Today* 6 (2018). https://www.asor.org/anetoday/2018/05/Marduk-Scribes-Neo-Assyrian.

Fitzpatrick-McKinley, Anne. *The Transformation of Torah from Scribal Advice to Law*. JSOTSup 287. Sheffield: Sheffield Academic, 1999.

Fleishman, Joseph. "Does the Law of Exodus 21:7–11 Permit a Father to Sell His Daughter to be a Slave?" *Jewish Law Annual* 8 (2000): 47–64.

———. "Exodus 22:15–16 and Deuteronomy 22:28–29—Seduction and Rape? Or Elopement and Abduction Marriage?" *Jewish Law Association Studies* 14 (2002): 59–73.

———. *Father-Daughter Relation in Biblical Law*. Bethesda: CDL Press, 2011.

———. "Offences Against Parents Punishable by Death: Towards a Socio-Legal Interpretation of Ex. 21:15, 17." *Jewish Law Annual* 10 (1992): 7–37.

Frahm, Eckart. "Family Matters: Psychohistorical Reflections on Sennacherib and His Times." In *Sennacherib at the Gates of Jerusalem: Story, History, and Historiography*, edited by Isaac Kalimi and Seth Richardson, 163–222. Leiden: Brill, 2014.

———. "The Neo-Assyrian Period (ca. 1000–609 BCE)." In *A Companion to Assyria*, edited by Eckart Frahm, 161–208. Blackwell Companions to the Ancient World. Hoboken: John Wiley & Sons, 2017.

Frame, Grant. *The Royal Inscriptions of Sargon II, King of Assyria (721–705 BC)*. RINAP 2. University Park: Eisenbrauns, 2021.

Fuchs, Andres. "Assyria at War: Strategy and Conduct." In *The Oxford Handbook of Cuneiform Culture*, edited by Karen Radner and Eleanor Robson, 380–401. Oxford: Oxford University Press, 2011.

Gallagher, William R. *Sennacherib's Campaign to Judah*. Studies in the History and Culture of the Ancient Near East 18. Leiden: Brill, 1999.

Gane, Roy E. *Old Testament Law for Christians: Original Context and Enduring Application*. Grand Rapids: Baker, 2017.

———. "Social Justice." In *The Oxford Handbook of Biblical Law*, edited by Pamela Barmash, 19–34. Oxford: Oxford University Press, 2019.

Garrett, Duane A. *A Commentary on Exodus*. Kregel Exegetical Library. Grand Rapids: Kregel, 2014.

Gelb, Ignace J., et al., ed. *The Assyrian Dictionary of the Oriental Institute of the University of Chicago*. 21 vols. Chicago: Oriental Institute of the University of Chicago, 1956–2010.

Gensenius, Wilhelm, E. Kautzsch, and A. E. Cowley. *Gesenius' Hebrew Grammar*. 2nd ed. Oxford: Clarendon, 1910.

Gerstenberger, Erhard S. "פלל *pll*." In *Theological Dictionary of the Old Testament*, vol. 11, edited by G. Johannes Botterweck, Helmer Ringgren, and Heinz-Josef Fabry, 439–49. Grand Rapids: Eerdmans, 2001.

Glanville, Mark. *Adopting the Stranger as Kindred in Deuteronomy*. Atlanta: SBL Press, 2018.

Godiwala, Dimple. "Postcolonial Desire: Mimicry, Hegemony, Hybridity." In *Reconstructing Hybridity: Post-Colonial Studies in Translation*, edited by Joel Kuortti and Jopi Nyman, 59–79. Amsterdam: Rodopi, 2007.

Goldingay, John. "Isaiah 56–66: An Isaianic and a Postcolonial Reading." In *Isaiah and Imperial Context: The Book of Isaiah in Times of Empire*, edited by Mark G. Brett, Andrew Abernethy, Tim Bulkeley, and Tim Meadowcroft, 151–66. Eugene: Pickwick, 2013.

———. *The First Testament: A New Translation*. Downers Grove: InterVarsity Press, 2018.

Goody, Jack. *The Logic of Writing and the Organization of Society*. Cambridge: Cambridge University Press, 1986.

Gottwald, Norman K. "Early Israel as an Anti-Imperial Community." In *In the Shadow of Empire: Reclaiming the Bible as a History of Faithful Resistance*, edited by Richard A. Horsley, 9–24. Louisville: Westminster John Knox, 2008.

Grabbe, L. L. Review of *Inventing God's Law: How the Covenant Code of the Biblical Used and Revised the Laws of Hammurabi*, by David P. Wright. *Journal for the Study of the Old Testament* 34, no. 5 (2010): 163.

Graupner, Axel. "„Ihr sollt mir ein Königreich von Priestern und ein heiliges Volk sein." Erwägungen zur Funktion von Ex 19, 3b–8 innerhalb der Sinaiperikope." In *Moses in Biblical and Extra-Biblical Traditions*, edited by Axel Graupner and Michael Wolter, 33–49. Berlin: De Gruyter, 2007.

Grayson, A. Kirk. *Assyrian Rulers of the Early First Millennium BC I (1114–859 BC)*. RIMA 2. Toronto: University of Toronto Press, 1991.

Grayson, A. Kirk, and Jamie Novotny. *The Royal Inscriptions of Sennacherib, King of Assyria (704–681 BC), Part 1*. RINAP 3/1. Winona Lake: Eisenbrauns, 2012.

———. *The Royal Inscriptions of Sennacherib, King of Assyria (704–681 BC), Part 2*. RINAP 3/2. Winona Lake: Eisenbrauns, 2014.

Greenberg, Moshe. "Some Postulates of Biblical Criminal Law." In *Y. Kaufmann Jubilee Volume*, edited by M. Haran, 5–28. Jerusalem: Detus Goldberg, 1960.

———. "נסה in Exodus 20:20 and the Purpose of the Sinaitic Theophany." *JBL* 79, no. 3 (1960): 273–76.

Greengus, Samuel. *Laws in the Bible and in Early Rabbinic Collections: The Legal Legacy of the Ancient Near East*. Eugene: Cascade, 2011.

———. "Legal and Social Institutions of Ancient Mesopotamia." In *Civilizations of the Ancient Near East*, vol. 1, edited by Jack Sasson, 469–84. New York: Scribner's Sons, 1995.

———. "Some Issues Relating to the Comparability of Laws and the Coherence of the Legal Tradition." In *Theory and Method in Biblical and Cuneiform Law: Revision, Interpolation and Development*, edited by Bernard M. Levinson, 60–87. JSOTSup 181. Sheffield: Sheffield Academic, 1994.

Greenstein, Edward L. "'If the Sun Shone on Him' (Exodus 22:2): A Different Approach." In *Ben Porat Yosef: Studies in the Bible and Its World: Essays in Honor of Joseph Fleishman*, edited by Michael Avioz, Omer Minka, and Yael Shemesh, 37–41. AOAT 458. Münster: Ugarit-Verlag, 2019.

Griffiths, Gareth. "Conversion, Identity, and Resistance in Colonial and Postcolonial Spaces: The Writings of Tiyo Soga 1829–1871." In *The Future of Postcolonial Studies*, edited by Chantal Zabus, 69–84. New York: Routledge, 2015.

Haak, Robert D. "Altar." In *Anchor Bible Dictionary*, vol. 1, edited by David Noel Freedman, 162–67. New York: Doubleday, 1991.

Hagedorn, Anselm C. "Local Law in an Imperial Context: The Role of Torah in the (Imagined) Persian Period." In *The Pentateuch as Torah: New Models for Understanding Its Promulgation and Acceptance*, edited by Gary N. Knoppers and Bernard M. Levinson, 57–76. Winona Lake: Eisenbrauns, 2007.

Hallo, William W., ed. *The Context of Scripture: Volume II Monumental Inscriptions from the Biblical World*. Leiden: Brill, 2003.

Halpern, Baruch. "The Housebreaking Law of Exodus 21:37–22:3: A Synchronic View." *Maarav* 20, no. 2 (2013): 247–50.

Hamilton, Victor P. *Exodus: An Exegetical Commentary*. Grand Rapids: Baker Academic, 2011.

Hayes, John H. *Interpreting Ancient Israelite History, Prophecy, and Law*. Edited by Brad E. Kelle. Eugene: Cascade, 2013.

Hays, Christopher B. *A Covenant with Death: Death in the Iron Age II and Its Rhetorical Uses in Proto-Isaiah*. Grand Rapids: 2011.

———. "Isaiah as Colonized Poet: His Rhetoric of Death in Conversation with African Postcolonial Writers." In *Isaiah and Imperial Context: The Book of Isaiah in Times of Empire*, edited by Mark G. Brett, Andrew Abernethy, Tim Bulkeley, and Tim Meadowcroft, 51–70. Eugene: Pickwick, 2013.

Hiebert, T. "Theophany in the OT." In *Anchor Bible Dictionary*, vol. 6, edited by David Noel Freedman, 505–11. New York: Doubleday, 1991.

Hirsch, Susan F. "Kadhi's Courts as Complex Sites of Resistance: The State, Islam, and Gender in Postcolonial Kenya." In *Contested States: Law, Hegemony and Resistance*, edited by Mindie Lazarus-Black and Susan F. Hirsch, 207–30. After the Law. New York: Routledge, 1994.

Hirsch, Susan F., and Mindie Lazarus-Black. "Performance and Paradox: Exploring Law's Role in Hegemony and Resistance." In *Contested States: Law, Hegemony and Resistance*, edited by Mindie Lazarus-Black and Susan F. Hirsch, 1–31. After the Law. New York: Routledge, 1994.

Hoffner, Harry Angier. *The Laws of the Hittites: A Critical Edition*. Leiden: Brill, 1997.

Holloway, Steven W. *Aššur is King! Aššur is King! Religion in the Exercise of Power in the Neo-Assyrian Empire*. Culture and History of the Ancient Near East 10. Leiden: Brill, 2001.

Holz, Shalom E. Review of *Inventing God's Law: How the Covenant Code of the Biblical Used and Revised the Laws of Hammurabi*, by David P. Wright. *Catholic Biblical Quarterly* 72, no. 4 (2010): 820–22.

Horowitz, Wayne. "Astral Tablets in the Hermitage, Saint Petersburg." *Zeitschrift für Assyriologie* 90 (2000): 194–206.

Horowitz, Wayne, Takayoshi Oshima, and Filip Vukosavović. "Hazor 18: Fragments of a Cuneiform Law Collection from Hazor." *Israel Exploration Journal* 62, no. 2 (2012): 158–76.

Horowitz, Wayne, Takayoshi Oshima, and Seth L. Sanders. *Cuneiform in Canaan: The Next Generation*. 2nd ed. University Park: Eisenbrauns, 2018.

Hostetter, E. C. *Nations Mightier and More Numerous: The Biblical View of Palestine's Pre-Israelite People*. Berkeley Institute of Biblical Archaeology and Literature Dissertation Series 3. North Richland Hills: BIBAL Press, 1995.

Houston, Walter. *Contending for Justice: Ideologies and Theologies of Social Justice in the Old Testament*. LHBOTS 428. London: T&T Clark, 2006.

Houten, Christiana van. *The Alien in Israelite Law*. JSOTSup 107. Sheffield: JSOT Press, 1991.

Houtman, Cornelis. *Exodus*. Historical Commentary on the Old Testament. 3 vols. Leuven: Peeters, 2000.

———. "Moses." In *Dictionary of Deities and Demons in the Bible*, edited by Karel van der Toorn, Bob Becking, and Pieter W. van der Horst, 593–98. 2nd rev. ed. Grand Rapids: Eerdmans, 1999.

Hundley, Michael B. "Of God and Angels Divine Messengers in Genesis and Exodus in their Ancient Near Eastern Contexts." *Journal of Theological Studies* 67, no. 1 (2016): 1–22.

Hurowitz, Victor Avidgdor. *Inu Anum Ṣīrum: Literary Structures in the Non-Juridical Sections of Codex Hammurabi*. Occasional Publications of the Samuel Noah Kramer Fund 15. Philadelphia: University of Pennsylvania Museum of Archaeology and Anthropology, 1994.

Ishida, T. *History and Historical Writing in Ancient Israel*. Leiden: Brill, 1999.

———. "The Structure and Historical Implications of the Lists of Pre-Israelite Nations." *Biblica* 60, no. 4 (1979): 461–90.

Jackson, Bernard S. "Ideas of the Law and Legal Administration: A Semiotic Approach." In *The World of Ancient Israel: Sociological, Anthropological, and*

Political Perspectives: Essays by Members of the Society for Old Testament Study, edited by R. E. Clement, 185–202. Cambridge: Cambridge University Press, 1989.

———. "The Problem of Exod. XXI 22–5 (*Ius Talionis*)." *VT* 23, no. 3 (1973): 273–304.

———. Review of *The Transformation of Torah from Scribal Advice to Law*, by Anne Fitzpatrick-McKinley. *Journal of Semitic Studies* 47, no. 2 (2002): 327–32.

———. *Wisdom-Laws: A Study of the Mishpatim of Exodus 21:1–22:16*. Oxford: Oxford University Press, 2006.

Jacobs, Sandra. "The Talionic Principle and Its Calibrations." In *The Cambridge Companion to the Hebrew Bible and Ethics*, edited by C. L. Crouch, 23–35. Cambridge: Cambridge University Press, 2021.

Jeremias, Jorg. *Theophanie: Die Geschichte einer alttestamentlichen Gattung*. Wissenschaftliche Monographien zum Alten und Neuen Testament 10. Neukirchen-Vluyn: Neukirchener Verlag des Erziehungsvereins, 1965.

Joüon, P., and T. Muraoka. *A Grammar of Biblical Hebrew*. 2nd ed. Rome: Gregorian & Biblical Press, 2013.

Kapur, Ratna. *Erotic Justice: Law and the New Politics of Postcolonialism*. New York: Routledge, 2016.

Kellerman, D. "גּוּר *gûr*; גֵּר *gēr*; גֵּרוּת *gērûth*; מְגוּרִים *meghûrîm*." In *Theological Dictionary of the Old Testament*, vol. 2, edited by G. Johannes Botterweck and Helmer Ringgren, 439–49. Grand Rapids: Eerdmans, 1975.

Kim, Uriah Y. *Decolonizing Josiah: Toward a Postcolonial Reading of the Deuteronomistic History*. The Bible in the Modern World 5. Sheffield: Sheffield Phoenix Press, 2005.

Kitchen, Kenneth A., and Paul J. N. Lawrence. *Treaty, Law and Covenant in the Ancient Near East, Part I: The Text*. Wiesbaden: Harrassowitz Verlag, 2012.

Knight, Douglas A. *Law, Power, and Justice in Ancient Israel*. Library of Ancient Israel. Louisville: Westminster John Knox, 2011.

Kraus, F. R. "Ein zentrales Problem des altmesopotamiscchen Rechtes: Was ist der Codex Hammu-rabi?" *Geneva NS* 8 (1960): 283–96.

Kwasman, Theodore. *Neo-Assyrian Legal Documents in the Kouyunjik Collection of the British Museum*. Studia Pohl: Series Maior 14. Rome: Editrice Pontificio Instituto Biblico, 1988.

Kwok, Pui-Lan. *Discovering the Bible in the Non-Biblical World*. The Bible and Liberation. Maryknoll: Orbis, 1995.

Lacan, Jacques. *The Four Fundamental Concepts of Psychoanalysis*. Translated by Alan Sheridan, 1977. Repr. London: Karnac, 2004.

Lafont, Sophie. "Ancient Near Eastern Laws: Continuity and Pluralism." In *Theory and Method in Biblical and Cuneiform Law: Revision, Interpolation and Development*, edited by Bernard M. Levinson, 91–118. JSOTSup 181. Sheffield: Sheffield Academic, 1994.

———. "Codification et Subsidiarité dans les Droits du Proche-Orient Ancien." In *La Codification des lois dans l'antiquité: Actes du Colloque de Strasbourg, 27–29 Novembre 1997*, edited by E. Lévy, 49–64. Travaux du Centre de Recherche sur le Proche-Orient et la Grèce antiques 16. Paris: De Boccard, 2000.

Lai, Chien-Kuo Paul. *Exodus (I)*. Tien Dao Bible Commentary. Hong Kong: Tien Dao, 2005. [Chinese]

Lambert, W. G. *Babylonian Wisdom Literature*. Winona Lake: Eisenbrauns, 1996.

Lauinger, Jacob. "Esarhaddon's Succession Treaty at Tell Tayinat: Text and Commentary." *Journal of Cuneiform Studies* 64 (2012): 87–123.

———. "The Neo-Assyrian *adê*: Treaty, Oath, or Something Else?" *Zeitschrift für altorientalische und biblische Rechtgeschichte* 19 (2013): 99–115.

———. "Neo-Assyrian Scribes, 'Esarhaddon's Succession Treaty,' and the Dynamics of Textual Mass Production." In *Texts and Contexts: The Circulation and Transmission of Cuneiform Texts in Social Space*, edited by P. Delnero and J. Lauinger, 285–314. Studies in Ancient Near Eastern Records 9. Berlin: de Gruyter, 2015.

Lazarus-Black, Mindie. "Slaves, Masters, and Magistrates: Law and the Politics of Resistance in the British Caribbean, 1736–1834." In *Contested States: Law, Hegemony and Resistance*, edited by Mindie Lazarus-Black and Susan F. Hirsch, 252–81. After the Law. New York: Routledge, 1994.

Lee, Bernon P. "Diachrony and Exegesis: Reading Exodus 21:18–27." In *From Babel to Babylon: Essays on Biblical History and Literature in Honour of Brian Peckham*, edited by Joyce Rilett Wood, John E. Harvey, and Mark Leuchter, 48–55. LHBOTS 445. New York: T&T Clark, 2006.

LeFebvre, Michael. *Collections, Codes, and Torah: The Re-Characterization of Israel's Written Law*. LHBOTS. New York: T&T Clark, 2006.

Leichty, Erle. *The Royal Inscriptions of Esarhaddon, King of Assyria (680–669 BC)*. RINAP 4. Winona Lake: Eisenbrauns, 2011.

Lenzi, Alan. *Secrecy and the Gods: Secret Knowledge in Ancient Mesopotamia and Biblical Israel*. State Archives of Assyria Studies 19. Helsinki: Neo-Assyrian Text Corpus Project, 2008.

Levinson, Bernard M. "The Case for Revision and Interpolation Within the Biblical Legal Corpora." In *Theory and Method in Biblical and Cuneiform Law: Revision, Interpolation and Development*, edited by Bernard M. Levinson, 37–59. JSOTSup 181. Sheffield: Sheffield Academic, 1994.

———. *Deuteronomy and the Hermeneutics of Legal Innovation*. New York: Oxford University Press, 1997.

———. "Is the Covenant Code an Exilic Composition? A Response to John Van Seters." In *Search of Pre-Exilic Israel*, edited by John Day, 272–325. JSOTSup 406. New York: T&T Clark, 2004.

———. "The Sinai Covenant." In *"The Right Chorale": Studies in Biblical Law and Interpretation*, 48–51. FAT 54. Tubingen: Mohr Siebeck, 2008.

Liverani, Mario. *Assyria: The Imperial Mission*. Mesopotamian Civilizations. Winona Lake: Eisenbrauns, 2017.

Livingstone, Alasdair, ed. *Court Poetry and Literary Miscellanea*. SAA 3. Helsinki: Helsinki University Press, 1989.

Loewenstamm, S. E. "The Trembling of Nature During the Theophany." In *Comparative Studies in Biblical and Ancient Oriental Literatures*, edited by S. E. Loewenstamm, 173–89. AOAT 204. Kevelear: Butzon & Bercker; Neukirchen-Vluyn: Neukirchener Verlag, 1980.

Lohfink, Norbert. "Fortschreibung? Zur Technik von Rechtsrevisionen im deuteronomischen Bereich, erörtert an Deuteronomium 12, Ex 21,2–11 und Dtn 15, 12–18." In *Das Deuteronomium und seine Querbeziehunge*, edited by Timo Veijola, 133–181. Schriften der Finnischen Exegetischen Gesellschaft 62. Göttingen: Vandenhoeck & Ruprecht, 1996.

Longman, T., III, and D. G. Reid. *God Is a Warrior*. Studies in Old Testament Biblical Theology. Grand Rapids: Zondervan, 1995.

Luukko, Mikko, and Greta Van Buylere. "Language and Writing System in Assyria." In *A Companion to Assyria*, edited by Eckart Frahm, 313–35. Blackwell Companions to the Ancient World. Hoboken: John Wiley & Sons, 2017.

Machinist, Peter. "The Man Moses." *Bible Review* 16, no. 2 (2000): 18–19, 53.

———. "The Rab Šāqēh at the Wall of Jerusalem: Israelite Identity in the Face of the Assyrian 'Other.'" *Hebrew Studies* 41 (2000): 151–68.

Malul, Meir. *The Comparative Method in Ancient Near Eastern and Biblical Legal Studies*. AOAT 227. Kevelaer and Neukirchen-Vluyn: Butzon & Bercker and Neukirchener Verlag, 1990.

———. Review of *Inventing God's Law: How the Covenant Code of the Biblical Used and Revised the Laws of Hammurabi*, by David P. Wright. *Bulletin of the Anglo-Israel Archaeological Society* 29 (2011): 155–59.

Mann, T. W. *Divine Presence and Guidance in Israelite Traditions: The Typology of Exaltation*. Baltimore: Johns Hopkins University Press, 1977.

Marshall, Jay W. *Israel and the Book of the Covenant: An Anthropological Approach to Biblical Law*. Society of Biblical Literature Dissertation Series 140. Atlanta: Scholars Press, 1993.

Mathew, Shiju. *Biblical Law Codes in Creative Tension: A Postcolonial Womanist Reading*. Biblical Hermeneutics Rediscovered 1. New Delhi: Christian World Imprints, 2016.

———. "Law, Land, and Gender in the Hebrew Bible: A Postcolonial Womanist Reading." *Asia Journal of Theology* 30, no. 2 (2016): 177–92.

Mathews, Danny. *Royal Motifs in the Pentateuchal Portrayal of Moses*. LHBOTS 571. New York: T&T Clark, 2012.

Matthews, Victor H. "The Anthropology of Slavery in the Covenant Code." In *Theory and Method in Biblical and Cuneiform Law: Revision, Interpolation and Development*, edited by Bernard M. Levinson, 119–35. JSOTSup 181. Sheffield: Sheffield Academic Press, 1994.

Maul, Stefan M. "Assyrian Religion." In *A Companion to Assyria*, edited by Eckart Frahm, 336–58. Blackwell Companions to the Ancient World. Hoboken: John Wiley & Sons, 2017.

McConville, J. G. "Singular Address in the Deuteronomic Law and the Politics of Legal Administration." *JSOT* 26, no. 3 (2002): 19–36.

Meek, Theophile James. *Hebrew Origins*. New York: Harper & Brothers, 1960.

Mendelsohn, Isaac. *Slavery in the Ancient Near East: A Comparative Study of Slavery in Babylonia, Assyria, Syria, and Palestine from Middle of the Third Millennium to the End of the First Millennium*. Westport: Greenwood Press, 1978.

Merry, Sally Engle. "Colonial and Postcolonial Law." In *The Blackwell Companion to Law and Society*, edited by Austin Sarat, 569–88. Malden: Blackwell, 2004.

Messick, Brinkley. *The Calligraphic State: Textual Domination and History in a Muslim Society*. Berkeley: University of California Press, 1993.

Miller, D. R. "The Shadow of the Overlord: Revisiting the Question of Neo-Assyrian Imposition on the Judaean Cult during the Eighth-Seventh Centuries BCE." In *From Babel to Babylon: Essays on Biblical History and Literature in Honor of Brian Peckham*, edited by J. R. Wood, J. E. Harvey, and M. Leuchter, 146–68. LHBOTS 455. London: T&T Clark, 2006.

Miller, J. Maxwell, and John H. Hayes. *A History of Ancient Israel and Judah*. 2nd ed. Louisville: Westminster John Knox Press, 2006.

Moore-Gilbert, Bart. *Postcolonial Theory: Contexts, Practices, Politics*. London: Verso, 1997.

Morrow, William S. "A Generic Discrepancy in the Covenant Code." In *Theory and Method in Biblical and Cuneiform Law: Revision, Interpolation and Development*, edited by Bernard M. Levinson, 136–51. JSOTSup 181. Sheffield: Sheffield Academic Press, 1994.

———. "Legal Interactions: The *Mišpāṭîm* and the Laws of Hammurabi." *Bibliotheca Orientalis* 70 (2013): 310–31.

———. "Resistance and Hybridity in Late Bronze Age Canaan." *Revue biblique* 115, no. 3 (2008): 321–39.

———. "'To Set the Name' in the Deuteronomic Centralization Formula: A Case of Cultural Hybridity." *Journal of Semitic Studies* 55, no. 2 (2010): 365–83.

———. "Tribute from Judah and the Transmission of Assyrian Propaganda." In *"My Spirit in Rest in the North Country (Zechariah 6.8):" Collected Communications to the XXth Congress of the International Organization for the Study of the Old Testament, Helsinki 2010*, edited by Hermann Michael Niemann and Matthias Augustin, 183–93. Frankfurt am Main: Peter Lang, 2011.

Morton, Stephen. *States of Emergency: Colonialism, Literature and Law*. Postcolonialism Across the Disciplines 11. Liverpool: Liverpool University Press, 2013.

Muraoka, T. *Emphatic Words and Structures in Biblical Hebrew*. Jerusalem: Magnes Press, 1985.

Naiden, F. S. "Gods, Kings, and Lawgivers." In *Law and Religion in the Eastern Mediterranean*, edited by Anselm C. Hagedorn and Reinhard G. Krakz, 78–104. Oxford: Oxford University Press, 2013.

Newson, Carol A. "Angels: Old Testament." In *Anchor Bible Dictionary*, vol. 1, edited by David Noel Freedman, 249–53. New York: Doubleday, 1991.

Ngũgĩ wa Thiong'o. *Decolonising the Mind: The Politics of Language in African Literature*. Oxford: James Currey, 1986.

———. *Wizard of the Crow*. New York: Anchor Books, 2006.

Nicholson, E. W. "The Covenant Ritual in Exodus XXIV 3–8." *VT* 32, no. 1 (1982): 74–86.

Niehaus, Jeffrey J. *God at Sinai: Covenant and Theophany in the Bible and Ancient Near East*. Studies in Old Testament Biblical Theology. Grand Rapids: Zondervan, 1995.

Noth, Martin. *Exodus: A Commentary*. Old Testament Library. Philadelphia: Westminster, 1962.

Novotny, Jamie, and Joshua Jeffers. *The Royal Inscriptions of Ashurbanipal (668–631 BC), Aššur-etel-ilāni (630–627 BC), and Sîn-šarra-iškun (626–612 BC), Kings of Assyria, Part 1*. RINAP 5/1. University Park: Eisenbrauns, 2018.

Nowicki, Stefan. *Enemies of Assyria: The Image and Role of Enemy in Assyrian Royal Inscriptions and Selected Textual Sources from the Neo-Assyrian Period*. AOAT 452. Münster: Ugarit-Verlag, 2018.

O'Connell, K. G. O. "The List of Seven People in Canaan." In *The Answers Lie Below: Essays in Honor of Lawrence Edmund Toombs*, edited by H. O. Thompson, 221–41. Lanham: University Press of America, 1984.

Osumi, Yuichi. *Die Kompositionsgeschichte des Bundesbuch Exod 20,22b–23,33*. Orbis Biblicus et Orientalis 105. Göttingen: Vandenhoeck & Ruprecht, 1991.

Oswald, Wolfgang. "Die Exodus-Gottesberg-Erzählung als Gründungsurkunde der judäischen Bürgergemeinde." In *Law and Narrative in the Bible and in Neighbouring Ancient Cultures*, edited by Klaus-Peter Adam, Friedrich Avemarie, and Nili Wazana, 35–51. FAT 2/54. Mohr Siebeck: Tübingen, 2012.

———. "Lawgiving at the Mountain of God (Exodus 19–24)." In *The Book of Exodus: Composition, Reception, and Interpretation*, edited by Thomas B. Dozeman, Craig A. Evans, and Joel N. Lohr, 169–92. VTSup 164. Leiden: Brill, 2014.

Otto, Dianne. "Subalternity and International Law: The Problems of Global Community and the Incommensurability of Difference." In *Laws of the Postcolonial: Law, Meaning, and Violence*, edited by Eve Darian-Smith and Peter Fitzpatrick, 145–80. Ann Arbor: The University of Michigan Press, 1999.

Otto, Eckart. "Aspects of Legal Reforms and Reformulations in Ancient Cuneiform and Israelite Law." In *Theory and Method in Biblical and Cuneiform Law: Revision, Interpolation and Development*, edited by Bernard M. Levinson, 160–96. JSOTSup 181. Sheffield: Sheffield Academic Press, 1994.

———. "Assyria and Judean Identity: Beyond the Religionsgeschichtliche Schule." In *Literature as Politics, Politics as Literature: Essays on the Ancient Near East in Honor of Peter Machinist*, edited by David Stephen Vanderhooft and Abraham Winitzer, 339–47. Winona Lake: Eisenbrauns, 2013.

———. "Book of the Covenant." In *The Oxford Encyclopedia of the Bible and Law*, vol. 1, edited by Brent A. Strawn, 68–77. Oxford: Oxford University Press, 2015.

———. "Das Bundesbuch und der „Kodex" Hammurapi: Das biblische Recht zwischen positive und subversive Rezeption von Keilschriftrecht." *Zeitschrift für altorientalische und biblische Rechtgeschichte* 16 (2010): 1–26.

———. *Das Gesetz des Moses*. Darmstadt: Wissenschaftliche Buchgesellschaft, 2007.

———. "Human Rights: The Influence of the Hebrew Bible." *Journal of Northwest Semitic Languages* 25, no. 1 (1999): 1–20.

———. "Kodifizierung und Kanonisierung von Rechtssätzen in keilschriftlichen und biblischen Rechtssammlungen." In *La Codification des lois dans l'antiquité: Actes du Colloque de Strasbourg, 27–29 Novembre 1997*, edited by E. Lévy, 77–124. Travaux du Centre de Recherche sur le Proche-Orient et la Grèce antiques 16. Paris: De Boccard, 2000.

———. *Körperverletzungen in den Keilschriftrechten und im Alten Testament: Studien zum Rechtstransfer im Alten Testament*. AOAT 226. Kevelaer: Butzon & Bercker, 1991.

———. "Laws of Hammurapi." In *The Oxford Encyclopedia of The Bible and Law*, vol. 1, edited by Brent A. Strawn, 500–508. Oxford: Oxford University Press, 2015.

———. "Town and Rural Countryside in Ancient Israelite Law: Reception and Redaction in Cuneiform and Israelite Law." *JSOT* 18, no. 57 (1993): 3–22.

———. *Wandel der Rechtsbegründungen in der Gesellschaftsgeschichte des antiken Israel: Eine Rechtsgeschichte des 'Bundesbuchs' Ex XX 22-XXIII 13*. Studia Biblica 3. Leiden: Brill, 1988.

Parpola, Simo. "Assyria's Expansion in the 8th and 7th Centuries and Its Long-Term Repercussions in the West." In *Symbiosis, Symbolism, and the Power of the Past: Canaan, Ancient Israel, and Their Neighbors – From the Late Bronze Age through Roman Palestina*, edited by W. G. Dever and S. Gitin, 99–111. Winona Lake: Eisenbrauns, 2003.

Parpola, Simo, and Kazuko Watanabe, eds. *Neo-Assyrian Treaties and Loyalty Oaths*. SAA 2. Helsinki: Helsinki University Press, 1988.

Patrick, Dale. "The Covenant Code Source." *VT* 27, no. 2 (1977):145–57.

———. *Old Testament Law*. Atlanta: John Knox Press, 1985.

———. "Studying Biblical Law as a Humanities." *Semeia* 45 (1989): 27–47.

———. "Who is the Revolutionist?" In *Theory and Method in Biblical and Cuneiform Law: Revision, Interpolation and Development*, edited by Bernard M. Levinson, 152–59. JSOTSup 181. Sheffield: Sheffield Academic, 1994.

Patterson, Richard Duane. "The Widow, the Orphan, and the Poor in the Old Testament and Extra-Biblical Literature." *Bibliotheca Sacra* 130, no. 519 (1973): 223–34.

Paul, Shalom M. *Studies in the Book of the Covenant in the Light of Cuneiform and Biblical Law*. Eugene: Wipf & Stock, 2006. First published 1970 by Brill (Leiden).

Peeler, Amy L. B. "Desiring God: The Blood of the Covenant in Exodus 24." *Bulletin for Biblical Research* 23, no. 2 (2013): 187–205.

Peiser, Felix E. *Texte juristischen und geschäftlichen Inhalts*. Keilinschriftliche Bibliothek 4. Berlin: Verlag von Reuther & Reichard, 1896.

Peled, Ilan. *Law and Gender in the Ancient Near East and the Hebrew Bible*. London: Routledge, 2020.

Perdue, Leo G., and Warren Carter. *Israel and Empire: A Postcolonial History of Israel and Early Judaism*. New York: Bloomsbury, 2015.

Perrin, Colin. "Approaching Anxiety: The Insistence of the Postcolonial in the Declaration on the Rights of Indigenous Peoples." In *Laws of the Postcolonial: Law, Meaning, and Violence*, edited by Eve Darian-Smith and Peter Fitzpatrick, 19–28. Ann Arbor: University of Michigan Press, 1999.

Petschow, H. P. H. "Die 45 und 46 des Codex Hammurabi – Bin Beitrag zum altbabylonischen Bodenpachtrecht und zum Problem: Was ist der Codex Hammurapi." *Zeitschrift für Assyriologie* 74, no. 2 (1984): 181–212.

Phillips, Anthony. "A Fresh Look at the Sinai Pericope: Part I." *VT* 34, no. 1 (1984): 39–52.

———. "The Laws of Slavery: Exodus 21.2–11." *JSOT* 9, no. 30 (1984): 51–62.

———. "Some Aspects of Family Law in Pre-Exilic Israel." *VT* 23, no. 3 (1973): 349–61.

Pixley, George. *On Exodus: A Liberative Perspective*. Maryknoll: Orbis, 1987.

Polak, Frank H. "Theophany and Mediator: The Unfolding of a Theme in the Book of Exodus." In *Studies in the Book of Exodus: Redaction – Reception – Interpretation*, edited by Marc Vervenne, 119–47. Leuven: Leuven University Press, 1996.

———. Review of *Inventing God's Law: How the Covenant Code of the Biblical Used and Revised the Laws of Hammurabi*, by David P. Wright. *Review of Biblical Literature* 12 (2010): 67–72.

Prabhu, Anjali. *Hybridity: Limits, Transformation, Prospects*. New York: State University of New York Press, 2007.

Pressler, Carolyn. "The Construction of Gender Roles in the Book of the Covenant and in Deuteronomy." In *The Cambridge Companion to the Hebrew Bible and Ethics*, edited by C. L. Crouch, 51–67. Cambridge: Cambridge University Press, 2021.

———. "Wives and Daughter, Bond and Free: Views of Women in the Slave Laws of Exod 21:2–11." In *Gender and Law in the Hebrew Bible and the Ancient Near East*, edited by Victor H. Matthews, Bernard M. Levinson, and Tikva Frymer-Kensky, 147–72. JSOTSup 262. Sheffield: Sheffield Academic, 1998.

Propp, William H. C. *Exodus 19–40: A New Translation with Introduction and Commentary*. Anchor Bible 2A. New York: Doubleday, 2006.

Purdy, Jeannine. "Postcolonialism: The Emperor's New Clothes?" In *Laws of the Postcolonial: Law, Meaning, and Violence*, edited by Eve Darian-Smith and Peter Fitzpatrick, 203–29. Ann Arbor: University of Michigan Press, 1999.

Radner, Karen. "Neo-Assyrian Period." In *A History of Ancient Near Eastern Law*, vol. 2, edited by Raymond Westbrook, 883–910. Handbuch der Orientalistik 72. Leiden: Brill, 2003.

Rainey, Anson F. "The Satrapy 'Beyond the River.'" *Australian Journal of Biblical Archaeology* 1, no. 2 (1969): 51–78.

———. *The El-Amarna Correspondence: A New Edition of the Cuneiform Letters from the Site of El-Amarna Based on the Collations of All Extant Tablets*. Handbuch der Orientalistik 110. 2 vols. Leiden: Brill, 2015.

Rajagopal, Balakrishnan. "Locating the Third World in Cultural Geography." *Third World Legal Studies* 15, no. 1 (1999): 1–20.

Ramírez Kidd, José E. *Alterity and Identity in Israel: The* גר *in the Old Testament*. BZAW 283. Berlin: de Gruyter, 1999.

Reiner, Erica. "Runaway – Seize Him." In *Assyria and Beyond: Studies Presented to Mogens Trolle Larsen*, edited by J. G. Dercksen, 475–82. Leiden: Nederlands Institut Voor Het Nabije Oosten, 2004.

Rendsburg, Gary A. *How the Bible is Written*. Peabody, MA: Hendrickson, 2019.

Rendtorff, Rolf. "The *Gēr* in the Priestly Laws of the Pentateuch." In *Ethnicity and the Bible*, edited by Mark G. Brett, 77–87. Biblical Interpretation series. New York: Brill, 1996.

Richardson, M. E. J. *Hammurabi's Laws: Text, Translation and Glossary*. New York: T&T Clark, 2004.

Rollston, Christopher. "Scripture and Inscriptions: Eighth-Century Israel and Judah and Writing." In *Archaeology and History of Eighth-Century Judah*, edited by Zev I. Farber and Jacob L. Wright, 457–73. Ancient Near East Monographs 23. Atlanta: SBL Press, 2018.

Roth, Federico Alfredo. *Hyphenating Moses: A Postcolonial Exegesis of Identity in Exodus 1:1–3:14*. Leiden: Brill, 2017.

Roth, Martha T. "Errant Oxen Or: The Goring Ox Redux." In *Literature as Politics, Politics as Literature: Essays on the Ancient Near East in Honor of Peter Machinist*, edited by David S. Vanderhooft and Abraham Winitzer, 397–404. Winona Lake: Eisenbrauns, 2013.

———. "Hammurabi's Wronged Man." *Journal of the American Oriental Society* 122, no. 1 (2002): 38–45.

———. *Law Collections from Mesopotamia and Asia Minor*. 2nd ed. Writings from the Ancient World 6. Atlanta: Scholars Press, 1997.

———. "The Law Collection of King Hammurabi: Toward an Understanding of Codification and Text." In *La Codification des lois dans l'antiquité: Actes du Colloque de Strasbourg, 27–29 Novembre 1997*, edited by E. Lévy, 9–31. Travaux du Centre de Recherche sur le Proche-Orient et la Grèce antiques 16. Paris: De Boccard, 2000.

———. "Mesopotamian Legal Traditions and the Laws of Hammurabi." *Chicago-Kent Review* 71, no. 1 (1995): 13–39.

———. "On *mār awīlim* in the Old Babylonian Law Collections." *Journal of Near Eastern Studies* 72, no. 2 (2013): 267–72.

———. "On Persons in the Old Babylonian Law Collections: The Case of *mār awīlim* in Bodily Injury Provisions." In *Extraction and Control: Studies in Honor of Matthew W. Stolper*, edited by Michael Kozuh, Wouter F. M. Henkelman, Charles E. Jones, and Christopher Woods, 219–27. Studies in Ancient Oriental Civilizations 68. Chicago: Oriental Institute of the University of Chicago Press, 2014.

Rothenbusch, Ralf. *Die kasuistische Rechtssammlung im 'Bundesbuch' (Ex 21,2–11.18–22, 16) und ihr literarischer Kontext im Licht altorientalischer Parallelen*. AOAT 259. Münster: Ugarit-Verlag, 2000.

Roy, Alpana. "Postcolonial Theory and Law: A Critical Introduction." *Adelaide Law Review* 29, no. 1 (2008): 315–57.

Said, Edward W. *Culture and Imperialism*. New York: Vantage Books, 1993.

———. "Michael Walzer's 'Exodus and Revolution': A Canaanite Reading." *Grand Street* 5, no. 2 (1986): 86–106.

———. *Orientalism*. New York: Vintage Books, 1979.

Sanders, Seth L. *The Invention of Hebrew*. Chicago: University of Illinois Press, 2009.

Sarna, Nahum M. *Exodus*. The JPS Torah Commentary. New York: JPS, 1991.

Satterthwaite, P. E., and D. W. Baker. "Nations of Canaan." In *Dictionary of the Old Testament: Pentateuch*, edited by T. Desmond Alexander and David W. Baker, 596–605. Downers Grove: IVP Academic, 2003.

Savran, George W. "Theophany as Type Scene." *Prooftexts* 23, no. 2 (2003): 119–49.

Schipper, Bernd U. "Egypt and the Kingdom of Judah under Josiah and Jehoiakim." *Tel Aviv* 37, no. 2 (2010): 200–226.

Schmid, Konrad. "The Biblical Writings in the Late Eighth Century BCE." In *Archaeology and History of Eighth-Century Judah*, edited by Zev I. Farber and Jacob L. Wright, 489–501. Ancient Near East Monographs 23. Atlanta: SBL Press, 2018.

Schniedewind, William M. *The Finger of the Scribe: How Scribes Learned to Write the Bible*. Oxford: Oxford University Press, 2019.

Scholz, Susanne. "The Complexities of 'His' Liberation talk: A Literary Feminist Reading of the Book of Exodus." In *Exodus to Deuteronomy*, edited by Athalya Brenner, 20–40. Feminist Companion to the Bible 5. Sheffield: Sheffield Academic, 2000.

Schwantes, Milton. *Das Recht der Armen*. Beiträge zur biblischen Exegese und Theologie 4. Frankfurt: Lang, 1977.

Schwartz, Baruch J. "The Priestly Account of the Theophany and Lawgiving at Sinai." In *Texts, Temples, and Traditions: A Tribute to Menahem Haran*, edited by Michael V. Fox, Victor Avigdor Hurowitz, Avi Hurvitz, Michael L. Klein, Baruch J. Schwartz, and Nili Shupak, 103–34. Winona Lake: Eisenbrauns, 1996.

Schwienhorst-Schönberger, Ludger. *Das Bundesbuch (Ex 20,22–23,33): Studien zu seiner Entstehung und Theologie*. BZAW 188. Berlin: de Gruyter, 1990.

———. "Auge um Auge, Zahn um Zahn." *Bibel und Liturgie* 63 (1990): 163–75.

Scott, James C. *Domination and the Arts of Resistance: Hidden Transcripts*. New Haven: Yale University Press, 1990.

Scurlock, JoAnn. *Magico-Medical Means of Treating Ghost-Induced Illnesses in Ancient Mesopotamia*. Ancient Magic and Divination 3. Leiden: Brill, 2006.

Segovia, Fernando F. "Introduction: Colonialism and the Bible: A Critical Stock-Taking from the Global South." In *Colonialism and the Bible: Contemporary Reflections from the Global South*, edited by Tat-siong Benny Liew and Fernando F. Segovia, ix–xxxi. New York: Lexington Books, 2018.

Seri, Andrea. "Domestic Female Slaves During the Old Babylonian Period." In *Slaves and Households in the Near East*, edited by Laura Culbertson, 49–67. Oriental Institute Seminars 7. Chicago: University of Chicago Press, 2011.

Sharrad, Paul. "Some Pacific Takes on Postcolonial Theory." In *Reconstructing Hybridity: Post-Colonial Studies in Translation*, edited by Joel Kuortti and Jopi Nyman, 99–120. Amsterdam: Rodopi, 2007.

Shohat, Ella. "Notes on 'Post-Colonial.'" *Social Text* 31/32 (1992). 99–113.

Silva, Roshan de. "An Ontological Approach to Constitutionalism in Sri Lanka: Contingency and the Failure of Exclusion." In *Laws of the Postcolonial: Law, Meaning, and Violence*, edited by Eve Darian-Smith and Peter Fitzpatrick, 181–202. Ann Arbor: University of Michigan Press, 1999.

Sinha, Manisha. *The Slave's Cause: A History of Abolition*. New Haven: Yale University Press, 2016.

Sinha, S. Prakash. "Perspective of the Newly Independent States on the Binding Quality of International Law." In *Third World Attitudes Toward International Law: An Introduction*, edited by Frederick E. Snyder and Surakiart Sathirathai, 23–31. Dordrecht: Martinus Nijhoff, 1987.

Sjöberg, Åke W., ed. *The Pennsylvania Sumerian Dictionary*. Philadelphia: Babylonian Section of the University of Museum. Available online, http://psd.museum.upenn.edu/nepsd-frame.html.

Ska, Jean Louis. "Biblical Law and the Origins of Democracy." In *The Ten Commandments: The Reciprocity of Faithfulness*, edited by William P. Brown, 146–58. Louisville: Westminster John Knox, 2004.

Skaist, Aaron. "Ancient Near Eastern Law Collections and Legal Forms and Institutions." In *The Oxford Handbook of Biblical Law*, edited by Pamela Barmash, 305–18. Oxford: Oxford University Press, 2019.

Smith, Gary V. "The Concept of God/the Gods as King in the Ancient Near East and the Bible." *Trinity Journal* 3, no. 1 (1982): 18–38

Sneed, Mark. "Israelite Concern for the Alien, Orphan, and Widow: Altruism or Ideology?" *Zeitschrift für die alttestamentliche Wissenschaft* 111, no. 4 (1999): 498–507.

Speiser, E. A. "The Stem *PLL* in Hebrew." *JBL* 82, no. 3 (1963): 301–6.

Spencer, J. R. "Sojourner." In *Anchor Bible Dictionary*, vol. 6, edited by David Noel Freedman, 103–4. New York: Doubleday, 1991

Spieckermann, Hermann. "God and His People: The Concept of Kingship and Cult in the Ancient Near East." In *One God, One Cult, One Nation: Archaeological and Biblical Perspectives*, edited by Reinhard G. Kratz and Hermann Spieckermann, 341–56. BZAW 405. Berlin: de Gruyter, 2010.

Sprinkle, J. M. *'The Book of the Covenant': A Literary Approach*. JSOTSup 174. Sheffield: JSOT Press, 1994.

Stine, C. A. "Your Name Shall No Longer be Jacob, but Refugee: Involuntary Migration and the Development of the Jacob Narrative." In *Scripture as Social Discourse: Social-Scientific Perspectives on Early Jewish and Christian Writings*, edited by Jessica M. Keady, Todd E. Klutz, and C. A. Stine, 51–69. New York: T&T Clark, 2018.

Strawson, John. "Islamic Law and English Texts." In *Laws of the Postcolonial: Law, Meaning, and Violence*, edited by Eve Darian-Smith and Peter Fitzpatrick, 109–26. Ann Arbor: University of Michigan Press, 1999.

———. "Palestine's Basic Law: Constituting New Identities through Liberating Legal Culture." *Loyola of Los Angeles International and Comparative Law Review* 20, no. 3 (1998): 411–32.

Streete, Gail Corrington. *The Strange Woman: Power and Sex in the Bible*. Louisville: Westminster John Knox, 1997.

Sugirtharajah, R. S. *Exploring Postcolonial Biblical Criticism: History, Method, Practice*. Chichester: Wiley-Blackwell, 2012.

———. *Postcolonial Criticism and Biblical Interpretation*. Oxford: Oxford University Press, 2002.

———, ed. *Voices from the Margin: Interpreting the Bible in the Third World Account*. Rev. and expanded, 3rd ed. Maryknoll: Orbis, 2006.

Tadmor, Hayim. "Hammurabi and His Age." In *"With My Many Chariots I Have Gone Up the Heights of Mountain": Historical and Literary Studies on Ancient Mesopotamia and Israel*, edited by Mordechai Cogan, 597–616. Jerusalem: Israel Exploration Society, 2011.

Tadmor, Hayim, Benno Landsberger, and Simo Parpola. "The Sin of Sargon and Sennacherib's Last Will." *State Archives of Assyria Bulletin* 3 (1989): 3–52.

Tadmor, Hayim, and Shigeo Yamada. *The Royal Inscriptions of Tiglath-pileser III (744–727 BC) and Shalmaneser V (726–722 BC), Kings of Assyria*. RINAP 1. Winona Lake: Eisenbrauns, 2011.

Teeter, David Andrew. *Scribal Laws: Exegetical Variation in the Textual Transmission of Biblical Law in the Late Second Temple Period*. FAT 92. Tübingen: Mohr Siebeck, 2014.

Tigay, Jeffrey H. "On Evaluating Claims of Borrowing." In *The Tablet and the Scroll: Near Eastern Studies in Honor of William W. Hallo*, edited by Mark E. Cohen, Daniel C. Snell, and David B. Weisberg, 250–55. Bethesda: CDL Press, 1993.

Toorn, Karel van der. *Scribal Culture and the Making of the Hebrew Bible*. Cambridge: Harvard University Press, 2007.

Tsai, Daisy Yulin. *Human Rights in Deuteronomy: With Special Focus on Slave Laws*. BZAW 464. Berlin: de Gruyter, 2014.

Tuell, Steven S. "The Southern and Eastern Borders of Abar-Nahara." *Bulletin of the American Schools of Oriental Research* 284 (1991): 51–57.

Turnham, T. J. "Male and Female Slaves in the Sabbath Year Laws of Exodus 21:1–11." *Society of Biblical Literature Seminar Papers* 26 (1987): 545–49.
Tzoref, Shani. "Knowing the Heart of the Stranger: Empathy, Remembrance, and Narrative in Jewish Reception of Exodus 22:21, Deuteronomy 10:19, and Parallels." *Interpretation* 72, no. 2 (2018): 119–31.
Ussishkin, David. *The Conquest of Lachish by Sennacherib*. Tel Aviv: The Institute of Archaeology, 1982.
———. "Sennacherib's Campaign to Judah: The Archaeological Perspective with an emphasis on Lachish and Jerusalem." In *Sennacherib at the Gates of Jerusalem: Story, History and Historiography*, edited by Isaac Kalimi and Seth Richardson, 75–103. Leiden: Brill, 2014.
Van De Mieroop, Marc. *A History of Ancient Egypt*. Blackwell History of the Ancient World. Malden: Blackwell, 2011.
———. *A History of the Ancient Near East ca. 3000–323 BC*. 3rd ed. Blackwell History of the Ancient World. Malden: Blackwell, 2016.
———. *Philosophy Before the Greeks: The Pursuit of Truth in Ancient Babylonia*. Princeton: Princeton University Press, 2016.
Van Seters, John. *A Law Book for the Diaspora: Revision in the Study of the Covenant Code*. Oxford: Oxford University Press, 2003.
———. "The Law of the Hebrew Slave." *Zeitschrift für die alttestamentliche Wissenschaft* 108 (1996): 534–46.
———. "Law of the Hebrew Slave: A Continuing Debate." *Zeitschrift für die alttestamentliche Wissenschaft* 119 (2007): 169–83.
———. *The Life of Moses: The Yahwist as Historian in Exodus-Numbers*. Louisville: Westminster John Knox, 1994.
———. "The Terms 'Amorite' and 'Hittite' in the Old Testament." *VT* 22, no. 1 (1972): 64–81.
Vaux, Roland de. *Ancient Israel: Its Life and Institutions*. The Biblical Resource Series. Grand Rapids: Eerdmans, 1997.
Venn, Couze. *The Postcolonial Challenge: Towards Alternative Worlds*. Thousand Oaks: Sage, 2006.
Viel, H.-Dieter. *The New Complete Code of Hammurabi*. Lanham: University Press of America, 2002.
Von Dassow, Eva. "Freedom in Ancient Near Eastern Societies." In *The Oxford Handbook of Cuneiform Culture*, edited by Karen Radner and Eleanor Robson, 205–24. Oxford: Oxford University Press, 2011.
Vroom, Jonathan. *The Authority of Law in the Hebrew Bible and Early Judaism: Tracing the Origins of Legal Obligation from Ezra to Qumran*. Supplements to the Journal for the Study of Judaism 187. Leiden: Brill, 2018.
———. "Recasting *Mišpāṭîm*: Legal Innovation in Leviticus 24:10–23." *JBL* 131, no. 1 (2012): 27–44.

Wafula, R. S. "The Exodus Story as a Foundation of the God of the Fathers." In *Postcolonial Commentary and the Old Testament*, edited by Hemchand Gossai, 10–26. New York: T&T Clark, 2019.

Wagenaar, Jan A. "The Annulment of a 'Purchase' Marriage in Exod 21, 7–11." *Zeitschrift für altorientalische und biblische Rechtgeschichte* 10 (2004): 219–31.

Walhout, M. D. "The *Intifada* of the Intellectuals: An Ecumenical Perspective on the Walzer-Said Exchange." *Soundings: An Interdisciplinary Journal* 74, no. 3/4 (1991): 327–50.

Waltke, Bruce K., and M. O'Connor. *An Introduction to Biblical Hebrew Syntax*. Winona Lake: Eisenbrauns, 1990.

Walton, John H,. and J. Harvey Walton. *The Lost World of the Torah: Law as Covenant and Wisdom in Ancient Context*. Downers Grove: IVP Academic, 2019.

Walzer, Micahel. *Exodus and Revolution*. New York: Basic Books, 1983.

Walzer, Michael, and Edward W. Said. "An Exchange: 'Exodus and Revolution.'" *Grand Street* 5, no. 4 (1986): 246–59.

Warrior, Robert Allen. "Canaanites, Cowboys, and Indians: Deliverance, Conquest, and Liberation Theology Today." *Christianity in Crisis* 49, no. 12 (1989): 261–65.

Watts, James W. *Reading Law: The Rhetorical Shaping of the Pentateuch*. Sheffield: Sheffield Academic Press, 1999.

Watson, Alan. *The Evolution of Law*. Oxford: Blackwell, 1985.

———. *Society and Legal Change*. Edinburgh: Scottish Academic Press, 1977.

Watson, Irene. *Aboriginal Peoples, Colonialism and International Law: Raw Law*. Indigenous Peoples and the Law. Milton Park: Routledge, 2016.

———. "Indigenous Peoples' Law-Ways: Survival Against the Colonial State." *Australian Feminist Law Journal* 8, no. 1 (1997): 39–58.

Weaver, Ann M. "The 'Sin of Sargon' and Esarhaddon's Reconception of Sennacherib: A Study in Divine Will, Human Politics, and Royal Ideology." *Iraq* 66 (2004): 61–66.

Ween, Renita J. *Battered Love: Marriage, Sex, and Violence in the Hebrew Prophets*. Overtures to Biblical Theology. Minneapolis: Fortress, 1995.

Weinfeld, Moshe. *Deuteronomy 1–11*. Anchor Bible 5. New York: Doubleday, 1991.

Weinstein, James M. "The Egyptian Empire in Palestine: A Reassessment." *Bulletin of the American Schools of Oriental Research* 241 (Winter, 1981): 1–28.

Wells, Bruce. "The Covenant Code and Near Eastern Legal Traditions: A Response to David P. Wright." *Maarav* 13, no. 1 (2006): 85–118.

———. "The Interpretation of Legal Traditions in Ancient Israel." *Hebrew Bible and Ancient Israel* 4, no. 3 (2015): 234–66.

———. Review of *Inventing God's Law: How the Covenant Code of the Biblical Used and Revised the Laws of Hammurabi*, by David P. Wright. *Journal of Religion* 90, no. 4 (2010): 558–60.

———. "What is Biblical Law? A Look at Pentateuchal Rules and Near Eastern Practice." *Catholic Biblical Quarterly* 70, no. 2 (2008): 223–43.

Westbrook, Raymond. "Biblical and Cuneiform Law Codes." In *Law from the Tigris to the Tiber: The Writings of Raymond Westbrook*, vol. 1, edited by Bruce Wells and Rachel Magdalene, 3–20. Winona Lake: Eisenbrauns, 2009.

———. "Biblical Law." In *Law from the Tigris to the Tiber: The Writings of Raymond Westbrook*, vol. 2, edited by Bruce Wells and Rachel Magdalene, 299–316. Winona Lake: Eisenbrauns, 2009.

———. "Codification and Canonization." In *La Codification des lois dans l'antiquité: Actes du Colloque de Strasbourg, 27–29 Novembre 1997*, edited by E. Lévy, 33–47. Travaux du Centre de Recherche sur le Procehe-Orient et la Grèce antiques 16. Paris: De Boccard, 2000.

———. "Cuneiform Law Codes and the Origins of Legislation." In *Law from the Tigris to the Tiber: The Writings of Raymond Westbrook*, vol. 1, edited by Bruce Wells and Rachel Magdalene, 73–95. Winona Lake: Eisenbrauns, 2009.

———. "The Female Slave." In *Law from the Tigris to the Tiber: The Writings of Raymond Westbrook*, vol. 2, edited by Bruce Wells and Rachel Magdalene, 149–174. Winona Lake: Eisenbrauns, 2009.

———. "The Laws of Biblical Israel." In *Law from the Tigris to the Tiber: The Writings of Raymond Westbrook*, vol. 2, edited by Bruce Wells and Rachel Magdalene, 317–40. Winona Lake: Eisenbrauns, 2009.

———. "Lex Talionis and Exodus 21:22–25." In *Law from the Tigris to the Tiber: The Writings of Raymond Westbrook*, vol. 2, edited by Bruce Wells and Rachel Magdalene, 341–60. Winona Lake: Eisenbrauns, 2009.

———. "The Nature and Origins of the Twelve Tables." In *Law from the Tigris to the Tiber: The Writings of Raymond Westbrook*, vol. 1, edited by Bruce Wells and Rachel Magdalene, 21–71. Winona Lake: Eisenbrauns, 2009.

———. *Studies in Biblical and Cuneiform Law*. Cahiers de la Revue biblique 26. Paris: Gabalda, 1988.

———. "What is the Covenant Code." In *Theory and Method in Biblical and Cuneiform Law: Revision, Interpolation and Development*, edited by Bernard M. Levinson, 15–36. JSOTSup 181. Sheffield: Sheffield Academic Press, 1994.

Westbrook, Raymond, and Bruce Wells. *Everyday Law in Biblical Israel: An Introduction*. Louisville: Westminster John Knox, 2009.

Wilcke, Claus. "Gesetze in sumerischer Sprache." In *Studies in Sumerian Language and Literature: Festschrift Joachim Krecher*, edited by N. Koslova, E. Vizirov, and G. Zólyomi, 455–616. Babel and Bible 8. Winona Lake: Eisenbrauns, 2014.

Williams, Peter J. "'Slaves' in Biblical Narrative and in Translation." In *On Stone and Scroll: Essays in Honour of Graham Ivor Davies*, edited by James K. Aitken, Katherine J. Dell, and Brian A. Mastin, 441–52. BZAW 420. Berlin: de Gruyter, 2011.

Williamson, James. "The Priority of the Laws Concerning Slaves at the Beginning of the Mishpatim in the Book of the Covenant—Coincidental or Purposefully Placed?" *Irish Biblical Studies* 28, no. 3 (2010): 98–124.

Williamson, Paul R. "Promised with Strings Attached: Covenant and Law in Exodus 19–24." In *Exploring Exodus: Literary, Theological and Contemporary Approach*, edited by Brain S. Rosner and Paul R. Williamson, 89–122. Nottingham: Apollos, 2008.

Wright, David P. "The Adaptation and Fusion of Near Eastern Treaty and Law in Legal Narrative of the Hebrew Bible." *Maarav* 24, no. 1–2 (2020): 85–136.

———. "The Covenant Code Appendix (Exodus 23:20–33), Neo-Assyrian Sources, and Implications for Pentateuchal Study." In *The Formation of the Pentateuch: Bridging the Academic Cultures of Europe, Israel, and North America*, edited by Jan C. Gertz, Bernard M. Levinson, Dalit Rom-Shiloni, and Konrad Schmid, 47–85. FAT 111. Tübingen: Mohr Siebeck, 2016.

———. "Holiness, Old Testament." In *Anchor Bible Dictionary*, vol. 3, edited by David Noel Freedman, 237–49. New York: Doubleday, 1991.

———. *Inventing God's Law: How the Covenant Code of the Bible Used and Revised the Laws of Hammurabi*. Oxford: Oxford University Press, 2009.

———. "The Laws of Hammurabi and the Covenant Code: A Response to Bruce Wells." *Maarav* 13 (2006): 211–60.

———. "The Laws of Hammurabi as a Source for the Covenant Collection (Exodus 20:23–23:19." *Maarav* 10 (2003): 11–87.

———. "Method in the Study of Textual Source Dependence: The Covenant Code." In *Subtle Citation, Allusion, and Translation in the Hebrew Bible*, edited by Ziony Zevit, 159–81. Sheffield: Equinox, 2017.

———. "The Origin, Development, and Context of the Covenant Code (Exodus 20:23–23:19)." In *The Book of Exodus: Composition, Reception, and Interpretation*, edited by Thomas B. Dozeman, Craig A. Evans, and Jael N. Lohr, 220–44. VTSup 164. Leiden: Brill, 2014.

Wright, Jacob L. "The *Raison d'Être* of the Biblical Covenant: Assessing Mendenhall's Emphasis on Kinship." *Maarav* 24, no. 1–2 (2020): 45–61.

Yaron, Reuven. *The Laws of Eshnunna*. 2nd ed. Jerusalem: Magnes Press, 1988.

———. "Quelques Remarques sur les Nouveaux Fragments des Lois d'Ur-Nammu." *Revue Historique de Droit Français et Étranger* 63, no. 2 (1985): 131–42.

———. "Stylistic Conceits II: The Absolute Infinitive in Biblical Law." In *Pomegranates and Golden Bells: Studies in Biblical, Jewish, and Near Eastern*

Ritual, Law, and Literature in Honor of Jacob Milgrom, edited by David P Wright, David Noel Freedman, and Avi Hurvitz, 449–65. Winona Lake: Eisenbrauns, 1995.

Yee, Gale A. "The Author/Text/Reader and Power: Suggestions for a Critical Framework in Biblical Studies." In *Reading From This Place: Social Location and Biblical Interpretation*, vol. 1, edited by Fernando F. Segovia and Mary Ann Tolbert, 109–18. Minneapolis: Fortress, 1995.

———. "Postcolonial Biblical Criticism." In *Methods for Exodus*, edited by Thomas B. Dozeman, 193–233. Method in Biblical Interpretation. Cambridge: Cambridge University Press, 2010.

Young, Lola. "Hybridity's Discontents: Rereading Science and 'Race.'" In *Hybridity and Its Discontents: Politics, Science, Culture*, edited by Avtar Brah and Annie E. Coombes, 155–70. London: Routledge, 2000.

Young, Robert J. C. *Colonial Desire: Hybridity in Theory, Culture and Race*. London: Routledge, 1990.

———. *Empire, Colony, Postcolony*. Chichester: Wiley-Blackwell, 2015.

Zaccagnini, Carlo. "The Enemy in the Neo-Assyrian Royal Inscriptions: The 'Ethnographic' Description." In *Mesopotamien und seine Nachbarn: politische und kulturelle Wechselbeziehungen im Alten Vorderasien vom 4. bis 1. Jahrtausend v. Chr*, edited by Hans Jörg Nissen and Johannes Renger, 409–24. Berliner Beiträge zum Vorderer Orient Texte 1. Berlin: Dietrich Reimer Verlag, 1987.

Langham Literature, with its publishing work, is a ministry of Langham Partnership.

Langham Partnership is a global fellowship working in pursuit of the vision God entrusted to its founder John Stott –

to facilitate the growth of the church in maturity and Christ-likeness through raising the standards of biblical preaching and teaching.

Our vision is to see churches in the Majority World equipped for mission and growing to maturity in Christ through the ministry of pastors and leaders who believe, teach and live by the word of God.

Our mission is to strengthen the ministry of the word of God through:

- nurturing national movements for biblical preaching
- fostering the creation and distribution of evangelical literature
- enhancing evangelical theological education

especially in countries where churches are under-resourced.

Our ministry

Langham Preaching partners with national leaders to nurture indigenous biblical preaching movements for pastors and lay preachers all around the world. With the support of a team of trainers from many countries, a multi-level programme of seminars provides practical training, and is followed by a programme for training local facilitators. Local preachers' groups and national and regional networks ensure continuity and ongoing development, seeking to build vigorous movements committed to Bible exposition.

Langham Literature provides Majority World preachers, scholars and seminary libraries with evangelical books and electronic resources through publishing and distribution, grants and discounts. The programme also fosters the creation of indigenous evangelical books in many languages, through writer's grants, strengthening local evangelical publishing houses, and investment in major regional literature projects, such as one volume Bible commentaries like the *Africa Bible Commentary* and the *South Asia Bible Commentary*.

Langham Scholars provides financial support for evangelical doctoral students from the Majority World so that, when they return home, they may train pastors and other Christian leaders with sound, biblical and theological teaching. This programme equips those who equip others. Langham Scholars also works in partnership with Majority World seminaries in strengthening evangelical theological education. A growing number of Langham Scholars study in high quality doctoral programmes in the Majority World itself. As well as teaching the next generation of pastors, graduated Langham Scholars exercise significant influence through their writing and leadership.

To learn more about Langham Partnership and the work we do visit **langham.org**

Milton Keynes UK
Ingram Content Group UK Ltd.
UKHW021007070524
442340UK00016B/721

9 781839 738807